POLITICAL THEORY

POLITICAL THEORY

N.D. ARORA
PGDAV College,
University of Delhi, New Delhi

S.S. AWASTHY
PGDAV College,
University of Delhi, New Delhi

HAR-ANAND
PUBLICATIONS PVT LTD

HAR-ANAND PUBLICATIONS PVT LTD
E-49/3, Okhla Industrial Area, Phase-II, New Delhi-110020
Tel.: 41603490
E-mail: info@haranandbooks.com/haranand@rediffmail.com
Shop online at: www.haranandbooks.com

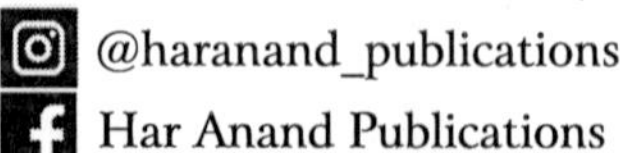

Eighth Revised Edition, 2007

Reprint, 2024

Published by Ashok Gosain and Ashish Gosain for Har-Anand Publications Pvt Ltd

Printed in India

Preface to the Second Edition

An author's greatest moment of pride is one when his/her work is well-received. It gives us immense pleasure in acknowledging our gratitude to both the teachers and the students who had welcomed the first edition of this book, despite its shortcomings.

In presenting the second edition, we wish to submit that attempts have been made to improve the sections which needed either elaboration or presentation/expression.

Any suggestion which helps in improving the present work would be welcomed.

N.D. Arora
S.S. Awasthy

Preface to the First Edition

Political theory, as a discipline of a wider subject, Political Science, has never been at rest. In fact, it should not be. For as long as political issues keep emerging, so long the discipline must offer remedies. Political Theory, to take but one instance, during the first half of the twentieth century, addressed itself to issues which, now, are no longer relevant, atleast some of them. Feminism, alongwith the concept of gender and patriarchy, the notion of sovereignty in relation to larger areas of power blocs and world economy, theories of citizenship, property, justice, and common good, subaltern studies, participatory democracy, the concept of development, environmentalism and many others did not bother the researcher much as they do now. That is one reason that newer works on Political Theory keep appearing from time to time. This study is an addition to the vast literature already available on the subject.

The occasion to undertake an exercise on the subject arose when the Department of Political Science (University of Delhi), under the chairpersonship of Professor Susheela Kaushik, decided to gi ve a new look to the Graduate and Honours Courses in 1995. So, the first word of gratitude goes to her and to her colleagues in the Department of Political Science, notably Professors Manoranjan Mohanty, S. Mukherjee, B.B. Sarkar, Neera Chandoke.

The present study is not the text book, dealt topic by topic as prescribed in the syllabus, though it does include all of them. In fact, it is more than a text book. It raises more questions than it solves them; it suggests more than it elaborates; it clarifies more than it presumes. The study, therefore, induces the teachers and the students alike to carryon from the point it leaves them off. It offers the inquisitive readers a list of readings which may, hopefully, help them to go in for a more detailed study on the subject. Though much attractive they look, the cumbersome footnotes are being avoided-for an introductory study like this.

While it is difficult, even if we try, to express our indebtedness to all our colleagues who, knowingly and unknowingly, some willingly while others unwillingly, helped us in the present endeavour. And yet, it would be doing injustice if we fail to acknowledge the kind cooperation of Dr. Sunder Raman, Dr. S.N. Talwar, B.S. Bagla, Dr. R.K. Anand, V.P. Pandey, Dr. B.N. Ray, Ram Bhatnagar, R.C. Vermani, Dr. Amita Singh, Dr. Sarah Joseph, Dr A.S Naraang who, in their wisdom, did much more than what they really did. While they deserve all the credit for what the study is worth, we, alone, are responsible for what it lacks.

Ms Kusum Chadha and Seema Kakran deserve special thanks for their useful suggestions in the task of writing this book.

We express our thanks to Shri O.P. Grover, our librarian, for making available the literature needed on the subject.

We thank our publishers, especially Shri Narendra Kumar, who made it possible for us to complete the project at the earliest possible time.

N.D. Arora
S.S. Awasthy

Syllabus in Political Theory

1. Nature and Significance of Political Theory
2. Power, Politics and Society
   (a) What is politics?
   (b) Different dimensions of Power.
   (c) Theories of power in society: class, gender and groups perspectives.
3. The State
   (a) The concept of the modern State, Sovereignty, Citizenship and Rights.
   (b) Dominant perspectives of the modern state.
   (c) Alternative perspectives.
4. The Concepts of Freedom, Liberty, and Equality
5. Theories of Property
6. Justice and the Common Good
   (a) Theories of Distributive Justice.
   (b) Notion of the Common Good.
   (c) Subaltern and Feminist Perspectives.
7. Democracy and Political Participation
   (a) Theories of Democracy
8. The Political Process and Social Change
   (a) Theories of social change, revolutionary change: concept of incremental change.
   (b) Development: Concepts of Development. Socialist, Liberal, Gandhian and others: Critiques of Development models: the debate on Welfare State.
   (c) Development and Environment: Contemporary debates.

Guidelines

Major Themes Under the above Topics:

1. Political theory-nature and significance. (See Chapter: 1)
2. What is politics? Politics as the conciliation of interests, politics as class struggle, politics as the pursuit of the common good. (See Chapter: 2)
3. Modes of power: political, economic and ideological. (See Chapter: 3)
4. Theories of power in society-class as the organising category for understanding power in society, gender and power, the

concept of patriarchy, pluralist theories of power in society. (See Chapter: 4)

5. The concept of modern nation-state; historical evolution. (See Chapter: 5)
6. The legal theory of sovereignty and its criticism, the concept of popular sovereignty, the nation-state in relation to power blocs and world economy, nation-state and imperialism. (See Chapter: 6)
7. Theories of citizenship, political and civil rights and citizenship. (See Chapter: 7)
8. Concept of democratic and human rights, their basis, justification of claims. (See Chapter: 7)
9. Liberal individualist perspectives on the modern state with special reference to the views of Locke, Bentham and contemporary libertarian theories: social democratic perspectives with reference to the views of Laski, Marxist and Gandhian perspectives. (Chapter: 8)
10. Equality: political, social and economic dimensions of equality, liberty and equality, equality and justice (See Chapter: 10)
11. The concept of liberty, negative and positive liberty, the Marxist concept of freedom (See chapter: 9)
12. The concept of property, theories of property (see Chapter: 11)
13. Theories of distributive justice with reference to Rawls, and Nozick (see Chapter: 12)
14. Socialist theories of Justice: Marxist, Anarchist and Democratic-Socialist.
15. Notion of the Common Good-Liberal, Communitarian, Marxian and Gandhian perspectives. (see Chapter: 13)
16. Subaltern and Feminist perspectives on Justice (see Chapter: 12)
17. Theories of participatory democracy, representative democracy including the pluralist-elitist theory of democracy, the concept of people's democracy (see Chapter: 14)
18. Historical materialism as a theory of revolutionary change: Popper's notion of incremental change (see Chapter: 15)
19. The concept of development, alternative concepts of development through the market, the welfare-state approach, socialist and Gandhian views regarding development, critique of development models (See Chapter: 16)
20. Development and issues of environment and conservation, the concept of sustainable development (see Chapter: 16)

Contents

1

Political Theory: Nature and Significance

Nobody debates the demise of Political Theory today, for its resurgence has been a fact of history, or atleast of recent history. There has been, since 1970s, David Held says, a revival of interest in Political Theory in Europe, the United States of America and in other parts of the world. The chief reasons for this revival are attributed to (a) break-up of the post-war consensus, (b) the consequential clash of values, and (c) changes in the humanities and social sciences, particularly a renaissance in Political Thought. It is, therefore, important to know as to what Political Theory is, or what it is about, and a host of other questions relating to its evolution, development, nature and significance.

I: Political Theory-Meaning

(A) What is Theory?

Before one attempts to know the meaning of Political Theory, it could not be out of place to know first as to *what a theory is*. Originating from the Greek word 'Theoria', *theory* means a well-focussed mental look taken at something in a state of contemplation with the intent to grasp or understand it. Arnold Brecht refers to the broad and the narrow meaning of the word 'theory'. In the broader sense, theory he says, means 'a thinker's, entire teaching on a subject (including description of facts, thinker's explanation, his conception of history, his value judgments, and his proposals of goals, policy and principles). In the narrower sense, theory, he continues, means 'explanatory' thought only or atleast primarily. It is the narrower meaning which Brecht prefers to assign to the word 'theory'.

Theory is oftenly confused with its related concepts for their boundaries overlap. Theory is not practice because, though we learn by doing, the latter has to work on some kind of base, the thinking.

Theory involves a theoretical frame which practice lacks. Theory is not description because "describing" is only a part of "thinking", its other parts include discovering, determining, augmenting, explaining and framing a phenomenon. Theory is not hypothesis, for hypothesis denotes a tentative assumption of facts and therefore, lacks what theory certainly has, definiteness. Theory is not philosophy because while theory is about 'something', philosophy is about 'everything'. Theory is not thought because it is a thought about thought and not an entire thought itself. There is much common between theory and reason, for both claim to be scientific, yet theory looks beyond reason, beyond science.

Accordingly, theory, as Karl Deutsch says, attempts to explain, order and relate disjointed data, identifies what is relevant and, therefore, points out what is missing in any phenomenon; predicts on the basis of observable facts. Theory is, therefore, a guide to practice, adds much to what is merely described, clarifies hypotheses, and as a part of philosophy explains an issue which meets the requirements of both reason and vision.

(B) Meaning of Political Theory

Political Theory is a theory about what is 'political', the science and philosophy of something that is 'political', A few definitions of Political Theory may be mentioned here:

(1) Broadly it means 'as anything about politics or relevant to politics' and narrowly as 'the disciplined investigation of political problems. (Sabine)

(2) "Political Theory is an explanation of what politics is all about, a general understanding of the political world, a frame of reference. Without one we should be unable to recognise an event as political, decide anything about why it happened, judge whether it was good or bad or decide that was likely to happen next." (Bluhm)

(3) Political Theory is 'a combination of a disinterested search for the principles of good state and good society on the one hand, and a disinterested search for knowledge of political and social reality on the other'. (Andrew Hacker)

(4) Political Theory is 'a network of concepts and generalizations about political life involving ideas, assumptions and statements about the nature, purpose and key features of government, state and society and about the political capabilities of human beings'. (David Held)

(5) "A body of thought that seeks to evaluate, explain and predict political phenomena. As a subfield of Political Science, it is concerned

with political ideas, values and concepts, and the explanation of prediction of political behaviour. In this broad sense, it has two main branches: one is political philosophy or normative theory, with its value, analytic, historical and speculative concerns. The other is empirical theory, with its efforts to explain, predit, guide, research and organise knowledge through the formulation of abstract models, and scientifically testable propositions." (Political Science Dictionary)

On the basis of above definitions, the major aspects of the meaning of Political Theory can be summed up as under:

(1) The area in which Political Theory works extends to the realms of politics only—political life of a citizen, his political behaviour, his political ideas, the government he establishes and the tasks the government performs.

(2) The methods, which Political Theory applies, include description, explanation, and investigation of any political phenomenon.

(3) Though Political Theory is all about what is 'political', yet it attempts to understand 'political' in relation to 'social', 'economic' 'pshychological', 'ecological', 'historical', 'moral' and the like.

(4) The object of Political Theory is to build ultimately, a good state in a good society and in the process create processes, procedures, institutions and structures historically tested and rationally attuned.

(5) As a body of thought, Political Theory seeks to explain, evaluate and predit political phenomena, and in the process builds not only scientifically testable models, but suggests values as rules of human conduct.

(6) Political Theory is both prescriptive as well as explanatory.

To sum up, one may say that political theory is an overview of what the political order is about. It is a shorthand, symbolic representation of what is 'political'. It is a formal, logical and systematic analysis of the processes and consequences of political activity. It is analytical, expository and explanatory. It seeks to give order, coherence, and meaning to what is described as 'political'.

(C) Political Theory: Subject Matter and Scope

For a better understanding of the meaning of Political Theory, it would be instructive to turn to its subject-matter and scope.

Politics as a political activity is usually associated with cynicism, and scepticism demonstrating self-seeking behaviour, hypocrisy, and manipulation of attitudes. Political Theory may, obviously, mean, then, a theory relating to all such negative connotations. But politics is neither politicking nor does Political Theory, a theory of political intrigues or subterfuge. If politics means what relates to 'political', then Political Theory may rightly claim to be a disciplined investigation of what constitutes 'political'. If Political Theory deals with what relates to the domain of 'political', then its subject-matter is bound to vary from time to time. From the early Greeks to about the end of the eighteenth century, Political Theory concerned itself mostly with what politics "ought to be." Almost during the nineteenth century and the first half of the twentieth century, Political Theory dealt, largely, with the nature, and structure of government as a decision-making body. Then came a period when some of the American Political Scientists, under the influence of scienticism, declared the death of Political Theory as against those, mostly the British traditionalists, who kept advocating the value and usefulness of Political Theory as a guide to political action. With the culmination of debate about the decline and resurgence of political theory, the two sides came to realise the process and the purpose of political activity. As such, the concern of Political Theory, today, has been both the nature and the proper ends of government.

Political Theory, as a disciplined investigation of political problems, implies those problems which are associated with the institution of government. Indeed, Political Theory is closely related to the study of what, and why of a government, but it is, on the other hand, associated inescapably with the relationship between the government and the outer world, Political system is a part of social system and social system exists within a particular environment. The environmental bearings are to be understood to the extent they influence the social system. The social system, encompassing in itself the whole variety of social sciences, moulds and gets moulded by the political system. Political Theory, while examining any political phenomenon, has to take account of what is non-political: be it economic, moral, geo-political, cultural, ecological and what not. We need to place political theory within the realm of political system, political system within the realm of social system, social system within the period it exists and under the environment it breeds. If Political Theory, David Held says, is concerned with "what is really going on" in the political world and, thereby, with the nature and structure of political practices', then a theory of politics today must take account of the place of the polity within geopolitical and market processes, that is, within the system of nation-states, international law and world political economy.

Political Theory docs not, and in fact, should not exist in isolation. It exists within a context. To understand political theory is to understand the context.

The subject-matter of Political Theory includes understanding of what is really 'political', to link political within what is non-political, and to integrate and co-ordinate the results of. the numerous social sciences for knowing its own nature. Its scope is not limited to what it constitutes, but to what exists in the periphery and beyond.

The focus of the scope and subject-matter of Political Theory is what goes on in political world. Accordingly, its basic components must be determined. Arnold Brecht refers to some units of Political Theory, especially the following.

(1) Group and not the individual is the real basic concept in Political Theory.

(2) As Political Theory deals with group, it is natural that there should be clash of interests not only among the individuals, but also among the numerous group. As a result, equilibrium or reconciliation of opposing interests has to serve the other component of Political Theory.

(3) The group life, in the realm of politics, lies at the heart of Political Theory. Accordingly the concepts with which it concerns itself are, or should be, power, influence, control, legitimacy, justice and the like.

(4) Another unit of Political Theory is action. Political Theory is not all philosophy, it is philosophy coupled with action. Any political theory not connected with action or policy can hardly be a political theory.

(5) To understand political theory is to know its agents and its actors. In politics, they are called the elite. Elite, therefore, constitutes another component of Political Theory.

(6) Choice and decision-making are also the units of Political Theory because they help know the seat where power rests.

Suggesting that the task of defining what is political as a continual one, Sheldon Wolin includes the following in the contents of political theory:

(a) a form of activity centering around the quest for competitive advantage between groups, individuals or societies;
(b) a form of activity conditioned by the fact that it occurs within a situation of change and relative scarcity.
(c) a form of activity in which the pursuits of advantage produces consequences of such magnitude that they affect in a significant way the whole society or a substantial portion of it.

(D) Political Theory: Evolution and Growth

Three major streams are mentioned while explaining the evolution and growth of Political Theory. These are as under:

(i) Classical Political Theory
(ii) Modern Political Theory
(iii) Contemporary Political Theory

(i) Classical Political Theory

Political theory, in its classical tradition, is not related as much to periodisation as is to the major themes of study. The classification of political theory into classical, modern and contemporary is, indeed thematic. What divides the classic or the traditionalist from the modern is the element of science in the latter and its absence in the former. Philosophy dominates the classical tradition of political theory whereas the science predominates the modernist. There may be an Aristotle and a Thomas, in the ancient and medieval periods of the West, who may emphasise on the science element while discovering the laws of public life and there may be a Strauss, in our times, who may see the utility of philosophy in the study of politics. Likewise modern political theory and contemporary political theory are to be distinguished. While all modern political theory may not be contemporary, most of contemporary political theory is always modern: modern political theory is empirical and scientific whereas contemporary political theory is philosophical and historical as well; modern political theory is present-oriented while contemporary political theory is future-oriented as well. Contemporary political theory attempts to synthesise the essence of both classical and modern political theory.

Political theory, in its classic form, emerged in ancient Greek culture, in the writings of Socrates, Plato and Aristotle, and continued until the beginning of the nineteenth century. The classical paradigm, according to Sheldon Wolin, relating to political theory, consisted of the following:

(1) The classical political theory was the practice of systematic enquiry whose aim was to acquire reliable knowledge about matters concerning the people. As a philosophical pursuit, theory sought to establish a rational basis for belief, as a politically inspired pursuit, it sought to establish a rational basis for action.

(2) The classical political theory identified the political with the common involvements, which men shared as partners. The Greek *Polis,* the Roman *res publica* and the medieval-times usage of *commonweal* denoted a sharing of what is common.

(3) Its basic unit of analysis had always been the *political whole:* the polis, the res public or the commonweal and in the process, attempting to specify the significant parts of the whole, how they

functioned and what their effect was on the quality of life in the political whole-the state. Political theory, in its classic form, came, thus, to view the state as composed of, and dependent upon, various interrelated structures, and the structures denoting activity, relationships and belief: *activity*, for example, may relate to ruling, warfare, education, religious practices, production of commodities; *relationships* may involve those between social classes, between types of superiority and inferiority, between the authorities and the subjects; *belief* may mean anything, i.e. concerning gods, justice, equality, natural law and the like.

(4) The notion that political theory related itself to the political whole, the state, gave way to an idea of system, an order and the resultant conceptions of balance, equilibrium, stability and harmony. No wonder if classical political theory tried to analyse the sources of conflicts, anarchy, instability, anomice and revolution and on it, attempted to enunciate the principles of justice which would form a guide for the discharge of duties in the political community.

(5) The classical political theory thrived on the significance of comparative studies for supplying a more comprehensive of explanation and a wider range of alternatives. That was the reason that the classical political theory developed a classification for political forms (e.g., monarchy, aristocracy, democracy, their variants) and a set of concepts such as law, citizenship, justice, participation so to prepare the way for an explanation that would account for differences or similarities.

(6) The classical political theory had been, largely, ethical in nature. Its response was rooted in a moral outlook: Plato advocated the ideal state, Aristotle, a state that can achieve the best possible, St. Augustine, the city of God. The classical political theory undertook to appraise the various constitutional forms, to determine the form most suitable for a particular set of circumstances, and to decide if any absolutely best form was possible.

(7) The classical political philosophers, by projecting the best form of polity as the ideal, revealed the boldness and radicalism of classical theorizing, though some dismissed such an idea as utopian and visionary. The project of the ideal states was no idle pastime, but was an invaluable means of practising theory and in the process, acquiring experience in its handling.

(ii) Modern Political Theory

Modern political theory encompasses in itself a host of diverse trends which include the institutional-structural, scientific, positivistic, empirical, behavioural, post-behavioural and even the Marxist. Thus, when one talks of modern political theory, one talks of all these trends, trends which dominated the greater part of our century. It is, since 1960s-1970s, that contemporary political theory starts.

The classical political theory, by and large, was philosophical, normative, idealistic and to some extent, historical. Ideologically, modem political theory can be classified into two opposing divisions—the liberal, including the individualist, the elitist and the pluralist on the one hand, and the Marxist, including the dialectical—materialist on the other. The liberal tradition, beginning from 15th-16th centuries, arose as a reaction against the classical political theory and after travelling through its institutional-structural voyage reached scientific-positivist-empiricist goals so to give way for the behavioural and the post-behavioural political theory. The Marxist political theory offered a diametrically opposite view to the one advocated in whole of the West.

Having found the classical political theory, sufficiently inadequate to answer the questions posed by the changing times of the 18th-19th centuries in the West, the modem political theory, as it came to be expressed in the institutional—positivist, imperialist—behavioural and post-behavioural trends, dubbed the whole classical tradition as dull. Their advocates, from Merriam and Key and down to Dahl, Lasswell, Easton, deplored the historical-normative-evaluative tradition of the classical political theory. Instead, they laid emphasis on the scientific-empirical-behavioural study as the most plausible one to understand the intricacies of politics. They sought to lay stress on 'present' rather on 'past', 'living' rather on 'dull', 'immediate' rather on 'remote': 'objective' rather on 'subjective': 'analytic' rather on 'philosophic': 'explanatory' rather on 'descriptive'; 'process-oriented' rather on 'purpose-oriented'; 'scientific' rather on 'theoretical'. They attempted to build a science of politics; objective, clinical, value-free, observational, measurable, operational.

Historically stated, modern political theory as it arose in the West, emerged from the shadow of positivism-empiricism. Until then, political theory, largely classical, was confined to a marginal role, being conceived at best as a body of classic texts of mostly historical interest, and usually found in philosophy, history, and logic. Positivism-empiricism denied the early political theory the status of a legitimate form of knowledge and enquiry. According to the positivist and empiricist outlooks, all knowledge is found in sensory observation; concepts and generalizations represent only the particulars from which they have been abstracted; values can not play any role in the formation of knowledge. As the meaning of concepts and theories, the positivist-empiricist believe, is directly tied to empirical observations, value-judgments, therefore, should not be accorded the status of knowledge. Accordingly, the normative statements of political theory may be characterized as mere declarations. Though positivism and empiricism did not last long, its legacy thrived for a long time to come, particularly in North America. This legacy was scienticism. The influence of scientism on the emerging behaviouralism and post-behaviouralism was both apparent and real. Behaviouralism, on its own, had certain features: it encouraged the systematic introduction of quantitative methods of analysis as the supreme methods of inquiry; it sought to displace the theoretical frameworks of normative political theorists by the development of empirical theory; and it decisively rejected the history of political theory as the primary source of interpretation. Post-behaviouralism was an extension of behaviouralism, adding the credos of 'action', 'relevance' and 'values' to behaviouralism. Thus, the challenge to behaviouralism came from within, from post-behaviouralism.

Modem political theory of the Western shade, as it developed over time, had certain features, particularly the following:

(1) Facts and data constitute the bases of study. Facts are accumulated, explained and are used for testing hypothesis.

(2) Human behaviour can be studied and regularities of human behaviour can be expressed in generalisations.

(3) Subjectivity gives way to objectivity; philosophical interpretation, to analytical explanation; purposive, to procedural; descriptive, to observational; normative, to scientific.

(4) Facts and values are separated. While in the early period, the facts were given all values, the values had no place in research, yet in the later period, values came to make the facts as relevant as possible.

(5) The methods adopted for research and study are to be self-conscious, explicit and quantitative.

(6) Political activity is an activity influenced by numerous other activities; social, economic, religious, moral, psychological, ecological and the like. Hence, inter-disciplinary synthesis is bound to yield rather better results.

(7) "What it is" is more important than either "what it was" or "what it would be", for the present is nearer to either past or future.

(8) Realism holds more weight than what is 'dull' or what is utopian. What and how and why a state does is more relevant than what is had been doing or is likely to do.

(9) Values are to support facts; substance, to forms; and theory, to research. This is the theme of post-behaviouralism.

(10) The journey from behaviouralism to post-behaviouralism is a journey from status quo to social change.

The Western modern political theory combines the merits of its empirical, formal and normative shades. It is concerned with both facts and values, both description and prescription, both explanation and valuation.

At the other end of modern political theory stands the Marxist political theory. The Marxist political theory, also called the dialectical-materialist or the scientific-socialist, is one which describes the general laws of motion in the development of all phenomenon. Its importance lies in change through the struggle between opposites: between relations of production and productive forces with a view to have a better mode of production; development from the lower stage to the higher one: from, say, capitalistic to socialistic and from socialistic to communistic. The dialectical-materialist theory provides a systematic and scientific framework of analysing and explaining, say, for example social and political change. It is a method of interpreting the past, understanding the present and projecting the future.

The major characteristics of the Marxist political theory can, thus, be summed up as under:-

(1) That every phenomenon is in a flux.

(2) It is in the nature of every phenomenon to attain its utmost development.

(3) As such, the direction of movement is from lower to the higher stage of development.

(4) The motion occurs through a dialectical method which is triple in essence. Hegel called it: thesis, anti-thesis and synthesis; Marx called it: relations of production, productive forces, and a new mode of production.

(5) Between mind and matter, it is matter that dictates. Matter only produces while mind merely reflects.

(6) Matter evolves because of its own law of evolution inherent in it.

(7) At the base of our whole superstructure, there is the base. The material base builds its own social, political, economic or educational super-structure. As is the base, so is the superstructure.

(8) Man, labour and nature constitute the essence of social development.

(9) Politics, as a class phenomenon, exists to justify the class character of a particular society. As and when class society is abolished, politics would lose all significance.

(10) Politics works both ways: it destroys the fabric and values of the earlier society, and builds, on the other, the new society.

It is, in this sense, that politics, as a power, is an instrument of social and political change. The dictatorship of proletariat would abolish the capitalist society and build the socialist society. As socialism would turn into communism, politics, as state, would wither away.

(iii) Contemporary Political Theory

The political theorists, after 1960s, and 1970s, have demonstrated the need of political theory in the fast changing world of ours. That is why that the interest in political theory is constantly growing in our times. This is partly because behaviouralism and post-behaviouralism, with their too much emphasis on science, have led us nowhere close to realities on the one hand, and partly because of the failure of the Marxism model in some parts of the world on the other. Soon, it came to be realized that political theory is more than a philosophy as it is also more than a science. Its mere reliance on philosophy robs it from being relevant and its too much stress on science obviates it from serving as a vision. It is not that we are parting away from our immediate past, but it is as if we are attempting to build on it.

If the task of political theory is, as it had been, to make us understand the political phenomenon, it is, therefore, necessary that it should confine itself to the explanation, investigation and ultimately comprehension of what relates to politics: concepts, principles and institutions. This is what contemporary political theory is doing. Brian Barry *(Political Argument,* 1965), while attempting to reconstruct and rediscover the role of political theory, attempts to 'study the relation between principles and institutions,' explanatory task of political theory should not lose sight of what it existed in the past. John Rawls *(A Theory of Justice,* 1971) refers to another task of contemporary political theory: a continuous search for truth, and suggests that the attempt can be made alongside the scientific-empirical methods. R. Nozick *(Anarchy, State and Utopia,* 1970), while rejuvenating on the recovery of political theory from its virtual demise, reverts to the individualist model of 'minimal' state and believes that contemporary political theory can solve many political problems by combining the classical ends with empirical means: The consensus, for example, (John Plamenatz; *Dcntocracu and illusion,* 1973) is that the empirical analysis and reflections of a logical and moral characters can co-exist in political theory.

Highlighting the characteristic features of contemporary political theory, David Held refers to the following:

(1) It has been renewed as the history of political thought, involving an attempt to examine the significance of text in their historical context.

(2) It has sought to revitalize the discipline as a form of conceptual analysis and in the process finding political theory as a systematic reflection upon, and classification of, the meanings of the key forms and concepts such as sovereignty, democracy, justice and the like.
(3) It has been developed as the systematic elaboration of the underlying structure of our moral and political activities: the disclosure, examination and reconstruction of the foundations of political value.
(4) It has been revitalized as a form of argument concerned with abstract theoretical questions and particular political issues.
(5) It has been championed as a critique of all forms of foundationalism, either post-modernists or the liberal defenders. It, accordingly, presents itself as a stimulant to dialogue and to conversation among human beings.
(6) It has been elaborated as a form of systematic model-building influenced by theoretical economics, rational choice theory and game theory, it aims to construct formal models of political processes.
(7) It has developed as the theoretical enterprise of the discipline of Political Science. As such it attempts to construct theory on the basis of observation and modest empirical generalizations.

Summing up, David Held offers a number of distinct tasks of political theory: "first, the philosophical-concerned, above all, with the conceptual and normative; second, the empirical-analytic-concerned, above all, with the problems of understanding and explanation; and third, the strategic-concerned, above all with an assessment of the feasibility of moving from where we are to where we might like to be. To these, one must add the historical, the examination of the changing meaning of political discourse—its key concepts, theories, and concerns—over time."

The post-1970s, while witnessing new developments in Political Theory, has given rise to four distinct views:

(1) With Rawls, political theory, as branch of moral philosophy has been described as essentially normative. Accordingly, the task of political theory is not only to develop general principles for evaluating the social structure, but also to design appropriate institutions, procedures and policies (see Ackerman, *Social Justice in the Liberal State,* (1980); Barry, *A Treatise* on *Social Justice,* 1989, and Beitz, *Political Theory and International Relations,* 1979).

(2) Political Theory is primarily contemplative and reflective enquiry concerned to understand human existence in general. So understood, as was really viewed in its older form, it is neither a branch of moral

philosophy nor normative in its orientation. (See Taylor, *Philosophical Papers,* 1985) Macintyre *After Virtue,* 1981; Connolly *Political theory and Modernity, 1988).*

(3) Political Theory is primarily concerned to articulate the self-understanding of a particular community, and that it is necessarily municipal in its scope and interpretive in its orientation. (See Walzer, *Sphere of Justice, 1983).*

(4) Political Theory needs to be tentative, exploratory, conversational, open minded, ironic sensitive. Such scholars draw inspiration from post-structuralist and post-modernist writers. (See Rorty, *Contigency, Ironys and Solidarity, 1989).*

II: Nature of Political Theory

The nature of political theory is closely related to the meaning one gives to it. As there is no agreement on the meaning of political theory, there is, therefore, no agreement about the nature of political theory. There are some who describe political theory to denote the works of numerous thinkers. But this assertion makes political theory more of political thought. There are others who equate political theory with political philosophy. While it is true that political theory constitutes a part of political philosophy, a part can never be a whole and as part, it remains a part of the whole. There are still others, mostly the modernists, who after incorporating science in political theory, prefer to call it political science. But political science is the science of politics and as such it is not a history of politics, or a culture of politics, nor even a philosophy of politics whereas political theory is a combination of all these. Political theory is usually confused with politics. The difference between the two is as much as is between theory and practice: a person may either be a politician, a political scientist, a political theorist, or a political philosopher, but he is never all in one, and seldom one in two or one in three.

(a) Political Theory: History

That political theory as history has been emphatically advocated by men like George Sabine, but all history is not political theory. That political theory is a science has been forcefully emphasised by men like Robert Dahl and David Easton, but all science is not political theory. That political theory is a philosophy has been sufficiently enunciated by men like Leo Strauss, but all philosophy is not scientific which means that philosophy can be unscientific as well. This is not to say that political theory is devoid of history, science or philosophy.

Political theory without history is a structure without a base. In studying and analysing politics, what we learn to understand is a political tradition, and a concrete manner of behaviour. It is, therefore, proper that the study of politics should essentially be a historical study. History, we should know, is more than the tale of the dead and buried, but is like a store-house of experience and wisdom, the sum-total, Rathore says, "and simultaneously the formation-head of a new development, something eternally significant and instructive, inseparably linked with contemporaneity in the perpetual progress of mankind, Ignore history and the delight of political theory is never to be retrieved."

(b) Political Theory: Science and Philosophy

Political theory without the quantum of science is unthinkable. If one defines theory as an explanation of a phenomenon, as Brecht really does, the phenomenon, without the element of science, would make it a matter of mere faith, a conviction or a belief. Theory has to have a 'science' in it, but only as much as theory needs. Too much scienticism in political theory robs the latter of its real essence. Its exponents, Rathore says, have not "succeeded in expending a cast-iron scientific theory of politics and what they have produced is a far from cohesive theory."

The sustenance of political theory depends on philosophy. Philosophy, as the sum-total of general laws (morals, norms, values etc. etc), has served political theory well through the ages. Philosophy, Kant says, has answered three questions: "What can I know?" "What must I do?", and "What can I hope for?" and this is what makes the philosophy a lodestar of life. Without philosophy, no political theory can ever hope to exist.

Science and philosophy, though stand on opposite poles, yet it is theory that combines the two. Theory, including political theory, has not only a philosophy, it also has a science. It is, therefore, in this background that one may say that a political theorist is both a political philosopher and a political scientist. It is, in this sense, that both political philosophy and political science are inadequate names for political theory. Brecht aptly says: "Political philosophy, political theory and political science arc no longer interchangeable terms." With the emphasis placed on science and a distinction from political philosophy, political science now refers to efforts limited by the use of scientific methods in contrast to political philosophy which is free to transcend these limits Likewise, political theory, when opposed to political philosophy, now is usually meant to refer to scientific theory only, and when opposed to scientific theory, now is usually meant to refer to a mere philosophy.

(c) Summing Up

In relation to history, political theory is the outcome of a peculiar set of historical circumstances and as such has a significance for all times to come. This makes the character of political theory respectable. In relation to philosophy, political theory is an attempt truly to know the nature of political things alongwith what is right, and good in them. In relation to science, political theory seeks to strive knowledge, as of facts or principles, gained by systematic study. Political theory, so understood, is philosophical as well as scientific, normative as well as empirical, evaluative as well as explanatory; historical as well as analytical.

Contemporary political theory is more of continuity than of change. When the political scientists, in the West, were trying to bring in scienticism and empiricism, they were not rejecting all that was the essence of traditional political theory. To an extent, they were giving a new development to what is considered 'political', in a way, they were liberalising political theory from its descriptive-interpretative shackles. They did realize the utility of knowing what politics had been in a particular time and under a particular situation. They did acknowledge the teachings of a particular political philosopher and his legacy. As such, they did not dismiss as worthless in all philosophy. Seen in this sense, the empirical-scientific (behaviouralism and post-behaviouralism including) trend in political theory was not a change, but a continuation of normative-philosophical tradition.

Likewise those who attempted to look at political theory more from a sociological point of view (de Tocqueville, Graham Wallas, Bagehot and others) or more from a psychological point of view (Hobbes, for example), they were merely adding numerous dimensions so as to understand political theory more clearly. Taken as this, the emphasis laid by the American scholars during the greater part of the post-war period, in the inter-disciplinary approach in politics was not an attempt to denigrate it, but was an endeavour to give politics a fuller meaning, making it more understandable and relevant.

Similarly, recent efforts to reject scientific jargons, purely empirical-drawn conclusions and techniques-oriented models are measures to set the worthlessness of political theory aright. Contemporary political theory is not condemning all empiricism or behaviouralism. Its science element is being retained to point out beneficial in social sciences as its philosophical content useful for understanding sciences related to society. So understood, political theory is not, and has never been, a break with the past, but is one that is in the state of constant continuity. We may conclude with Isaiah Berlin, in a rather lengthy statement:

"Neo-Marxism, neo-Thomism, nationalism, historicism, existentialism, antiexistential liberalism, and socialism, transportation of doctrines of natural rights and natural law into empirical terms, discoveries made by skillful application of models derived from economic and related techniques to political behaviour and the collusions, combinations, and consequences in action of these ideas indicate not the death of a great tradition, but, if anything, new and unpredictable developments."

III: Political Theory: Significance

A theory is described as one that enables us to organise our knowledge, orient our research and interpret our findings. But it is theory seen as a science, as a methodology and as a technique for reaching a goal seen as a philosophy, a theory is the enunciation of general-rules and laws as to how a man must live, a state be ordered and a society be organised. So seen, a theory is an end in itself. But theory, as we have seen earlier, is both a science as well as a philosophy. It is, therefore, an end, (philosophy) and an end to be achieved through the means (science). Political theory is a part philosophy and a part science. It is, therefore, neither a complete political philosophy nor a full political science. Defining political theory as the "critical study of the principles of right order in human social existence," Germino declares that political theory is "neither reductionist behavioural science nor opinionated ideology." It is, we must remember, a science but not a science which confines itself to propositions capable of sensory verification, but a science that fulfils the requirements of any social science Political theory, as a science, comprehends both the knowledge of facts and the insight with which this knowledge is comprehended and evaluated. As a political philosophy, political theory is not a utopian construction, but is one that finds out the truth of life. "Turning his back at distortions, over-simplifications, sloganeering, and demagoguery," Germino writes, "the political theorist speaks out with honesty on the perennial problems confronting man in his existence in society." Political theory, as a philosophy, attempts to find out what the truth is in a particular situation, to generalize from that what the truth would be in a different state of circumstances and then to advocate views with all the passion at its -command, Accordingly, political theory would continue to be needed as is needed science, or art, for it is, as Plamenatz says, "not fantasy or the parading of prejudices; nor is an intellectual game. Still less it is linguistic analysis." For Plamenatz, political theory is "an elaborate, rigorous, difficult and useful undertaking," and "as much needed as any of the sciences."

The importance of a political theorist. Brecht says, "is to see, sooner than others and to analyse, more profoundly than others, the immediate and potential problems of the political life of society; to supply the practical politician, well in advance, with alternative causes of action, the foreseeable consequences of which have been fully thought through; and to supply him not only with brilliant asides, but with a solid block of knowledge on which to build." He continues, "when political theory performs its function well, it is one of the most important weapons in our struggle for the advance of humanity. To imbue people with correct theories may make them choose their goals and means wisely so as to avoid the roads that end in terrific disappointment."

As a science, political theory can perform certain useful functions. David Easton mentions some such functions:

"(1) To identify the significant political variables and describe their mutual relations. To ensure this, an analytical scheme is essential. This would render research meaningful and arrange facts leading to generalizations.

(2) The existence, and wide acceptance of and consensus by workers in the field, on a theoretical framework, would enable the results of the various researches to be compared. It would help in the verification of conclusions drawn by the earlier researches and may also reveal the areas of research which require more empirical work.

(3) Finally, the existence of a theoretical framework, or at least, a relatively consistent body of concepts, making research more reliable."

But this is what a theory does as a science. Though such functions of political theory, in themselves, are, indeed, important, yet they help understand a phenomenon, not the phenomena; a part and not the whole.

Theory is not merely a science, it is a philosophy as well; not a phenomenon, but phenomena as well; not a part, but a whole as well. Indeed, political theory does make people understand as to what the present is and for what the present exists. But it does more than that. Accordingly, it rises above being the attendant of the status quo: it deals with larger functions of how the present has come to stay, on what assumptions does it exist and where would it, in future, lead to. Political theory, no doubt, arises from a specific context, but its significance extends beyond that. It, to a great extent, contributes to the capacity of man to understand himself, his system, his society and his history. Its job is not merely to understand the system around him, but is one through which he is to take the command of his own affairs himself.

Political theory serves as a teacher, a guide and a philosopher of men is general in their attempts to comprehend and control the whole environment—both social and natural. It is worth-noting the significance of political theory as indicated by C. Wright Mills:

(1) Political theory is itself *a social reality:* it is *an ideology* in terms of which certain institutions and practices are justified and others attacked, it provides the phrases in which demands are raised, criticisms made, exhortations delivered, proclamations formulated, and at times, policies determined.

(2) Second, it is an *ethic,* an articulation of *ideals* which at various levels of generality and sophistation is used in judging men, events and movements, and as goals and guidelines for aspirations and policies.

(3) Third, it designates agencies of *action,* of the *means of reform, revolution and conservation.* It contains strategies and programmes that embody both ends and means. It designates, in short, the historical levels by which ideals are to be won or maintained after they have been won.

(4) Fourth, it contains *theories* of man, society, and history, or atleast assumptions about how society is made up and how it works; about what are held to be its most important elements and how these elements are typically related; its major points of conflict and how these conflicts are resolved. It suggests the methods of study appropriate to its theories. From these theories and with these methods, expectations are derived.

By way of conclusion, we may say that political theory builds a model of the political order, serves as a guide to the systematic collection and provides an analysis of political data. As science, political theory describes political reality without trying to pass judgement on what is being depicted, either implicitly or explicitly. As philosophy, it describes rules of conduct which help secure good life for all.

Political theory is no easy and simple an enterprise. It is an elaborate and a consistent exercise, at that, aiming to achieve a better world of politics. Philosophy and science have no privileged cognitive status in political theory. All political philosophy makes claims about the operation of the political world—claims which require detailed examinations within model of enquiry which go beyond those available to philosophy alone. All political science raises normative questions which a dedication to the normative-explanatory does not eliminate. Political theory, if it has to be successful, requires the philosophical analysis of concepts and principles, and the empirical understanding of political processes and structures. Neither philosophy nor science, in their individual capacity, can easily replace the other in the projection of political theory. This is so because systematic political knowledge embodying generalizations about patterns of political life is possible and that efforts to achieve it are the major tasks of political theory today.

SUGGESTED READINGS

1 Connolly, W., *Political Theory and Modernity* (Oxford: Blackwell, 1988)
2 Finifter, A.(ed), *Political Science: The State of Discipline* (Washington D.C. American Political Science Association, 1983).
3 Held, D. (ed), *Political Theory and the Modern State* (Cambridge: Polity, 1989)
4 ________*Political Theory To-day* (Cambridge: Polity 1991)
5 Kavanagh, D. *Political Science and Political Behaviour* (London: Allen and Lenwin, 1983)
6 Kymlicka, W., *Contemporary Political Philosophy* (Oxford: Oxford University Press, 1990)
7 Leftwich, A. *(ed.)New Dimensions in Political Science* (Aldershot, Edward Elgar, 1990)
8 Lloyd, C. (ed), *Social Theory and Practical Practice* (Oxford: Clerendon, 1983)
9 Miller, David (ed), *The Blackwell Encyclopaedia of Political Thought* (Oxford: Blackwell, 1987)
10 Miller, D., and Siedentop, L. (ed), The Nature of Political Theory (Oxford: Clarendon, 1983)
11 Ricci, D.M., *The Tragedy of Political Science* (New Haven: Yale University Press, 1984)
12 Weisberg, H. (ed) *Political Science: The Science of Politics* (New York: Agathon, 1986)

2

Politics: Meaning and Nature

I. What is Politics?

Politics is a widely observed phenomenon. Whether one likes it or not, one finds oneself in politics, directly or indirectly, knowingly or unknowingly; willingly or unwillingly. To attribute any activity to be 'political' is not, therefore, astonishing. In fact, it has become almost a fashion, if not a habit, to address any simple human activity as 'political'. No wonder, if there are references like the 'university politics', 'church politics', 'politics in sports', or 'Congress politics'. So excessive has been the use of the word 'politics' that it has lost its real meaning.

The negative meaning of politics is gaining currency. It is, quite often equated with 'cynicism', 'scepticism', 'mistrust', a 'dirty' word associated with 'self-seeking behaviour, hypocrisy and the manipulation of attitudes'. That is why that some describe 'politics' as 'the technique of compromise' while others call it as 'the art of possible', 'the last refuge of the scoundrel', 'the art of looking for trouble, finding it-whether it exists or not-diagnosing it wrongly, and applying the wrong remedy', and the like. Though there is not much truth in the meaning of politics negatively understood, but this does not, and in fact, should not prevent us to know what politics is.

Consider politics ethically and one would say with Plato and Aristotle that it is a means to attain a 'good' and 'just' life. Consider it. legalistically as with the ancient Romans, one will find politics another name for 'administration'. With St. Augustine, politics becomes 'a city of man' acting as a bridge with 'the city of God'. Consider it as most of the traditionalist scholars. do, politics becomes a study of the state, the government or both. Consider it as some of the modern scholars do, it emerges as the study of power. The liberals, over time, have ended up by regarding politics as the reconciliation of antagonistic interests and thereafter as the pursuit of common good. The Marxists, while describing "politics" as a class concept and therefore 'dirty' declare it as an instrument of social and political change. With Aristotle, some would say that politics is a 'master science', while with Buckle, others would pronounce it as 'the most backward of all the arts'. In short, politics, to different people in different circumstances and at different times, means differently.

1. Politics: Traditional and Modern Meanings

Politics is both described traditionally and scientifically. The traditional meaning of politics is different to its meaning understood in scientific manner. It would, therefore, not be out of place to give a brief description of the traditional and modern meanings of politics.

(a) *Traditional Meaning of Politics:* For a long time in the history of political thought, politics has been regarded as a study of the state. Highlighting the traditional meaning of politics, the Dictionary of Political Science describes it as a systematic study of the state and of the processes governing its internal and external relations. No wonder if some scholars regard state as synonym of politics. Garner says that politics 'begins and ends up with the state.' Bluntschlli holds the view that politics "is concerned with the state which endeavours to understand and comprehend the state in its fundamental conditions, in its essential nature, in its various forms of manifestations, its development." According to Gettell, politics "is the historical investigation of what the state has been, an analytical study of what the state is and a political and ethical discussion of what the state ought to be."

There are the traditional scholars who regard politics as the study of government. Seeley says that politics "investigates the phenomena of government as Political Economy deals with wealth; Biology, with life; Algebra, with numbers and Geometry, with space and magnitude." Leacock describes it as a study which deals with government only. Macmillan's Modern Dictionary considers politics as something 'dealing with the organisation and administration of government.'

There are also the traditional scholars who regard politics the study of both the state and government. Gilchrist says that politics deals with the state and government. Paul Janet declares it as a 'part of social science which treats the foundations of the state and the principles of government.' David Easton's description of politics as 'the science of authoritative distribution of values in a society' is, more or less, a view that equates politics with the science of the state and government.

Politics as the study of the state or the government or of both does contain an element of truth. For centuries, politics has been regarded as something that is associated with political organisation—the way it is composed and the way it works. Politics as the study of political community conceals more than it reveals about politics. Politics is more than a mere description of the state or the government; it is how it works and with the force it works. It is more than a mere association; it is an institution as well. This is where the traditional meaning of politics fails to deliver goods. The meaning of politics, as something revolving around political association is, indeed, not wrong, but it is, surely, incomplete.

(b) *Modern Meaning of Politics:* If the traditional meaning of politics as the study of the state or government or both IS incomplete, so is incomplete the modern meaning of politics as the study of power.

The modern scholars, mostly under the influence of science, attempt to give politics a meaning in which it is described as an activity. From Hobbes and Max Weber and down to modern political scientists, mostly Americans (men like Merriam, Lasswell, Shils, Catlin, Dahl, Easton and others), politics has been described as the study of power. These scholars define power as 'a relation among actors in which one actor induces other actors in some way they would not otherwise act' (Dahl) or as the ability to produce intended effects as directly involve other persons' (Lasswell) or 'a relationship in which one person or group is able to determine the actions of another in the direction of the former's own ends' (Easton). These scholars hold the view that the power of the state, in politics, lies in and with the state. Robert Dahl, therefore, concludes. "The government is any government that successfully upholds a claim to the exclusive regulation of the legitimate use of physical force in enforcing its rules within a given territorial area. The political system made up of the residents of that territorial area and the government of the area is a state." Some definitions relating to politics as 'power' may be mentioned here. Lasswell and Kaplan say that politics is 'an empirical inquiry in the study of the shaping and sharing of power.' According to Dahl, politics 'deals with power, rule or authority.

That politics as power, contrary to what the traditionalists say it as the study of the state, is an inadequate meaning as is the one advocated by the modern scholars. What is more peculiar to the modernists is the fact that they have come to consider politics as the central theme which revolves around power, an arena of grabbing power or what Hobbes had said long ago: '... a general inclination of all mankind, a perpetual and restless desire of power after power that ceaseth only in Death.'

2. Attempts to Give Politics a Meaning

Serious difficulties arise when attempts are made to give politics a meaning. As men try to give politics a meaning, they confront themselves with a number of alternatives, especially the following.

One alternative designs to embrace, in the meaning of politics, a host of activities thought to be 'political' in nature. For some, politics consists of those human behaviours which are centred on the institutions and practices of government. There are others who see politics as the process by which human organisations solve their problems, i.e., with the obstacles they perceive to exist between their present conditions and the goals they wish to pursue. There are still others who think of politics as those human interactions involving the use, or the threat of use, of power or authority. David Easton hints at a perspective in which politics is regarded as a process by which scarce resources (human, or material) are allocated within a social unit (a city, a state, or a nation) for the purpose of providing for human needs and desires.

Another alternative worth consideration in the process of giving politics a meaning is to ask certain questions and find their answers in politics. Some such questions may be mentioned here: How do the artifacts of human organisation (formal groups, political parties, nation-states, international organisations, for example) persist through situations of strains, stresses and changing circumstances? How do some individuals or groups first achieve and then maintain preponderant influence or power? What social, cultural and economic conditions nurture different types of political order (e.g., anarchy, democracy, authoritarianism, totalitarianism)? The second alternative is less an attempt at defining politics than an endeavour to describe what it does.

The third alternative attempting to give politics a meaning concentrates on the major or important categories of activity or behaviour that constitute politics. According to some, conflict is the essence of politics. Dahl, therefore, says: "Politics and conflicts are born as inseparable twins." Likewise, power and influence demonstrate certain relationships and activities that become a part of the study of politics and therefore, are included in what constitutes the meaning of politics. Leadership, decision-making process and the like are the other categories of activities or behaviour among individuals and groups, and therefore, are considered while giving politics a meaning.

William Bluhm attempts to combine, as nearly as possible, three alternatives explaining the meaning of politics, when he says: 'Politics is a social process characterised by activity involving rivalry and cooperation in the exercise of power, and culminating in the making of decisions for a group.'

3. Characteristics Constituting the Meaning of Politics

Without attempting to define politics, one can identify, to mention a few, certain characteristic features which may be found in any meaning of politics.

(i) Politics involves an activity, a practical activity performed by the individuals in public life. It is something related to public, the people, the group at large, and their relationships and interactions.

(ii) Politics is related to what is political or what influences it. As such, Economy is not all entirely non-political. So, for example, is History which is, again not all historical. It is interdisciplinary in the wider sense of the term:

(iii) Politics is about power, i.e., about the capacity of social agents, agencies, and institutions to maintain or transform their social or physical environment. It is, as David Held says, 'about the resources which underpin this capacity (power) and about the forces that shape and determine its exercise.'

(iv) Politics is found in a system which is 'political' in nature. It works where political system is found or where political action is undertaken. This means that the extent of politics extends to political patterns of human relationships.

(v) Politics involves a pattern of political relationship—those who command on the one hand and those who obey on the other.

(vi) Politics includes government and its institutions, rules and procedures but it, at the same time, thrives within a broader system, called the social system.

(vii) Politics as the study of political system, itself a part of social system, studies problems which affect the whole fabric of human society.

By way of conclusion, one may like to say with William Welsh:

We study politics, then, as it occurs in political systems. These systems (though abstractions)—consist of persistent patterned sets of relationships among human beings, relationships that have to do with power, rule, or authority.

Because of its omni-presence, it is easy to understand that politics is substantially influenced by many elements of the broader social system (and one may add, ecological system) of which it is a part.' Stephen Wasby rightly regards politics as one aspect of the society. He says: "Even if special institutions are developed to perform political functions, politics is never separate from the larger society. In a sense, it is simply a facet of social system ... ", He continues: "To study politics is to take the social whole in order to examine one part of its structure and operation. When we do this, we need to know what the political aspect of society—the political subsystem, or polity—does for the entire society".

II. Politics as the Conciliation of Interests

The conciliation of interests is characteristic of liberal political theory, either classical or contemporary. The classical liberalism took upon itself the task of resolving conflicting interests as they existed among the individuals whereas the contemporary liberalism attempts to bring about conciliation of antagonistic interests as they are found among the numerous groups. What was individualism in classical liberal political theory, so has been pluralism in contemporary liberal thought. It is not, therefore, surprising to equate classical liberalism with individualism and contemporary liberalism with pluralism. Within the framework of individualist theory, individual interests' weighed more than the social interest whereas pluralism seeks to highlight what is "social" in the individual. In both, politics is an effort to bring about the rule of law in which power guarantees the general interest and the common good against the pressure of private interests. Maurice Duverger says: "Politics is a means of realising the integration of all citizens into the community and of creating the just state," a state that acts as an umpire in the resolution of opposing interests.

Contemporary liberalism is an improvement over classical liberalism, as pluralism is, over individualism. Between the state as essentially an evil and the one that is an institution of service, there stood a state that was regarded a positive good. Between Locke, Smith and Bentham on the one hand, and Laski, Maclver, Barker, Lindsay and Tawney on the other, there stood John Stuart Mill rightly described as a philosopher in transition and Thomas Hill Green who provided a bridge between classical liberalism and contemporary liberalism. If Locke, Smith and Bentham took up the cause of *Laissez-jaire* state on the one hand, Laski, Maclver, Barker, Lindsay and Tawney thought of the state as a positively good institution necessary for the development of man's personality on the other. Between these two, Mill and Green removed all doubts about the evil nature of political power. Mill, as an individualist, was closer to classical liberals than to the modern ones and Green, on the other hand, as an idealist, was nearer the contemporary liberals than to the classical ones.

(a) From 'Individual' Good to *'Social' Good: An Historical Brief*

The journey from an era of 'individual' good to that of the 'social' good is a journey from individualism to pluralism, both constituting liberalism either of the past or of the present. The classical liberalism, i.e., the liberalism of the 17th-18th centuries, as reflected in the writings of Locke, Bentham or Adam Smith, was a reaction to the medieval thinking of extolling "the whole" at the cost of "the part"; 'body' at the cost of the 'organ'. The result was the dominance of the state, the Church, the community and the family with individual having no 'individual life' of his own or/and liberty which he could enjoy. Armed with the strength of renaissance and reformation and enlightenment, the classical liberalism, as the philosophy of the rising industrial class, came to be associated with 'individualism'. The doctrine of individualism as a philosophy of the early liberals extols the value of the individual human being, upholding liberty and the equal rights of all individuals to equal freedom. In Locke, individual possesses the right to engineer a revolution. In Adam Smith, there should be minimum governmental interference in individuals' economic activities (i.e., *laissez faire)* if the "wealth of nation" has to be enhanced. In Bentham what is real in an aggregate is the "individual" interest, the social interest being nothing more than a nonsense (the word fondly used by Bentham). It was obvious that a free economy, then, was regarded most conducive to the satisfaction of human beings and their interests, the state contenting itself with minimal functions. That was precisely the idea inherent in the dictum: "That the state is a necessary evil". This was a period of negative liberalism—a period when the state was construed to be a negative institution: the more it is, less is the individual.

From late 1880s, liberalism entered a new phase. John Stuart Mill and more than him, Thomas Hill Green made possible, through their writings, what may be called 'social' liberalism. Social liberalism was different from 'individual' liberalism (i.e., early, classical, economic) in so far as the good of the individual came to be thought as tied to the good of the whole community The atomism of the formal classical view came to be regarded as morally and sociologically naive. Poverty, unemployment and ill-health came to be regarded, no longer, as the concerns of the isolated individuals, but had become social issues which had to be dealt with by the state as well. Liberty was no longer a *laissez-faire* affair, but had come to be regarded as best only when regulated or controlled.

Social liberalism of the late 19th and the early 20th century, (Graham Wallas, in particular) had paved way for a pluralist society with contemporary liberalism as its philosophy. The period between the two great wars (1919-1939) and the one that followed them, as also the impact of the socialist movements, created a state that was to be welfare; a society that was to be pluralist and a politics that was to resolve conflicting interests of the groups. That is how liberalism, in its numerous shades (first as 'individual' liberalism, then 'social', and ultimately 'welfare') have reached 1960s and 1970s. This is not to say that liberalism, now, has attained its demise, for an attitude and a mental frame as liberalism is, never dies. The latest and probably the recent variation of liberalism- goes a step backward and exalts 'individual' within a broader frame of the society. This, atleast, is the essence of what has come to us through the writings of John Rawls, Robert Nozick, Michael Walzer, Friedrich Hayek and a host of other scholars like them.

(b) Classical Liberalism and Modern Liberalism: A Distinction

One is tempted to raise points of differences between the classical liberalism and modern liberalism or between individualism and pluralism:

(1) The classical liberalism regards individual as the starting point of liberal philosophy whereas the modern liberals begins with the group. The subject of the two differs; for the individualists, it is the 'individual' while for the pluralists, it is the 'group'.

(2) The classical liberals think the individual activity as the moving spirit of society whereas modern liberals, the pluralists particularly, regard group activity as the basis on which the social fabric is interwoven.

(3) The classical liberals give importance to individual interest while the modern liberals believe in the dominance of the social interest over particular interests of the people.

(4) For the classical liberals, the individualists especially, society, as an aggregate of individuals, is only an imagination; for the modern liberals society is not only 'natural', it is real as well.

(5) The classical liberals, zealous as they are about the autonomous individual, speak of rights as inviolable and liberty as the absence of all restraints. The pluralists or the new liberals as one may like to call them, do not think of liberty as unbridled.

(6) The classical liberalism had expelled government from the market place; modern liberalism brought it back, so to protect people from an unfair economic and exploitative system.

(7) The individualists advocate a limited state with limited functions and limited powers whereas the pluralists neither doubt the efficacy of the state nor its potentialities. Both, of course,

maintain that politics exists to resolve the conflicting interests among people.

(8) The advocates of both shades of liberalism do no fit together neatly into the same school. Hume, de Tocqueville, Burke, Hayek, for example, are liberals as well as conservatives; and Hobhouse, Hobson, Dewey, Rawls are liberals as well as socialists.

And yet, there is a view that the two schools of liberalism, classical and contemporary, are not distinct. The basic tenets of the classical liberalism were worked and so reworked that they remained the fundamental principles of the contemporary liberalism. Many of the ideas that were associated with classical liberalism were flexible enough to be used by the new liberals. That is why that no liberal, either of the past or of the present, ignores individual autonomy, disrespects human personality, hates man's initiative and/or wants a totalitarian and authoritarian state.

(c) *Individualism, Individual Interests and Limited State*

The liberals, particularly the classical ones, are formally committed to individualism. *Individualism* revolves around individual. For the individualists, individual is both more real, than and prior to society. The individual, in the classical liberal format, is usually understood as a single, self-enclosed being 'shut up in his own subjectivity.' In terms of natural rights, the individual, the classical liberals would say, 'own his own body', the proprietor of his own person', as Macpherson uses the term and is, therefore, linked with 'possessive individualism'. Individualism or the classical liberalism, is primarily a philosophy of man, about him by highlighting his individual interests and for him in so far as it demands the fulfilment of his interests. It, thus, begins with the individual and ends up with the individual. For the individualists, the individual is selfish because he has his particular interests; he becomes social because he finds others as instruments for the satisfaction of his interests. In this setting, he is social. Because he is social, he knows how to extract from others what he himself needs, and also because he can distinguish between what is good and what is bad, he becomes rational. The individualist argument runs like this: As the individual, with his particular interests, wants to satisfy and maximise his interests, he finds himself in the society of people. Before the individuals, eager to fulfil their interests, break their heads, a body of rules and regulations is brought in to set the conflicting interests to order. This is from where politics starts.

For the early liberals, politics acts as the arbiter and the balancer. It reconciles the antagonistic interests of the individual and attempts to bring a state of balance.

Beginning with *the individual and his individual interests,* individualism builds itself on the following *assumptions:*

(1) It is natural for an individual to have his own interests. Equally natural is the fact that the individual must seek ways and means to attain and maximise them.

(2) Individuals live together (and therefore, are social) so to satisfy their interests.

(3) It is natural, under the circumstances, that the interests of an individual may (or are bound to) clash with those of the others.

(4) Politics comes in to resolve and conciliate the conflicting interests of the individuals. It becomes the law-maker, the law-enforcer and the arbiter posted with the task of maintaining law and order.

That the individual is egoistic and, therefore, attempts to fulfil his interests while in association with others is the beginning from where the classical liberal theory starts. His selfishness forces him to become social; his sociability teaches him to act in a certain manner, making him, thus, a moral as well as a rational being at the same time. Thus, man's sociability, morality and rationality emerge from his urge to satisfy his interests. The individuals' interests, among themselves, clash because demands always outweigh the supplies.

The interests among the individuals clash because they have to. Selfish as individuals are, their interests must take to antagonism. As John C. Calhoun rightly puts it: "The constitution of our nature ... makes us feel more intensely what affects us directly than what affects us indirectly through others," and this "necessarily leads to conflicts between individuals." Divergence of interests puts people in different positions. Temperamentally, people are not all alike; there can be no meeting point between a radical and a conservative and, if for this reason, there is the clash of interests between the two, it is understandable. Differences between two persons on the procedure to be followed for attaining an agreed object may also lead to conflicts among them. More such reasons responsible for conflicts among individuals can well be offered. The important point worth remembering is that the individuals must have their own interests and that the conflicting character of interests is more natural than apparent.

If individualism is what an individual ego is, and if the individual interests alone bind individuals together, there have to be minimum possible rules and regulations regulating the affairs and relations of the people. Liberty, as the absence of all restraints, popular as its meaning was during the 17th-18th centuries, could not admit any or more laws. It is, therefore, not surprising that the classical liberals were, quite naturally, committed to *a limited state.* The minimal state, as advocated by the individualists, was necessary in so far as its task was limited to the maintenance of law and order and security from external invasion. For all other tasks, the state was dubbed as an evil. John Locke (1632-1704) assigned to the state the lone job of protecting property of the people. Adam Smith (1723-1790), the economist, propounded a *laissez-faire* state. Jeremy Bentham (1748-1832), the utilitarian thought that a non-interventionist state alone could promote "greatest happiness of the greatest number."

(d) Criticism

The classical liberalism has its inherent *weaknesses.* Individualism, as the philosophy of classical liberals, over-estimates the potentialities of the individual by regarding him all social, all moral and all rational. Conversely, it underestimates the capabilities of the state which the later liberals were soon to realise. The concept of individual ego can not be stretched too long and too far. Individual, indeed, is one who has a world of his own, but there is no denying the fact that he lives in the world which is not entirely the one he makes. There is the fact when Aristotle declared man as a social animal. Sociality is as important a part of human nature as is individuality. It is difficult to assume society as a mere aggregate of people or a crowd consisting of individuals. Leave individuals in their solitary setting, they would never be better than brutes. Peter Self describes the frustrating effects of individual egoism when he says: ".... a group of villagers graze their livestock upon a common pasture. Once social constraints get broken, each individual has a progressive incentive to expand his share of grazing, and no new equilibrium point can be reached until the pasture is completely ruined."

(e) Pluralism, General Interest and Welfare State

Positive liberalism, as a reaction to negative liberalism of the early liberals, sought to reconcile individuality with community-individual good with general good. T.H. Green, as the most significant exponent of positive liberalism, argued that society was a means for individual self-realisation and development, and that politics exists to draw forth the potentialities inherent in the individual. Self-realisation and development of the individual, Green emphasised, could be made possible only within the framework of social institutions, state including. Mill before and Hobhouse after him propagated Green's point of view that in individual's own good also lies the good of the community.

We cannot divorce our own good from the good of others. Mill had rightly observed that if a government was to be a government for the people, it has to be a government of all the people, representing all the interests of the society. Thus the way was paved for pluralism which was, more or less, a variety of the 20th century liberalism. Kariel says: "As the exclusively proper way of ordering and explaining public life, it (pluralism) remains the heart of the liberal ideology of the Western world." Hence, in the changed conditions of the 20th century, a welfare state and the concept of 'general interest' were to be, obviously, associated with the pluralist theory.

The pluralist politics is, essentially, group politics. *Pluralism* is no longer a theory against the absolute nature of state sovereignty as it had initially emerged in the writings of Laski, Maclver, Lindsay or Barker. It has come to incorporate, as the 20th century American scholars, like Robert Dahl would suggest, a network of groups competing for capturing political power. David Held says: "Pluralists put particular weight on the processes creating, and resulting from, individuals combining their efforts in groups and institutions in the competition for power." Hence, the pluralist politics is mainly concerned with sets of individuals maximizing their common interests. Schmitter defines pluralism "as a system of interest representation in which the constituent units are organised into an unspecified number of multiple, voluntary, competitive, non-hierarchically ordered and self-determined (as to type or scope of interest). Categories which are not specifically licensed, recognised, subsidised, created or otherwise controlled in leadership selection or interest articulation by the state and which do not exercise a monopoly of representational activity within their respective categories."

So understood, the *characteristics ofpluralism* may be stated asunder:

(1) A pluralist system consists of a large number of groups, com peting for (a) members, and (b) resources. More are the members, greater are the chances for attaining more resources.

(2) Competition is natural because the conflict of interests among the groups in the society is inevitable.

(3) The pluralist politics is the politics of compromise and one that attempts to achieve an equilibrium of conflicting powers. As such, power is a matter of contest.

(4) The pluralist politics is not only group politics, it is interest politics as well. There are group which oppose one another because they differ in their objectives. Politics is an attempt to discover the interest common to all the groups and thereafter promoting what is called the general interest.

Though the democratic elitists sing the same chorus of general interest as the pluralists do, yet the two differ, drastically, on the following:

(1) There is a many-sided emphasis on politics in pluralism whereas in elitism, the emphasis is one-sided.
(2) The pluralists do not over-emphasise, as the elitists do the capacities of the politicians in shaping contemporary life.

As individual interests find expression in group interests for purposes of fulfilment, it is, therefore, natural that there must exist clash of interests among the groups. Pluralism is a political theory of competing and mutual opposing groups. If resolution of conflicting interests among the individuals has been a characteristic of classical liberalism, the conciliation of conflicting interests among the groups is characteristic of modern liberalism or what may rightly be called pluralism. Individuals, without owing anything to the society, attempt to fulfil their interests and in the process, maintain a balance in the society-all this in the *laissez-faire* atmosphere. Groups, without owing anything to the society, attempt to compete and control power over other groups so to promote their own interests, but in the process, create an equilibrium. Accordingly, if the individual good was the motive to cover the risk of wholesale violence in individualistic era, the general good is the motivating force to cover the risk of wholesale anarchy in the modern times.

General interest, public interest or common interest are interchangeable words. What each of them indicates is something where interest of all is inherent. It is, therefore, a meeting point of all the conflicting interests, the compromise of the varying and opposing interests. It is not the interest of one individual or one group at the cost of all others. It is an interest which has, at its core, the interest of all, the 'interest common to all. It, being a general and common interest, is one that unites people. It is a unifying force. More implicit or explicit it is, more stable is the system. It, therefore, is one that provides to a system, order or/and a fabric not only a sound base, but also a sufficient strength to support itself.

The pluralists link themselves with the idea of general, public or common interest. They usually, Peter Self says, confine it to rules for conflict management and dissolve its substantive meanings into the interests of actual or latent groups. If interest is a way of referring to the common concerns of a given set of individuals, it is, then natural for them to find themselves in a group, and likewise, if the groups find themselves united in a given community, it is natural that the groups, by doing so, are trying to preserve and promote the common interest. In pluralistic theory also, the task of politics remains, as in the individualistic one, the conciliation of interests. In the latter case, it is the conciliation of interests among the individuals where in the former case, it is the conciliation of interests among the groups.

From the pluralist point of view, as with the classical liberals too, the state appears to be a neutral arbiter, impartially controlling the conflicts of social groups. Politics, Schwarzmantel says, supervises and regulates social antagonism, without taking sides. Politics, Bernard Crick says is a process of "ruling divided societies without undue violence." In the words of Duverger, "Politics is an attempt to resolve the individual and group conflicts without physical violence." As the pluralist theory is a group theory, its politics, as such, is competitive and not consensual, but in no way restricts politics to act as an umpire, for the personnel of the state do not favour anyone set of social or economic interests. The pluralistic politics, being competitive, gets reflected in more than one way—in elections, in dialogues, in legislative debates. "The pluralist view sees politics as a process of choice and competition ... is marked by choice between, and competition among, a variety of political parties and pressure groups" ensuring "the diffusion of power", says Schwarzmantel.

The neutrality of the state, as the axiom develops in pluralist theory, is oftenly linked with a view of the state as an agent of reform. The pluralist state is becoming, increasingly, *a welfare state* is no longer an instrument of the capitalist class, but is one that puts into effect schemes of social welfare and has, as in most of the European countries, assumed a more active and interventionist role than ever before. Hobson, Hobhouse. Dewey have viewed the state as an integral part of the economic and social life of the community. It was not just concerned, as in the heydays of *laissez [aire,* with freeing individuals from obstacles to their economic activity, but was actively involved in the promotion of a better life for its citizens. This is, in fact, the essence of the welfare state as the pluralists view it.

The scholars have, however, divided pluralism into classical pluralism and nee-pluralism. David Held points out the following distinction between the two:

(1) The classical pluralist theory admits of diverse, and even overlapping, interest groups seeking political power. Nee-pluralism admits multiple pressure groups, but political agenda is biased towards corporate power.

(2) In the classical pluralist theory, politics mediates and adjudicates between demands. In nee-pluralism, politics forge its own sectional interests.

(3) Power is shared and bartered by numerous groups in society as the classical pluralists would argue. On the other, according to the nee-pluralists, power is contested by numerous groups.

(4) Within the framework of classical pluralism, balance between active and passive citizenry is regarded sufficient for political stability while in nee-pluralism, there is unequal involvement in politics.

Truman and Dahl represent classical pluralism and Charles Lindblom and Pollitt, the neo-pluralism. Dahl's *A Preface to Democratic Theory* (1956) puts him among the classical pluralists whereas his *A Preface to Economic Democracy* (1985) enlists him among the .neo-pluralists.

(f) Criticism

The modem liberalism or for that matter pluralism is subject, briefly, to the following observations:

(1) The pluralist theories underrate the power of the state. Though they accept the interventionist role of the state, yet that role is confined only to the resolution of interests.

(2) The interventionist role of the state tends to diminish its arbiter role. The state, under pluralism, does not appear to be neutral because it is not equally accessible to all the social forces.

(3) The pluralist view that there is the diffusion of power in a pluralist society owing to numerous group is untenable because power, at the top, is always held by a small cohesive group.

(4) The pluralist system, being competitive, represents diverse and conflicting interests, for groups nowhere compete on equal terms, Business group, usually have an edge over other groups. The welfare state, as claimed by the pluralists, becomes, more or less, a capitalist state.

(5) Consensus and not the competition, is the platform on which the society rests. This fact fades away the pluralist vision altogether.

It is clear that pluralism has been under strong attack in the country (that is the USA) where it is most entrenched. *McConnell* (1966) contends that American distrust of the uses of public power has led to its widespread fragmentation and appropriation by private interests. *Lowie* (1979) argues that the same process has eroded the rule of law, undermined the principle of equal rights and ended in 'a hell of administrative boredom'. *Keriel* (1961) concludes that the ethical appeal of pluralism has collapsed and that the 'public interest' needs to be vigorously reasserted. *Dahl* (1982), now, believes that the pluralist system can only be rescued by basic changes in political and economic institutions.

III. Politics as Class Struggle

Politics as, class struggle, is characteristic of the Marxist theory as the conciliation of interests has been that of liberalism. The liberals, of either yesteryears or of to-day, consider individual and group interests, and conflicts among them, as natural. The Marxists, on the other, regard these conflicts as man-made. If the liberals, pluralists including, believe that the conflicts among the individuals or groups are resolvable, the Marxists hold the view that these conflicts are irreconcilable. So the Marxists, as Duverger tells us, declare that politics "is conflict, struggle, in which power allows those who possess it to ensure their hold on the society and to profit by it."

The basic assumptions of liberal politics as the conciliation of interests are unacceptable to the Marxists. The Marxists, unlike the liberals, do not think that the conflicts among the individuals or the groups are natural; that there is something called as the general, common or social interest; that the state acts as the balancer of interests and is, therefore, non-partisan. On the contrary, the Marxists hold the view that the common interest, for all practical purposes, becomes, and always is, the interest of the economically dominant class; that politics is, and has always been, a class category. Politics, according to the Marxists, arose in class society and would remain until there exist mutually antagonistic classes in the society. The class society is represented by class politics where mutually opposing classes would continue to remain in the state of struggle against each other. It is only in the classless society that politics would disappear, wither away as Marx had once announced.

(a) What is *a Class?*

The Marxists give a definite connotation to the terms 'class' or 'classes'. In his work, *A Great beginning,* Lenin had defined classes "as large groups of people which differ from each other (i) by the place they occupy in a historically determined system of social production; (ii) by their relation to the means of production; (iii) by their role in the social organisation of labour, and consequently, (iv) by the dimensions and mode of acquiring the share of social wealth." So understood, they are either (i) masters or slaves; feudal lords or serfs; capitalists or workers; (ii) owners or non-owners; (iii) non-doers or doers; (iv) profiteers or wage-earners. The Marxists recognise two broad or what the Marxists call, basic classes in any given class society; one that owns the means of production and another that does not. In the first category, there are the masters, the feudal lords, the capitalists, in short the expropriators and in the second the slaves, the serfs, the workers, in short, the expropriated, and therefore are correspondingly, the owners, non-doers, and profiteers on the one hand, and on the other, the non-owners, the doers, the wage-earners.

(b) How do the Classes Originate?

The Marxists believe that the classes, in the sense they use the term.. have not always existed. In the most primitive society, when the means of production did not exist, there were no classes opposing each other. As people, in course of time, began producing and, as a result, owning the means of production, and as and when they produced more than they consumed, there arose the possessing class on the one hand and the non-possessing class on the other. This was the beginning of the class society, of also the opposing classes, those who owned and those who did not own.

With the gradual development of productive forces and increase in labour productivity, the people began to identify the means of production, to produce more than what was needed. As a result, accumulation of material wealth and appropriation of the means of production became possible. This was the beginning of private property (one that has the capacity to produce), owning class and the exploitation of those who did not own. That is how that the masters exploited the slaves in the slave-owning society, the feudal lords, coercing the serfs in the feudal society, and the capitalists, oppressing the proletariat. Because the owners own the means of production, they, therefore, own the non-owners and strike them at their whims.

(c) Theory of Class Struggle

The opposing classes have to oppose each other. These antagonistic classes stand against each other in state of confrontation. They differ in every aspect. Their interests are irreconcilable, their economic and political positions are apart; their life-styles are different; they differ in their thinking, in their consciousness, in their attitude. In fact, there is nothing common between the two. The antithetical position of classes in society is the source of their bitter struggle and an endless struggle at that. So Marx and Engel. wrote in the *Communist Manifesto:*

"The history of all hitherto existing society is the history of class struggle: freeman and slave, patrician and plebian, lord and serf, guildmaster and journeyman, oppressor and oppressed, stood in constant opposition to one another, carried out an uninterrupted, now hidden, now open fight, a fight that each time ended, either in a revolutionary reconstitution of society at large, or in the common ruin of the contending classes.".

What is clear and in fact, remarkable is the unity of humanity on the one hand, and the continuity of history on the other. What maintains this unity and continuity is the war, the continuous war between classes in a class society. The actors change but the war always has the same character. The class struggle ends here and then begins from there. It is, Claude Lefort says, "a single war fought out in many episodes."

The class struggle is a phenomenon characteristic of a class society. The classless society would not have struggle because there would be no classes to fight with each other. The socialist society, built on the ruins of the capitalist society, and later the Communist society would not experience any struggle because in each of these societies, there would be but only one class – the working class.

The class struggle is of positive character in so far as it launches the beginning of a new era from primitive communist society to the slave-owning society; from the slave-owning society to the feudal society; from the feudal society to the capitalist society and from the capitalist society to the socialist society and then to the communist society.

(d) Classes and Class Struggle – their Characteristic Features

From above, the following characteristic features can be seen in the Marxian concepts of 'classes' and 'class struggle':

(1) The conflict among the individuals and groups are not natural. They are the result of the class society.
(2) The common interest is nothing more than the interest of the economically dominant class.
(3) The state is never a neutral institution. It is what its base wants it to be. It is partisan in so far as it protects and promotes the dominant class and conversely oppresses the weaker one.
(4) Classes originate because of the origin of private ownership of the means of production.
(5) As these classes stand in opposition against each other, they keep fighting. The change in the actors does not result substantially, in the nature of class war.
(6) The class struggle phenomenon exists only in the class society. In the classless society, there is no class struggle.
(7) Revolutions, as the culminating stage of the class struggle, serve as the engines of social development, from the lower stage to the higher one.
(8) The future of classes is their virtual abolition as and when the class society moves into classless society. In the interim period (the socialist society) between capitalism and communism, the working class would attempt to exploit the capitalists – the earlier expropriators.

(e) Forms of Class Struggle

The Marxists speak of, as in the capitalist society, three forms of class struggle: (i) *economic,* (ii) *political* and (iii) *ideological.*

(i) In economic terms, the two opposing classes—the capitalists and the worker—confront each other. Each is conscious of its economic interests and each attempts to protect and maximize them. The capitalists stall all efforts of the workers in bringing about economic equality, and the workers demand higher wages, shorter hours of work and build their organisations to create and strengthen their struggle and solidarity.

(ii) The political struggle revolves around political power, each class striving to capture it. As the capitalist class mans and masters political power, the workers have to fight resolutely for attaining it. In capturing power, the workers have to employ the most diverse means: peaceful parliamentary struggle if possible and armed struggle if necessary.

(iii) Of great importance is the ideological struggle between the capitalists and the workers. There is much that the capitalists possess in advancing the cause of their ideology, The control over the agencies of public opinion is one such means. The workers have to wage a relentless war against bourgeois ideology which dominates the whole capitalist system, and in the process, organise themselves in a cohesive class and build its ideology.

(f) Politics and Class Struggle

For the Marxists, the state is no impartial institution. They say that the state originated at a particular stage of social development, the stage when there emerged opposing classes. Until then, there was no state, no state apparatus, no political activity. Politics, the Marxists hold the view, was, thus the result of the class society. It arose to serve the economically dominant class and conversely, exploit the non-owning class. the state, in any class society, is a class institution, an oppressive organ, a partisan organisation, an executive machinery for purposes of exploiting the poor. The state, being a class instrument, remains as long as there remains the class society. The existence of the dictatorship of the proletariat in the socialist society, following the capitalist one, is a transnational phenomenon, existing until the overthrow of the capitalist system lock, stock and barrel and the establishment of the socialist society. That is why the Marxists regard politics not merely an instrument of class struggle but also a means for bringing about socio-economic changes in the society, transforming the class character of the society into its classlessness, from the capitalist society to the socialist one.

(g) Criticism

Politics as class struggle has remained a subject of attack from many quarters. The *anti-socialists* emphasise, not on the class struggle, but on the natural harmonies of society. The *sociologists,* regarding the Marxian concept of class struggle as limited, highlight numerous types of struggles in the society—racial, social, cultural, civilizational. The *revisionists* in Germany, the *Fabians* in England and the *syndicalists* in France dubbed the marxian theory of class struggle as inadequate, narrow or not radical enough. The existence of politics as an instrument of class struggle on the one hand and as an apparatus for socio-economic transformation of society on the other: one negative and the other positive: one as destructive and the other as constructive makes confusion more confounded than removing it.

IV: Politics as the Pursuit of Common Good

Politics invariably implies, among other things, political power-power to make laws, take decisions, enforce them and punish the guilty. But in doing all this, it does not and, in fact, can not set aside its attempts to first search and then seek the fulfilment of common interest. No state, if it avows to be democratic, can survive for long unless it promotes what is in the interest of all or most of them.

To equate common interest with common good is .not uncommon. The problem arises only when one endeavours to know as to what common good is. Common good may mean common interest, social justice, welfareism or good and just life for all alike. It may also imply good of all or/and good for all, actions done impartially or done without prejudice to others. Vague as the term is, common good means many things to many people.

(a) Meaning of Common Good

The idea of common good is not new. The ancients, whether eastern or western did point out as to what constitutes the common good. "If all communities (meaning here associations, numerous groups) aim at some good," Aristotle once wrote of the *polis* "the state or political community, which is the highest of all, and which embraces all the rest, aims and in a greater degree than any other, at the highest good." Much later, Rousseau thought of common preservation and the general well-being as the very essence of common good. But this is not enough!

Common good, as is what it is, needs to be understood more than what meets the eye.

Certain governmental functions such as defence, order, prevention of epidemics, good roads, though benefit all or nearly all, do not constitute the whole of common good. This is so because the idea of common good is associated, primarily and essentially, with services such as education, old age pensions, medical facilities and the like. The essence of common good lies in what is done in the interest and welfare of all the people. It is closer to the promotive, more than protective, functions of the state.

But this is what we understand common good as an objective. Surely, the properties of common good include the promotion of the interests of the people. We would not call a certain action of the government as promoting common good if it harms more than it benefits the people. None would challenge the fact that the idea of common good must incorporate in itself the realisation of some goal. There is yet something more to it. If common good means the realisation of some goal or aim, the question which assumes importance is the number of people whose interests are to be realised. Would we say that the promotion of the interests of majority is a common good? Benn and Peters say:

"Neither is the common good merely the good of the majority; for we often think it right, for example, to tax the majority to relieve a needy minority; and we should condemn majority action if it took no account of suffering inflicted on the few merely because they are a few." For them, to seek common good means "to try to act justly." "deciding impartially between all claims and trying to satisfy those for which the best case can be made out."

So understood, common good is both an objective to be realised and a procedure to be followed. It is an objective in so far as it can be defined precisely and achieved through the medium of the state. It is a procedure is so far as it demands of the state to act in the most impartial manner.

Common good, both as. an objective and a procedure, is closely associated with a state democratically constituted. Opinions may differ with regard to the contents of common good or what functions and services should or should not be enlisted as part of the common good, but unless a state is a state of all the people, it can not be a state for all the people. The idea of common good has emerged and developed with the evolution and growth of 'democracy'. To talk of 'common good' prior to our modern democratic age is a mere phantasm. In ancient times, the idea of common good was merely an ethical idea, a sheer ideal and a model to be adopted in real life. During the medieval monarchical days, 'common good' existed either in the religious precepts or in the philanthropy of the autocratic czars as expressed in certain relief measures. It is only with the advent of 'democracy' that the idea of common good assumes importance as a matter of peoples' claim on the state. The liberals touched the 'common good' mark after travelling through *laissez faire* and welfare state. The socialists, especially of the Marxian type, soon discovered the totalitarian state turning into an authoritarian one, and, therefore, pushing a step back-ward, contented themselves with the ideal of common good.

The goal of common good is more relevant to the developing nations than to the developed ones. The developed nations see in 'common good' state's efforts to act as impartially as possible. They find it in its procedure. The developing countries, economically and socially backward as they are, regard 'common good' as an objective as well as procedure. The tasks of nation-building and modernisation being undertaken in the developing nations, reflect, in ultimate, nothing but the realisation of 'common good'.

(b) Characteristics of Politics as the Pursuit of Common Good

The following characteristics of politics as the pursuit of common good are notable:-

(1) Politics is not merely an agency for reconciling the-conflicting interests of the individuals. The emphasis is not on 'the individual' but on what is 'common' for all the individuals.' Politics discovers what is 'common' for all and thereafter, promotes the spirit of commonalty.

(2) Politics is not 'class struggle' as the Marxists insist. If it were so, the dictatorship of the proletariat, howsoever transitional it might be, would not have been, as Lenin said, better than the bourgeois state quantitatively or well as qualitatively. Class permeation, and not class conflict, is the essence of the state.

(3) The idea of common good presupposes a state that serves and not the one that orders. Benn and Peters say that the state alone is peculiarly fitted to achieve common good.

(4) Politics exists to pursue common good. The range of common good lies between protection on the one end and development-conservation on the other. It begins with the establishment of social order and ends up in a state that serves all.

(5) As an objective, the state has to achieve the common good; as a procedure, it has to act justly and impartially. The developed countries adopt common good more as a procedure than as an objective whereas the developing nations accept it both as an objective as well as a procedure.

(6) Common good, as a concept, is a modern democratic phenomenon. Its geneses can be traced back in the writings of the individualists, utilitarians, idealists, socialists-both utopian and scientific. The latest to join the race are the communitarians.

(c) Communitarianism and 'Common Good'

The notion of 'common good' has cut across all modern ideologies, for it has been the goal set to be achieved by all of them. The individualists like John Locke and Adam Smith saw good of the society emerging from the good of the individual. The utilitarians like Jeremy Bentham found common good in the 'greatest happiness of the greatest number.' T.H. Green, the idealist, held the view that common good is attained when the state becomes an obstacle against all obstacles. The utopian socialists like Saint Simon thought the good of community as a condition for the good of the individual. Marx insisted that common good could be realised only in a classless society.

The communitarians like Michael Sandel, Michael Walzer and Charles, Taylor were not the first to invoke the idea of community as a reaction against the idea of 'individual'. Hegel, Green, Bosanquet, Tawney, Williams, Wolff had, in their different ways, provided their critiques on what was mischievous in liberalism. The communitarians can, at best, be regarded as the latest critics of liberalism.

The communitarians believe that common good can not be determined by abstract reasoning, nor are they freely chosen by atomized moral agents, but rather arise out of and are implicit in the ways of life of particular communities. Condemning the liberals for having built individualism, subjectivism, atomism, elevation, instrumentalism, contract-based and market-oriented liberalism, the communitarians declare community as the source of political values and of common good. The communitarian argument can be summed up as under:

(1) Common good, the communitarians say, can not be developed by abstract philosophical reasoning. Nor is it the product of individual preference or emotional attitude. Rather, it is embodied in the community itself. So understood, community serves as the basis of practical reason and political judgement, including common good itself.

(2) The liberal theory of the self and the conception of the human condition flowing from it have been criticized by the communitarians. They argue that the self does not exist in isolation and that it, atleast, is, in part, constituted by the values of community within which the self finds himself or herself.

(3) The development of community can not be, the communitarians tell us, secured by agreement on abstract principles, but rather has to trade on values which are implicit in the way of life in community as it exists. Walzer points out: "Justice and equality can conceivably be worked out as philosophical artifacts, but a just or egalitarian society cannot be. If such a society isn't already here—hidden as it were in our concepts and categories—we shall never know it concretely or realise it in fact."

Conclusion

Common good relates itself to the interests of the community as against those of the individual Fairly old as the concept of common good claims itself to be, it has grown and developed with the idea of 'democracy. 'Common Good' sets a goal and a way to achieve it. Politics, if it has to respond to the values of democratic norms, it has to throw all its weight in pursuing the good 'common' to all.

The notion of 'common good', on both theoretical and practical grounds, is too weak to withstand its own vagueness. This is because the idea raises more questions than solves them. One is never sure as to where the boundaries of 'common good' start and where do they end. Again, one does not know the satisfaction of the interests of how many people in a society would constitute 'common good'. The government can always, including Rousseau's government based on general will, resort to arbitrariness in the name of 'common good'.

Despite all the limitations which the idea of 'common good' is supposed to contain, there is a ground and that too, a profound ground in favour of 'common good' both as a concept as well as a concrete category. The philosophers, by invoking the idea of common good, show a path to be followed by the rulers. Though 'common good' may be a distant goal, yet nothing stops any state to make an attempt approaching it. The notion of 'common good', like those of justice, equality, freedom and others, act as trend-setters and keep strengthening the idealist stream which is no less important in political theory.

SUGGESTED READINGS

1 Bellamy, R, *Theories and Concepts of Politics: An Introduction* (Manchester: Manchester University Press, 1993)
2 Blondel, J., *The Discipline of Politics* (London: Butter-worths. 1981)
3 Gray, H., *Liberalism: Essays* in *Political Philosophy*, (London: Routlege, 1989)
4 _________; *Liberalism* (Milton Keynes: Open University Press, 1986)
5 Kymlicka. W., *Liberation, Community and Culture*, (Oxford: Cloredon, 1989)
6 Leftwich, A., (ed), *What is Politics?* (Oxford: Blackwell, 1984)
7 Cevitas, R (ed), *The Ideology of the New Left* (Cambridge: Polity, 1986)
8 McLennan G., Held, D., Hall, S., (eds), *The Idea of Modern State* (Milton Keynes: Open University Press, 1984)
9 Mouffe, c., *The Return of the Political* (London: Verso, 1993)
10 Offe, C; *Contradictions of the Welfare State* (London: Hutchison, 1984)
11 Pierson, c., *Marxist Theory and Democratic Politics* (Cambridge: Polity, 1986)
12 Plant, R, *Modern Political Thought* (Oxford: Blackwell, 1991)
13 Rosenblum, N., *Another Liberalism* (Mass., Harvard University Press, 1987)
14 Sandel, M., *Liberalism and Its critics* (Oxford: Basil Blackwell, 1989)
15 Walzer, M., *Spheres of Justice* (Oxford: Martin Robertsn, 1983)
16. Wasby S., *Political Science: The Discipline and Its Dimensions* (Calcutta: Scientific Book Agency, 1972)

3

Power

The concept of power is central to the understanding and practice of politics. Machiavelli pioneered the study of power and its application in the political system. Thomas Hobbes wrote that "There is a general inclination of all mankind, a perpetual and restless desire of power after power, that ceaseth only in death."

I: Power: Meaning and Definitions

A standard definition of power is very difficult, as it is one of the most complicated concepts in political science. The dictionary meaning of power gives little insight into its definition. According to Oxford English Dictionary, power is the "ability to do or act" and 'control, influence, ascendency'. Webster's Dictionary defines it as the possession of control, authority, or influence over others. To Arnold Wolfers, power is defined as the ability to move others by the threat or infliction of deprivation. It is also "the ability to move others or to get them to do what one wants them to do and not to do, what one does not want them to do." Robert Dahl defines power as "a relationship among actors in which one actor induces other actors in some way they would not otherwise act." To Morganthau power is "man's control over the minds and actions of other men". Easton opines that power is a "relationship in which one person or group is able to determine the actions of another in the direction of the former's own ends." Bertrand Russel viewed power "as the production of intended results".

Power is not physical force; Physical force may be an instrument of power but equating both would tantament to a mere confusion, for power is always legitimate. Power is not influence also, as Arnold Wolfers point out that influence means "the ability to ... move others ... through promises or grants of benefits." 'Authority' is closely connected with power, but it is more than power. It means besides the legitimate right to use force, the holders of power has a moral right to rule and use coercion. In fact all the governments strive to replace power with authority which makes the governance easy and the employment of coercion becomes minimum so far as society in general is concerned.

The word 'power' is derived from the Latin word *'Potere'* meaning 'to be able'. The concept of power has affinities with the concept of domination (from latin 'dominium' meaning mastery or control). It is also close to the concept of authority. And yet, the three do not mean the same. While the concept of power is agnostic; domination, on the other connotes an asymmetry, and authority suggests a kind of concent or authorization.

Over the years, there have developed models of power. Mention is being made about the following four:

(i) *Volunatarist model of Power,* as advocated by Dahl (1968) regards power as a capacity to get others do what they would not otherwise do, to set things in motion, and 'change the order of events. Power is a force that brings movement. It is a cause-effect relationship, and asumes a ruler on the one hand and the ruled on the other; a two-way traffic.

(ii) *Hermeneutic model of Power,* as advocated by Bernstein, 1974 and Taylor, 1979), holds that power is constituted by the shared meanings of given social communities. Thus the emphasis of this model of power is on norms, i.e., power is embedded in a system of values. It is power as norms, and more than this, i.e., norms as power.

(iii) *Structuralist model of Power,* as advocated by Ball 1975; Bhaskar, 1975; Isaac, 1987) and traced back to Marx and Durkheim, defines power as the capacities to act in a pre-given reality of structural forms. It assumes that power is closely related to structural rules, resources, positions and relationships. Following Marx, this model holds the view that the individual is a social being who can individuate himself only in the midst of society.

(iv) *Post-modernist model of Power,* as advocated by Flax, 1987; Ferguson, 1987; Faucault, 1977), regards power as complex and ambiguous and believes that it is located in a multiplicity of social spaces.

Summing up the above, we may say that the concept of power would have the following characteristics:-

1. Power assumes a relationship of domination and subordination among men.
2. It is relative depending upon the capacity to influence others.
3. It is used to achieve desired ends.
4. State or the government is the repository of power with a legitimate right to use force.

However no power can claim to be absolute, no matter how ruthless or autocratic, the ruler is. There cannot be, as. Panton and Gill remark, "a simple one way relationship between governor and governed." There are limits to tolerance and no ruler can rule for long without the significant support form some section of the people, whose interests have always to be considered. History has witnessed the saga of many powerful rulers who even claimed themselves to be God but were eventually overthrown. Accounting and responsiveness on the part of the government is very important. This is more so in case of democratic governments who are chosen by the people and their governance is based on consent and persuasion. The exercise of power is also subjected to a variety of pressures from interest group, political parties, public opinion and international arena. The capacity or capability to exert obedience is also important as many governments have failed in doing so. Morality, ethics, religion, customs and traditional beliefs further constitute limitation on power. Last but not the least is the performance, successes and failures in realising the desired ends, which affect the operation of power.

II: Forms of Power

There is no unanimity regarding the number of forms of power in political science. However generally, power is said to have three forms. They are:-

1. Political Power.
2. Economic Power.
3. Ideological Power.

Political Power: Approaches

Political power means the power of the state or government. The state through its agency-the government exercises control over the individuals and associations in its territory. However here we are more concerned with the people who man the government rather than the study of government. As E.P. Allens puts it, "Political power is evidenced by the ability of those who control the instruments of government to secure obedience to their decisions."

History has witnessed fierce struggle for the control over political power in different periods. Initially the tribals fought among themselves followed by the great ambitious kings who desired to expand their rules even to unknown frontiers. Later this struggle took place between king-feudals on the one hand and Church on the other. The modern era saw the conflict between king and the capitalist class and the rivalries between the capitalists and the workers since 18th century.

This long history only proves that obtaining political power has been the key issue in politics.

There have been a vide variety of governmental systems. However the form of government decides the allocation of power. In monarchy, the king is at the helm of affairs and the decision making is affected by him and the feudal lords. In dictatorship the political power is vested in the hands of dictator and his henchmen. Democracy, on the other hand, believes in wide participation and the political power is controlled and exercised by the vast electorate.

Formally, the political power is vested as per the constitutional arrangements in a polity. The executive, legislative, judiciary, bureaucracy, pressure groups and the political parties control and direct the operation of political power. An indepth study of politics would however, take into account the informal elements which act behind the scene and dominate the political system. Regarding this, there have been in modern times mainly three approaches to the pragmatic study of political power. They are

(i) Marxist approach
(ii) Elitist approach
(iii) Pluralist approach

(i) Marxist Approach

Marxists believe that political power is in the hands of the ruling class for the protection and enhancement of its economic interests. The basic assumption behind this belief derives from the fact that mode of production determines the political superstructure of the society. In; this, as Andrew Cox says, "Individual acting as politically relevants actors .... have very little scope at all to shape the economic base of society on its political and social superstructure." Moreover the personnel who control the state apparatus belong to represent the same class. Thus the state is nothing but the executive committee of the ruling class incapable of achieving harmony in the society. Changes in the political power structure do take place but that is "not because of conscious efforts by committed individuals at the political and social levels of society but because the existing mode of production is challenged by an alternative and technically more efficient 'mode of production. This is how the power structure changed in the slave-owing society, feudal society and capitalist society. In capitalist society, according to Marx, the state "is a committee for managing the collective affairs of the bourgeoisie." However the working class as it becomes increasingly organised also demand participation and is finally accommodated in the political power structure. But with the highly centralised structures. and complex bureaucratised state machinery, it is, incapable of giving any challenge to the capitalist system. Thus political power may be shared by the workers but they have very limited role in its working. Finally in Marxist scheme of things. State is to wither away which means ultimately political power with all its structure will have no role to play. It will not be required at all.

(ii) Elitist Approach

According to the elitists, the political power is controlled and exercised by few people who acquire dominance as a result of their wealth, power, moral and intellectual abilities. The prominent advocates of elite theory are Mosca, Pareto, Mitchells, C. Wright Mills and Schumpeter. The theory believes in the presence of elites in every political system. Criticising the basic tenet of democracy, Pareto says. "We will not linger over the fiction of popular representation ... let us rather see what is the substance beneath the various forms of power in the governing class. Discounting exceptions, which are few and of short duration, there is everywhere a governing class, not large in membership, which maintains itself in power partly by the consent of governed." Sometime the elite has to resort to force to remain in political power. To Schumpeter, "Democracy means only that the people have the opportunity. of accepting or refusing the men, who are to rule them.' The members of this elite who govern the political power are not exclusive. There is 'circulation of elites' in which new members join and old leave. Even the so-called revolution is nothing but a change in the composition of elites. "The elite," according to Mosca, "performs all political functions, monopolises power and enjoys the advantages that power brings .... " The identification of elite, however, has been a critical problem. Different theorists of elite theory have identified them differently. In general, if all are to be accepted, this ruling elite is composed of politicians, army generals, bureaucrats, big industrialists, intellectuals and high officials of public corporations.

Like the Marxists, the elite theory maintains that political power does not subserve the common good. But they do not accept the Marxian view of political power being an instrument of oppression. On the contrary they believe that the purpose and objective of political power is to reconciliate and harmonise the conflicting interests in the society.

(iii) Pluralist Approach

Modem liberals have advocated pluralist approach to political power. They stand for the autonomy of political power as distinct from economic power. Political power is not the monopoly of few as elitists and Marxists assert, but is widely distributed. Prof Laski remarks that power should be plural as society itself is plural. Beginning from the assumption that society being composed of different groups, Norsis says... "no one group always dominates to the exclusion of others. Interaction such as industrialists and workers, businessmen and consumers, housewives and unionists, students and pensioners check and balance each other in the pursuit of their own ends." To pluralists, government acts as honest broker or umpire, independent of any particular interests.

The pluralists view power in the decision making perspective. They would study and identify different groups which played their respective roles in a particular decision making. For this, detailed information is to be collected and conclusions arrived at. In this way, as Panton and Gill opine, "it may well be possible to identify clearly who wields influence or power and with respect to what areas of policy. Steven Lukes suggests three dimensions of operation of political power. Firstly only such decisions with respect to key issues are made which are desired by the possessors of power. Here the preferences of people who hold power are important. The second dimension involves the failure of power holders to act at all. This is a conscious decision and power is used for taking no action as the holder of power are not just interested. Lastly, the third dimension of power in which it is influenced is by changing the minds or as Barry Barrens suggests, "...its possessors may secure their interests not by winning a contest or even by avoiding a contest, but by transforming the consciousness of their political opponents, and weakening their grasp upon the nature of their real interests so much that no contest threatens." To Lukes, only the first dimension is very clearly observable in politics, the other two act from behind the scene and what people fail to do and what they fail to think of or perceive, is the only evidence for their existence ... " In such a situation, power becomes an essentially contested concept in which people will always disagree in deciding the actual operation and even definition of power.

Thus the political power is used by different groups in different times depending upon a variety of factors. However, such a group politics also creates crisis in the political system, especially when there is a strong minority whose interests are not taken care of and which starts questioning the very legitimacy of the political system, along with the threat of cessation from the polity.

III: Types of Political Power

In a political system, the political power is manifested in, what Anthony H. Birch calls, a four-fold typology:

(i) The most -obvious form of manifestation of political power is coercion, in which the government uses force to make its presence felt. Here citizens have no choice. Examples could be the police lathi charging a demonstration, imposition of curfew and demolition of encroachments on public property.

(ii) Secondly, there is political authority which means the exercise of power by the lawful authorities to make and implement decisions, that are binding within the political system. The law making function is performed by the legislature, the executive and bureaucracy implement them, and the courts interpret and adjudicate.

(iii) Political power is also manifested in political influence. Influence is exercised by various pressure-groups and political parties on the decision-making authorities, so that their demands are met and grievances redressed.

(iv) Lastly is the political manipulation defined "as the activity of shaping the public opinion, values and behaviour of others without the latter realising that this is happening." The mass-media being used for political interest of a particular political party or leader and a teacher teaching politics in a biased manner can be examples of such type of political manipulations.

Another characteristic of political power is its exclusive right to use physical force to exert obedience. The rules and laws framed by the political power are binding on every citizen. No one can claim immunity from observation of laws. Violation of laws invite punishment and coercion by the political power. Robert Dahl rightly puts it, "The government is any government that successfully upholds a claim to the exclusive regulation of the legitimate use of physical force in enforcing its rule within a given territory. The political system made up of the residents of that territorial area and the government of the area is a state." In fact, State is differentiated from all other organisations by its legitimate power to use force. The organisations may pursuade or influence but not coerce their members for the desired results. The government not only makes rules and laws but also possesses the effective machinery to enforce them.

The basic function of political power is to maintain law and order and dispense justice. However, in modern times, political power has to deal with a wide range of issues and problems. It has to bring about a reconciliation between conflicting interests and to look after the common good in the society. In developing countries, the political power has been associated with achieving the gigantic task of socio-economic development. The concept of welfare state and planned economy have increasingly expanded the activities of political power where it has to involve and decide issues relating to society, economy and even culture. The goal of common good being objective, political power not only controls and regulates the economy but it also runs factories and industries.

IV: Economic Power

Economic power is the material power. It can also be called as the power of wealth. To Marxists, the political power has always remained in the hands of possessing class and the possessing class has always exercised political power for its own benefits. The liberals, however, stand for autonomy of political power from economic power.

In liberal democracies, the economic power is vested in the capitalists. They control the means of production and distribution of goods and services. However, the liberal democracies have also witnessed managerial revolution where the economic power has been transferred from the capitalists to the professional managers. "With the management", as Ashim Gill puts it," and the labour being able to own shares in the parent organisation, the distinction between owner and worker has also blurred and the system has become closer to the Marxist ideals of collective ownership." However, the democratic society is based upon economic inequality. As a result of this economic inequality the society witnesses class conflicts. With the passage of time, the economic inequality came to be considered as natural and on the basis of this claimed truth the society acquired speed for its growth. It is a fact that this phenomenon of economic inequality did attain certain degree of success. But such successes were primarily individual successes. In the process, certain states also become rich but the humanity as a whole did not develop. The problem with capitalism is, as Ashim Gill puts it, "that it results in a fragmentary view of the world." Everybody is competiting against each other and self aggrandisement is the motto." No one has an overall view of progress, but all have self-centred views of progress." There is no planning as law of supply and demand satisfies the requirements of market economy. But this also puts individual at the mercy of market forces, where the competition is ruthless and even inhuman. Modern democrats have defended the liberal democratic model by suggesting that no longer the ruthless capitalism exists and there is a greater participation in economic activity. Consequently economic power has been widely distributed and prosperity is the fact of modern life.

In a socialist state, economic power is in the hands of people who control political power. The entire economy is handled directly by the state, right from the ownership of means of production to the distribution of goods and services. This is because the Marxist ideology does not believe in the autonomy of political power, rather political power is subservient to economic power and fundamental changes in the society are determined and caused by the economic forces or the mode of production. Any change in the mode of production will affect the corresponding changes in political and social superstructure. Thus the hand mill creates feudalism, while the steam mill, a capitalist-industrial society. To quote Marx, "The mode of production in material life determines the general character of the social, political and spiritual processes of life. It is not the consciousness of man that determines their existence, but on the contrary, their social existence determines their consciousness. Ideas and ideologies and other factors also play their role, but they are essentially the part of the dynamics of material life, devoid of any independent existence. Thus, history can be understood as the study of different modes of production and their conflicts. "Change occurs", as Cox puts it, "as one particular means of production (and the classes to which it gives rise) comes into conflict with an alternative means or mode of production (and with the classes which this in turn generates). As one mode of production is superseded by another, the ruling class which owns the newly dominant means of production will reshape the state structures to serve its own ends." Thus political power is controlled and exercised by the ruling class for their own ends. In history, feudalism was based on the ownership of land, which was the dominant mode of production and the political power was dominated by absolute king and feudal overlords. Wealth and position in the society derived from the landownership and the landowners dominated the different state structures. This dominance ensured the class character of the state. The feudalistic mode of production was challenged by the capitalist mode of production, resulting into the transfer of political power from kings and feudal overlords to the capitalists. In capitalism, the capitalists constitute the ruling class. To conclude, political power is the means of dominance and oppression in the hands of possessing class to further their class interests.

There is no denying of fact that economic power has affected and subjugated the political power. "In Western societies," says Durverger. "today money is still the strongest political weapon." This is true of all democracies where political power is slave to the economic power and democracy a prisoner of the possessing class, Therefore, a proper analytical understanding of economic power is necessary for a precise evaluation of political power.

However, to say that economic power governs the political power, will be a half-truth only. The interplay of economics and politics is a very complex dynamics. The political power also influences the economic forces. The .modern state has turned into welfare state in which the economic system is highly regulated and controlled by the political power. With the rise and development of political consciousness, as a result of universal adult franchise, the political power has turned economics into welfare economics and the political power is not exclusively the domain of holders of economic power.

V: Ideological Power

Ideological power is the rationalisation of any system in terms of ideas and beliefs with the desired objective of justifying that system. Strictly speaking it is not an end itself but a means to the realisation of welfare of mankind. Ideology dictates direction as it motivates people to be committed to its cause. Thus ideological power becomes an instrument for the justification of political power.

Since, the objective of ideology is the 'overall progress of mankind,' Ashim Gill points out that... "Different ideologies have devised different means to achieve this end, and no one ideology is or can be, absolutely applicable and relevant to all times, places and circumstances. Every particular idea or ideology has a particular time and a place... No one can stop the march of an idea whose time has come and ideas that are out of time with ground reality are fated to die." Thus in medieval times, the kings took the plea of divine rights of kings by asserting the divine origin of state. This ideology projected kings as breathing idols of God and any violation of their rule tantamounted to sin and would invite divine punishment.

However, in modern times, the ideologies have been secular. As Fredrick M. Watkins points out, "Their vision is not of a blissful life in the hereafter, but of a perfectible life on earth." Inherent in this, is their unshaking faith that they can achieve a perfect state and therefore, their goals are utopian. According to Watkins "oversimplification is the primary characteristic of modern ideologies. This is their strength and also their weakness." They control the-minds and actions of men by advocating their ideas to be holding universal application and that they are the only repository of truth and goodness to the exclusion of others. Therefore, the unique characteristic of an ideology is to demand blind loyalty from its followers.

Throughout history, ideologies have been divided between two opposite camps— "the liberals and the authoritarians; the radicals and the conservatives, the upper classes and the lower classes, the capitalists and the communists, the state and the church, the socialists and the fundamentalists." They coexist and according to Ashim Gill, every state is in a situation of dynamic equilibrium. Any increase in one part of the state creates an imbalance in other part." The balance is restored either by the reforms within and if the imbalance becomes too great, revolution follows. The dominant ideologies of modem age have been democracy and communism. Democracy emphasises the rationality and autonomy of the individual by declaring freedom, equality and fraternity as universally accepted values on which any system of government is to be based. But this is also the ideology of ruling class-the capitalists, which is shared by all the people, irrespective of their class division. Marx called this false consciosness, as the class which owns the means of production also controls the means of mental production and the ideas generated from such production are universally accepted as true. This is necessary for the people in general, living in society because as Cohen asserts, "If the exploited were to see that they are exploited, they would resent their subjection and threaten social stability. And if the exploiters were to see that they exploit, the composure they need to rule confidently would be disturbed. Being social animals, the exploiters have to feel that their behaviour is justifiable." To Marxists, the origins of ideology lay in materialist base of the society. Therefore, their objective is to affect change in materialistic base to bring about a revolution.

The ideology of communism with all its varieties speaks of exploitation by a small minority over the big majority throughout history. Marx's *Communist Manifesto,* which has been hailed as the Bible of Communism contains the important tenets of this ideology. To Laski, it gave direction and philosophy to what had been before little more than an inchoate protest against injustice. Marxism aims to remove this injustice by the establishment of a socialistic society which eventually will give way to a communist society where there will be a total elimination of exploitation and injustice.

Thus the ideological power is the power of ideas and beliefs designed to legitimise and maintain a particular political and social system in its totality. It is vested in the ruling class which, as Marx said, is also the 'ruling intellectual force.' The ideological power is propagated through the family environment, education system, culture, religion, ethics, morality and the means of formulation of public opinion. The mass media also plays a substantial role in moulding and planting the ideology into people's minds.

VI: Ideological Power, Political Power, Economic Power: The Interrelation

Ideological power is intrinsically related to political and economic power. Ideas have been crucial to politics and have been responsible for political changes. They brought democracy in various parts of the world and subsequently affected socialism in Soviet Union and in other countries. The political power for its own safety also propagates and protects the ideology. The Marxists, after seizing power in Soviet Union vowed to expand the communist ideology beyond their frontiers. Stalin declared that Soviet Union was an island in midst of a vast capitalist sea and therefore, communist ideology must be exported to other countries as well, so that Soviet Union ceases to remain an island. Thus he saw the preservation of his political power in the expansion of communist ideology internationally.

A large part of ideology contains economics. This shows the relationship between the ideological power and economic power. The ideologies of democracy or capitalism and communism carne as a result of economic changes in the society. As Ashirn Gill says that "capitalism and communism had to wait till the industrial revolution, before they could be fully developed into the powerful ideologies of their times."

In fact both the ideologies were associated and affected by the industrial revolution. On the other hand the Industrial Revolution also, as. Watkins says owed "much to the power of ideology." Ashim Gill comments that, "The fall of communism today is a sign of the times that the factors that were ripe for the rise of communism and existed at the beginning of the century are no longer relevant." Ideology is a vision which needs a plan or programme of action in different fields of politics and economics. If the action fails, the whole ideology would fall as the house of cards. This is evident from the collapse of communism in different parts of the world. Hence, economic, political and ideological powers are inseparable parts of one whole with the objective of maintaining or changing a particular system.

SUGGESTED READINGS

1. Ball, T., "Power, Cousation and explanation", *Polity*, 2., 1975. "The Changing Face of power", in Ball, T., *Transforming Political Discourse* (Oxford: Basil Blackwell, 1988)
2. Barry. B., *Power and Political Theory: Some European Perspectives* (London: Wiley, 1976)
3. Bernstein, R., *Praxis and Action* (Philadelphia University of Pennsylvania Press, 1974)

4. Bhaskar, R., *A Realists Theory of Science* (Brighton: Harverster Press, 1975)
5. Dahl, R., "The Concept of Power", *Behaoioural Science,* 2., 1957
--------- *Who Governs?* (New Haven: Yale University Press, 1961)
-------- "Power", *International Encyclopedia of the Scoial Sciences* (New York: Free Press, 1968)
6. Isaac, J., *Power and Marxist Theory: A Realist View* (New York: Cornell University Press, 1987)
7. Lasswell, H. and Kaplan, A., *Power and Society* (New Haven: Yale University Press, 1950).
8. Lukes, S., *Power: A Radical View* (London: Macmillan 1974)
9. Nagel, J., *The Descriptive Analysis of Power* (New Haven: Yale University Press, 1975)
10. Poulantzas, N., *Political Power and Social Classes* (London: New Left Book, 1973).

4

Theories of Power in Society

Numerous kinds of power are usually referred to. The power of objects (like magnets), natural processes (like the fall of water), artifacts (like the engines), and human beings collectively constituted (like the power of groups and organisations) are some such examples of the types of power. But in social and political theory, power, in politics and society, is regarded aa the ability to do anything or the capacity for producing an effect. Robert Dahl, while describing power keeping in view its *nature, social location,* and *effects of its exercise,* says: "(individual) A has power over (individual) B to the extent that A can get B to do something which B would not otherwise do" Power expresses itself through force, manipulation, persuasion and authority and is said to have forms like *political, economic* and *ideological* on the one hand, and on the other derived through status, class and party (to use Marx Weber's description of distribution of power). Barry Barnes identifies four kinds of power as are. understood in social and political theory: *political-military, economic, social* (status-based) and *cultural,* somewhat close to Michael Mann's classification of power into: *military, economic, political* and *ideological.* According to Michael Mann, the ideological power is derived from the monopolization of norms, rituals, and practices; economic power, from the control of the means of production, distribution and exchange and is possessed by those who monopolise these means; military power, from the military elites; and political power; from the state.

Power, in Political Science, has its peculiar features. Notable among these are: power is *relational* in the sense that it involves a relationship between one who holds it (the ruler) and the one who accepts it (the rule); it is *situational* in the sense that its expression varies from situation to situation; it is *coercive* in the sense that it has, behind it, the use of force or of compulsion; it is *legitimate* in the sense that it designates in accordance with prior determined law, a set of persons and institutions to make and implement rules and decisions, it is subject to *pressures:*

diffused and direct on the one hand, and specific and indirect on the other.

Power, in politics, means power of the state as expressed in its laws and as made by the legislature, enforced by the executive or applied by the judiciary. These are but the formal agencies which exercise power as permitted by the law of the land in a society. In addition to these formal agencies—legislature, executive, and judiciary—there are the informal or what may be called as the extra-constitutional agencies which control the very nerves of the whole administration. These include the political parties: the invisible governments, and the interest-pressure groups: the makers and unmakers of the ministries. Beyond these informal agencies, there is, in every democracy, the political sovereign—the electorate, not as is found in the individuals individually, but as is found in the individuals in a collectivity, in a body, in a class or in a group. The electorate, we must know, is sovereign only in the rhetorical sense of the term. It is able to express its power through numerous agencies (organised or unorganised) by influencing those who exercise it on behalf of the people.

Theories of power in a society are numerous, so are numerous its varying perspectives. For purposes of understanding power, it would be useful to discuss it, especially in the light of the following aspects:

(a) Class and Power
(b) Gender and Power: the Concept of Patriarchy
(c) Pluralist Theories of Power

I: Class and Class Theory of Power

The existence of 'class', by and large, is a universal phenomenon in human societies. What may differ from society to society is the nature or content of the class. Obviously in a peasant society, no one would expect a class of the industrialists. With the change in the social structure of society, there may occur changes in the forms of classes, or atleast the dominant classes. That is why that Marx and Engels talked of 'masters and slaves' in the slave-owning society; 'the feudal lords and the serfs' in the feudal society; 'the capitalists and the proletariat' in the capitalist society. There may be feudal lords in a capitalist society, but they would not constitute a dominant class there. Likewise, there may be entrepreneurs in a feudal society, but they would not make a dominant class in such a society. Class, thus, is universal: singular in a classless society, and plural and in a way mutually antagonistic in a class society.

The word class' has a different meaning, for a Marxist as well as a non-Marxist. A Marxist regards class as an economic category whereas a non-Marxist considers it as. a social one. For a Marxist classes as Lenin had said are a large groups of people distinguished by their position in the historically determined system of social production, by their relationship to the means of production, by their role in the social organisation of labour, and consequently the methods by which they receive their share of social wealth. For a non-Marxist, classes, as Bauer says, are "groups of individuals who had received an equal education, developed in a similar environment and engaged in the same occupation". The Marxists categorise classes as masters and slaves (in a slave-owning system of production), feudal lords and serfs (in feudalism), capitalists and workers (in capitalism). The non-Marxist on the other hand, offer, for purposes of convenience, numerous criteria of classes such as: (i) wealth, property or income; (ii) family or kinship; (iii) location of residence: (iv) duration of residence; (v) occupation; (vi) education; (vii) religion.

The basic difference between the Marxist and the non-Marxist perspectives is the way they look at the classes. Because the Marxists view classes as economic groups divided into possessing and non-possessing, and therefore are mutually opposed. The non-Marxists, on the other hand, regard classes as social groups united by something common from within, and therefore, are mutually friendly. The Marxists see antagonism among the classes, i.e., basic classes (capitalists and the workers in a capitalist society, for example). The non-Marxists see in them permeation. For the Marxists, the division of classes into haves and have-riots is not only sharp, it is complete as well; for the non-Marxists, the division of society into classes is never complete, is always flexible, and hence, loosely drawn up.

These differences between the Marxist and the non-Marxists views throw up some prominent similarities as well and these can form the basis of how we understand by the world 'class'. To begin with (i) a class implies a set of people bound together by something common; (ii) it bestows a status for the individual in the group; (iii) it assigns a role that an individual is expected to perform; (iv) it provides a system of reward/punishment.

A class is not a number of people born, say, on first of March in a particular year, for there is nothing that brings them together. What makes a group a class is the fact that its members are conscious or aware of each other. They mayor may not have social interaction; and mayor may not have organised themselves in a social organisation, but they must possess the element of the consciousness of kind. The females, the aged, the white for example, constitute a class. So do the workers and the capitalists, the teachers and the taught, the rulers and the ruled. And if among themselves, they develop social relations at any level, macro or micro, and if they decide to form a social structure for themselves, they find themselves in a group called the class. The first necessary component of a class, therefore, is the consciousness of the kind, and on it are built, in order of propriety, the elements of 'social relationships' and 'social organisation'. No social organisation would be formed unless its members have social interactions among themselves, and no interactions among the people are possible unless they are conscious or aware of their kind. Consciousness of kind is the foundation, the starting point of any class. It is this element from where there begin relations and interactions. The consciousness of kind is the element where a class is born; its life depends on how its members relate themselves in relation to one another; its survival is assured when it is structurally and institutionally shaped.

Society is not an aggregate of one class, but is a multitude of numerous classes: in a way, a web of social classes.

(a) Class: Its Role and Nature

Class is not a structure only and nor merely a relationship, but also is a function. Every class, as against or in cooperation with others exists for a purpose. No family would have existed if the reproduction of species would not have been a necessity. No political party, in a democracy, would have existed if capturing of political power would not have been the goal to be achieved. A class, like any group, is a people organised for a purpose: specific or general. Had there been no purpose, there would have been no groups/classes. Every class, therefore, has a corresponding role, though with the passage of time the role a class performs becomes general or assumes what becomes general alongwith its traditional role. Family's traditional role has been the reproduction of the species, but alongwith this role, the family does other functions as well: nurturing the children, caring for their health and education, planning their career and the like. The state's traditional role, to give another example, has been the maintenance of law and order, but it now does many more things. The state performs welfare functions, protects the social system, provides a score of amenities, exploits the natural resources, maintains the ecological balance and the like. The passing of time has revolutionised the nature of every class: from single to complex; from specific to general.

There is no need to go into the details of the role that a class performs. Suffice it is to state that every class-exists for its corresponding purpose.

A class is a function in so far as it exists for a purpose. It is a structure in so far as it is an organisation. What it means is that every class is organised in accordance with a set procedure and functions within a defined frame. In other words, a class is an institution as well. As an institution, a class survives and in fact, thrives on a body of rules and regulations. The rules and regulations, written or unwritten, of a social class define the relations of the members among themselves, create a hierarchical system of functionaries, provide a procedure in accordance with which the class functions, bestow a status on its members, and explain the ways it would conduct itself with other classes in the society.

The strength of a class depends on how it is organised and how it disciplines its members. More disciplined the class is, better are the results it yields. The worth of a class lies in its capacity to organise people, for more organised and disciplined people produce more effect, and therefore, possess more potential and more powers.

The organising role of the class is to organise its members in a cohesive body; bind them through its rules; and unite them in the objectives for which a class stands for. The more is the capacity of a class to organise itself, more influence does it exert and more powers it is likely to wield. Speaking within the peculiar Russian condition of pre-revolution years. *Rabochaya Mysl,* a newspaper, explains the importance of the organising role of a class: "Organise! Organise, but not only in mutual benefit societies, strike funds: and workers' circles; organise also in a political party; organise for the determined struggle against the autocratic government and against the whole capitalist society. Without such organisation, the proletariat will never rise to the class-conscious struggle; without such organisation, the working-class movement is doomed to impotency."

A class deliberately formed for a purpose with all the class-consciousness at its support, organises its members as strongly as is the class that evolves slowly through the ages. Class-consciousness is a common factor in the class that is formed and in the class that evolves. The Communist Party is an example of a class that is formed and the capitalist class is an example of the class that evolves. The former organises people explicitly and the latter, implicitly; in the former case, organisation is a matter of deliberate intention with an avowed objective; in the latter case, there is neither any formal organisation to bind its people nor any formal body to speak for it. But the unity in such a capitalist class is as strong as in any well-formed (say the Communist party) class, for all capitalists speak the same language at all places. Consciousness of the kind is the unifying element for all classes: Capitalists' or workers'; black and the white; the males and the females. Classes differ in their goals, tacits and nature.

To sum up, one may say that a class is an aggregate of people with a similar consciousness; that each class stands for a purpose, functions through a set of rules, and regulations, . and accordingly adopts ways and means to achieve its goal; that each class organises itself for producing maximum possible results.

(b) Class Theory of Power

Marxism presents the class theory of power. It regards a class more than a group of organised people. For the Marxists, class is, in itself a power. The Marxists hold the view that power is a class concept; that it arose with the development of antagonistic classes in the society; that it is a phenomenon of a class society; that it has been the monopoly of an economically-dominant class in the class society; that the workers, in the capitalist society, would organise themselves and capture power so to abolish it altogether by establishing the classless society; that power would, ultimately, cease to function in the classless society. The Marxist theory of class as power can be summed up as under:

(1) Individual is no abstract being; he is not what *he is as such,* but is what he does; he is not an isolated being, but is one who exists in interaction with and in relation to others; he is not the first, but is one who is the product of what is there all around; he is thus, the product of history, though he makes history as well; individuals live not individually, but they live in relations to one another; the key to understand individuals and their nature and relations lies in class structure.

(2) As individual is the product of history, so is the class. Classes had not existed in all ages and would not, therefore, exist in all future. They emerged at a particular stage of material development.

A class is not only a historical category, it is economic as well. This is not to say that there are no classes other than the economic. But what is being emphasised is that other types of classes are the off-shoots of the economic class whose nature and role change with the changes in the economic structure of the society.

As a class is essentially a historical product and also an economic one, it is connected with a certain stage in the development of production, with a certain type of production relations. The changes in the mode of social production result in the changes in the whole social system of a given time.

(3) Men do not choose their society, they are born in it, for society and its mode of production already exist. History produces individuals in a particular setting, though in the course of development, they change

the setting itself. Individuals, when born, find themselves in a group which has a particular status in social production: some may find themselves as owners of the means of production while others, without them; some may find themselves as managers of the social labour while others, as labour-wagers; some may find themselves as masters who take away all profit while others, as workers who take merely wages to subsist themselves. That is how antagonistic classes arose and would remain as long as there are class societies.

(4) Those who own means of production in a particular stage of material development possess both the society (therefore, a society is the society of the masters', of the feudal lords, or of the capitalists) and power. The economic wealth generates power, for one generation's wealth becomes the power of the generation that follows. The economically dominant class makes the rulers as its maid, for economic power dictates the political power while its corresponding culture builds ideological frame to legitimise what it possesses.

(5) Class antagonism is characteristic of a class society and, therefore, all hitherto recorded history (excepting the early primitive-communist society—an unrecorded account of man's history), Marx and Engels declared, is the history of class struggle: struggle between the masters and the slaves; the patricians and the plebians; the feudal lords and the serfs; the guildsmen and the journeymen; the bourgeoisie and the proletariat, and in short the exploiters and the exploited—the struggle is open at times and hidden at others, resulting, ultimately, in the formation of a newer society.

(6) In Marxian literature, the class struggle is said to be natural because of the clear-cut and sharp division, resulting from the opposing class-consciousness. The forms of class-struggle, in a capitalist society, for example, are described economic, political and ideological. The economic struggle is an effort of the proletariat to improve their material and working condition. It is also an effort of the capitalists to resist and stall the workers' demands. The political struggle is the struggle for the demolition of capitalism by the working class and the equal efforts of the capitalists to maintain its system. The ideological struggle is the struggle between two opposing ideologies—of workers and the capitalists. For Marx, and therefore, for the Marxists, the proletariat in the capitalist society, being a revolutionary class, would emerge victorious.

(7) Power, as a result of class society, remains the monopoly of the possessive class in every class society. The economically-dominant class wields power in the real sense of the term, state acting only as an agency of oppression for the owners of the means of production. To put an end to the class antagonism and, therefore, class divisions,

power (state and political power) would have to be used. And for this, power would have to be captured by a revolutionary class which is none else but the working class in the capitalist society. Power has, thus, to be used to abolish all power-power that coerces, power that punishes and the power that compels.

The Marxian theory of class has been under strains from numerous quarters. Marx is usually condemned for having oversimplified the character of a society by stating that there exist two broad classes in a class society. Indeed, economic base constitutes one ground for classifying states. But there may be other bases as well. Weber, for example, suggests status as an important factor in the classification of classes. It is argued that Marx had totally ignored the element of permeation of classes. The clash of interests brings classes in confrontation against one another, but the relationship between all classes is not always the relationship of 'touch me not', To say that it is the class consciousness which unites the capitalists, and also the workers: the exploiters and the exploited and that they always find themselves at war with each other is a falsification of what one sees in the society. By virtue of their common situation, workers may be found 'objectively' in conflict with the capitalists while, subjectively, they may lack this class-consciousness, and in the process, a particular worker 'A' may not find his particular employer 'B' exploiting him. What is being emphasised is that a similar situation is not likely always to produce a class. Marx's theory of power speaks less of the theory of class and more of the theory of social development. His main concern was to explain historical epochs of material development and it was, under this larger frame, that he came to speak of class and of the owning class that possessed power. The description of the forms of power into economic, political and ideological is, indeed, understandable. But what is not understandable, in the Marxian theory, is the importance attached to each of these forms which keeps changing: sometimes it is the economic power which makes and unmakes the political power while at others, it is the political power that shapes the social structure of the society. Marx says that in the classless society, antagonistic classes would disappear and that the classes which remain are friendly classes. The latest development of Marxism proves otherwise: the ruling class, in socialist states, has alienated itself from the ruled after having usurped all economic benefits.

II: Gender and Power: Feminism and Patriarchy

Feminism is a revolt against patriarchy. It is a protest against male domination. It is a reaction against the idea that women are men's delight. It is an ideology whose basic goal, as Dahlerup paraphrases, is to remove the discrimination against and the degradation of women and to break down the male dominance of society. It is committed to women's emancipation, seeking equality between men and women in all aspects of life, be its personal, private, familial or public.

Feminism is a gender phenomenon. Gender and sex are likely to be confused as one. What is 'sex' in biology is 'gender' in social sciences. Gender, is the social institutionalisation of sexual inequalities. It is a concept which, on social plane, refers to males and females, assigns to them their relative roles in the society, and thus, accords a corresponding social position. So understood, gender, in social sciences, implies social construction of males and females identity. It is a social recognition of biological differences. In the context of patriarchical societies, the concept of gender is understood as an ideological mechanism in the subordination of women.

(a) Distinction between Gender and Sex

Though usually confused as one, the two, gender and sex, are distinct. Their distinction, however, mainly on academic plane, may be summed up as under

(1) Gender is the method of classifying people in the society on grounds of sex; sex is the method of classifying people in the society on grounds of structural differences. Gender is 'social classification' of people; sex is 'biological classification' of human beings.

(2) Gender is made whereas sex is born. A child is born as a boy-baby or a girl-baby, but develops into a man or a woman when assigned a particular role in the society. Gender is the functional aspect of sex; sex is the biological aspect of gender.

(3) The characteristics of gender (say masculinity or femininity) are culturally and socially constructed whereas in the case of sex, they are biologically and naturally founded.

(4) Gender reflects nurture whereas sex, nature. In other words, gender develops as a result of nurture while the development of sex is the result of nature. A male gender is attuned. through nurture, to his corresponding role; a female one, to her own.

(5) The nature of women, as also of men, when biologically determined, relates to the domains of sex. the nature of women, as well as of men, when socially constructed, relates to the domain of gender.

(6) The task of feminism is the abolition of gender inequality, and not of the sexual one. Feminism, as the ideology of female gender,

advocates gender equality within the framework of sexual inequalities.

(7) Gender discrimination is a social problem whereas sex-inequality is an inborn phenomenon.

(8) The distinction on the basis of sex into man and woman speaks of statistical categories: men belonging to one category, the women, to the other. In itself, the statistical categories are only sociological terms and therefore do not mean much in society relations. It is only then when these categories assume social forms and are assigned peculiar roles that they enter the arena of gender problem.

However, it would be wrong to overemphasise the distinction between gender and sex. The distinction here made is only an academic discourse and should not be taken too far. The fact, on the other hand, is that biological and gender distinctions are hollow. The argument is that biological differences should not be made a basis for gender distinctions. Women have to be mothers, but they need not accept the responsibilities of motherhood. Child-bearing and child-rearing are two differents things. Men can assume the duties of motherhood and can help in child-rearing. Furthermore, it is wrong to regard childbirth as a social disadvantage or a disqualification, denying women a role in public life. It is also wrong to assume that what is personal, private, domestic, and familial is always non-political. To insist men as public and women as private is to limit the boundaries of politics. That is why that the feminists advocate "The politics of everyday life" as Simone de Beauvoir points out, "Women are made, they are not born", the gender differences, it may well be argued, are merely manufactured by male chauvinists.

III: Feminist Critique of Mainstream Power Theories

Feminism refers to a theory which sees the relationship between the sexes as one of inequality, subordination and oppression and which sees this as a problem of political power than a fact of nature. What it means is that the distinction between men and women is not merely biological, but is also made sociological and thereafter political: men and women are biologically different, but they are seen, regarded and structured socially as different gender. The masculine gender, being physically strong and having made himself as the incharge of the external or what may be called 'public', exploits woman by considering her as an inferior being, a slave, and a commodity.

Feminism of the *liberal* shade advocates equality between men and women and thus argues that both be given equal legal and political rights. The *Marxist* feminists deplore the fact that women, like most men, in any class society, are oppressed and would continue being oppressed by the capitalist system of production; only communism would relieve them, like the exploited men as well, of their exploitation. Basing their argument on the ground that the age-old patriarchal power has enslaved the women, the *radical feminists* say power, politics and public life are the domains of men and they, therefore, need to be re-defined and reworded so to put an end to all types of male domination. There are the *socialist feminists,* while combining the best of both the radical and the Marxist feminists arguments deplore male domination over female and insist on the fact that all areas of life be seen political on the one hand and seek to declare the patriarchal power a fact of male domination on the other.

The chief characteristic of feminism is that it regards gender divisions as political rather natural, refecting a 'power relationship', between man and woman. The feminists, furthermore, insist that politics is an activity which takes place within all social groups, family including and is not confined to the affairs of government called the 'public' affairs by male chauvinists. They say that politics exists wherever social conflicts exist and they exist at the family levels and are, for example, related to the questions of sexual cruelty.

Feminism, though belongs to the twentieth century, the feminist views have been expressed since long, dating back to the ancient civilizations of Greee and China. Christine de Pisan's *Book of the City of Ladies (1405)* foreshadowed many of the ideas of modem feminism. It was only in the nineteenth century that an organised women's movement developed. The first text of modem feminism comes from Mary Wollstonecraft's *Vindication of the Rights of Women* (1792). By mid-19th century, the women's movement acquired a central point indicating campaign for female suffrage. This period is known as the "first wave" of feminism, seeking equal rights for women. The "second wave" feminism emerged since 1960s when a considerable literature on feminism came up through Betty Friedan *(The Feminine Mystique* —1963). Kate Millet *(Sexual Politics* —1985), and Germaine Greer *(The Female Eunuck,* 1970). It was a period when political emancipation of women and their liberation became the objectives of Feminism. The 1980s and 1990s may well be described as the period of post-feminism when claims were made to have achieved some of the goals of women's movement in the West, though a lot has yet to be done in the rest of the world.

(a) The Feminist Tirade

Feminism attempts to demolish the whole fabric and all the ideas which justify male superiority. It sees history as the history of patriarchy, male's ill-treatment of women in all domains from say family to the society as a whole. It is, therefore, at war against everything that smacks of masculinity. It does not believe competitiveness and aggressiveness as men's qualities, but regard them having created numerous problems in society. On the contrary, it admires womanly virtues of peace, temperance and empathy—virtues that can change the whole face and nature of society.

The feminist accusation lies in its tirade against each aspect of life, political power including. It affirms the view that "the state is but one manifestation of patriarchal power, reflecting other deeper structures of oppression and women's well-documented exclusion from its formal institutions as a symptom of gender inequality" (Bryson, 1992). The feminists do not think that the state or its power is public, political and therefore autonomous in itself; they rather think that it is inextricably related to areas of life such as the family and sexuality which are believed to be private' as well as non-political. Their argument is that the exclusion of women from power is not just unfortunate and therefore can be remedied, but is deliberate because all the structures and institutions of power have been made of men, by men and therefore, exist for men and their interests as against those of the women. The feminists, and particularly the radical feminists, disapprove the whole idea of competitive pursuit of power (pluralist view) as an embodiment of male values, and therefore, on this plea, reject all conventional politics, and bureaucratic hierarchical system, and instead, as Bryson says, separatism should be favoured over participation in existing organisations or institutions. The more radical feminists advocate the disciplined organisation of the female bodies to fight out the patriarchal power within the framework of patriarchy itself. As against the Marxists, the feminists regard female gender, not the economic class, as a power and also capable of grabbing power in its own right.

Bryson sums up the feminist argument: For radical feminist, therefore, state power is not to be understood in its own terms, but as part of a ubiquitous system of patriarchal power. This means that it is not a neutral tool, considering men and women equally, to be changed not through the changing of incumbents of power, but is one where the patriarchal domination of women by men is the central and defining feature of state power.

Feminism has developed into a general critique of social relationships of sexual domination and subordination or as an opposition to any form of social, personal or economic discrimination which women suffer because of their sex.

The feminist attack on the concept of equality dates back to fairly a long past. But it was Wollstonecraft's criticism of Rousseau who, despite having lauded equality, excluded women and thought of them as men's delight. The exclusion of half of human race from public life, and therefore, from the citadels of power, was unethical, immoral, and undemocratic. When some (almost half of mankind) do not have the same excesses to public life and are coerced, they can not be equal like those (i.e. men) who possess all these facilities. The feminists challenge the validity of a democratic value, called the right to vote, being denied to women and if granted, are to be shadowed by their men-folk on grounds, that the 'personal' or 'private' has no relation with what is 'public'. The democratic right of participating in power has been denied to women, most of them in most part of history. Pluralism and also nee-pluralism do not regard women as a sufficient group to be a participant in the exercise of power in the society. Dahl, a known pluralist feels contented if all men are replaced by words like 'all men and women', a simplification of the problem which is too intricate.

The Marxian theory of class, described as in economic terms, does not regard women as a class worth considering in any system of production. To say, as the Marxists do, that women would be emancipated once there develops a classless society is to say not much. They do not see or understand any non-economic sources of oppression and that is why they regard, women like most men as exploited by the possessing classes. In the Marxian frame, the whole issue of women's exploitation, in different types of society, has not been explored fully. Marx had organised International Working men's Association and had not formed International Working Women's Association. The Marxists have, thus, ignored women as a class or women as a power.

(b) Gender and Power: A Plea for Women's Rights

One of the objects of feminism is its advocacy of women's rights. Feminism incorporates in itself a set of ideas relating to the lot of women: agitation for political and legal rights (now won), equal opportunities (being fought now) and sexual autonomy (a future programme). The rise of the feminist movement has its roots in the social recognition of the subordination of woman, from the existence of discrimination and inequality based on sex. It is a set of ideas seeking to bring about a social change in favour of the females. It is and has been a movement with changing aspects of campaign for women from time to time, phases which, notably, include suffragette, women's emancipation, women's liberation and the like.

The history of the feminist movement can be traced to a number of traditions. Respect for women had been a characteristic feature of the oriental societies. In the medieval Europe, the defenders of women's nature included Jean de Meung, Christine de Pisan, Marie de Gournay, Aphra Behn and Mary Astell. The period between 1790-1860 may be called the period of the beginning of the feminist movement in the West. Dominated by the Enlightenment ideas, people talked about the rights of man (representing woman as well), reason, natural law and equal rights. In both the French and the American revolutions, issues relevant to women's rights were raised, a feminist document coming from Mary Wollstonecraft's *A Vindication of the Rights of Women (1792).* The early activists in both the USA and Britain, were Elizabeth Cady Stanton, Margaret Fuller, Lucretia Mott, and the like and who were concerned with securing legal rights for women in matters relating to marriage, education, employment etc. The 19th century witnessed the association of feminism with the unitarian and Quaker traditions. As against the bourgeois and the individualist feminism, there arose the socialist feminism in late 19th century and early 20th century. Radical feminism of 1970s, 1980s and 1990s goes to the extent of advocating separatism.

The three chief trends of feminism can distinctly be noticed. *One* is related to suffragette movement (1860-1930). Under it, feminism campaigned for women suffrage separate from and independent of political parties and other organised groups. Its argument was that women could not rely on political parties and other organised groups for support to the women's cause and that they would have to fight themselves for equality and justice, close to it was *another* trend developed by Freud who sought to shift the thrust from suffrage to sexuality. He did not seek to understand what a woman is, but how she comes into being and in the process raises questions of women's oppression. The *third* trend grew in the shadow of movements launched by the students and the blacks in 1960s. It was a trend that sought women's liberation, protesting against the relegation of women to a secondary role in the society on the one hand, and on the other, emphasising the concept of sisterhood.

The feminist movement has stood against the worsening conditions of women. Wollstonecraft says: "Women are everywhere in a deplorable state; for in order to preserve their innocence, truth is hidden from, them, and they are made to assume an artificial character before their faculties have acquired any strength." As they are denied the necessary education to develop their reason, they are relegated to the performance-- of task such as bringing up the children and managing the households, confining their domain to what is usually termed as private' or 'personal'. John stuart Mill, as a great advocate of females' rights, regarded women's subordination, Valerie Bryson says, as "a barbarous relic of an earlier historical period, far from being the inevitable outcome of natural attributes, it originated in force and was now sanctified by custom so as to appear natural". Stating the Marxian position on the subject, Engels had remarked: "In the family, he (man) is the bourgeois; the wife represents the proletariat", one, the exploiter and the other, the exploited.

Condemning the Rousseauian observations about women's submissiveness, dependence, voluptuousness and amusement for males, Wollstonecraft believes that women are more than merely sexual beings; they are human beings at that. Giving a theological arguments, she says that the rational God would not create one half of the human race virtually mindless and, thus, stressed that all, both men and women, are as they were, equal before God. Condemning the principle that divides people on the basis of sex, Mill insists that the existing social relations between the sexes should be replaced by a principle. of perfect equality, "admitting no power or privilege on the one (male) side, nor disability on the other (female)". The Marxists associate women's subordination with class society and affirm that the classless society would put an end to it.

It may be argued that sex is no disability for women and that it does not make them inferior to men. There is hardly any difference between the psychology of men and women. Nor does maleness give men a superior status and femaleness, an inferior place to women.

History has been cruel to the female gender. Women, because they belong to a sex other than that possessed by men, have not been given a public exposure ever since the beginning of the patriarchical system. The public affairs have therefore, been regarded affairs of men, and not of women. Like any other possession, woman has been considered nothing more than a commodity. Aristotle would not grant them citizenship because their job was restricted to the reproduction arid nurture of children. For a long period in history, man remained the incharge of the external world, women experiencing disadvantages in all spheres of life.

The feminist argument stands for the plea that the distinction between men and women is a biological fact and that women need not be structured as inferior beings. All discrimination, Mill had pointed out, against women should be abolished and that they should be given the same opportunities as are given to men. Mill also favoured the ideas of women's access to education and employment, besides their contribution in public and political life. All feminist thought condemns differences on grounds of sex and argues in favour of gender equality.

It is, indeed, difficult to argue for the denial of rights (political and non-political) and opportunities (education, suffrage and employment) to women, so is difficult to build barriers against women in the world of politics. But it is also a fact that women's special role in the family can hardly be challenged. Even the recent feminists have also realized that women have special responsibilities in the family. Thus, it may be stated that if "the personal is political" (a feminist slogan), the personal, it may be added is "rersonal" after all.

(c) *Gender and Power: The Concept of Patriarchy*

The fact of women's oppression is closely related to the term 'patriarchy'. Patriarchy may be described as a political structure which favours 'man' and propagates women's subordination as natural and inevitable The New York Redstockings manifesto of 1969 says: "Women are an oppressed class. Our oppression is total, affecting every facet of our lives. We are exploited as sex objects, breeders, domestic servants, and cheap labour. We are considered inferior beings whose only purpose is to enhance men's lives—we identify the agents of our oppression as men. Male supremacy is the oldest, most basic form of domination."

Man's domination and woman's subordination are the two sides of the same coin. Both relate themselves to the term 'patriarchy'. Patriarchy represents male chauvinism and therefore, man's domination and hence results in the oppression of women. Feminism is associated with female sex and therefore, with the female gender whereas patriarchy is associated with male sex, and therefore, with male gender.

The literature on feminism and patriarchy overlaps. Notable readings on both include, among others, Shulamith Firestone's *The Dialectic of Sex* (1970), Germaine Greer's *The Female Eunuch* (1970), Eva Figes *Patriarchical Attitudes* (1970), Robin Morgan's *Sisterhood is Powerful (1970),* Michelle Wand or's *The Body Politic* (1972). Kate Millett's *Sexual Politics* (1985) is important in so far as it provides a theoretical frame to the concept of Patriarchy and on whose analysis of this term, later theories have developed.

(d) Patriarchy to *be understood sociologically*

Derived from the Greek word *pairiarches,* the term means "head of the tribe", more specifically, male head of the tribe. So understood, patriarchy means the rule of the head of the family, of the father, of the male, and in short, of man. The word patriarchy' gained usage in the 16th-17th centuries during the hey-days of the absolutist monarchical powers when the power of the King, absolute as it was, over his people was regarded similar to be one of the father over his family.

The essential principle of patriarchy, Millett notes, is the fact that male would dominate the female. So understood, patriarchy is associated with the rule of man over women: man is the ruler; woman, the ruled, sexual inequalities are transformed into genders, each gender performing a specific role, and man getting the larger share than the woman. Relatively weak physically, the woman comes to be regarded socially inferior—a means to serve 'man'. So were the beginnings of man's domination; so were also the beginnings of woman's exploitation.

Patriarchy is not the term that denotes something related to male-being, it is something that implies a measure of power. Patriarchy is a male power; it is the power of man over woman. Millet writes: "..... in all known societies, the relationship between the sexes has been based on power, and that they are therefore political. This power takes the form of male domination over women in all areas of life; sexual domination is so universal, so ubiquitous and so complete that it appears 'natural'."

Patriarchy, as the rule of man over woman, is not only the oldest, but is the deepest as well. Its characteristic values are ingrained in socialisation that starts from childhood and is reinforced by education, literature, religion and the like. Man whether boy, youth, mature person or an old one, keeps possessing far greater a position than a woman in all domains of social life and all this because he has the power of the male gender. The female, on the other, is so tutored from the day she is born until the day she dies, that she finds her 'colonisation' by man as a God-willed command. Such a state for women, Millet says, "leads to self-hatred, self-rejection and an acceptance of inferiority." The patriarchy argument runs as: man has the power, because he is a man; because he is more intelligent, rational, resourceful and masculine than woman; because God has gifted him talents far more than possessed by a woman; and because, unlike woman, he has led history, guided it and has, in fact, made it. Millett touches the near truth when she says: "The patriarchal power of men over women is therefore basic to the functioning of all societies and it extends far beyond formal institutions of power." The gender relations are so structured that a woman has to depend on man for purposes of satisfying her basic needs, and in the process has to accept her virtual servitude. Sexual violence, and rape are not regarded uncommon in patriarchal frame, because sexual relations between men and women are considered as an expression of male power. Patriarchy, therefore, is not only the rule of male over the society, but is also the rule of man over woman. Regarding history as a record of man's inhumanity to woman, Millet concludes: "..... thousands of women who die in the

United States each year as a result of illegal abortion are victims of the same system as is the Indian woman forced to die on her husband's funeral pyre, the Chinese woman crippled by foot-binding and the African girl whose clitoris is cut out."

IV: Pluralist Theories of Power

There is no specific pluralist theory of power, but 'theories'. Mention may be made about atleast three shades of pluralism: (i) Pluralism as expressed in the writings of Lindsay, Laski, Barker, Maclver and others; (ii) Pluralism which took shape in the early post-war (1945) period in the writings of the American scholars such as Truman and Dahl (1956); and (iii) Neo-Pluralism (since 1970s) as has developed in the writings of Lukes, Dahl again (1978, 1985), Lindblom, Nordlinger, Pollitt and others. The first of these shades builds its theory as a reaction against the absolutistic state and emphasises the role of numerous associations in the society. It seeks to explain that there exist associations and groups independent of the state, performing important functions and that the state, as an association, acts as a coordinator only. The second shade admits diverse range of overlapping groups which seek to obtain political influence, state only mediating and adjudicating among them, and in which system, power is shared and bartered by such groups. The third shade admits numerous pressure groups competing for political power and in which the state, as an embodiment of power, attempts to build itself. One may hasten to add that all these shades of pluralism are, essentially, parts of the on-going liberal ideology. Describing pluralism, in generic form, as a historical phenomenon, Kariel says: "As the exclusive proper way of ordering and explaining public life, it (pluralism) remains at the heart of the liberal ideology of the Western world."

Neo-pluralism, as the recent and third shade was built on the second, as was second built on the first. The pre-war pluralism (of Lindsay, Laski, Maclver, Barker ana others) was more or less a critique of the Austinian absolute state, and as such had no theory of the state. But the second shade, one may call pluralism proper (or classical pluralism, if one likes) provides a theory of state and explains the location and exercise of power. Neo-pluralism, if not extension, is pluralism as has adapted itself in the changing conditions of 1970s and thereafter.

Pluralism proper has its roots in American history and it is in the United States of America that it developed and took a concrete shape. The pluralist theories of power (the classical or the neo-classical) are being discussed as have emerged on the American soil.

(a) Pluralism: Meaning

Pluralism, as different from corporation, can be, Schmitter says, defined as "a system of interest representation in which the constituent units are organised into an unspecified number of multiple, voluntary, competitive, non-hierarchically ordered and self-determined categories which are not specially licenced, recognised, subsidized, created or otherwise controlled in leadership selection or interest articulation by the state and which do not exercise a monopoly of representational activity within their respective categories." This long definition of pluralism leaves the following features:

(1) Pluralism represents interests of numerous organised units.
(2) These organised units are voluntary, competitive and non-hierarchical: voluntary because they originate from specific interests of their own; competitive because they compete in satisfying the interests they stand for as also in exerting influence on the decision-making processes; non-hierarchical because they do not represent any kind of a pyramid.
(3) These units or groups do not play or play the least role in the selection of the state mechanisms.
(4) The state assumes upon itself the role of an arbiter in adjudicating and reconciling conflicts and promoting common interest as against the particular interests of such groups.
(5) These groups are the basis, and not the engines of power.

(b) Pluralism and Groups

The pluralists regard groups extremely important in the political process. They say that the individuals, sharing common interest, form groups. These groups seek to make claims and demands on the government. They make their claims and demands by exerting influence through resources such as organised and disciplined membership. For the pluralist politics, there is the government at the centre of the political fabric. Groups are part of the fabric, but not part of the government. They develop within a system and become pressure groups so as to make demands upon the government. Latham, in his book *The Group Basis of Politics* (1965), asserts that pressure group is the basic political form and that the political process is essentially a struggle between such groups. He says: "The legislature refrees the group struggle, ratifies the victories of the successful coalitions, and records the terms of the surrenders, compromises, and conquests in the forms of statutes .... The legislative note on any issue tends to represent the composition of strength, i.e. the balance of power, among the contending groups at the moment of voting. What may be called public policy is the equilibrium reached in this struggle at any given moment."

(c) Pluralism and Location of Power

Power, as the capacity to achieve the desired end, does not reside in an individual, but exists in the relationships between the individuals and the groups they form. It is the power of the groups to influence the policies of the government and make the latter adopt policies which favour a group or a particular set of groups. It is also the power of the government to seek obedience of its laws from the individuals belonging to numerous groups.

The pluralists say that power is non-hierarchically and competitively arranged. It exists as a part of the endless process of bargaining between groups with their relative interests. Power, the pluralists say, is not hierarchical because it does not flow from one group to the other. It is, they insist, competitive in the sense that numerous groups compete among themselves in influencing and controlling the decision-making process. Competition, among groups, may not necessarily end up in the victory of one group over other groups: the contest is not a one-to-one contest. It may end up in balancing the interests of the various groups. Pluralism is a group politics, but not all groups are involved in politics.

The central idea of pluralism, the pluralist studies reveal, is that power and influence, as Alan Cawson says, can be understood in terms of the resources which individuals and groups are able to command in a political market place, and for which they compete in politics. As economic resources, the political resources, are too limited. Therefore, competition among the groups to attain maximum of them is natural. So in a pluralist frame, groups are necessary components and it is the competition which ultimately decided things. Hence, power, in pluralist theory, is the ability to participate in decision-making successfully. As each group has its own power, though restricted, the system so structured prevents the centralisation of power. The power relations among the groups are never permanent in a pluralist society, for they keep shifting with the change in the claims and demands of the numerous groups.

(d) Features of the Pluralist View of Politics

An analysis of pluralism highlights certain features and prominent among them are:

(1) No single groups, in a society, can claim to represent all the interests. Each group represents its own interests: more the groups, more are the interests which are represented. A society, thus, consists of numerous groups with their corresponding interests.
(2) Though the numerous groups are in competition with one another for seeking fulfilment of their interests, it is not necessary that they lead to conflict among themselves. The pluralists forsee a type of equilibrium which maintains the whole fabric.
(3) The pluralists do not subscribe to the view that political power and control of the state are linked with the dominant economic class. They are of the view that both, political power and economic power, though related to each other, stand distinct from each other.
(4) From the pluralist point of view, the state acts as the neutral arbiter, controlling the conflicts of the numerous groups impartially. The pluralists say that the state supervises and regulates social antagonisms without taking side, representing the interests which make it.
(5) Pluralism admits competition as a method of reaching a decision, consent as the underlying basis of the decision reached, and accountability of the ruling groups towards the society as a whole.

A discussion of pluralism would be incomplete without a reference to nee-pluralism. Pluralism and nee-pluralism have much in common. Both believe in citizenship rights: one-person, one-vote, freedom of expression and others. Both insist on a system of checks and balances so that no organ of the government can assume arbitrary powers. Both favour the competitive electoral system. And yet the two exhibit important contrast as well. Under pluralism, governments mediate and adjudicate between demands; under nee-pluralism, the government stands for its own interest. In the former, power is shared by numerous groups while in the latter, it is contested by them. In the former, there is the balance between active and passive citizenry whereas in the latter, there is unequal involvement of citizens in politics.

SUGGESTED READINGS

1 Banks, O., *Faces of Feminism,* (Oxford: Basil Blackwell, 1986).
2 Bryson Valeria; *Feminist Political Theory* (New York, Paragon House, 1992).
3 Coole, D., *Women in Political Theory* (Brighton: Wheatsheaf, 1988).
4 Coward, R., *Patriarchal Precedents: SexlLal and Social Relations,* (London: Routledge and Kegan Paul, 1983).

5 Dahl, R.A., *Who Governs? Democracy and Power in* all *American City* (New Haven: Yale University Press, 1961).
6 ________*Pluralist democracy in United States* (Chicago: Rand McNally, 1967).
7 ________*A Preface to Economic Democracy* (Barkeley: University of California Press, 1985).
8 Elshitain, Jean Bethke., *Public Man, Private Woman in Social and Political Thought* (Princeton, N.J., Princeton University Press, 1981)
9 Jagar, Alison and Rothenberg, P.S. (eds) *Feminist Frameworks* (New York: McGraw Hill, 1984)
10 Latham, E., *The Group Basis of Politics* (New York: Octagon Books, 1965).
11 Lukes, S., *Power: A Radical View* (London: Macmillan, 1974).
12 Mackinnon, C., *Towards a Feminist Theory of the State* (London: Harvard University Press, 1989).
13 Mann, M., *The Sources of Social Power* Vol. 1 (Cambridge: Cambridge University Press, 1986).
14 Martin, R.M., 'Pluralism and the New Corporatism', *Political Studies, 1983.*
15 Miliband, R., *Class Power and State Power* (London: New Left Books, 1973).
16 Okin. S; Women in *Western Political Theory* (Princeton: Princeton University Press, 1979).
17 Poulantza, N., *Political Power and Social Class* (London: New Left Books, 1973).
18 Truman, D., The *Governmental Process* (New York: Knopf, 1951).

5

The Modern Nation State

The concept of state is the very essence of Political Science. No wonder if some scholars regarded State and Political Science as synonyms. But the concept of State has not been static in all times. It kept changing from one period to another. In terms of its relation with other countries, what has emerged is not merely a state but a nation-state. From the very beginning of modem period in the West, state underwent colossal changes as a result of which the absolute monarchies changed into constitutional monarchies: the loyalty towards the king as a person was replaced by loyalty towards the king as an institution. This is what is at the depth of saying that the King and Crown in England are two different concepts. From 17th century onwards, particularly in Europe, there have emerged political sovereignties in the form of constitutional monarchy in England, the Republic in France and unification of states in Italy and Germany, The concept of sovereignty became the dividing line between the nation-state on the one hand and the idea of world state on the other. These are some of the areas with which we are concerned here.

I: State – Definitions and Its Elements

There have been numerous definitions of state. Some of the definitions are as follows:

"The state is an association of families and villages for the sake of attaining a perfect and self sufficient existence." *–Aristotle*

"A state is an association of families and their common affairs, governed by a supreme power and by reason." *–Bodin*

"The state is the politically organised people of a definite territory."

–Bluntschli

A State is "a people permanently occupying a fixed territory, got together by common laws, habits and customs into the body politics, exercising through the medium of an organised government, independent sovereignty and control over all persons and things within its boundaries, capable of making war and peace and of entering into all international relations within the communities of the globe."

- Robert Philimore

State is "a community of persons, more or less numerous, permanently occupying a definite portion of territory, independent, or nearly so, of external control, and possessing an organised government to which the great body of inhabitants render habitual obedience."

-Garner

"The state is an association which, acting through law as promulgated by a government endowed to this end with coercive power, maintains within a community territorially demarcated the universal external conditions of social order." *-MacIver*

State is "a territorial society, divided into government and subjects, whether individuals or associations of individuals, whose relationships are determined by the exercise of this supreme coercive power."

- Laski

"By 'the state' we mean a particular and special association, existing for the special purpose of maintaining a compulsory scheme of legal order, and acting therefore through laws enforced by prescribed and definite sanctions." *-Barker*

Thus the state has been defined variedly. As Maclver says, "It may seem curious that so great and obvious a fact as the state. should be the object of quite conflicting definitions. Yet such is certainly the case." Indeed, the state has not been a unified entity. It is, as David Held holds, a multi-dimensional phenomenon, the nature of which varies across time and space.

The word 'state' derives from the Latin *Stare* (to attend) and *status* (a standing or condition). The Roman writers, Cicero and Ulpain, and also the medieval lawyers used terms such as *status Civitatis* or *status regni,* referring to the condition of the ruler, the fact of possessing stability. "Standing" or "status" is the word associated with the state.

The English word "state" is in fact, a contraction of the world 'estate', similar to the old French word 'estat' and modern French *'eiei'*, both of which imply a profession or social status. The Spanish *estudo* gives the same idea of state or stability, status.

Though the state as used to convey 'status', 'standing', goes back to the twelfth century, it was Machiavelli who coined the word state in the modern sense of the word, i.e., the state as power, as authority, symbolising / stateliness}.

(a) *State and its elements*

State has four essential elements without which u can not exist. They are people, territory, government and sovereignty.

1. *People:* People or population is the human element of state. It is impossible to conceive a state without people. Therefore, population is very important. But then, how much population should be? For Plato, it should be 5040, which excludes the slaves who constituted a significant number of the population in his times. Rousseau thought the population should not exceed 10,000 people. It is very difficult to fix population of a state. In modern times, we have India and China with huge population and countries like San Marino with a very small population. Thus modern states differ greatly in terms of population. One can safely say that the population must be enough to constitute governing and the governed classes, sufficient to support a political organisation. The population should be in proportion to the available land and resources. The composition of the population is also important. A state with a homogenous people can be governed easily.

2. *Definite territory:* According to Prof. Elliot, "Territorial sovereignty or the superiority of the state over all within its boundaries and complete freedom from external control, has been a fundamental principle of the modern state life." The territory has to be definite because it ensures the exercise of political authority. Nomadic people may have some form of political organisation but they do not constitute a state as they do not have a definite territory. The Jews had been living in different countries. They did not constitute state until when they got a definite territory in Israel Territory may be large or small, but it has to be definite. In modern times we have large states like Brazil, USA and Russia and also small states like Monaco whose area is less than 200 square kilometers. The quality of land is also important. The states in Middle' East were insignificant, but with the discovery of oil, they acquired prominence. A large area with the abundant availability of natural resources makes a state powerful However, it

should be proportionate to the population. Large size of a state also gives strategic and military advantage. Usually, the territory of a state has to be compact and contiguous. However, there are exceptions also. Before the creation of Bangladesh, Pakistan was divided into two territories miles apart from each other. Alaska and Hawaii, are member states of USA, but are far from her. The territory of a state includes land, water and the sky over it. The territorial limit in the sea is an issue of controversy in International Law. Traditionally it has been three miles from the coast. But now the countries are claiming more. India has extended its territorial jurisdiction to twelve miles from the coast.

3. *Government:* The government is a political and legal arrangement in the society. Without government, there will be a crowd of people and not state. In fact, the state expresses itself through the government. State is abstract while the government is state's concrete shape. It is a means by which the society is governed. The collective life is impossible without a government. It is a condition for any civilised life. The major function of the government is to maintain peace lawfully.

The government acts through three main organs-legislature, executive and judiciary. The legislature enacts laws, the executive implements them and the judiciary adjudicates.

There may be different forms of government right from one man rule to the rule by majority. In monarchy, the king rules. Dictatorship including the militarism is the rule a dictator. Aristocracy is a rule of the few. However, by the end of 20th century, generally it is felt that the democratic system of government is the best. Direct democracy in which the people directly rule, being impossible given the size of states in terms of population and area, as also the representative government or indirect democracy is practiced in almost the entire world barring few exceptions.

4. *Sovereignty:* Last but not the least is sovereignty. The term sovereignty has been used from the middle ages which meant 'to rule over.' Originally it meant the power of a monarch to rule over his kingdom. Later the term was broadened to mean the national control of a country over its territory. Sovereignty is the supreme power of state both internally and externally, by which the state commands and exerts political obedience from its people. Internally there is no parallel authority to state and externally it is free from any foreign control. It is this attribute of state which distinguishes state as one association' from other associations.

Without sovereignty, statehood is not achieved. India before independence had a definite land, population and a government but had no sovereignty. Therefore, it was not a state. Destruction of sovereignty means destruction of statehood.

All the four elements of state are indispensable to its existence. The absence of even one of them would mean the negation of state.

From above, the essential characteristics of the state may be summed up as under:

(i) The state possesses a geographically identifiable territory with a body of citizens.
(ii) It has to have authority over all citizens and groups within its bowdaries.
(iii) In embodies more comprehensive and general aims than other associations within and beyond the state.
(iv) The authority of the state is legal, and more than that, it is supreme. Sovereignty is the attribute of the state, and no other related concept such as society, country, nation, government, and other associations has it.
(v) It is based on procedural rules which have more general recognition in society than other rules.
(vi) It has maximal control of resources and force within a territory: its monopoly of force is based on legitimacy.
(vii) It is seen as a sovereign internally supreme within its territory, and externally as a distinct, but an equal member of the international community.
(viii) It is a continuous public power, separate and district from the rulers and the ruled.

(b) Changing Concept of the State

In terms of history, we may identify three general perspectives of the history:

(i) The first perspective about the history of the state dates back to the early Greeks who used the word 'polis' samething that integrated in itself something of society, government, schools, ethics, art, religion and the like. That is why that the Greeks never made any distinction among concepts stated above. For Aristotle, Political Science was study of 'polis'. There were conceptions of territory, citizenship, revolution authority, law in vogue, but there was no conception of separate powers of government, no conception of a separate civil society, and no precise idea of a legal constitution.
(ii) The second. perspective dates back when the state from the early Middle Ages, Roman and Canon law had established ideas of transcendent public welfare; power and law were associated

with the office of the monarch; concepts of citizenship and the rule of law. But then, the word state was not used until the sixteenth century, numerous other associations such as the nobility, church, guilds existed to challenge sovereign's position. The idea of a state as a defined territorial unit with loyal population did not exist then.

(iii) The third perspective on the history of the state dates back to the emergence of the state from the late Middle Ages. It was from here that the state appeared as a power, and as an higher authority associated with the state followed by the absolutist monarchy, the constitutional monarchy, constitutional state, democratic one, and lastly, the kind of state in its forms as we find today.

The perspective on the history of the state does give the idea of how the state has developed, especially in the West. To understand the concept of the state more clearly, it is important to know the *approaches* to the study of the state. These, mainly, are:

(i) ***Juristic or Legal:*** This approach to the study of the state is the oldest, and dates back to the ancient Roman period. Words like power, authority and legitimacy, as were used in relation to the state from the sixteenth century, had their roots in Roman Law. The early critiques of feudal state, initially by the Papal lawyers, derived from the Roman Law sources, forming, later on, the basis for notions of authority and law associated with the central rule. That the state is something as the hierarchy of legal rules as also the embodiment of legal positivism is the Roman contribution to the Western Political Thought.

(ii) ***Historical:*** This approach to the study of the state studies the growth of the state, laying emphasis on the factors connected with the rise of the state, as in the growth of the Ranaissance city-states, the Reformation, the break-up of the Holy Roman Empire, the growth of centralised salaried bureaucracies, standing armies, dynastic and religious wars as in the West, and the Oriental state as in the East. There are others who lay emphasis on the history of certain ideas accompanying the events in the growth of the state, ideas such as social instinct, kinship, religion, force, power, citizenship, political consciousness and the like.

(iii) ***Sociological/Anthropological:*** This approach to the study of the state tends to view the state as a way of organising society, i.e., 'state soceities' as subspecies of the genus of society. Another way of putting this is that the state is a subspecies of government. State organisation, in this approach, is made one form in which human beings have organised their social existence. Marx, Durkheim, Duguit, Weber, and MacIver have viewed the state in this manner, explaining the state through the broad study of the society.

(iv) ***Political-scientific:*** This approach to the study of the state sees the state to be a specialised agency which comes about to perform certain functions in changing economic and social situations. This approach refers to a variety of theories to explain the state, especially the following:

(a) Empirical pluralists and neo-pluralists view society as constituted by groups, and the state as synonymous with government where it becomes the centre of pressure or interest groups activity. In this theory, power is the control over resources by groups are in the competitive market where the state government reflects the dominat coalition (Latham: *The Group Basis to Politics,* 1965) or it acts as an impartial umpire or neutral arbitor (Dahl, *Polyarchy: Participation and Opposition,* 1971). As against society-centred state, there was developed a state-centred state (Nord linger, *On the Autonomy of the Democratic State,* 1981) where the state is regarded as an important actor, relatively autonomous from societal interests and whose processes are independent from societal preferences and choices, and one which moulds individual choices.

(b) Elitism, from Mosca, Pareto, Michels to Bachrach *(The Theory of Democratic Elitism,* 1967), assumes the rule of democratically chosen minority over many as an empirical, scientifically verifiable fact. The state, with classical elitists such as Mosca Pareto and Michals, was a rule of the few over many, 'the iron law of oligarchy' or 'the continuity of elites in politics'. With democratic elitists such as Bachrach, elite is democratic so far as the state is controlled by few duly chosen from and responsible to many: democratic in so far as avoids the risks of direct rule of the people.

(c) Corporatists and neo-corporatists are pluralists in so far as they admit the role of the competitive groups in politics; they are not pluralists in so far as they talk about a more limited number of groups competing to capture the reign of governments. Cawson *(Corporatism and Political Theory,* 1986) sees the role of the state within the capitalist society, where interests are organised and interact with the state where a new form of economy, different from capitalism and socialism, functions under the supervision of the state.

(d) Marxists regard the state as a class institution and as such, the product of class society so to defend private property and eventually capitalist accummulation. They view the state as an instrument of exploitation or what Marx called the executive committee of the exploiting class and one which would be abolished with the class society (capitalist society, so to say). But they too talk about the state (in the form of the dictatorship, of the proletariat) in the transitional period between the out-going capitalism and in-coming communism, and it is during this period that the state would act as an instrument of social and political change which eventually would wither away in the communist society.

(e) Individualists, liberals and neo-liberals view the state embedded in individual choice. They believe that the state emerges from the logic of self-interested individual choice and exists for the fulfilment of individual interests, performing varying tasks within the framework of the autonomy of the individual. That is .how developed *laissez faire* state (Bentham), welfare state (Laski) and minimal state (Nozick).

(v) ***Philosophical/normative:*** This approach to the study of the state lays emphasis on two basic things: philosophical in so far as it demands of the': state to reflect on the right, the best or most just order: nonnative in so far as it is bound up with values and ideas of civil existence.

II: Nation and Nationality

Nation is a collective noun which means an aggregation of people having special ties which bind them. People possessing distinctive features and united by special ties of sentiments are referred to as nation. To J.S. Mill it is 'the identity of political antecedents, the possession of a national history, and consequent community of recollections; collective pride and humiliation, pleasure and regret connected with the same incidents in the past.' Nation is constituted by a geographical unity, a common past, a common language, a common religion common history, common hopes and aspirations. It is an emotional feeling and sentiment of a people that they are one and exclusive from others. It differentiates an English man from a French or an Indian. The presence of a political organisation is not a must for nation; state may not coexist with a nation. However, whenever they coexist, a strong national feeling is created. A nation devoid of state has also demanded statehood as an inherent right. After the First World War, many nations were given statehood.

However, there is an obvious differentiation between state and nation. State is a political entity; nation a cultural and psychological concept. Nation is a stable historical community and cannot be expanded at will while state may expand as a result of war or some other factor; it may shrink also unlike a nation. The people of a state may belong to more than one nation. Members of a nation may be divided into different states. The post-world war period witnessed the division of Korean nations into two different independent states.

Yet a precise definition of nation is very difficult. The political theorists have also been using the term nation to connote different meanings. A distinction is also made between nation and nationality. To James Bryce, nationality means a group of people who are not independent While a nation is a nationality, which is organised politically and is either independent or desires to be independent. Thus, here nation is considered to be an advanced form of people's organisation. Stalin also held this view and to him nationality was formed in feudal and ancient periods with the fusion of various tribes and racial groups who had a bond of unity in terms of common language. Nation is more consolidated by economic forces. However, he felt that at times there may be need for multinational state.

MacIver says that it is useless to search for any common quality or definite interest in the creation of nationality and nationhood. The Swiss and Indians have no common language, the Jews had no common territory and common race is nearly always a delusion. According to him, "Nationality is the sense of community which, under the historical conditions of a particular social epoch, has possessed or still seeks expression through the unity of a state." People belonging to one nation have intensive love and devotion to it and during the crisis there emotions are stirred so high that they forget their differences, become one and are prepared to sacrifice their lives. Let us see various factors that accounts for such nationality. Some of them are as follows:

(i) ***State***—The existence of state itself creaks national spirit. People living in a particular state are knit together by the law and administration. The evolution of common order foster the sense of being one and development of sense of likeness. This common order separates them for the people belonging to other states. Wars between states develop these feelings and as MacIver says, appeal 'in the process to the strongest emotions of love and hate, through common peril and common triumph.'

(ii) ***Idea of belongingness* to *a group or social unity***—This is a historical factor. People of a nation live together in a particular geographical territory from the time immemorial. This gives them a distinct identity as race. The Poles, Persians, Greeks, Romans are some such examples. These communities emerged as a result of fusion of different tribal groups in ancient times. However, in modern times, race is not important factor for we have countries like Switzerland, India, USA, Canada and many other countries which are multi-racial.

Further, the concept of racial unity is dangerous also. Hitler advocated the doctrine of racial supremacy of Aryans and perpetuated genocide on Jews. Lastly, as Mussolini said, "Race is a feeling, not a reality. Nothing will ever make me believe that biologically pure races can be shown to exist today."

(iii) ***Common language***—Language is the medium of expression, and a common language means comfortable channels of communication and interaction among the members of the community. Common language also means common literature and a common heritage of historical traditions. A common language creates a cohesive society. Countries lacking common language constitute weak nations. In India national unity has suffered because we have no common language and non-Hindi states have resisted to the spread of Hindi as official language. It is also true that the lack of common language may not prove dangerous to national unity if other factors are strong. Moreover, as Ashirvatham points out that several nationalities do not possess a common language. People of Switzerland speak atleast three distinct languages. Further the people of the USA and Canada speak a common language but they never intended to become one nationality.

(iv) ***Common culture*** – Culture as a means of propagation of national ideas plays a very important role in the creation of nationalities. Common culture means common historical traditions and literature, common heroes and a common way of living together. These factors create an unshaking unity among the people. National literature is also significant, as it contributes largely to the development of nationality, as Joseph Bernard points out, by striving to create and maintain national traditions and by endearing the national history to the nationality. It is the vehicle of national tradition. Religion also binds the people into one. However, it is not regarded as indispensable because modern states are multi-religious. Moreover, religion is considered to be the private affair of individuals and secularity of political organisations have been accepted. However, religious strifes have hampered the growth of national unity in many countries like India.

(v) ***Economic Factor***—Marxists believe that nations emerged as a consequence of fusions of various tribes and clans, under the stress of developing capitalist mode of production. Nations could not have emerged in slave or feudal society. According to Asirvatham, "Common economic interest has been one of the strongest factors in the maintenance of the Japanese and Australian nationalities." The economic motive knit people together and created a consciousness of kind. But economic interests alone cannot create nationality. In fact, every nation strives to effect unity by cutting into economic ties. During the crises, people of a nation become one irrespective of their economic status.

(vi) ***Common subjugation***—This factor has been responsible to a great extent in the creation of nations in the developing World. In India, common subjection to British created common nationality. Most of the countries in Africa are characterised by the absence of any political history before colonialism. In fact these countries were created by the Western imperialist powers. The very basis of the existence of these countries have been the common subjugation. Common slavery created a feeling of oneness among the people.

State, race, common language, common culture, economic ties and common subjugation are some of the objective factors that help the creation or evolution of the nation. However, all of them are not indispensable. Their significance varies from nation to nation and also as MacIver points out that ... "scarcely any two nationalities seem to find their positive support in the same objective factors."

III: The Development of Nation-State

Modem nation-state is a highly complex phenomenon. It is the result of a long historical evolution. But this evolution has not been uniform and continuous. Even the origins of state is a mystery. Historically it is difficult to find out as to when and how the state came into being. However, we have sufficient evidence to trace the development of state from the primitive times to the modem nation-state. The following have been the forms of evolution of modem nation-state.

1. The Tribal Formations
2. The Oriental Empires
3. The Greek city-state
4. The Roman Empire
5. The Feudal state
6. The Modern Nation-State

(i) *Early Tribal Formations:*

The earliest form of political organisation has been the early tribal formations in the primitive society. These tribes did not stick to a particular piece of land; they were mobile subject to the availability of food and water. These tribal organisations must have been matriarchal, as the nature has bestowed on woman the responsibility of upbringing the children. However, later on, the patriarchal society came into existence, a society headed by the male member of the tribal community. This was because man developed pastoral and agricultural habits. Consequently many of these tribes did not remain nomadic. They settled on a definite piece of land.

Kinship or blood relation was the basis of tribal communities. Blood relation, real or assumed created an organisation where the bonds of unity were traced from a common ancestor. It created, as Henry Maine points out, a common consciousness, common interest and common purpose. To MacIver, "kinship creates society and society at large creates the state."

Although these tribes were scattered in different parts of the world, yet the primitive society, again to quote MacIver, "has certain common factors under the most diverse conditions of environment and among peoples the most remote from each other." Some of the characteristics of these tribal communities, as pointed out by MacIver are as follows:

1. Tribal communities were 'all small and relatively isolated groups.' They were close to nature and were entirely dependent upon the nature for their survival. There were no professional jobs except for men making bows and arrows or witch doctors etc. There was no division of labour and little exchange of products. Man was totally helpless before the fury of nature.

2. The "apparatus of civilisation" was also very poor. There was no system of education, no written script and no record of science. There is a folk-culture and within each tribal community, there is "an identity of customs, manners and morals ... rigorously prescribed by and for the folk."

3. The tribal community is governed by the customs and the observance of them is a must for all its members. In fact the whole life is controlled by the customs in which the primal facts of birth, marriage and death are given an elaborate social setting. The violators of the customs are ruthlessly dealt with because of the apprehension of the fury of ghosts, village God and other unknown forces. The primitive man is highly scared of such unknown forces which existed in the absence of any scientific knowledge and explanation.

4. Under the circumstances, life is communal and there is no cause for individual initiative. In fact the individual has neither the capacity nor the social sanction for liberty as every aspect of his life is totally regulated by the custom. 'Morality is the fulfilment of custom' and blind observance, of prevailing social values only alternative. In short there is a total subordination of the individual to the communal life. However, the cohesion in this communal life is not because of any economic factor. It is the spiritualism which is the basic social organisation. 'Its feasts and solemn occasions, its love, its songs and

dance, its whole armaments of traditions and customs, bind each member within the narrow circle of social security.' In such a system the tribal chief was very powerful who would enforce his discipline vigorously. In some tribes, the chief was elected, while in others it was a position held as a matter of heredity.

Such tribal formation did not create state. Ashirvatham rightly says that "conquest and domination were necessary before tribal man could accustom himself to larger loyalties and to political authority and obligation." However, the origins of state can be traced from the tribal communities as rudimentary concept of political authority and subordination arose. To MacIver, "it is the slow beginnings of the state."

(2) The Oriental Empires

The second phase of development of state saw the emergence of empire in Orient. The empires developed around the valleys—the Tigris and the Euphrates, the Nile, the Yellow river, Yangtse and the Indus. These valleys have been called cradles of civilisation. The empire came into existence as a result of accumulation of surplus wealth, which the primitive society was lacking. Therefore, the primitive society is characterised by the absence of any class struggle. According to MacIver, the surplus of wealth was due to "progress in the domestication of animals, in the cultivation of the soil, in the techniques of the arts of peace and war, of production and of exchange." Together they created a new instrument of power which came into the hands of the state.

These empires were situated in Sumeria, Assyria, Persia, Egypt, China and India. They were centred around the cities where the wealth had accumulated. To MacIver, "The presence of the city is witness to the fact that a group has liberated itself from the immediate necessity of wresting a livelihood from the soil, that it has found a means by which to command the fruits of the labours of other men." The city provided the heart of the empire. They were subjected to raids and even destruction by the nomad tribes. But the nomad tribes on their own could not form an empire. Only the settled population with enough wealth and the concentration of power created an empire.

These empires were dominated by a king and his nobles who had full authority over their subjects, who were servants to the political power. The authority was based on fear and despotism. The kinship of primitive society is replaced by class organisation. 'Religion crystallises into temple worshipping overshadowing the ancient sites of the household.' A priesthood develops, as MacIver points out, and becomes an exclusive and highly organised instrument of social control. A military order with a permanent armed force and professional officers who organise a rigorous system of subordination and make unquestioned and graded authority and obedience the rule of life. The king is God and principle of common service on the part of subjects is enforced. With the free labour, temples and palaces were built. The early empires were not highly centralised. They were made up of different tribes which paid tributes and furnished soldiers to the king. However, they were autonomous in their local affairs. The principal governors also attempted to become independent of the empire whenever opportunity arose.

These empires rose and fell, but they never attained political stability. There was no cohesion and common purpose. In fact their primary functions were to collect taxes and recruitment of soldiers. Yet the empires played an important role in the development of state and its institutions. The state acquired the territorial character and narrow kinship bond broke down. The empires also taught people obedience to the political authority.

(3) Greek City States

The third important stage in the development of state was the Greek city-states. Nature has given a unique geographical setting to Greece where a sophisticated system developed in the form of Polis or city-state. The country consisted of a series of numerous valleys, maintained barriers and sea which gave the people, on the one hand the opportunity to contact the outside world by trade, on the other, a natural climate to develop autonomous activities of the city-states. These city-states emerged as a result of unity of villages into one political unit. The important city-states were Athens, Sparta and Syracuse.

The population of city-state was small; approximately a few thousand people lived in a city-state. However, this population was divided into three classes. Firstly, were the slaves who constituted a large segment of population. They constituted one-third of all the inhabitants. Slavery as an institution was universally accepted. Even Aristotle, the father of Political Science justified it. The second class consisted of resident foreigners or metics. The metics did not take part in the political life of city-states. But he was a free man. Thirdly, was the body of citizens who were free and participated in the political life. To Greeks, citizenship was not something of a possession or a right but, as Sabine says, as something shared much life like membership in the family. Participation in political activities was a must for every citizen.

The Greek city-states had a variety of governmental systems. Sparta had aristocracy, Athens democracy while Syracuse experienced dictatorship. Some city-states also had monarchy. However, the governmental system of Sparta alone remained constant. In other city-states we find political dynamism, switching over from monarchy to aristocracy, from aristocracy to tyranny and from tyranny to democracy.

The city-state of Athens is still remembered for the civic harmony, inculcated through the democratic institutions. Sabine has quoted Pericles stating: "An Athenian citizen does not neglect the state because he takes care of his own household: and even those of us who are engaged in business have a very fair idea of politics. We alone regard a man who takes no interest in public affairs, not as harmless, but as a useless character; and if few of us are originators, we are all sound judges of policy." People participated in the state activities without any discrimination of rank and wealth. Political power was vested in the Assembly of adult masters above the age of twenty and the government functionaries were ultimately responsible to it. All major matters like declaration of war and peace, the forming of alliances, and general laws were decided by the Assembly. The citizen population of Athens was very less. In a particular time it was only a few thousand, while one thousand nine hundred officials posts existed. Thus every citizen had the opportunity to occupy offices. The citizen also took active part in various ceremonies and festivals that used to take place from time to time. Thus "The life of the citizen," MacIver rightly states, "was the life of the city. His good was ... totally identified with that of the commonwealth." Athens can rightly be called as the foundation of Western model of democracy. It laid great emphasis on the freedom of individuals which has to be the basis of any political system. Every Greek political thinker agreed that the tyranny was the worst type of government because it was unlawful and destroyed the self-government, while, as Sabine says, "In the free state the law and not the ruler is sovereign, and the law deserves the citizen's respect, even though in the particular case it injures him."

However, as Barker puts it, "... the city-state was something more than a political system; and it went beyond the legal purpose of declaring and enforcing a body of rules for the control of legal relations. It was state and society in one, without distinction or differentiation...." This was the greatest mistake of the Greeks. To them law and custom or convention were one and the same and city-state was state, religion, culture and economy all in one. MacIver comments, "Under such a theory no form of life is safe, no religion, no opinion, unless its adherents control the government."

Another defect of city-state was that it overpowered the family which was devoid, of its rightful place in the community. The importance of household activities diminished and family lost its primary position.

The city-state did not look after the education and other needs of the people. The position of woman also suffered. Instead of being an equal partner of man, the role of woman was relegated to internal household chores. MacIver points out that, "In the majority of Greek cities women filled so small a part that we cannot even obtain information about them."

(4) The Roman Empire

The end of first century BC saw the emergence of the great Roman Empire which had united almost the entire Western nations into one political system. Initially Rome was a city-state with a monarchy ruling over it. The common people called plebians fought against the monarchy and acquired political authority alongwith the patricians, the nobles who were already enjoying political power. In 510 BC monarchy gave way to aristocratic Republic. This Republic also witnessed the struggle between the plebians and patricians which was solved amicably by democratising the political authorities and structures, and by introducing the concept of popular sovereignty. However, by the middle of 5th century, the Republic was again in crisis. Julius Caesar gave a decisive blow to the Republic. Eventually the Roman Empire was proclaimed under the emperorship of Augustus in 27 BC The Roman Empire extended from England in the West to modem Israel, Syria, Egypt, Sudan etc., on the northern coast of Africa, included whole of Italy, Portugal, Spain, France, some parts of Germany and South Eastern Europe.

The Roman Empire was characterised by effective centralised administration led by the Emperor. The people of the empire had a common citizenship of Rome which gave them political and civil rights. However, the Romans had always differentiated between civil rights and political rights. Civil rights meant right to equality before the law, while political rights, right to membership in the sovereign body. Some towns were given civil rights but no political rights. The empire had a well knit civil service with an elaborate system of hierarchy in which civil service offered a career. There was freedom of travel and trade throughout the empire. It also established courier system. The great cities especially on the coast, were cosmopolitan in their population. The system of slavery existed, but they were allowed to have property of their own. They owned land, property, ships and interests in business concern and their rights were protected by law. Augustus, the founder of the empire, wanted to rejuvenate society by admitting to it the best element of slavery and he put them in highest circles and the most important positions.

The most important contribution of the Roman empire had been in the field of law. The law was codified and from time to time changes affected according to the changed circumstances. The Romans also went ahead and thought about law among nations. This was necessitated by the expansion of Rome and the growth of foreign trade. The law was based on reason and justice defined as the constant and perpetual will to give each man his right: Respect for human personality and human relationships, freedom of man are some of the aspects of the Roman law which are even valid today.

Augustus, the founder emperor of the Roman empire called himself as 'First Citizen' and claimed that he derived power from the Senate (the Assembly) and people. In fact initially law-making was done by the Senate but later on they were transferred to the emperor whose words became law. The empire was divided into various provinces which were given decent governments. Taxation was reasonable, and land tax was collected directly by responsible officials; Diets were formed in the provinces. The Roman army was a highly professional army.

Rome never sought to impose uniformity on her subjects. Within the framework of empire, the provinces were free to develop their life in their own way.

The cities were a necessary part of the imperial administration. In the first two centuries A.D., the cities, free from war and other crisis, competed against each other in the splendour of their public buildings and the luxury of their social services. Under Diocletian, the empire was made an aristocracy. The empire was unified and the provinces became equal to Rome. Apprehension of any rebellion on the part of provincial governors was avoided by an elaborate political subdivision of the whole empire and a strict separation of the civil and military power.

The main weakness of the Roman empire was that its Western and Eastern parts always remained apart politically. In the later times, the military dictatorship had almost replaced the civil government, while in the east, civil administration controlled the army. The emphasis on unity led to the negation of democracy. Gettel remarks, "The Greek had developed democracy without unity; the Rome secured unity without democracy." Despite their statesmanship and intellectual capabilities, the Romans could not develop a sound basis of political organisation. Yet in an age of slow communication, they proved that a large state could be stable and an effective government possible.

(5) The Feudal State

The downfall of the Roman Empire created confusion in Western

Europe where the state had died. It seemed as if the achievements of the Roman empire had gone into waste. The Roman ideas of uniformity of law, centralised administration and common citizenship were set aside. Instead the idea of individualism, liberty and local self-government became prominent. These ideas were cherished by the Teutonic tribes who had invaded and brought about the downfall of Roman empire. Feudalism arose as a compromise between the two ideologies of Roman empire and the Teutonic tribes. Feudalism had been criticised on the basis of argument that it was no system at all or as a confusion organised.

The word feudal is derived from fief which means estate or land held on condition of homage and service to superior lord. Feudalism is a system in which political authority is derived from land. In feudalism, state was submerged in the community. The imperial unity of Roman empire gave way to imperial hierarchy, with the king at the top. Under the jurisdiction of the king, the feudal overlords called counts, marquises and dukes ruled the land. In return they were to pay dues and render military services.

The feudal state envisaged the king at the centre and the country divided into the feudal nobles. The land under nobility was divided among the tenants. The tenants further divided their lands among the vassals and serfs. Essentially it was an hierarchy based on land holding.

The control of kings over the serfs and farmers was indirect; they were directly controlled by the tenants who were in turn controlled by the feudal overlord. The feudal overlords had a direct relationship with the king who controlled them. Thus a rigid system of classes was established in which personal loyalty to the immediate superior was the rule. The feudal overlord would hold the land till he fulfilled his obligation to the king. The tenancy rights were transferred to the heirs of the lord after his death. In short, feudalism had the following features:

(i) Existence of a king at the top of the hierarchy with the ability to exert obedience from the lords.
(ii) The lords having necessary authorities over their land and its population.
(iii) The vassals or serfs had a personal loyalty to the lord.

The king had three competitors to his authority. Firstly, the Church which claimed immunity in both civil and criminal cases. The Church not only survived the disintegration of Roman empire, it also emerged as the most organised group in medieval times. It had amassed a considerable amount of wealth and landed property. The Pope as head of Church claimed superiority over the kings. The Church took up many functions of state including the preservation of law and order. Church had become the state itself and civil authority was, as Figgis points out, merely the police department of the Church. Secondly, there were feudal nobles who individually acted sovereign in their respective areas. Sometimes they collectively formed a baronage ready to dispute king's authority. The last and the final challenge came from the local communities or commons in the town. They asserted autonomy for their local municipal governments. They also joined together in the assembly of commons and would pose challenge either to king or feudal baronage by joining the estate. Thus feudalism was a state of three estates or as Barker aptly puts it, "a paradise of estates rather than a pattern of a state." The state's authority was disputed and divided and it was incapable of enforcing law and order in the society. However, society existed in abundance, association based on religion, class or profession carne into existence, 'each making its own law and order in a time of general self-help' and the authority of state was sidelined.

IV: The Modern Nation-State

The nation state comes into being when the territorial nation provides the space, area and the human material for the creation of state. Social cohesion, with a common tradition and sentiment makes the state a formidable power. Barker has defined the nation-states thus, "a modem state is generally a territorial nation organised as a legal association by its own action in creating a primary body of constitutional law (such action often being a process along a line of time rather than an act at a point of time) and functioning in that capacity under that primary body of law for the purpose of declaring and enforcing a secondary body of ordinary law."

However, three aspects of nation-state must be clearly borne in mind. Firstly, the nation continues to exist in the nation-state and 'remains active in the formation and expression of public opinion, social manners and national character.' It also acts through other channels to fulfil the requirements of individuals. Secondly, the nation-state is not always a unitary national society. India is the best example of such a nation-state. The minorities exist and follow their own language, customs and religion. Sometimes, these minorities become a real problem to the nation-state. Thirdly, the nation-state acts, through a Constitution which is a bridge between the nation and state. The Constitution is the creation of the nation, directly or indirectly. It is a 'nationally endorsed scheme of rules', Barker rightly puts it, 'which makes the state what it is today, controlling and constituting its character. Thus by its very value, nation-state is a limited state. David Held says that "All modern states are nation states-political apparatuses, separate from both the ruler and the ruled, with supreme jurisdiction over a demarcated territorial area, backed by a claim to a monopoly of coercive power, and enjoying a minimum level of loyalty from their citizens."

(a) Causes of the rise of Nation-States

Out of the confusion and chaos of feudalism the modern nation state originated. The nation-state first came into existence in England. Later on it expanded to other parts of Europe. However, in Germany and Italy, it came only in late 19 century. The following were the causes of the rise of modern nation state.

A. *The renaissance:* The fourteenth and fifteenth centuries Europe witnessed the great Renaissance which broke its deep slumber and signalled the end of dark age of medieval times. Renaissance was the revival of ancient Greek knowledge, which the Europe had forgotten under the tutelage of feudalism.

Renaissance heralded the age of reason, where beliefs and superstitions had to give way to rational arguments. It meant the study of ancient Greek theorists like Plato and Aristotle. The education system would include not only the religious education, but it had to be all comprehensive, which meant study of man and his problems. Thus subjects like history, geography, law, logic, philosophy and other social sciences also came to be studied in different universities. The religious faiths and beliefs were also examined through reason. The character of literature also changed. The monopoly of Latin in literature was replaced by the local languages of English, Italian and French etc. Sir Thomas More wrote his famous work *'Utopia'* in English. The world was also discovered and interaction with Far East, India, America and other countries of new world started.

Renaissance asserted the individuality and that the man has a right to seek pleasures in life. Renaissance started a process in which people achieved liberation from the dominance of the Church and created an environment where man could think about himself and his surroundings. This process ultimately led to the nationalistic feelings.

B. *The rise of nationalism:* The most important cause of the origins of nation state was the rise of nationalist feelings in Europe. According to MacIver, "The preconditions of nationality were being laid in the later middle ages." Europe could be divided into different areas where there were common religion, common language and common history. The dawning of modern age saw their assertion as nation.

In England, Angles, Saxons, Jutes and others had asserted themselves into a single national kingdom. Since the Norman conquests of England in 1066, England had possessed a large part of France. She even claimed the crown of France. But the Hundred Year War decided this issue and England was expelled from the French territories. Henry VII while establishing his new monarchy in England declared that he was not interested in the French territories. Thus formed was a true English nation fermenting patriotism among its population.

Similarly, a French nation-state was created among the French speaking people in France. Various feudal ducats areas which had been enjoying complete independence were merged into a nation-state of France. Spain and Portugal, Poland, Sweden, Denmark and Russia also witnessed this national upsurge and consolidated into nation-states. However, Germany and Italy took a very long time. It was only in late 19 century that they could acquire nation-states status.

C. *Crusades:* Jerusalem, the capital of Palestine became a unifying force in Europe. In Western Asian countries, including Palestine, Islam had taken deep roots. The Christian pilgrims and missionaries who visited Jeruselam, the holy place of Christianity, were subjected to oppression and harassment by the Turks. The people of Europe—kings, feudal lords and common people set aside all their differences and united as one in fighting these crusades. Although these crusades failed because Palestine could not be liberated from the Turks, yet the Crusade created a mew environment, in which the various kings and feudal lords who had been fighting with each other joined hands as one supported by all the sections of population. This process of unity accelerated the idea of nation state.

D. *The disintegration of the Church:* During the middle ages, the Church dominated, as MacIver says, "to a degree unparalleled in the history of Western civilisation before or since." In 800 AD, the Holy Roman Empire was created which replaced the imperial unity of Rome. It had become a state in itself where it could impose tax, enact its own laws and punish the violators. The king had to bow before the Pope because the latter could even overthrow the former, Pope's temporal powers rested on the support from the believers of Christianity and no king could afford to challenge his authority. However, a new development took place within the Church in which its unity was broken and its universal claim over both spiritual and temporal power was defeated. This was Reformation movement started by Martin Luther in Germany but which soon swept the entire Europe. The movement succeeded because the Church had become a symbol of evil; corruption was rampant and the standards of morality had sunk very low. As a result of the Reformist movement, the Holy Roman Empire disintegrated and nation-state emerged.

E. *The ambitions of kings:* In history, changes take place because of ambitions also. The powerful church with its right to exert obedience from the king was a matter of insult and shame to the ambitious kings. There was a case in which a king had to do penance, barefooted in the snow for three days and nights before the Pope. "The power of Pope," according to MacIver, "touched too nearly the pride and the power of kings." There was no demarcation of authorities between the Pope and the king, and Pope was dominating everywhere. The division of country into different feudal lords also made king uncomfortable. He had no direct connection with the people and the feudal lords could be a challenge to his authority. Under the circumstances the king decided to assert himself. In the 14th century, the king of France got the Pope arrested in Rome itself, when latter decided to excommunicate the former from Christianity. In England, when the Pope refused King Henry VIII to permit divorce from his wife, the King broke all relations with the Church and created the Church of England of which he himself was the religious head. Similar development took place in some of the principalities of Germany. The King also became the head of the state's Church.

F. *Development of trade and commerce:* The advent of modem age, witnessed the discovery of new world. America was discovered and new routes to Far East were identified. This resulted in commercial revolution in Europe. Trade and commerce increased manifold. The king's treasury also flourished by way of collection of taxes. Now the kings no longer needed the assistance of feudal barons as they themselves could afford to maintain a big army. In England, King Henry VII built up a powerful army and with a strong hand enforced law and order. Other kings also followed him.

The development in trade and commerce also created a new middle class which supported a strong king for its own interests, as the confusion of feudalism was an impediment to the development of trade and commerce. The strength of the new middle class was its accumulated wealth. This class was eager to secure new markets in order to make more wealth. It was constituted mainly from the ranks of emancipated and enterprising peasants who had suffered at the hands of both clergy as well as nobility. The trading class also wanted security from the sea pirates. The feudal system with its decentralised structure was incapable of providing protection to the newly emerged middle class. Only a centralised political system could do so. Therefore, they supported the king. This gave a death blow to the feudal state.

G. *The role of peasantry:* Under the feudal order, the peasants were isolated and ignorant from the rest of society. They were highly isolated and poor. A serf was practically bound to the estate where he worked; he could leave village with great difficulty. He could also be ejected from his dwellings at the will of the baron. The absence of money economy prevented the free exchange of service and assured the dependence and the immobility of labour. There was no reward for the labour. Further, feudalism was characterised by a continuous armed battle in which peasantry had to participate and sacrifice for their masters. There was no peace in society. The dissatisfied peasants and common people looked to the king for the maintenance of law and order, and peace.

H. *New methods of warfare:* The nation-states also owe their origin to the new methods of warfare. The supremacy of feudal lords was due to the big castles which in the age of swords, bows, arrows, and spears were invincible. However, the development of large siege cannon rendered the high thin walls of barons indefensible. Other sorts of firearms also became important. The handguns which could be used by everyone after a little training but was more effective than spears, arrows, bows or swords. As a result, the large progessional armies were at the disposal of the Kings rendering the feudal lords incapable of resisting them.

(b) The evolution of Nation-State

The modern nation-states has passed through three phases of evolution. They are:

(a) Political Absolutism
(b) Democracy
(c) Imperialism

(a) *Political Absolutism:* According to Gettel, "A national state with centralised, government in the hands of an absolute monarch-organisation again without freedom-was the immediate out-growth of the decaying feudal state." The king became the state and all powers were concentrated in him. Law became the will of the king and this was justified by involving the doctrine of divine origin of state. The God created the state and the king is chosen by Him, who is his breathing idol on earth. Therefore, violation of his authority is not only illegal but also a sin which may invite His punishment. The theory of divine origin of state thus paved way for king's divine rights. The king had support from all sections of the people. In Denmark and

France, conflict took place between king and the feudal nobility and people supported the king. As MacIver points out that "Monarchy was their first refuge against feudal privilege, the exploitation of the nobles and their exemption from the burdens of taxation." England under Tudors, Spain under Philip II and France under Louis XIV are the classical examples of such political absolutism.

b. *Democracy:* However, political absolutism was not to remain for ever. Democracy was gaining ground. The monarch tried to take help from the feudal nobility which was now no longer a threat to him to oppose the growing power of democracy. The people demanded more active political participation in state activities. In England a fierce battle was fought between the king and the parliament for supremacy in which a king lost his life and another had to fled from the country to save his life. The Glorious Revolution took place in 1688 and England became a constitutional monarchy. The powers of the king became nominal and Parliament acquired sovereignty. Some other states followed the English way, while few like France threw away the monarchy and established the Republican form of government.

But democracy did not usher immediately. It came in through stages. The universal adult franchise came only in the first quarter of 20th century in England and much later in other countries.

Alongwith the universal adult suffrage, a strong feeling developed that there are definite limitations on the state authority. The purpose of state was the general welfare of the people and the state was an agency within the society for the specific purpose. The autonomy of individual was assertea and he was to be given maximum freedom. The economy and religion were divested from state's sphere of activities and put into the individual's domain.

c. *Imperialism:* Alongwith the development of democratic institutions, the nation-state in Europe also became imperialistic. England had the biggest share in imperialism. The sun in the British empire never used to set. Flance was the second biggest empire. Germany, Holland, Belgium-in fact all the nation-states tried to expand their territories beyond their frontiers. The First World War erupted because of the struggle between different imperialists to take possession of different colonies. However, post-second world war era witnessed the general weakening of the imperial powers. The nationalist *movement* in colonies also grew stronger and a decolonisation process was set in; new nation-states in Africa and Asia came into being. Most of these newly independent states followed the western model of democracy, but except in few countries this model did not succeed. The imperialism in its classical form now is not possible. However, neo-colonisation has replaced it and western domination is being maintained in free nations.

V: The Socialist States

The Marxists refuse to accept the concept of nation-state. Instead they advocate internationalism. They have interpreted Western concept of democracy in material terms. They believe that the economic factor has been the dominant factor and the changes in the history take place as a result of interplay of material forces. Nation-state, according to the Marxists, is just like any state based on class collision and democracy, a bourgeois democracy. The state power is used for the oppression of one class by another; the democratic capitalist state is to be over-thrown by the socialist states which is a transitional phase, eventually giving way to communism where state will cease to exist; it will fade away.

In 1917, the socialist revolution took place in Russia. Later on socialist revolutions took place in many countries like Poland, Hungary, Cuba, Romania, East Germany, North Korea and China. However, these countries also functioned like any other nation-states. Only difference was the exercise of complete control over economy by the state in these socialist countries. The socialist states were also characterised by the monopoly of political power in the hands of few people who controlled the communist parties in their respective countries. There was no freedom. The people of these socialist states did not appreciate the sacrifice of political freedom for the sake of economic emancipation. Further, economies of these countries did not give any impressive performance. All these factors made socialist system a short lived affair.

Summing up

We find two contrary trends. Firstly, there is a trend towards creation of supra-national state. Regional groupings like European Union, NAFTA, APEC, ASEAN etc. are becoming very important. Secondly, democracy is in trouble in many nation-states because minority groups within nation states are asserting their separate identity and demanding secession.

Thus the nation-state is being challenged both from within and without. The emergence of international economy, the multinational corporation and an international movement for human rights have all eroded the sovereignty of nation states. The regional, ethnic, communal identities and religious fundamentalism are the biggest challenges to the nation-state within. Consequently, nation-states are in danger. In

1989 there were nine states in Communist Europe, now we have 27 states in the same area. The disintegration of such a large number of nation-states have created fear that the same fate awaits for the countries like India, Canada and many other nations. However, it is also a fact that democratic countries have so far survived the disintegrative threats. They have remained united. It is also a fact that the organisations, as Ash Narain Ray points out whose field of action was effectively bounded by the frontiers of their territory like Parliament, national broadcasting firms lost as a result of dominance of transnational economy and the organisations which are free from national boundries like multinationals, the international currency market and globalised media have gained.

Yet it will be improper to suggest that the age of nation-state has come to an end. The international forces have been able to erode the sovereignty of nation-states to an extent only. The nation-states, on their, part have also become conscious of new trends.

SUGGESTED READINGS

1. Badie, B. and Birnbaum, P., *The Sociology of the State* (Chicago: Chicago University Press, 1983)
2. Carnoy, M., *The State and Political Theory* (Princeton: Princeton University Press, 1984)
3. Cassirer, E., *The Myth of the State* (New Haven: Yale University Pres, 1946)
4. D'Entreves, A.P., *The Notion of the State* (Oxford: Clarendon Press, 1967)
5. Dunleavy, P., and O'Leary, *Theories of the State: The Politics of Liberal Democracy* (London: Macmillan, 1987)
6. Jassay, A. de, *The State* (Oxford: Basil Blackwell, 1985)
7. Jordon, B. *The State, Authority and Autonomy* (Oxford: Basil, Blackwell, 1989)
8. Krader, L., *The Formation of the State* (Englewood Cliffs, N.J. Prentice-Hall, 1968).
9. Lowie, R.H. *The Origins of the State* (New York: Harcourt Brace, 1927)
10. Lubasz, H., (ed.) *The Development of the Modem State* (New York: Macmillan, 1964)
11. MacIver R.M. *The Modern State*, (Oxford: Oxford University Press, 1926)
12. Mclellan, G., Held, D., Hall, S., (eds.) The Idea of the Modern State (Milton Keynes: Open University Press, 1984)
13. Miliband, R, *The State in the Capitalist Society* (London: Quartet Books, 1973)
14. Poggi, G., *The Development of the Modern State* (London: Hutchinson, 1978)
15. Vincent, A.W., *Theories of the State* (Oxford: Basil Blackwell, 1987)

6

Sovereignty

Sovereignty is one of the four essential elements of state without which there is, no state. The terms 'sovereignty' is derived from the Latin word *superanus* which means supreme. It is the supreme power of the state by which it commands obedience from the people. It means the independence of state from interior as well as exterior forces. No individual or any association within the state can claim immunity from sovereignty, everybody is subject to its control and supervision. Similarly in international field, the states interact on the basis of respect for each other. Sovereignty and states are free from control of any external forces. But the pluralists reject this concept of sovereignty and stand for a limited sovereign power to the state. They want to divide this sovereign power of state between the state on the one hand and the associations on the other. However with the fast changing world, the concept of sovereignty has also undergone many changes and the international forces are gradually evading state's sovereignty. These are some of the issues with which the present chapter is related. First, let us study the development of the concept of sovereignty.

I: Development of the Concept

Sovereignty as the supreme power of the state has been a modern concept. It came into existence as a result of rise of nation-states in Europe and was used to assert the need for central authority of powerful monarchs in the transition from feudalism to nation-state. However the idea of sovereignty can be traced back to Greek-city states. Aristotle, the father of Political Science, accepted it as the supreme power of the state. But he never discussed the nature of sovereignty. He was more concerned with the location of sovereignty. Here he had two views. Firstly, according to him, the deliberative body of the state should be sovereign and secondly, that law should be sovereign. He preferred sovereignty to be vested in law. The Romans viewed sovereignty as fullness of the power of state. It was generally accepted that state should be final authority in solving the disputes among the citizens and law of the state was binding upon them.

The medieval age saw the disappearance of state. There was the absence of a unified authority. Feudalism, in fact, was the antithesis of any unified authority. The loyalty was based on personal dependence. The Church had become very powerful and usurped state functions. The authority of king was challenged by not only the Church, the barons and the commons were also his formidable rivals. Under such circumstances there was no place for the modem concept of sovereignty. Further, the law of God which was supposed to be superior to human law also restricted the development of sovereignty as absolute and indivisible.

Jean Bodin is the first political thinker who propounded the modem concept of sovereignty. He defined sovereignty as "supreme power over citizens, unrestrained by law." He also defined citizenship as subjection to a sovereign. To Bodin, sovereignty is undelegated, perpetual and unlimited. Sovereign is the source of law and has the unconditional right to make, interpret and execute laws. The location of sovereignty depends upon the specific form of government. Thus according to him, sovereignty is vested in the king in a monarchy, while in democracy, it resides in popular bodies. Yet Bodin's sovereignty is limited by the law, customary and constitutional law and the institution of private property.

Jean Bodin's views reflected the sixteenth century political and social situation of Europe where the religious war had destroyed the unity of Church and the modern nation states came into being. As a result, the monarch became dominant and the centre of the unified authority of state. Sovereignty came to be regarded as an attribute of state, vested in the monarch.

The theory of sovereignty found its perfection in Thomas Hobbes. For Hobbes, sovereignty is the creation of social contract and the sovereign is that individual or assembly who is authorised to will for the general purpose of a peaceful life. Hobbes gave vast powers to his sovereign. He is the only source of laws and interpreter of laws; His command is law; He is above the law of nature and divine law and the individual has no right to disobey him. Thus his authority is absolute and unlimited. However, Hobbes conceded one limitation on the sovereign's power. The sovereign cannot command an individual to kill, wound or maim himself. He also made it clear that the state existed to protect the lives of the people and this itself constituted a limitation on sovereignty. He conceded the right to revolt in exceptional circumstances. In fact his theory of unlimited sovereignty is a necessary compliment to his individualism.

Hobbes preferred monarchy to any other system because an assembly of men may disagree with each other and produce a civil war. But to Rousseau, sovereignty was located in the people, expressed in General Will and voiced in the direct assemblage of all citizens. Rousseau's concept of popular sovereignty was his most notable contribution to political thought. The government to him, is merely the agent of people who as a corporate body are sovereign. Sovereignty has the same rigorous absolutism as Hobbes' sovereign had. Like Hobbes, Rousseau advocated an unlimited sovereignty, leaving to the individuals only the duty of citizenship. Both Hobbes and Rousseau argued that this was no deprivation because the sovereign 'bears the person' of the citizen and acts of the sovereign are the act of the citizen himself.

Both Hobbes and Rousseau laid down the foundations of a totalitarian state. It was left to Locke who stood for a limited government. He justified the results of Glorious Revolution of 1688 which snatched from the monarchy its absolutist powers and advocated doctrine of popular sovereignty, supremacy of Parliament, constitutional government, limited monarchy and the rule of law. For Locke, sovereignty is neither absolute nor indivisible. However Locke is not consistent in his views on sovereignty. At times, he suggests that sovereignty is located in the people; at times it is the legislature which is supreme. He also says that "where the executive power is vested in a single person who has also a share in the legislature then that person may in a tolerable sense be called the supreme power." The weakness in Locke was that he recognised the force of political sovereignty but did not give adequate recognition to legal sovereignty. However his ideas found full expression in the French Revolution, which declared people to be sovereign. The importance of the French Revolution in the development of the modern concept of sovereignty. is that it reasserted absolutist and unlimited nature of sovereignty on the ground that people being sovereign, there is no need to restrict the supreme power. The newly emerged nation-states claimed total sovereignty, both internally as well as externally. They also asserted their rights to expand "It the expense of others. Further as a result of Industrial Revolution, the activities of state expanded enormously which meant a significant increase in the importance of state as supreme law maker. As a result of these developments, all traces of limited sovereignty, even those that remained in Locke's theory of civil government vanished. In England, Parliament became supreme. There was no barrier to its omnipotence except, as De Lolme said, it could not make a man a woman, or a woman, a man.

Thus the stage was set for Hegel to advocate his views on state and sovereignty. Initially he said that sovereignty lies in the person of monarch as he was a great admirer of Alexander, Julius Ceaser and Napolean. The downfall of Napoleon compelled him to set aside his glorification of dictatorship or absolutism. Instead he advocated constitutional monarchy. The movement of history, he said, is from despotism to a republic and then to a constitutional monarchy. However he gave the monarchy the absolute power to veto over legislation. According to Hegel "The State is perfected rationality, the eternal and necessary essence of spirit, the rational in itself and for itself, an absolute fixed end in itself." The society is to be regulated by the state. The state is supreme over all associations and groups." McGovern aptly points out that, "The state Hegel conceives is a mystic transcendental entity, the mysterious union of all with all, the great whole which embraces, but is greater than, any or all of the individual selves. Compared with this supreme reality, the state, all other things, whether the individual, the family, the corporation, society as a whole sink into insignificance." To him state is the work of God. It is the Divine idea as it exists on earth". he completely subordinated the individual to the state's will. The state has the highest right over the individual and his freedom is a gift of the state. The state not only allows but also enlarges the freedom. The organised moral life is possible only in a state. At the same time, Hegel's state is not arbitrary. As Sabine says, "its absolutism reflected its superior moral position and that Hegel permitted the state to monopolize the ethical aspects of society." State acts through laws which must be rational. It must apply equally to all. A constitutional government excludes lawlessness and provides security. The exercise of authority is according to rules which limit the discretionary powers of officials and functionaries; Hegel also glorified war. The state of war reflected the omnipotence of state and it was perfectly natural for states to go on war. The victorious state could claim to be the agent of world spirit. Thus Hegel's notion of sovereignty is exclusive of any control. Morality and international law also do not constitute any limitation on sovereignty

Hegel's concept of sovereignty had a veil of mysticism. John Austin, an English jurist, made his concept of sovereignty free from any mysticism and advocated a legal view in which sovereignty was absolute, unlimited and indivisible. Austin's views were later on challenged by the pluralists. We shall discuss Austin's, and pluralist's view of sovereignty in detail. First let us understand the meaning of sovereignty.

II: Definitions and Meaning

Sovereignty is "the supreme power over citizens and subjects unrestrained by law". *–Bodin*

Sovereignty is "the supreme political power vested in him whose acts are not subject to any other and whose will cannot be overridden." *–Grotius*

Sovereignty is "the supreme, irresistible, absolute, uncontrolled authority in which the supreme legal power resides. *–Blackstone*

Sovereignty is the commanding power of the state: it is the will of the nation organised in the state; it is the right to give unconditional orders to all individuals in the territory of the state." *–Duguit*

"Sovereignty is the supreme will of the state." *–Willoughy*

Sovereignty is the exercise of final legal coercive power by the state. *–Soltau*

Sovereignty is the concept which maintains no more-if no less-than that those must be an ultimate authority within the political society if the society is to exist at all. *–Hinsley*

Sovereignty means "the political authority within a community which has the undisputed right to determine the framework of rules, regulations and policies within a given territory and to govern accordingly." *–David Held*

The above mentioned definitions project the traditional view of sovereignty. The following conclusions can be drawn from them:

1. Sovereignty is an attribute of state.
2. It is the supreme will of the state.
3. It is a legal coercive power of the state.
4. Sovereignty makes the law and exert obedience from the people.
5. Sovereignty lies in a person or a body of persons.
6. The sovereign power is absolute and is without any limitation.

III: Sovereignty: Internal and External

Sovereignty has two aspects—*internal* and *external.* Internal sovereignty means that the state is the supreme power in its territory. It makes laws which are universally applicable within the boundaries of the state. No individual or association can claim immunity sovereign power; everything is under its supreme command. Its power to force obedience has no legal limitation, for the sovereign is the creator of law. The external sovereignty gives total freedom to the state in international field. Externally, sovereignty is absolute and free from any outside interference. The relations among different states in international politics are based on respect for mutual sovereignty. Membership of United Nations or entering into an alliance or treaty is also no limitation on sovereign because obligations so created are accepted by sovereignty willingly. The sovereignty may choose to reject them at any time. If at all there are limitations, they are self-imposed limitations and do not destroy sovereignty.

IV: Characteristics of Sovereignty

The traditional view of sovereignty has in it the following characteristics:

1. *Permanence:* Sovereignty is permanent as it co-exists with the state. Any change in government does not effect the continuation of sovereignty. In English constitution there is a maxim—'The king is dead, Long live the king'. This means that the king as a person is dead but king as an institution always remains in existence. With the death or overthrow of a government, sovereignty does not cease to exist. It shifts to the next bearer immediately.

2. *Absoluteness:* The sovereign power is absolute and subject to no restraint. Both internally as well as externally, it is free from any limitations. Within the boundaries of a state, the sovereign is over and above any individual, association or institution. None can claim immunity from the sovereign. He is the source of law and foundation of justice. Externally also, there is no pressure or restrain on sovereignty. It is free from customs, traditions, morality and practices. Absoluteness is the supreme characteristics of statehood. Gettel rightly puts if, "If sovereignty is not absolute, no state exists."

3. *Universality:* According to Gamer, "Sovereignty is co-extensive in its operation with the jurisdiction of the state and comprehends within its scope all persons and things in the territory of the state." Sovereignty is all comprehensive and extends to all individuals and

association in the state. The existence of embassies which enjoy extra-territorial facilities is no erosion of sovereign's universality as it is a matter of international courtesy to facilitate international relations among the states. Moreover this facility may be withdrawn and history provides many such examples. Sovereign may accept some limitations on its own. But there cannot be any compulsion. The state reigns supreme.

4. *Inalienability:* Sovereignty can never be alienated from the state. Its alienation from the state would mean state's suicide. According to Leiber, "Sovereignty can no more be alienated than a tree can alienate its right to sprout or a man can transfer his life or personality to another without self destruction." The state and sovereignty are essential to each other. The cessation of a territory of a state to another means the transfer of sovereign power over that portion of land. If a part of the territory becomes independent, it means existence of two states. If the entire territory of a state is invaded by another, it means the destruction of both state as well as sovereignty. Inalienability of sovereignty also means that sovereign power cannot be lost due to its non-exercise. According to Gamer, "Sovereignty cannot be lost by mere lapse of time, as property in land may be lost by prescription at private law."

5. *Exclusiveness:* Exclusiveness means that only state possesses the sovereign power and is legally competent to exert obedience. To accept the existence of more than one sovereign is to destroy the basic unity of the state. State may delegate some of its power to some association or individual on its discretion. But that does not means that the said association or individual have acquired sovereignty. The sovereignty remains with the state.

6. *Indivisibility:* In every political society, there exists only one authority which is legally competent to command. The sovereign power is one unit and cannot be divided. To Jellinek, notion of a divided fragmented, diminished, limited, relative sovereignty is the negation of sovereignty. Gettel says, "If sovereignty is not absolute, no state exists: If sovereignty is divided, more than one state exists." Kalhoun also says, "Sovereignty is an entire thing. To divide it is to destroy it. It is the supreme power in a state and we might not as well speak of half a triangle or half of a square as half of sovereignty." The existence of many sovereigns would result in conflicting commands and chaos in society eventually leading to the extinction of state. Gettel rightly says that, "A divided sovereignty is a contradiction in term." However many writers do not believe in the indivisibility of sovereignty. According to them the sovereign power in a federation is divided between the units and the centre. The United State's Supreme Court accepted this view in *Chisholm* Vs *Georgia* (1792) case and held that both

the Union as well as States are sovereign in their respective areas. But this is not true. Gettel rightly states, "What is divided in federal system is not sovereignty, which resides as a unit in the state as a whole, but the exercise of its various powers, which are distributed in accordance with a constitutional system among various governmental organs." The pluralists have also strongly objected to the indivisibility of sovereignty. But they have also committed the same mistake by confusing the sovereign power as governmental powers.

V: Types of Sovereignty

The term sovereignty has been used variedly in political science which creates difficulty in its real comprehension. Here we will discuss some of the types of sovereignty.

(a) Real and Titular Sovereignty: A distinction is often made between real and titular sovereignty. This distinction has a historical connotation. There was a time when the king in England was absolute. He possessed as well as used his powers. With the strengthening of democratic movement, gradually the king's powers were transferred to the institution called the Crown. The king became titular or nominal sovereign as all the powers were used in his name but he himself as a person did not use them. Therefore the maxim in England—the king can do no wrong' because he is not supposed to act. The powers of the kings are used by the Crown (the Prime-Minister, his Cabinet and the Parliament) which is real sovereign. In United States, there is no such distinction as the President is real as well as titular sovereign.

(b) Legal and Political Sovereignty: The concept of legal sovereignty is a constitutional concept which means the identification of the holder of supreme power in legal sense. It has to be a person or body of persons who exercise the sovereign powers in the state. The Constitution in the state prescribes the legal arrangement according to which the power is to be used. Legal sovereignty thus is the determinate person or body of persons empowered to make laws and issue commands. The judiciary also recognizes such person or body of persons. Disobedience to the commands of legal sovereign invites physical punishment. The legal sovereign also possesses coercive power within the boundaries of the state. The authority of the legal sovereign is thus characterized by legal sanctity and it is unlimited, and all the individuals and associations are bound by its decisions. None can claim immunity from the legal sovereign. The best example of legal sovereignty is the King-in-Parliament in England. According to Dicey, the British Parliament "can adjudge an infant of full age, it may attain a man of treason after death; it may legitimise an illegitimate child,

or if it sees fit, make a man a judge in his own case." Jennings also points out that "Parliament may remodel the British Constitution, may prolong its own life, may legalise illegalities. .... may give dictatorial powers to the government...., may introduce communism, or fascism, entirely without legal restriction."

However, in practice legal sovereign is limited and controlled by the political sovereign. Dicey aptly puts it, "Behind the sovereign which the lawyer recognizes, there is another sovereign to whom the legal sovereign must bow." Political sovereign is not recognised by the courts of law, it is not determinate person or body of persons also, yet its existence cannot be ignored. The legal sovereign also recognises its existence However the definition of political sovereignty is very difficult. Gilchist defines it as "the sum total of the influences in a state which lie behind the law." According to Garner, "In a narrow sense the electorate constitutes the political sovereign, yet in a wider sense it may be said to be the whole mass of population, including every person who contributes to the moulding of public opinion whether he is a voter or not." In direct democracy where people as a whole constitute a body which is supreme and makes law, the distinction between legal and political sovereignty is blurred. In indirect democracy or the representative form of government, which is widely in operation these days, the political sovereign makes it presence felt during the general elections. The legal sovereign is chosen by the political sovereign and is ultimately responsible to it.

De Jure and De Facto Sovereignty: The distinction between *de Jure* and *de facto* sovereignty is based on the actual exercise of sovereign power and the legal claim over it. *De Jure* sovereign is a person or body of persons who is legally competent to issue commands, while *de facto* sovereign is in actual command of the situation who really enforces his command. Bryce aptly puts it," the person or body of persons who can make his or their will prevail whether with the law or against the law; he or they constitute the *de facto* ruler, the person to whom obedience is actually paid." The basis of the authority of a *de facto* sovereign is force, rather than the law. Normally *de jure* sovereign is the same as the *de facto* sovereign. The authority which is issuing commands and enforcing them has also the legitimate power to do so. However the differentiation between the two becomes real as a result of *coup* or the violent overthrow of existing government. In 1917 after the communists overthrew the Tsar government, they were the *de facto* sovereign while the law still recognised the Tsar government as the *de jure* government. Same is true of *de facto* government of Ayub Khan in Pakistan. During the first and second world wars, many countries in Europe came under the German rule .The German rulers became *de facto* sovereign while the laws still recognised the overthrown governments in the respective countries. It has also been observed that the distinction between the two do not remain for long and both merge into one. The *de facto* rulers make necessary changes in the Constitution to make their rule legitimate or *de jure,* because legal sanction ensures a moral claim to authority. On the other hand it has been observed that .authority based on brute force invites natural opposition. However as the *de facto* sovereign acquires legal sanctity, this opposition softens considerably and people's acquiescence is realised.

Austin and other jurists have criticised the notion of *de facto* sovereign as the law can only recognise legal sovereign. Austin would better like to use the terms *de jure* and *de facto* sovereigns in respect of government.

VI: Popular Sovereignty

Modem democracy is based upon the concept of popular sovereignty which means that the ultimate authority rests with the people: The doctrine of popular sovereignty can be traced to Cicero who said that the state is the "people's affair". To him state was a moral community, a group of persons who, in common, possess the state and its law, and the authority arises from the collective power of the people. The state exists because it provides the advantages of mutual aid and just government. However, the doctrine of popular sovereignty is a modem concept which arose as a reaction against the absolutism of the monarchs.

Althusius gives a clear statement of popular sovereignty. For him, sovereignty resides in the people as a corporate body, which cannot be transferred to any other person or organisation. Thus, no, king or ruling class can be rightly called sovereign. The people as, a corporate body give power to administrators through a contract to make the purposes of the corporation effective. This power can be reverted back to the people if somehow the holders of power forfeit it. Althusius gives right to resist tyranny to the people.

John Locke, having analysed the state's origin in terms of social contract, gave all authority to the people. He believed that the supreme power of the state rests with the community permanently. The community alone is competent to lay down the fundamental law of the land which the government cannot violate. The government exists in the interest of the people and there cannot be any arbitrary rule. Although Locke never expanded a doctrine of popular sovereignty, yet he was clear that government was constituted for specific purposes i.e. the protection of life, liberty and property and that the government is a trust. Locke permitted people to remove a government which forfeited their trust. However, the problem with Locke, as Asirvatham points out was that "the people are in the nature of a sleeping partner. They let the government carry on the sovereign authority within certain limits till it begins to abuse its power, and when it does that, the sovereign people raise themselves from their slumber, overthrow the existing government, and set up another government in its place." Locke has justified revolution, only when it is supported by the entire community.

Rousseau may will be regarded as the father of the concept of popular sovereignty. According to Maxey, "...it is beyond dispute that in the sphere of political thought, he performed a service of incalculable importance that was his formulation of plausible and largely realisable theory of popular sovereignty." Sidgwick says: "Rousseau's concept of popular sovereignty is based on three principles:

(i) Men are by nature free and equal;
(ii) The right of government must be based on some compact freely entered into by these equal and independent individuals;
(iii) As a result of compact, the individuals become an indivisible part of a body of sovereign people *which* has an alienable right of determining its own internal constitution and legislation.

Rousseau made a clear was distinction between the state and government. To him, government was merely an agent having delegated powers which could be withdrawn or modified as the will of the people dictates. Undoubtedly, the government had limited authority.

Rousseau's sovereign acts only for the welfare of the people and aims at achieving common good. He wrote, "It is impossible for the sovereign body to hurt its members. The sovereign for its part cannot impose upon its members any fetters that are useless to the community." In his scheme of things, Rousseau made the General will as supreme, which is the will of the people.

The concept of popular sovereignty reached its peak during the American and French Revolutions. The American Declaration of Independence declared, "We hold these truths to be self-evident that all men are created equal, that they are endowed by their creator with certain inalienable rights that. among these are Life, Liberty and the pursuit of Happiness. That to secure these rights, Governments are instituted among Men, deriving their just powers from the consent of the governed." The Declaration explicitly recognised the people's right to alter or to abolish any government which is destructive to the inalienable rights of life, liberty and pursuit of happiness. It also spoke of the British king who had become a 'Tyrant' by his acts and therefore "...is unfit to be the ruler of a free people." The French Declaration of the Rights of Man and Citizen declared that, "The source of all sovereignty is essentially in the nation; nobody, no individual can exercise authority that does not proceed from it in plain terms." It also said that "The aim of every political association is the preservation of the natural and imprescriptible rights of man. These rights are liberty, property, security and resistance to oppression."

The American Constitution echoed the concept of popular sovereignty. According to Gettel, "The American Constitution represented the first successful attempt of a people to create consciously and deliberately, a system of government, and to enact consciously and deliberately, a system of government, and to enact the principles of a political philosophy into law. The idea of a fundamental document, created by a special representative body created for the purpose, and formally approved by the people was one of the most important contributions of the period." The American and French Revolutions made the concept of popular sovereignty as the basis of modem democratic state.

According to Dr. Asirvatham, the concept of popular sovereignty contains following features:

1. Government does not exist for its own good. It exists for the good of the people.
2. If people's wishes are deliberately violated, there is a possibility of revolution.
3. Easy means should be provided for a legal way of expressing public opinion.
4. Government should be held directly responsible to the people through such means as frequent elections, local self-government, referendum, initiative and recall.
5. Government should exercise its authority, directly in accordance with the laws of the land and not act arbitrarily.

We may conclude that the concept of popular sovereignty is essentially a democratic doctrine which puts immense faith on the people, their rights and capabilities. They constitute a corporate body which is supreme and source of all authority in the state. The governmental authority so created is limited in nature, subservient and responsive to the wishes of this great corporate body.

The weakness of popular sovereignty can not be denied. Gettel rightly points out that the sovereignty of the people by its very definition is contradiction in terms. Certain writers have equated people with electorate and to them popular sovereignty means power of the electorate. But the electorate cannot be considered as one political entity. the elections are won on the basis of majority. According to Gamer, "The sovereignty of the people, therefore, can mean nothing more than the power of the majority of the electorate in a country, where a system of approximate universal suffrage prevails, acting through legally established channels, to express their will and make it prevail." But then the number of electorate is very small in any country and they cannot be regarded as legally sovereign. The concept becomes further confused if we study the dynamics of modem democracy. As a result of revolution in the means of communication, the electorate in particular and people in general are fed with readymade ideas which are accepted by them as their own. People and their votes are manipulated through a variety of ways and means. Democracy has become a mobocracy in which the crowd dominates. Popular sovereignty may faithfully reflect in direct democracy where the people really exercise their sovereign powers through referendum and other means. But that is not possible in the modem age given the large population and size of the state. Moreover, to Laski, "the business of the modem state is far too complex to be conducted by perpetual referenda." If the popular sovereignty means that government should act according to the wishes of the electorate, many problems would follow. Practically, it may lead to confusion and chaos in the state, as the opposition may charge a government to be acting against the interest of electorate and the government refusing to accept such a proposition. Thus, the concept of popular sovereignty when really applied in politics may lead to instability in political systems.

VII: Austin's theory of Sovereignty-The Legal View

John Austin (1790-1859) was an English jurist. He belonged to Bentham's school of utilitarianism and believed that the state owed its existence to its utility to the people. The end of state is the maximum good of the maximum number. He propounded the theory of sovereignty in his book '*Lectures on Jurisprudence* (1832) which has been his contribution to the political science. John Austin has defined sovereignty in judicial/monistic/legalistic term.

According to Austin, "If a determinate human superior, not in the habit of obedience to a like superior, receives habitual obedience from the bulk of a given society, that determinate superior is sovereign in that society and the society (including the superior) is a society political and independent." Austin also believed that law is the command of the sovereign and every law is "set directly or circuitously, by a sovereign person or body to a member or .members" in the state.

The following propositions can be derived from Austin's view of sovereignty:

1. Sovereignty is necessary for the state. One of the four attributes of state is sovereignty. The existence of state is impossible without its sovereign power. Every independent political community has a sovereign power which is as essential as the centre of gravity in mass of matter. The end of sovereign power means the end of state.
2. Sovereignty resides in a determinate person or body of persons. To Austin, state is a legal order in which the sovereignty can be identified. It vests either in a person or a body of persons as per the legal arrangements in the state. It cannot be found in "General will" as Rousseau argued because "General Will" is a very vague concept. Sovereignty does not reside in God. Even the electorate does not possess sovereignty because they are not a determinate body. According to Henry Maine, "He is not necessarily a single person; in the modem western world he is very rarely so; but he must have so much of the attributes of a single person as to be determinate".
3. Sovereignty is the supreme power in the state. Sovereign is the determinate human superior who is the source of all authorities in a state. His authority is unlimited and absolute. He does not obey any superior authority. He is supreme and commands all individuals and associations within the state. Nobody can claim immunity from him. He cannot be subjected to any direct or indirect control. Sovereignty is free from any external pressure also. The law is not a limitation on sovereign as he is above the law. In fact he is the source of law. He is not subject to any limitation except those which he sets up himself.
4. The sovereign receives habitual obedience from the bulk of the society. People habitually obey the sovereign. The authority of sovereign is not casual. If a significant part of the population refuses to render obedience to the sovereign, then he is not sovereign in the true sense. Similarly a short time obedience is also not a attribute of sovereignty. According to Austin, the obedience to sovereign must be continuous, regular, undisturbed and uninterrupted. Sovereign power is permanent in a given society.
5. Law is the command of the sovereign. According to Austin; sovereign is the source of law. He defined law as a command given by the superior to an inferior. The sovereign has a right

to legitimate use of physical force to enforce its laws. Violation of law may invite penalties. Sovereign is above customs and conventions. They exist with the permission of sovereign and do not constitute a limitation on laws. The rights and liberties of the individuals also emanate from the laws of the sovereign. Thus law is the will and command of the sovereign.

6. Sovereignty is indivisible. The power of sovereignty cannot be divided between two or more persons. It is one unit and incapable of any division. Division of sovereignty means destruction of state.

Thus, according to Austin, sovereignty is the supreme power of state which is determined, comprehensive, absolute, unlimited, permanent and indivisible. Austin's concept of sovereignty has been criticised on the following grounds:

(i) *Identification of sovereign is a difficult task:* For Austin, sovereign is a determinate human being or body of persons. but it is almost impossible to locate such a person or body of persons in modem times. This might have been possible in old times when the kings ruled with absolute power. The modern age has witnessed the expansion of democracy in all parts of the world. Democracy envisages the concept of popular sovereignty in which the people are supreme and the governments are responsible to them. But then to Austin, neither the people nor the electorate can be called sovereign as they are not a determinated human authority. In a federation where there is a division of power between the centre and the states, sovereignty can never be located. In such a system the constitution is supposed to be supreme, but the constitution is not human, hence 'cannot be sovereign. Even the British Parliament which is supposed to be supreme cannot be truely called sovereign, as it also works under limitations. In fact the real rulers of a society are undiscoverable.

(ii) *Sovereignty has never been absolute:* Every state works in a social perspective and the sovereignty is limited by the customs and conventions of the society. Historically speaking, no sovereign has been absolute. Henry Maine gives the example of Maharaja Ranjit Singh of Punjab who exercised despotic power over his subjects. Smallest disobedience of his commands invited ruthless punishment in the form of death or mutilitation. Yet he never issued a command which Austin could call a law. Even he could not violate the customs and conventions of the society. The customs and conventions are the result of a long historical process and are binding on sovereign. Even in the West, according to Maine "no sovereign, however despotic, could disregard the entire history of the community, the mass of its historic antecedents, which in each community determines how the sovereign shall exercise or forbear from exercising, irresistible coercive power." According to Bluntschli, "Sovereignty is limited, externally by the right of other states and internally by its own nature and by the rights of its individuals." It is difficult for any state to be absolute. International law puts limitations on sovereignty externally while social customs, religion, morality and ethics restricts its operation internally. The concept of popular sovereignty is in vogue these days which gives ultimate power to the people and the legal sovereign has to bow before them.

(iii) Austin's notion of law as the command of the. sovereign and as command given by a superior to an inferior have also been criticized as *erroneous.* There are many laws which owe their origins to the customs and traditions of the society. According to MacIver, "The state has little power to make customs and perhaps less to destroy it..." "Customs when attacked by the law retaliate in return and in this retaliation, they attack not only the particular law hut also the 'spirit of law-abidingness'. The notion of law as command is also wrong because it exaggerates the coercive power of state. We obey law not because there is a physical force behind it to compel its observance: laws are obeyed because they serve our common interests. Duguit rightly says that "Law is the product of our social life. We obey law because they are for social interest and that it is impossible to maintain social order without them." The absence of law would mean the rule of anarchy where no human existence is possible.

(iv) *Sovereignty is not indivisible:* Every political society is characterised by division of functions without which an effective political order can never be created. The legislature, the executive and the judiciary work in their respective fields and the sovereign power is divided among them. In a parliamentary form of government, one may say that the legislature is sovereign because the executive and the judiciary follow the legislature. But in a federal government, the legislature cannot be sovereign because it cannot alter the constitution entirely on its own. Further, the pluralists have vehemently opposed the indivisibility of sovereign power. They believe that state is an association, like any other associations, in the society created for specific purposes and the sovereign power should be divided among the various associations and the state.

(v) *Austin ignores the concept of political sovereignty.* In fact he failed to make a distinction between the legal and political sovereignty. In case of England, he could not decide as to where the sovereignty resided. On the one hand he says that the parliament is sovereign, then he says that the electorate is sovereign. At times, to him, the

House of Commons is sovereign. Gamer rightly states that, "It is great mistake on the part of Austin that he has laid much emphasis on the legal aspect of the sovereignty. He has ignored other aspects and influences. It was natural from the lawyer to make such a mistake."

We shall discuss more objections to Austin's concept of sovereignty in the pluralist criticism of such a legalistic view. However in defence of Austin, one can say that his views are strictly legal and Gamer aptly says "as a conception of the strict legal nature of sovereignty, Austin's theory is, on the whole, clear and logical."

VIII: The Pluralistic Attack on Austin's Theory of Sovereignty

Austin's concept of sovereignty is also called monistic view of sovereignty as it envisages a single source of sovereignty in state. According to Austin, state and sovereignty co-exist and are absolutely inalienable. But the pluralists stand for many sources of sovereignty. They want to distribute the sovereign. power between different associations in the society.

There is a long list of pluralist writers. Some of them are: Dr. J. Neville Figgis, Paul Boncour, Durkheim, Maclver, Laski, Barker, Duguit, Krabbe, G.D.H. Cole and Miss Follet. The pluralistic concept of sovereignty rose because of the following main factors.

(i) The pluralistic philosophy originated as a reaction against the state absolutism, which gave all powers to the state and completely subjugated the individual. To Hegel, the state was the march of God on earth which should be worshipped. His school of idealism regarded state as a vehicle of all individual development and progress. Austin did not share his views with the idealists, yet his legal view of sovereignty made the state absolute.

(ii) The expansion of democracy and the rise of welfare state are also responsible for the assertion of pluralism. Democracy stands for decentralisation and accountability of the power-holders. The use of welfare state witnessed the expansion of state activities. With the result, modem state is overburdened with work. It has penetrated into almost all the human activities. The result has been confusion and inefficiency, as the state could not perform the expanded functions satisfactorily. Ward aptly puts it, "To remove the congestion at the centre and to increase social efficiency, pluralists put forward proposals which aim at decentralisation of authority."

(iii) In their revolt against monistic sovereignty, the pluralists were highly influenced by the guilds of medieval ages which had come up as a result of confused situation of feudalism where there was no unified authority. These guilds wielded enormous powers. The pluralists' desire to revive these guilds in the form of associations which should share the sovereign power.

(iv) The growth and development of federations in different states also contributed to the spread of pluralism. It is very difficult to locate the human determinate sovereign in a federation where the powers are divided between the centre and the units. Moreover, in such states, sovereignty is always limited.

(v) Lastly, the development of internationalism and the consequent demand for maintenance of peace in world helped the origin of plusalism. It was believed that the two world wars were the result of politics of arrogant sovereign states which brought about untold miseries for the people, in the form of death and destruction. The question of the survival of human beings on the earth was raised and a need was felt for the creation of an international organisation to maintain international peace and security. This was only possible if the states surrender their absolute right to decide everything. Laski maintained that there should be limits on external sovereignty in the interest of world peace. He also declared, "It would be of lasting benefit to Political Science, if the whole concept of sovereignty was surrendered."

The pluralists have criticised Austinian view of sovereignty on the basis of following three arguments:

a. The existence of associations or organisations in the society;
b. International Relations; and
c. Law.

(a) Associations and State Sovereignty

The pluralists view state as an association. According to them, it is one of the many associations in the society. Society thus is composed of many associations, as human life is multi-dimensional Associations are formed for the development of various aspects of human personality. Gierke and Maitland maintain that there is a real personality of associations and sovereignty should be divided between the state and other associations. Associations are not the creation of state; by their very nature they are original, formed for specific purposes. They also operate independent of state. Therefore they should be given functional freedom and state should not monopolise sovereignty. For Lindsay, state has no personality of its own. At the most, it is an "organisation of organisations". It is true that the membership of state is compulsory and normally this membership is also not by choice but by birth, while the membership of other associations is voluntary and may be surrendered at will. But this alone cannot justify the doctrine of absolute sovereignty of state.

The pluralists maintain that there are associations which originated before the origin of state like the family and the Church. Figgis writes, "The state did not create the family nor did it create the churches, nor even in any real sense can it be said to have created the club or trade unions, nor in the middle ages, the guilds or the religious order, hardly even the universities or colleges within the universities; they have all arisen out of the natural associative instincts of mankind, and should all be treated by the supreme authority as having a life original ... " According to Figgis, human society is not a sand heap of individuals related only through the state, but an ascending hierarchy of groups.

As an association, the functions of the State are limited. Its primary function is maintenance of law and order and preservation of peace.

Other associations exist to develop the various aspects of individual's personality. No doubt by preserving peace, state performs a very important function, but that is not the end of everything. Moreover in the ultimate analysis, the state only provides the basic conditions; actual development of the human personality is through other associations only. Thus the structure of the society is federal, therefore the authority must also be federal. According to Lipson, "Not only is society a pluralistic union of groups, but the ways in which every human being is associated are also plural." Since the state is only an association in the society, therefore the whole of sovereignty cannot be given to it.

As other associations or groups are as important as the state itself, the pluralists demand non-interference in the activities of associations by the State. They assert that the state has no right to claim total loyalty from its citizens. In case of conflict between an association and state, the individual should be free to choose. Coker aptly puts it, "The state is confronted not merely by unassociated individuals but also by other associations evolving independently, eliciting individual loyalties, better adapted than the state-because of their select membership, their special forms of organisation and action for serving various social needs." The various associations must be treated by the state on the basis of equality and should be allowed complete autonomy in their respective affairs.

However, the pluralists do not want to abolish the state. They want the state to perform its own specific function and to coordinate the activities of different associations. For Lindsay, the state can have 'control over other associations within it only if and so far as, the citizens are prepared to give it such power'. According to Barker, "The state, as a general and embracing scheme of life, must necessarily adjust the relations of associations to itself, in order to maintain the integrity of its own scheme to other associations, in order to preserve the equality of associations before the law; and to their own members in order to preserve the individual from the possible tyranny of the group".

Maxey sums up the major thrust of the pluralistic attack on sovereignty as follows:

(i) that the state is but one of numerous social, economic, political and other groupings through which men in society must seek to satisfy their interests and promote their welfare;

(ii) that these different groupings are not mere creatures of the state but arise independently and acquire power and authority not given by the state;

(iii) that the functions of such voluntary associations as churches, labour unions, trade organisations, professional societies and the like are as necessary and important as those of the state; (iv) that the monistic state is not only incapable of wielding absolute authority over such bodies but is incapable of regulating their affairs intelligently or administering them efficiently;

(v) that the monistic concept of sovereignty is a mere legal fiction which not only misses the truth but does incalculable harm in obstructing the evolution of society along more natural beneficial lines.

(b) Law and State Sovereignty

Austin's concept of law as will and command of the sovereign has been vigorously criticised by the. pluralists. They hold law as independent and anterior to state. Law is not the command of the superior to the inferior. According to MacIver, "The state is both the child and the parent of law." The origins of laws lie in their social requirement. Man is a social being and as such he has to observe social discipline and follow rules which are necessary for social life. Laws are followed not because of the fear of punishment but because they are necessary for collective existence. Duguit says that "Law is primarily the product of social psychology, depending upon the physical, mental and moral needs of society." If the advantages of social life are to be maintained rules are to be observed, otherwise the society will disintegrate. For Duguit, laws are the condition of social solidarity. Laws are obeyed because they represent necessary conditions of society. They are inherent in society. They serve social ends. The state itself is subject to legal obligations. Duguit regards the state as pure abstraction while the government as a reality. The acts of the government are the acts of the people who constitute it and these acts are valid if they conform to the norms of social solidarity. To Krabbe, the source of law is the feeling or sense of right. He defines law as the "totality of rules, general or particular, written on unwritten which springs from men's feeling or sense of right." He further elaborates that law should be demanded by the majority. Krabbe assigns sovereignty to the law and according to him the state owes its authority due to law. The state thus is subordinate to law. According to pluralists, laws are made not because the sovereign wills it; they are made because they are required and the state only promulgates the laws according to the social requirements. State does not create law, it only promulgates. Moreover there are customs and traditions in the society which are enforced, although they do not have any legal sanction. In England, writes F.A. Ogg, "The common law is the vast body of legal precepts and usages which through the centuries has acquired binding and almost immutable character."

Thus for the pluralists, law means following:

(i) Law is not the command of the sovereign.
(ii) The origins of law is in its social requirements.
(iii) The state is under the law.
(iv) The state acts through the government and government's act should serve the social ends.
(v) The associations should have the power to make laws in their respective areas.

(c) Internationalism and State Sovereignty

According to Laski, "The notion of an independent sovereign state is, on the international side, fatal to the well-being of humanity." The pluralists are highly critical of external sovereignty which resulted in two world wars in the present century. With the stock-pilling of nuclear arms which have the capacity to destroy world many times and which can only lead to MAD i.e. mutually assured destruction, the state has no option but to surrender its absolute, unlimited and indivisible sovereignty. Articles 2 and 24 of the Charter of United Nations put limitations on state sovereignty. The U.N. Declaration of Human Rights is another step in the direction. The International law is becoming a fact of international life. The Nuremberg trials after II world war refused to accept the waging of aggressive war as a prerogative of state sovereignty. The pluralists give importance to preservation of world peace and for this they want the destruction of external sovereignty.

(d) Laski's Criticism of Austin's Theory

Laski's attack on Austin's theory of sovereignty is contained in his various works particularly in *A Grammar of Politics, The State in Theory and Practice* and *The Foundations of Sovereignty.* His critique can be summed up under the following points:

(i) *Historically invalid:* According to Laski, Austin's concept of absolute sovereignty is historically false statement of facts. Historically, sovereign power has been subjected to limitations. Nowhere do we find such an absolute and unlimited sovereignty. Laski says that the power of the state is used by the government and will of the state is the will of the government. Therefore the state cannot have unlimited powers. Every government is built upon 'a contingent moral obligation.'

In history, there is a very small period when we really had a sovereign in Austin's sense. This was the period when the nation-states arose and the kings asserted their authority. In fact the territorial and omnipotent state was the offspring of the religious struggles of the 16th century and the emergence of sovereign state vindicated the 'supremacy of secular order against religious claims'. Thus there were certain historical factors which were responsible for the absolute sovereignty of the state.

In modem times also the sovereignty is limited. The only example could be of King-in-Parliament in England but 'everybody knows that to regard the King-in-Parliament as a sovereign body in the Austinian sense is absurd.' No Parliament can defranchise the Roman Catholics or prohibit existence of trade unions. The British Parliament is subject to external and internal limitations. Moreover in a federation it is impossible to locate a human determinate where the constitution is based on separation of powers and no organ of the government can be termed as supreme. In modem democracy the electorate is ,supposed to be sovereign. But the electorate is an indeterminate body in Austinian sense. In fact to Laski, the real rulers in .a society are undiscoverable. Thus to Laski, "No sovereign has anywhere possessed unlimited power; and the attempt to exert it has always resulted in the establishment of safeguards. Even the Sultan of Turkey in the height of his power was himself bound down by a code of traditional observance, obedience to which was practically compulsory upon him." (ii) *Ethically indefensible:* According to Laski, Austin makes the individual slave before his sovereign. This is ethically wrong because it retards the individual's development and moral stature. Thus the idea of state sovereignty is ethically indefensiible and a barren concept Laski says, "The only state to which I owe allegiance is the state in which I discover moral adequacy, and if a given state fails to satisfy that condition I must, to be consistent with my own moral nature, attempt experiment .... our first duty is to be true to our conscience".

(iii) *Fallacies of the Austinian Law:* Laski is highly critical of Austin's concept of law. To Austin, law is the command from a superior to inferior. To Laski this is ridiculous. He says, "To think of law as simply a command is to strain the definition to the verge of decency." He says that laws are universal in character and applied to both the law- makers and the subjects. Moreover to Laski, law is an instrument for satisfying social needs. They are obeyed not because of any coercion but because they satisfy the requirements of the people. The objective of a good law is the maximum possible satisfaction of desire and only such law should be obeyed.

(iv) *Pragmatically faulty:* Laski also: criticises Austin's concept of sovereignty on pragmatic grounds. Austin's theory has lost its utility particularly in view of the growing challenge of powerful groups from within and some kind of international organisations from without. The theory played a remarkable role in the past in securing the independence of state organisation from religious domination and sought political allegiance of the people for a common sovereign in the state. However in modern times, this theory has lost its value.

(v) *Anti-internationalistic:* Austin's sovereignty is criticised on the basis of internationalism. The concept of absolute sovereignty is incompatible with the interests of humanity as it leads to destructive wars which may even annihilate the entire mankind. Laski writes, "Internationally it is not difficult to conceive the organisation of an allegiance which reaches beyond the limits of the state. To leave with a handful of men, for instance, the power to make war may well seem anachronistic to those who envisage the consequences of war. When state sovereignty in international affairs was recognised, there was no authority existent to which that type of control might be entrusted. It is atleast arguable now that an authority predominant over states may be conceived which is entrusted to the regulation of those affairs or more than national interests. It involves at any rate, on the international side abolition of state sovereignty." Laski firmly believes that the concept of the sovereignty of the state would also pass away, just as the divine rights of kings had. To him, state sovereignty is an obstacle in the path of international order. The Austinian state, says Laski, is a state unto itself and as such has no concern for world peace and security. Laski is so opposed to the concept of sovereignty that he wants to delete it from the discipline of Political Science.

(vi) *Austin's sovereignty curbs the individual liberty:* As Austin's theory of sovereignty admits an absolute sovereign, Laski fears that such an absolute sovereign would never grant any liberty to the individual. Laski had great distrust of power and those who exercised it. Therefore, he stood for decentralisation and argued that the state should be responsible for its action. The state should also protect and respect certain rights of the individual without which he cannot develop his personality. Laski reminds that 'the state is not itself an end, but merely the means to an end, which is realised only in the enrichment of human lives. Its power and allegiance, which it can win, depend always upon what it achieves for that enrichment.'

(vii) *State as an Association:* Like other pluralists, Laski clearly differentiates between state and society. State is one of the associations in the society created for a specific purpose. The objective of an association is to develop human personality in the specific area for which it is formed. He says, "Associations exist to fulfil purposes which a group of men have in common. They support and imply functions." Thus every association serves certain interests in the society. State also looks after certain interests in the society. All these associations including the state have their own distinctive identity and personality. To Laski, "The group is real in the same sense as the state is real. It is that is to say, an interest to promote, a function to serve. The state does not call it into being. It is not outside the categories of law, dependent upon the state. It grows in the whole environment as a natural response to factors in that environment. It lives and moves as its surrounding circumstances seem to warrant." These groups or associations like political parties, churches, trade unions, golf clubs, dramatic societies, determine- the individual's choice 'of friends, of opportunities, of a career.' Thus for Laski 'there is no necessary unity in society. Society is essentially pluralistic and we are not a universe but a multiverse'. Society is composed of a variety of associations working at different levels.

Thus the structure of the society is essentially federal. Therefore Laski argues that the authority must also be federal. It is wrong to confine all the sovereign powers to the state. In the matter of law-making, all should be consulted. Laski also feels that allegiance to various associations depended upon their performance. Men belong to many groups, including the state and a competition for allegiance is continuously possible; and no group including the state can claim total loyalty from the individual. The state as an association can not regulate the total life of man. Its function is merely to coordinate the activity of different associations in the society.

(e) MacIver's Attack on Austin's Theory of Sovereignty

R.M. MacIver has criticised Austin's theory of sovereignty from sociological view in his two books namely, *The Modern State* and *The Web of Government.* He criticises Austin's concept of absolute and unlimited sovereignty on following grounds.

(i) The legalist doctrine of sovereignty is formal. "Legally the state is unlimited, because it is the source of legal enactment..." But then same is true of the church 'because it is the source of ecclesiastical law, or the Royal and Ancient Club,' because it alone prescribes the laws of golf .... The state is one of the organs of community. According to MacIver sovereignty" is the attribute of an association and no more absolute than the association itself.

(ii) The legalist theory of sovereignty speaks in terms of power and not service. But the power is only an instrument of service. The state performs specific functions. It cannot take the place of society and usurp its functions. The state services are not unlimited and therefore 'the conception of unlimited sovereignty is dangerous. To attribute power to government beyond the limit of its capacity for service is the grave error on which all tyranny is based.'

(iii) The concept of unlimited sovereignty has also been criticised by MacIver on the basis of history. Historically speaking the state never possessed absolute sovereignty. The Greek city-state were not really states. During those times, 'the state was still an aspect, not yet a form of society.' The concept of sovereignty arose to assert the need of centralised authority in the transition from feudalism to the nation-state. MacIver points out that 'the great difference between the political thought of our times and that of the past is the definite assertion of the limited and relative character of sovereignty.' Earlier sovereignty was limited mainly on moral grounds or 'will of the God' on the welfare of his subjects, which the rulers ought to obey.' As a result of social development in nineteenth century which came about due to Industrial Revolution, associations became a force to be reckoned with. "The real powers exercised by the numerous and often vast associations of the new age confounded the idea of a single all comprehensive authority." The 'first wave that broke over the doctrine of absolutism came with the withdrawal of the state from the control of the church. "It has been succeeded by others and in our own days the conflicting currents of strong economic interest may well be said to have overthrown it altogether," as 'the state could no longer pretend to be the one all-powerful agency of the social life.'

(iv) Thus for MacIver, the state is an association. In the first place Maciver distinguishes state from the society. According to him "To identify the social with the political is to be the guilty of the grossest of all confusions, which completely bars any understanding of either society or state." State came into existence much later than the society. The state exists within the society but it is not even the form of society. For MacIver society is composed of different associations and the state is one of them. MacIver is aware of differences between the state and other association. he says, "The essential difference between other associations and the state lies just in this: that the other associations are limited primarily, by their objective, which is particular, whereas the state is limited primarily by its instrument, which is particular, while its objective is general, within the limits so imposed." State's laws are universal and they have coercive sanctions unlike associations. Therefore the state "can only concern itself .... with those interests which can reasonably regarded as universal: Further tile state is permanent. "If a state dissolves: it is like a convulsion of nature. If it breaks into two; it is with violence and fierce repulsion." This is not true in case of other associations. However despite the differences state remains an association, although, 'unique in its kind' among other associations in the society. The family, the church are examples of other associations which are as natural as the state is. State has not created them. These "association have an inner life which is at least as autonomous as that of the state." MacIver is ready to give state the power of regulation only in respect of their common external attributes. The state cannot control the internal affairs of the associations. He says "... the state does not regulate the internal affairs of other corporations, it does not and can not determine their purposes or for the most part their methods." Human life and culture are diversified and the doctrine of absolute sovereignty if actually practised, 'would be fatal to the harmony of social life.' The associations which represent this diversity cannot be controlled by

State 'because they are neither its parts nor its subjects.'

(v) MacIver also criticises Austin's concept of law. According to him, there are many kinds of laws. There is social law which is expressed in customs and traditions. Part of this in turn is reinforced, reaffirmed, and enlarged as the law of the state.' The Austinian idea that law is the command of superior to inferior is, to MacIver misleading, "since it conceals and even denies two of the attributes which law everywhere exhibits, its universality and its formality." These attributes 'are necessary consequences of the structure and operation of every political system.' According to MacIver "Law is the very antithesis of command .... " because "command separates the giver and the receiver, separates their states always and sometimes their interest as well." but law is universal and is applied to both-legislator and the people, "when an army officer issues a command, he does not have to obey it himself, any more than an employer who gives instructions to his employees. Further command belongs to the sphere of administration, as it is a means of execution. Command does not belong to legislation; it is not a form of enactment, law is permanent and fundamental as compared with command."

MacIver believes that the state is a corporation and subject to legal obligation. "... in the great book of the law the state merely writes new sentences and here and there scratches out an old one. Much of the book was never written by the state at all, and by all of it the state is itself bound, save as it modifies the code from generation to generation." The authority of law is greater than the authority of the state. The 'state is more the official guardian than the maker of law'. It has to uphold the rule of law.

(f) Criticism of Pluralist view of Sovereignty

The pluralist assumptions and their critique of Austin's monistic view of sovereignty have been criticised on many grounds. *Firstly,* the pluralists suffer from an inner contradiction. On the one hand they stand for decentraisation of sovereign power and autonomy of groups or associations, on the other they want state to play a coordinating role and regulate the activities of association. Thus they themselves give precedence to state vis-a-vis other associations. Modern society is highly complex and the state and its supremacy as the final judge in reconciliating the interests of divergent and conflicting interests is above any challenge. *Secondly,* the concepts of welfare state and planning have increased the state activities and state control to a great extent

Thirdly, the plura lists assume that there cannot be overlapping of functions among the groups. The fact is that they do not run on parallel lines. To avoid chaos and disorder, the state must have supreme powers to control them. *Fourthly* Austin himself will not object to what the pluralists stand for. He has only given a legal view of sovereignty which is essential for any civilised existence. International law is yet in its developing stage and cannot be regarded as a limitation on state sovereignty. Laski later on himself criticised the concept of pluralistic sovereignty. He believed that the pluralists failed in understanding the state "as an expression of class-relations". Laski said, "Legally no one can deny that there exists in every state organ whose authority is unlimited."

The significance of pluralism lies in their assertion of importance of group life in modern society. The pluralists stood for democracy and decentralisation against the absolutist state. However, state sovereignty cannot be done away with as it may lead to chaos and confusion in the society. We may conclude with Sabine, "For my own part, then, I must reserve the right to be a monist when I can and a pluralist when I must."

IX: Nation-State and Imperialism

The emergence and growth of the idea of nation-state are closely related to the development of the concept of sovereignty. In fact, each supplemented and strengthened the other so much that the two concepts have become synonyms. To talk of nation-state in the absence of the characteristics of sovereignty is to talk of sovereignty without its base. Happily, the fast-changing developments in national and international politics are bringing about the corresponding far-reaching changes in both nation-states and the concept of sovereignty.

During the most part of the early modern period and until a larger part of the 20th century, the idea of nation-state got rooted so deeply in the minds and activities of the scholars and rulers that there had appeared what may be called aggressive, extreme and narrow nationalism, leading, thus, to dictatorial regimes fighting against one another.

Industrialisation, capitalism and then colonisation followed each other: At the base of this development, extreme nationalism played its vital role in bringing one sovereign state against another. If extreme nationalism is one end, its another end is imperialism. To borrow Lenin's phrase, imperialism is the highest stage of nationalism (for Lenin, capitalism). Ebenstein says that imperialism is a chief distortion of nationalism. He writes: "Love of oneself becomes hatred of others, and enslavement of others is clothed in such masks as 'the white man's burden', or the need for 'living space'." According to Schuman, "Imperialism is the imposition by force and violence of alien rule upon subject people, despite all moralizing and pretensions to the contrary." Schumpeter defines imperialism as an "atomistic force, ancient in inception, decadent and self-conscious in an age of nationalism, yet still powerful enough to lord it over its rival, the upstart capitalism." In .economic terms, imperialism is the result of colonisation while politically it aims at creating, organising and maintaining an empire, subject to a single, nationalistic and centralized will.

Trade, investment of surplus capital, colonisation and ultimately political control are the numerous causes which help in the development of imperialism. In any type or form, imperialism implies a subject who is usually economically, politically and militarily a weak country on the one hand and a strong country on the other. The Western imperialisation of Asia, Africa and to some extent of Latin America came through industrialisation, search for new markets, urge for obtaining raw-material and colonisation. Extreme nationalism, which guided the destinies of the industrial Western nations, brought them against one another. Imperialistic rivalries, militarism, armaments-all led to wars, both regional as well as global.

As imperialism breeds imperialism, and as it, ultimately, ends up in wars, it is difficult to justify it on any ground. With extreme nationalist feelings as the motivating force, imperialism finds expression in either direct political control in the form of 'protectorates' or indirect political control in the form of extending the areas of influence. For the colonial people, imperialism brings discrimination and regression; for the mother country, it brings nationalist pride, arrogance and socio-cultural superiority.

Nation-state and imperialism are good companions. When together, as they usually are, they result in discrimination, coercion and war. Andrews asks the question: "How can you be a friend of the man who insists on always keeping you in a semi-inferior position." "An imperial power", Asirvatham says, "is always on pins and needles, and the mentality which it exhibits is inimical to the maintenance of normal human relations." Both, the concepts of nation-state and imperialism are the enemies of the basic idea of globalisation. Where these exist, it is difficult to imagine the simplest form of any international organisation. As the world is drawing closer, nation-states and the imperialistic tendencies are becoming irrelevant. Abolition of the imperialistic tendencies demand the minimisation of nation-state, and hence a rewording, if not complete removal, of the concept of sovereignty in the light of insistent claims of globalisation.

X. Nation-State and Globalisation: Disjunctures of Power Blocs, World Economy and the like

The sovereignty of the nation-state is, and has never been, in doubt; but it has always been under strain. The challenges to state sovereignty have never been so demanding as are now, especially at a time when global inter-connectedness has become not only a reality but also a necessity. State sovereignty, today, does not mean state autonomy-the right of the state to do anything it likes. It may be remembered that the state sovereignty has never been absolute, except legally. The limitations on state sovereignty were even recognised by Bodin, Hobbes and Austin during the days when globalisation was not on the agenda of internationalism.

Today, globalisation has become a fact of our times, a fact that has brought nation-state and its sovereignty to order. David Held has summed up the argument in favour of globalisation as follows:

1. With the increase in global interconnectedness, the number of political instruments available to governments and the effectiveness of particular instruments has shown a marked decline; border controls have lessened; and flow of goods and services, ideas and cultures has increased. The result is a decrease in policy instruments which enable the state to control activities within and beyond its borders.
2. States can experience a further diminution in options because of the expansion in transnational Forces and interactions which reduce and restrict the influence particular governments can exercise over the activities of their citizens. The impact, for example, of the flow of capital across borders can threaten anti-inflation measures, exchange rates and other government policies.
3. In the context of a highly interconnected global order, many of the traditional domains of state activity such as defence, communication, and the like cannot be fulfilled without resorting to international forms of collaboration. As the demands on the state have increased in the postwar years, the cooperation of other states has become necessary.
4. Accordingly, states have had to increase the level of their political integration with other states so to control the destabilising effects that accompany global interconnectedness. They have to strengthen, for example, organisations like International Monetary Fund (IMF) and the General Agreement on Tariffs and

Trade (GATT).

5. With the growth of a vast number of institutions and organisations, a basis for global governance has already been laid. The new global politics-involving, among other things, multibureaucratic decision-making within and between governmental and international bureaucracies, and the like-has created a framework in and through which the rights and obligations, powers and capacities of states have been redefined.

The sovereignty of the nation-state continues, but the sovereign structure of nation-state is heavily influenced by global tendencies, besides those found within the boundaries of the state itself.

(a) Nation-State and Power-blocs

The development of the global system of states as appears in the form of numerous power blocs has immensely influenced state's authority and integrity. This is clear from the following:

(i) The rise of the U.S.A. and the USSR as world powers during the post-war years (and until the disintegration of the USSR in 1991) had restricted many states in making their decisions on their own whether those were related to domestic politics or relations with other countries. Within the ambit of the changed scenario of unipolar or multipolar world, the states have come to depend on each other. The U.S.A. exerts a large measure of influence on the domestic and foreign policies of weaker and smaller states.

(ii) The dominance of the USA and the USSR with their power alliances too had constrained numerous states for making their decisions themselves or independent of the bloc-leader. The NATO (North Atlantic Treaty Organisation), the SEATO (the South East Asia Treaty Organisation), one-time CENTO (the Central Treaty Organisation), the ANZUS (the Australia, New Zea Land, the United States), the OAS (the Organisation of the American States), all under the American influence, and the Warsaw Pact under the Soviet patronage gave meagre international options to their respective member-states. Held says: "A state's capacity to initiate particular foreign policies, pursue certain strategic concerns, choose between alternative military technologies and control certain weapon systems located on its own territory are restricted by its place in the international system of power relations".

(iii) Each of these military alliances has its own structure, its own procedure and method of functioning and its own policy as developed by the member-states. But the influence of the member-leader goes unquestioned and the other member-states have limited options to operate on. Giving the NATO example, Professor Held says: "its (NATO's) concern with collective security has trodden a fine line between, on the one hand, maintaining an organisation of sovereign states, and, on the other, developing an international organisation which operates *de facto,* if not *de jure* according to its own logic and decision-making procedures." The NATO is an example of a supranational organisation in which the USA commands while the other member states merely submit.

(iv) Even without a commitment to a NATO armed conflict, Held says, "state autonomy as well as sovereignty can be limited and checked." This is because, he continues, "the routine conduct of NATO affairs involves the integration of national defence bureaucracies into international defence organisations." Such organisations, creating transgovernmental decision-making systems, escape the control or even consultation of any single member-state. They lead to establish informal, and yet very powerful, trans governmental personnel networks or coalitions outside the control of and accountability to any national mechanism.

(v) The membership of NATO, and for that matter, of any other power-bloc, does not abolish sovereignty of each member state, but it certainly compels the member-states to compromise on issues where they are in clash with one another. Under the circumstances of mutual conflicts relating to scarce resources, arms contracts and others, the member-states negotiate and renegotiate their sovereign power within the framework of the broader power-bloc.

(b) Nation-State and World Economy

No country is economically self-sufficient, not even the U.S.A. The compulsions of world economy attempt to limit the power or scope of sovereignty of the nation-state. It is clear from the following:

(i) The internationalisation of production has been made possible through the organisation of the multinational corporations. These corporations work across the borders and function outside the domains of national sovereignties. The Multinational Corporation (MNCs), it is argued by people like Professor Held, "plan and execute their production, marketing and distribution with the world economy firmly in mind." Though these MNCs have a national base, the nations from where they originate, their interest is always global as is their strategy. The nation-states do little in controlling these corporations while these corporations have much to guide the policies of the states where they operate.

(ii) The financial organisations such as banks are becoming global progressively, no matter from where they function: London, New York or Tokyo. A greater role is being played by the New Information Technology in so far as it helps in the mobilisation of economic units—currencies, stocks, shares and the like-for financial and commercial organisations of all kinds.

(iii) With the technological advancement in communication and transportation, the separate market-boundaries, necessary for independent national economic policies, are losing importance. Inspite of the fact that the distinctive identities are kept preserved, markets and societies are becoming more sensitive to one another. To a great extent, the possibility of a national economic policy has, accordingly, reduced so to suit itself to the claims of international financial and fiscal system. Likewise, Held says: "the levels of employment, investment and revenue within a country are often subordinated to the decisions of MNCs ... ".

(iv) We do not live in the shadow of keynesianism, for it is hard for individual nation-states to intervene and manage their economies in the face of global division of labour and monetary system. What is usually found is the increasing interconnectedness of the various sovereign states which operate within the international framework, which usually all the states operate.

(v) As no country is self-sufficient, especially in economic matters, the nation-states have to organise themselves regionally and globally. There are such groups, though loose, as West-West, North-South, South-South, East-West, the developed and the developing. These groups do affect the economy of each individual nation-state.

Thus we see that the internationalisation of production, finance, management and distribution is unquestionably eroding the capacity of each individual sovereign state to do what it wants to do. No country, howsoever strong it may be, has control over its future economic policies, for it has to affect and get affected by the economic policies as they are pursued globally. There is a definite diminution of state autonomy in the face of world economy.

(c) Nation-State and International Organisation—International Law

The sovereignty of the state is never absolute and in fact, it can never be. Power-blocs, world economy and the like erode the absolute power of the state. International Organisations and International Law provide other disjuncture to state sovereignty.

As the number of *international organisations* increase, so increase transnational links and so is eroded the right of the state to decide its own fate on its own. A brief summary of such argument is given below:

(i) The growth and development of international organisations have led to important changes in the decision-making structure of world politics. There are new forms of international organisations to play their role in matters relating to world affairs. No nation-state can take the United Nations for granted and that each sovereign state has to work within the framework of the UN Charter. Additionally, a whole variety of international organisations and numerous pressure groups do influence the activities and policies of the national states.

(ii) There are international organisations of technical types. These include the Universal Postal Union (UPU), the International Telecommunication Union (ITU), the World Meteorological Organisations (WMO) and the like which are, generally, non-controversial, but they do supplement the services offered by the individual states to their respective citizens. These non-political and technical organisations do influence some notable aspects of the foreign policies of nation-states and as such do not allow them to act arbitrarily.

(iii) In addition to these non-political and technical international organisations, there are political and even controversial organisations such as the World Bank, the IMF, UNESCO, and the UN which, while occupying a greater measure of powers in their own spheres, bestow, if not intervene, influence the policies of the sovereign states.

(iv) The operations of the IMF goes a step further and almost grab the sovereign rights of a nation. While giving loan to a particular nation-state, the IMF may insist on certain conditions such as a cut on public expenditure, devaluation of currency and a substantial cut on the welfare programmes and all this, obviously, put premium on state sovereignty of the concerned state. The most of the developing countries have to tolerate the intervention of IMF.

(v) The case of the European Community (EC) Provides a bigger threat to the sovereignty of the states. The EC can make laws which are, or can be, imposed on the member-states. The EC has become, more or less, supranational agency, for within it, the Council of Ministers has the power to make and enact policies. Accordingly, the member-states of the EC are no longer the sole centres of power within their own borders. Held says: "..... within the community (i.e. EC), sovereignty is clearly divided: any conception of sovereignty which assumes that it is indivisible, illimitable, exclusive and perpetual form of public power—embodied within an individual state—is defunct."

International law, as has developed over time, has also put the state sovereignty in right perspective of the changing international situations. This is clear from the following:

(i) By state sovereignty we mean the right of the state to act independently and under no explicit influence of any other foreign government. It implies, among other things, two points: (a) that a state is powerful enough to protect its own autonomy in all matters of foreign policy, and (b) to prevent domestic courts from ruling on the behaviour of foreign states. Such aspects of state sovereignty are under strenuous stresses. The EC law, for example, through its Single European Act, does hardly ensure national sovereignty to any of its members.

(ii) The UN's Universal Declaration of Human Rights urge the UN members to introduce rights incorporated in the Declaration in their respective states-rights which are not the result of the states acting individually. The UN Declaration though does not take away the state sovereignty, but certainly fashions it.

(iii) The European Convention for the Protection of Human Rights and Fundamental Rights is a typical case which does not fit in the framework of the claims of state sovereignty. Any citizen belonging to any state which is the member of the European Community can demand the introduction of any right included in the Convention, but not incorporated in the Constitution of the concerned state. Obviously, the European Community does no longer leave the state free to treat its own citizens as it thinks fit.

(iv) The idea of membership of a national state bestowing rights and duties on the individual and the creation of new liberties and obligations in international law have opened up a significant issue which strikes at the concept of state sovereignty directly and with all force at its command. The International Tribunal at Nuremberg, for example, clearly says that when international rules which protect humanitarian values come into clash with state laws, individuals must transgress the state laws.

(v) International law is no longer a law between the states only and exclusively. It is and, in fact, has been changing and is basing itself increasingly on the norms of co-existence and cooperation. Unlike the traditional international law which assumed the separateness of the individual states, the new international law is building itself on the concept of 'togetherness' and 'closeness' of the numerous states.

SUGGESTED READINGS

1 Held, D., *Models of Democracy* (Oxford: Polity Press, 1987).

2 __________(ed.) *Political Theory Today* (Oxford: Polity Press, 1991).

3 Jordan, B., *The State: Authority and Autonomy* (Oxford: Basil Blackwell, 1985).

4 Kegley, Charles W. and Wittkopf, Eugene R., *World Politics* (London: Macmillan, 1989)

5. Nordlinger, E.A., *On the Autonomy of the Democratic State* (Canbridge Mass: Harvard University Press, 1983).

6 Ray and Bhattacharya, *Political Theory Ideas and Institutions,* (Calcutta: The World Press Private Ltd., n.d.)

7 Rosenau, James N., *The Study of Global Interdependence* (London: Pinter, 1980).

8 Soroos, Marvin S., *Beyond Sovereignty* (Columbia: University of South Carolina Press, 1986).

9 Stankiewicz, W.J., *Aspects of Political Theory* (London: Collier Macmillan, 1976).

10 Wallerstein, Immanuel, *The Modern World System* (New York: Academic Press, 1974).

7

Citizenship and Rights

Citizenship, rights and duties are intrinsically connected with one another. Citizenship does not merely mean a set of rights to be enjoyed by a person. Nor does it mean that the idea of citizenship implies the existence of certain claims of a person on the state. Citizenship is, indeed, a matter of rights, but it also is a matter of duties. If we claim rights, we must also shoulder responsibilities. If, for example, we seek right to vote, we must vote for the right person or for the right political party. The one end of citizenship is a set of rights enjoyed by an individual and the other end is a set of duties an individual has to perform. The idea of citizenship, at one end, is what we *own,* and at the other end, is what we *owe:* rights we own; duties we owe. To think of citizenship in terms of rights only is as mistaken as is when we relate citizenship to duties only.

I: Citizenship-Meaning and Nature

The words 'citizen' and 'citizenship' owe their origin to the Latin word 'civis' which means a resident of a city. Citizen, therefore, is one who lives in a city and citizenship is the status of the citizen, a symbol that gives recognition to the fact that a citizen is a resident of a city. But this is what we understand citizenship etymologically. Such a meaning of citizen, and therefore, of citizenship is narrow and does not include in it the characteristics we normally attach to them in our times.

Citizenship implies membership of a political community called the state. We, as members of community or society, are social beings; we become political beings only after having acquired membership of the state, or having born in a state. Our membership of the state, if we extend the meaning of citizenship, grants us a legal status, a status behind which there are set and well-defined rights and duties. This is not to say that as social beings, we are without rights or are absolved of our social responsibilities. What we do not have in society and what we have in a state is the legal sanction. Our right to vote is a legally recognised right whereas our right to help the poor has a social or moral bearing.

So, citizenship is not merely the membership of the state, it is the legal recognition of the person as citizen. Social recognition implies our membership of the society; legal recognition, membership of the state, for to be a social being is one thing, and to be a political being, altogether different. All social beings are not citizens, though all citizens are social beings. A subject is a social being but he/she is not a citizen; a national is a social being, but all nationals are not citizens; an alien is a social being, but all aliens do not constitute citizen-body. A citizen is a special being, member of a state and so recognised.

Citizenship implies membership of the state and bestows a status, and grants a recognition, but with these, it demands participation in the affairs of the state. The status that turns an individual into a citizen also expects a citizen to make or unmake, and in short, participate in the activities of the state. Participation in the making, and functioning of the state by the members of a political community make them citizens and this is what distinguishes citizens from all others who are non-citizens in a state; democracy from all other forms of government. We find citizens only in a democracy; there are no citizens in a monarchy, there are only subjects there. Participation of the people, called the citizens make a system a democratic one. Citizenship and democracy go hand in hand. The growth of one means the growth of the other. As monarchies changed into democracies, so changed subjects into citizens.

Participation in the affairs of the state is a characteristic feature of citizenship. Residence within the territorial jurisdiction does not entitle one to be a citizen of that state. One has to participate in the making of the government i.e., exercise franchise, contest elections, hold public office, express opinion and so on. A subject has no such rights and so he/she is not a citizen; a national because of lower age or any other disability does not contribute in any governmental activity, and so he/ she is not a citizen. An alien is not a citizen because no alien possesses any political right. An alien is a social being and in a way, is like a guest and by this logic, enjoys certain facilities not available to the citizens. But he/she remains a guest and hence is not a host. He! she is respected as a guest, but this does not bestow ownership rights on the aliens. No alien participates in building, repairing or renovating the house. So mere residence in a state does not qualify anybody to be a citizen of a state. Membership of and participation in the state constitute virtues of citizenship.

Participation in the state implies sharing and shouldering responsibilities as members of the political society. This means that those who share some responsibilities must possess certain rights which help citizens perform their duties. It is here that participation in the affairs of the state implies the existence of certain rights for the citizens. These rights are rights which help citizens participate in the formation and functioning of the government. These are the political rights-rights which include franchise rights, contesting elections, holding public offices, censuring rulers, expressing opinions and so on. These rights, in a state, are available to citizens only. This means that those who do not have these rights are not citizens. Thus, citizenship implies membership, participation, as a consequence of these, enjoyment of political rights.

There is yet another aspect which has a particular importance in understanding what citizenship really means. Citizenship implies claims that one has on others, but it also implies that there is something that state expects of a citizens—the duties. Citizenship is not only an arrangement of rights, it is also a system of duties. The quality of citizenship is both the right use of the available political rights and the faithful performance of the duties so demanded. So there is a right-based citizenship as well as a duties-based citizenship. Highlighting the rights-duties syndrome, Brigan says: "Citizenship has two aspects: (i) that every citizenship has the right to be consulted in the conduct of political society and the duty to contribute something to the general consultation, and (ii) the reverse. The citizen who has a right to be consulted is bound by the results of that consultation."

By way of conclusion, one may, for sake of brevity, sum up the characteristic features of citizenship as under:

(i) Membership of a political community and legally recognised;
(ii) A status which is exclusive property of the citizen;
(iii) Participation in the affairs of the state;
(iv) Provision and exercise of political rights so to ensure participation; and
(v) Performance of duties as members of the state.

II: Citizenship-Growth and Development

(i) Citizenship in ancient times

Democracy, despite Aristotle's love for the rule of law, was a perverted form of government. If anyone is seeking the idea of citizenship in ancient Greece (from where all Western political thought is said to have begun), one may not find there all about citizenship. Aristotle's definition of citizen as one who possesses virtues of a law-maker and a judge is a great joke on the idea of citizenship—atleast in our times. Everyone, in ancient Greece generally and in Athens particularly, was a law-maker in so far as he participated in law-making, but each one was not a magistrate or an official. Through a system of rotation and a lot, every voter, Maclver says, "had the opportunity to be magistrate, judge or other official. .... On all political issues the citizens freely decided in their assembly." But the citizen-body, in Greek democracies, was the smallest fraction of the entire population—so it was of Attica the territory of the Athenian state. Maclver points out: ".... the citizens constituted in effect a privileged class. The citizen-roll was jealously guarded and only the sons of free Athenian parents were admitted. The outlying population of Attica, for the most part illiterate, could hardly .... exercise the rights of citizens. Resident aliens were debarred from citizenship, and below them were the slaves, constituting more than a third of the population, who had no rights whatever. As for women, they were still kept .... all except the high class *hetairai* or courtesans .... in a kind of oriental seclusion." Thus, ancient Greece hardly gave the idea of citizenship, particularly where the idea of democracy was not only strictly limited (women were excluded), but had, to a great extent, an anti-democratic stance.

In ancient times the ancient Rome including, where slavery was an inevitable part of society, the idea of citizenship could hardly find any expression worth noticing. Wherever there had, existed the institution of slavery, those engaged in menial toil were regarded inferior and thus were debarred of civil and political rights. Citizenship, then, was restricted to cities and citizens were only the city-dwellers.

(ii) Citizenship in medieval times

The medieval age was characterised by contradictions particularly in matters relating to state-society. On the religious plane, all were considered equal-brothers because all were thought to be the sons of God. But on the social and political planes, there was hardly any equality, hardly any idea of universal brotherhood, hardly any democratic value. The medieval society was a religion-based society, hierarchical and rigid where lordship or serfdom was a matter of birth-hereditary. The individuals played no role in politics, for kingship was divinely ordained and king's right to rule went unchallenged. Where, despite all claims of equality in Christianity, there had existed inequality between man and man and where politics was an activity of the few, restrictively few, one could hardly imagine any democracy, and therefore, hardly any citizenship.

(iii) Citizenship and modern age

The idea of citizenship has grown with the idea of democracy. In fact, attempts at democratization preceded the franchise efforts, for much before universal male voting right, the attempts were, for example, made to make legislative bodies as representative as possible in England. Though representation, in the beginning, was not the representation of number and actually was that of interests, yet ground was being prepared for the on-coming era of democracy.

The credit must go to the medieval times for having contributed, though in a limited way, to the ideals of democracy. Christianity, highlighting the universal ethical principles, had pronounced that every human being has a value and a personality in himself. The medieval concept of the worth of human personality became the cornerstone of the basis of democracy that was to follow in the coming centuries.

There was yet another development during the medieval times and this was the evolution of the representative system. Representation, in medieval times, was representation of the interests. Following the great Magna Carta (1215) of England, there was the rudimentary, discriminatory and restrictive introduction of the representation system when, in 1265, Simon de Montfort, the Earl of Leicester had summoned two citizens from every borough as well as two knights from every county to sit in the Parliament with peers and the prelates. That is how representation was introduced and the beginning—of the House of Common in England was made. Do not we recognise the English Commons as the matrix of modern democracy? The later events. confirmed the introduction of representative devices, the House of Lords, representing feudal Lords, priests and the higher classes whereas the House of Commons, representing the commoners, the knights, the townsmen. As circumstances moved, the House of Lords remained as undemocratic as it was and therefore gradually surrendering political power to the commons, and the House of Commons as democratized it came to be, got all the powers, so much that the House of Commons became the Parliament in the real sense of the term. The idea of representation, medieval as it was in its origin, became an important ingredient of democracy that followed in later years.

The idea of representation did not come as a design in the history of England, the country where democracy was bornand later flourished. History as it came up in conflicts and struggles moved towards democratic norms, mostly as a result of accidents. The initial struggles were not. struggles for introducing democracy as they were struggles against tyranny and despotism. England provides a remarkable and in fact a representative example: the theory of two swords of medieval times not only brought religion in tune with politics, reformation following, it also abolished the trio: king, feudal lord and the priest, bringing the king-feudal lord combine as the victorious. This combine, ultimately, led to absolutism of monarchical system and the advocacy of the divine rights theory of kings. The whole Stuart period (1603-1688) was a period of civil war where the parties now were the king-feudal lords on the one hand, and the merchant and manufacturing classes on the other. The glorious revolution (1688) was the victory of the capitalists. But that was not the beginning of democracy as was the beginning of liberalism—the classical liberalism as we would call it now. The course of history in France, Germany, Italy, and other European countries was, more or less, the repetition of the English events. Macpherson, therefore is right in pointing out that the Western system became liberal first and democratic later. As different aspects of democracy came to be introduced, so were introduced the various forms of citizenship in the West. The beginning had already been made with the French "Liberty, Equality and Fraternity" and the American declaration of "Rights of Man".

The growth and development of idea of citizenship as it came about in the writings of the great English philosophers can be summed up as under:

John Locke (1632-1704), as the forerunner of liberalism, was no democrat, and in fact, every liberal, then, need not be a democratic. His concern was his attack on political power. His whole philosophy, while justifying the English revolution of 1688, revolved around his thesis that political power was limited because its task was limited. He had built a limited state, giving it the only task of protecting the property of the people and by this logic, advocated limited powers. Individualist as he really was, Locke declared the state as a means and the individual as an end. Thus Locke was concerned more with the functions of the state than with its structure. Hence, we do not see the introduction or the development of any democratic institutions in his writings.

Jeremy Bentham (1748-1832) lived at a time when the question of the origin of the state had lost all weight and people had turned their attention on the structuring and restructuring of democratic institution. Non-interventionist as Bentham was, he did not go all out to give the state all functions and, therefore, all powers. Nor was he much enthusiastic about laying down the principles of representative institutions. Between 1791 and 1802, he was for a limited franchise, excluding the poor, the uneducated, the dependent, and the women. In 1809, he was for a householder franchise, one limited to those paying direct taxes on property. By 1817, he was virtually talking about universal franchise minus under age, and those who are unable to read, and of course, excluding women. By 1820, he was for manhood franchise. So, we see Bentham according no importance or less importance to either citizen or citizenship. His idea of citizen and contents of citizenship were kept changing from time to time, and from one of his writing to the other.

If Bentham was too less enthusiastic in matters relating to franchise, John Stuart Mill (1806-1873) was too eager to grant it to everyone, including women and in fact, to some, more than one vote. Participation in the affairs of the state was according to Mill, the greatest task of citizenship. In his *Thoughts on Parliamentary Reforms* (1859), Mill advocated the idea of plural voting, saying: "that a perfect electoral system required both that every person should have one vote and that some should have more than one vote." In his *Representative Government* (1861), Mill urged plural voting for some along with the exclusion of others from any vote all-the poor especially. However, in Mill's scheme what was noteworthy was the idea of plural voting. He had justified plural voting on the ground (i) that it would prevent class legislation; and (ii) that it would be beneficial by giving more votes to those whose opinion is entitled to a greater weight.

The later part of the 19th century and the first quarter of the 20th century changed the concept of citizenship from an idea to movement. The franchise movements began everywhere in the West from England to the United States, and in the process suffrage once based on 'qualifications of property, education, residence, sex' and so on came down to what we call universal adult franchise.

Citizenship implying political participation with the right to franchise as the starting point had been acquired in most of the liberal world by the middle of the 20th century. In the Marxian thought, citizen and citizenship were class concepts to be found only in the class societies and in their political systems. For the Marxists, capitalist societies produce only the bourgeoisie and the proletariat: the exploitors and the exploited and that political equality, in such societies, is only a mask of bourgeois domination. The Marxists hope to find the real worth of man and, his personality only in the classless society where individual would meet as free human beings.

With advancing years, the significance of the idea of citizenship and citizenship itself has immensely increased. More we find ourselves in the state, more we realize our worth as citizens. This makes the notion of citizenship a matter of discussion as well as a debate. There are the nee-liberals, Hayek and Nozick, who are zealous of individual's rights, but do not admit a full state, much less the theory of citizenship. On the other, there are the communitarians' whose idea of citizenship, covering both rights and duties, springs from individual's membership of a community. The feminists, critics of the male notion of citizenship, urge citizenship for women as *women*. The subaltern advocates lament the progressive ill-treatment of the weakest and the most backward in the society and ask for an equally genuine citizenship for all.

III: Theories of Citizenship: Marshall and Giddens

The concept of citizenship has been, if not neglected, a concept so well known and understood so easily that it escaped the attention of many philosophers and scholars. It is, really, easy to dismiss the idea of concept by arguing that a citizen, as a permanent member of a political society, has certain rights to exercise and certain duties to perform and that with the growth of democratic ideas, there has been a corresponding expansion. of citizenship together with its contents. Citizenship is no more a set of political rights, it is also a set of social and economic rights. Its historical growth is not merely traced to the advent of democracy, but to the origin and development of capitalism. It is not merely a formal observance of laws, but is the eternal association with the society as a whole, state including.

Numerous scholars have drawn attention to various aspects of democracy. Their theories or what may be called their contribution to the concept of citizenship can be summed up below:

It is difficult to say whether *Aristotle* had any *theory of citizenship,* and if at all he had any, it is still more difficult to have its application on the modern national states. There are two reasons for that: (i) For Aristotle, citizenship was the privileged status of the ruling group of the city-state, and hence had excluded mass of the people; (ii) For Aristotle, the status of citizenship was confined to the effective participation in the deliberation and exercise of owner, and hence had excluded participation in the form of exercising franchise or of system of representation.

Over the ages, citizenship, after having its long oblivion, came to the fore with the modern period beginning since capitalism. Its area has been fairly expanded now. It, today, means that all persons as citizens are equal before law and therefore that no person or group is legally privileged. But there is a meaningful criticism against this meaning by the *Marxists* who say that despite legal membership of the state, legal equality may not help the disadvantaged people in a class society to participate in the affairs of the state fully and completely. Marx says: "The state in its own way abolishes distinctions (of) .....birth, rank, education and occupation .... where it proclaims that every member of the people is an equal participant in popular sovereignty.... Nevertheless, the state allows private property, education, and occupation to act and assert their particular nature in their way ..... Far from abolishing these factual distinctions the state presupposes them in order to exist."

Marx is no enemy of the theory of modern citizenship, for he describes its achievements as a big step forward, but he insists and his thesis is that mere political emancipation in citizenship is inadequate and instead advocates a great human emancipation in which persons are freed from the determining power of private property and its associated institutions. Social revolution, Marx declares, can bring about human emancipation.

The theories with regard to citizenship arose firstly through two-in-one question: should social inequalities be made irrelevant for membership in the status of citizenship or should these be abolished through social revolution? As Marx had suggested, and secondly through the growth of labour movements which ultimately expanded the area of citizenship. Two opposing views, in this regard, are: one by Ossowski *(Class Structure in the Social Consciousness,* 1963) who says that as the movement for citizenship grows, it makes the class system an anachronism, leading thus to the gradual reduction of social inequalities. Another view is by Goldthorpe in his article 'Social Inequality and Social Integration in modem Britain' 1974) published in Wedderbun (ed), *Poverty, Inequality and Class Structure* who says that advances in citizenship are likely to leave class structures intact.

Marshall *(Citizenship and Social Class,* 1960) offers a systematic. theory of citizenship. His general understanding of citizenship is entirely conventional. He says that (i) citizenship is a status attached to full membership of a community and that (ii) those who possess this status are equal with respect to the rights and duties associated with it. He adds that different societies would attach different rights and duties to the status of citizen, for there is no universal principle of rights and duties of citizenship in general.

Marshall provides a synthesis of the historical evolution of modern conception of citizenship and rights in Britain. He divides this process into *three* phases or elements: civil, political and social. The *first* phase, Marshall says, took place roughly speaking. in the eighteenth century and saw the consolidation of civil rights, such as 'liberty of the person, freedom of speech, thought and faith, the right to own property and to conclude valid contracts, and the right to justice. The *second* phase, occurring generally during the 19th century, witnessed the consolidation of political rights such as participation in the exercise of political power either as a voter or an official *Finally,* the third phase, a 20th century phenomenon, involved the creation of social rights expanding from the right to economic welfare and security to share to the full in social heritage. and to live the life of a civilised being according to the standards prevailing in society.

Marshall does not regard these three categories as distinct or exclusive but as complementary. Our exercise of political rights, for example, entails not only the civil rights ensuring our freedom of speech, but also a sufficient level of education. The three phases, he says, form part of a dialectical process whereby rights as privileges of feudal system are changed into universal entitlement of all the members of society. He approaches a near communitarian view when he shifts his view of citizenship from status to contract where people possess human rights as persons pursuing their own lives in their own way.

Marshall's another important contribution to the theory of citizenship is the relationship between citizenship and social class. He notes that the development of the institutions of modern democracy coincided, as in England, with the rise of capitalism. In the early phase, capitalism tended to undermine citizenship as was found in the customary privileges of landed classes, but with its development, citizenship rights came to be ensured for the propertied (capitalist) classes. Thus Marshall says: "In undermining one type of class system, citizenship, promoted and secured a second." "During the period of the 18th and the 19th centuries, the rights of citizenship", Marshall explains, "were entirely harmonious with the class inequalities of capitalist societies," for rights were basically civil in nature. "Capitalists and workers,". Marshall argues, "are indistinguishable from the perspective of, civil rights in. having the same right to enter into market exchanges and contracts with each other." It is only then when citizenship comes to incorporate .in itself political and social rights that conflicts in the class system come to the fore. Surveying the whole historical process of class conflict between the capitalists and the workers, Marshall says that the passing of Reform Acts, emergence of the workers in trade-unions, the Chartist movement, in England, established the claim of the workers that they, as citizens, were entitled (in addition to political rights already won) to certain social rights. The inclusion of social rights in citizenship rights meant, as Marshall says, a war between citizenship and the capitalist class system. It is therefore, argued that social citizenship has not destroyed class, nor social inequalities, but has, as Marshall concludes, "imposed modifications on' class with the result that changes are being made in the class system through the exercise of citizenship rights by the working class movement.

Barbalet sums up Marshall's contribution to citizenship in these words: "In summary then, Marshall sees the development of citizenship and of the class system in terms of interactions between them. Through their antagonistic relationship, citizenship and class inequality each contribute to changes in the other. Unlike most theorists of class structure, Marshall recognises the possible impact of citizenship on aspect of class inequality and therefore on class loyalty and class resentment, both of which tend to affect the nature and incident of class conflict. Marshall sees such possibilities because he understands citizenship in terms not only of its legal and political dimensions, but also of its social component."

Marshall's theory of citizenship invited more critics than admirers. Ralph Dahrendorf, for instance, while commenting on Marshall's work, refers to the gradual expansion of citizenship from the legal to the political and social sphere,' but adds that the process as 'still unfinished', for new dimensions of citizenship may, according to him, be discovered by political organisation and social groups. Anthony Giddens, no admirer of Marshall, takes strong exception to Marshall's characterisation of industrial rights. He affirms the significance of Marshall's analysis of citizenship for contemporary social and political theory, he has a number of criticism to make (see 1981, pp. 226-9; 1982. pp. 171-3; 1985. pp. 204-9). It is critical of what he sees as the teleological and evolutionary elements in Marshall's analysis (see especially 1982. p. 171). Giddens criticizes Marshall for treating the development of .citizenship as if it were something that unfolded in phases according to some inner logic within the modern world. In Giddens's account, Marshall tends to overstate the extent to which citizenship rights can be understood in terms of a threefold staged process. In addition, Giddens sees in Marshall's account an oversimplification of the role of politics and the state. Marshall, according to Giddens, understood the unfolding of citizenship rights from the eighteenth to the twentieth century as a process which is supported and buttressed by 'the beneficent hand of the state'. In Giddens's analysis, Marshall seriously underestimated the way 'citizenship rights have been achieved in substantial degree only through struggle'. The industrial rights, i.e., fight to form unions or to go on strike are not mere extensions of the civil rights as Marshall makes us believe, but, Giddens asserts, were achieved through struggle by the workers. Giddens attacks the evolutionary account of the development of citizenship for suggesting that the battle for civil and political rights has been won. According to Giddens, the battle continues into the future. Gidden's argument, as against Marshall's, is that the citizenship rights have been achieved only through struggle. He says: "the extension of citizenship rights, in Britain as in other societies, was in substantial degree the result of the efforts of the unprivileged to improve their lot and that the groups previously excluded had to struggle for attaining it."

More fundamentally, Giddens maintains that each category of citizenship right should be understood as an area of contestation or conflict, each linked to a distinctive type of regulatory power or surveillance, where that surveillance is both necessary to the power of superordinate groups and an axis around which subordinate groups can seek to reclaim control over their lives.

From Giddens's writings, the following classificatory scheme of rights, and the modes of power and institutional sites to which they are related, is suggested:

	Types of right			
	civil	economic civil	political	social
Type of regulatory power or surveillance	policing	control of work-place	political	'management' of population
Institutional centre or locale where rights are championed and fought over	law courts	work-place	parliament or legislative chamber	(state administrative offices?)

Giddens is in disagreement with Marshall on the chronology of the three categories of rights: civil rights first, political rights later and social rights still later. His theory, rather, is that civil and political citizenship rights developed together, civil rights consolidating capitalist class power, and political rights adding and strengthening it. According to him, citizenship, rising from the shadow of democracy, developed with the growth and expansion of state sovereignty.

In sum, in Giddens's assessment, class conflict has been and remains the medium of the extension of citizenship rights and the basis of the creation of an insulated economy, polyarchy and the welfare state. The forging of state sovereignty was a critical impetus to the struggle for rights and to the remoulding of citizenship. The increase in state administrative power led to the creation of new aspirations an demands and to the development of institutions which were responsive to them. *Bruan Turner (Citizenship and Caritalism,* 1986), as opposed to Marshall's historical development of citizrnship in terms of elements or phases, describes the development of citizenship in terms of the consequences or what he called the waves. For him, there have been four such waves: first had the consequence of removing property from the definition of citizen; the second removed sex; the third wave redefined the significance of the age and kinship ties in the family for citizenship rights; and a fourth wave, as Turner says, is currently expanding citizenship by ascribing rights to nature and the environment.

IV: Citizenship – Rights-based and Duties-based

Citizenship, as a status, characterises a set of rights. Rights are important because they .attach a particular capacity to persons by virtue of a local though conventional as well, status. When persons have capacities or opportunities for particular actions, say certain powers, they are supposed to possess rights: status provides capacity, and capacity provides power and power, ultimately, a right. This, however, does not mean that all rights spring from citizenship and that citizens alone have all types of rights. There are aliens who, as aliens, possess civil and social rights. So is true about the national. What they do not possess and what all citizens, with civil and social, possess political rights. Hence, while all rights are not citizenship rights, all citizenship rights are rights.

Citizenship rights, as rights of a person in a state, are ultimately secured by the state. Barbalet writes: "Citizenship rights impose certain limitations on the state's sovereign authority." Right to vote, for example, is a citizenship right of a person, but it is a duty of the state to protect this .right of the citizen.

Right-based citizenship does not specify rights to be ensured and secured by the state, it also demands a restraint on the one who exercises it and also on others in whose frame the right is exercised. Right to property is not merely a right to hold property, it is also a right to acquire it, possess It and/or dispose it of. But such a right puts a restraint on the one who enjoys property right in so far as the enjoyer of the right does not obtain or acquire property through anti-social and anti-national activities. Likewise such a right of 'A' puts a restraint on all others to demonstrate their regard for A's property. Citizenship does not mean the existence of a right as a licence, it means a claim, a social claim at that. It demands of the person who possesses it a high level of wisdom to use it in the best interests of the society as well as in his/her own. Citizenship implies an obligation as well; it is both a claim as well as a duty. Right-based citizenship does not merely mean a set of rights, it also means the provision of duties as well. This means that rights are to be enjoyed within the framework of duties.

Likewise duties-based citizenship is citizenship high and of good quality. Such a citizenship would mean the adoption of those forms of conduct that are compatible with those of the others. Citizenship involves a right and a duty simultaneously. Liberty, Mill had said once, means pursuing our own good in our own ways provided we do not harm the like liberty of the other. 'Pursuing our own good in our own way' is a right coupled with a duty of not harming the like liberty of the other. What is a right, therefore, for a person also becomes a duty for him/her. Our rights are the duties of others and others' rights are our duties. As are our rights social, so are our duties. Rights and duties do not exist before or against society: rights are our claims on other and duties are others' claims on us. We obtain rights only after having performed our duties. Citizenship is not only the ordering of our facilities, it is also the ordering of our loyalties as well. Rights and duties put together constitute what is called citizenship. Citizenship means the right exercise of our rights; it also means the right use of our conduct as well. Both, rights and duties, are two sides of citizenship.

The concept of citizenship is both a concept of rights on the one hand, and of duties on the other. It is a citizenship with rights whose base are the duties; a citizenship with duties whose object is individual and social welfare. In any case, the concept of citizenship is a concept about human relationships in a society. If, for example, a person has a right to something, other members of his society have an obligation to respect that right. If, again, it is a right of action such as a right to engage in political dissent, fellow citizens and the government have an obligation to tolerate expressions of dissent. But this is what we. understand citizenship as rights-based.

There is the other, and perhaps more important aspect of citizenship: it is a citizenship as based on duties, on obligations of the holder of rights. We do not have a right to do any thing we like. We have rights as emanate from society and we exercise them in a social framework. We have a right to express our dissent, but in doing so, we do not have the right to block the way which approach the hospitals, but rather, we have the duties not to do so. Citizenship, we may conclude, involves social claims as are enjoyed by the people, but they also place responsibilities on them as well. To talk of citizenship with rights and without duties is as meaningless as is citizenship with duties and without rights.

V: Rights-Democratic and Human

Rights are social claims which help individuals develop their personality. If democracy is a government of the people, and also a government for the people, it must, then, exist to serve the individual. Such a democractic government can best serve the people if it maintains and provides a system of rights. States never give rights, they only recognise them; governments never bestow rights, they only protect them. Rights emanate from society and belong to the individuals as members of the society but they exist to help individuals attain the development of the human personality. State comes in to provide an atmosphere for the due enjoyment of the rights. It is in this sense that the functions of the government provide conditions for the exercise of rights and it is also in this sense that rights exist to provide a source from where all governmental activities begin.

(i) Rights-Meaning and Nature

Right is a claim, a social claim necessary for the development of human personality. It is not an entitlement a person is possessed with. In the ancient and medieval times, people—some people—were entitled to enjoy privileges, but we do not call them rights. Rights are not privileges because they are not entitlements. There is a difference between rights and privileges: rights are our claims against others as are others' claims on us; entitlements are privileges granted to some but denied to others; rights are universal in the sense they are assured to all who live in the society, privileges are not universal in the sense that they are possessed by the few; rights are granted to all without any discrimination, privileges are showered on some, the selected few; rights are obtained as a matter of rights, privileges, as a matter of patronage; rights emnate in a democratic structure, privileges are found in undemocratic structure—be it absolute monarchy, oligarchy or despotism. That is why we say, rather insist, that rights are always democratic. Undemocratic rights are contradictions in themselves. Because rights are social, because they exist in society and because they are available to all to be exercised for the good of all, including the holder, they are democratic in character, always.

To prepare a list of democratic rights for all times is to prepare a list, however, exhaustive, which would both be incomplete and inadequate. This is so because the levels of democracy differ from society to society as also from time to time. Hence, such an exercise is left as it is.

(ii) Bases of Rights

There are the *contractual* rights. They are contractual in so far as they are legal because they are the result of the contract. Any contract, except the social contract which nobody is sure of its conclusion, confers rights and obligations on the signatories. By its very nature, the contractual rights are legal and therefore binding and have behind them a measure of force and compulsion.

There are the *positive as well as the negative rights,* maintained by the laws of the state. A right is positive when it expects a citizen to participate in political activity; it is negative when it refrains the individual from doing anything. Such rights, positive and negative, are contextual in nature for they are stated on the particular people by a particular authority and in a particular situation. It is, in this sense, that rights are always dynamic, their contents change with the changing circumstances. These rights like the contractual rights are both social, and civil.

There are *moral rights* as well, deriving their authority from a code of morality shared by the members of a community. These rights are not enforced by the state, but by the conscience of the individual or the customs which prevails in a community at a given time. Like the positive and negative rights, moral rights are also contextual, exist within the context of a particular frame. The Muslims, residing in Britain are not permitted to have four wives, although they belong to societies where such is the right of a Muslim. The context in Britain is different and hence a different moral right. Likewise the British in Saudi Arabia cannot, and in fact, do not celebrate wedding with champagne.

There is yet another category of rights, called the *political rights* These rights usually include the rights to vote, to organise political parties, to contest elections, to petition, to resistance, to compete and hold public office and so on. Like any other rights, political rights are contextual.

(iii) Society, State and Rights

Rights are not the products of the state, though there are rights given to us through laws. But the rights from legislation are merely a recognition of what already exists in the society. Our rights are social in the sense that they emnate from society at any given point of time; they are social because they are never anti-social; they are social because they had never existed before the emergence of society; and they are social because they cannot be exercised against the common good perceived by the society.

What is, then, the role of the state? As our rights are inviolable, it is the duty of the state to maintain, extend and protect them. The state is not the originator, but is the defender of our rights. If it were to be the 'giver' of our rights, it would grant them to us through a law made by it. By the same logic, the state would become the 'taker' of our rights by passing just another law. In that case, our rights are out rights but to be exercised at the mercy of the state.

Our rights are the result of our membership of a political community as also the return of our service, say the obligation, done to the society. Rights are the returns given to us by others in response to the performance of our duties towards others. Duties are the seeds of which rights constitute a crop.

(iv) Rights: Theories

Rights constitute the sum-total of those opportunities which ensure the enrichment of individual personality. Rights relate to the individual, to the development of his personality. "Rights are, thus, those conditions of social life", Laski says in his *A Grammar of Politics,* "without which no man can seek, in general, to be himself at his best". Rights arise in society. They originate in society. There are no rights before, beyond, and against society. There are no rights before the emergence of society. Rights emanate from socially desirable conditions. No man, for example, has a right to murder or theft. Rights are social because they promote social good or social welfare. The state does not create or grant rights, so it cannot take away them. The state only recognises rights, so it only secures them. Society grants rights and the state maintains them.

So understood the characteristics features of rights are:

1. Rights are related to the individual. Rights are rights of the individualss. They are related to the individual in the sense that they promote the development of the individual and his personality;
2. Rights are social by nature. This means that rights are given by the society. It also implies that rights originate in society. There are, therefore, no rights where there is or there was no society;
3. Rights are social in another sense as well. They are social because rights are not, in their contents, against social good. That is why that there have never been rights which are either anti·, social or immoral;
4. Rights are granted by society while the state recognises them, maintains them and secures them;
5. Rights emanate in social framework. Rights are granted by society only after obligations are fulfilled. Before rights, duties are performed. Rights and duties go together in the sense that rights come after duties. Because duties are offered, so rights are given; and

6. Rights are never permanent. They change with the changing time. As such, they are dynamic in nature. It is, therefore difficult to present any list of rights once for all.

Theories of Rights

Various theories with regard to rights have been there from time to time. Some such theories are:

1. Theory of Natural Rights

The theory of natural rights had been popular during the 17th-18th centuries and mainly in the writings of Hobbes (*Leviathan,* 1651), Locke (*Two Treatises of Government,* 1690) and Rouseau (*The Social Contract,* 1762). These contractualists say that there were natural rights possessed by man in the state of nature. Rights, the contractualists believe, were independent of organised society because they were the possession of man in the state of nature. Rights, according to them, were attributed to individuals as if they were essential properties of men as men. They are, the contractualists declare, inalienable, imprescriptable and indefeasible rights.

The theory of natural rights is criticised mainly on the following grounds:

1. The theory of natural rights is basically non-juristic. The natural rights are not basically sanctioned claims enjoyed by a man in a politically organised society;
2. The natural rights, as this theory emphasises, exist in pre-social period. The fact is that rights can never exist before or beyond society because rights before society are mere physical energies;
3. The contractualists say that men had natural rights in the state of nature and that society was organised to guarantee their realisation. This is basically wrong in the sense because it is society that grants rights and it is the government or the state that maintains and secures them.

The theory of natural rights had exercised a great influence during the days of American and French Revolutions. Yet the theory came under attack later. Bentham denied the existence of pre-social rights. Rights,. he insists, exist only in an organised society. Laski criticised the natural rights for their being a permanent bundle of privileges and held, "no permanent and unchanging catalogue of rights can be complied". The idea of rights is essentially dynamic, changing with the social changes.

2. *The Legal theory of Rights*

The legal theory of rights holds the view that the rights are granted by the state. It says that it is the state, the government that grants rights to the people. Among the various advocates of this theory, the names of Bentham, Hegel and Austin can be mentioned. The theory regards right as a claim which the force of the state grants to the people. The essential features of this theory are: (i) that the state defines and lays down the bill of rights. Rights are not prior or anterior to the state, because the state is the source of rights; (ii) that the state lays down a legal framework which guarantees rights and that it is the state which enforces the enjoyment of rights; (iii) that as the law creates and sustains rights, so whenever the content of law changes, the substance of rights also changes.

The legal theory of rights suffers from various defects such as the following:

1. The state does maintain rights, it does not create them. Our rights emanate because of our membership of the society. The state comes to give the rights their guarantees and realisation;
2. If for once, it is admitted that the state creates rights as this theory affirms, it would have to be admitted that our rights are what the state wants them to be ours' and not what we want for ourselves; and
3. If the state grants a right through one law, it can take away that right through another law. Under such circumstances, our rights would be on the mercy of the state.

3. *The Historical Theory of Rights*

The historical theory of rights regards the rights as products of a long historical process. It holds the view that rights grow from traditions an customs. As traditions and oustoms stabilise owing to their constant and continuous usage, they take the shape of rights. The historical theory of rights originated in the 18th century in the writings of Edmund Burke and was later adopted by various sociologists.

The historical theory of rights is important in so far as it condemns the legal theory of rights which suggests that the rights are the creation of the state. It is also important because it denies the theory of natural rights. The state, the advocates of the historical theory emphasise, has only to recognise those rights of men which have already come into vogue through long usage.

But the historical theory of rights suffers from its own difficulties. It cannot be admitted that all our customs have resulted in our rights. In that case, the Sati system should have been the right of the Indian women and the child-marriage, the right of the children. Again, it is also not true that the present rights have all been derived from traditions and customs. The economic rights, right to work, right to social security etc., can not be related to any tradition or custom.

4. The Social Welfare Theory of Rights

The social welfare theory of rights presumes that rights are the conditions of social welfare. The theory believes that the state should recognize only such rights as go to promote the social welfare. Among the modern advocates of the social welfare theory, Roscoe Pound and Chafee are worth mentioning. Chafee believes that law and custom and natural rights etc. etc. should all yield to what is socially beneficial or essential. Rights should be determined through the dictates of the social conditions.

Apparently the social welfare theory of rights seems to be valid theory, but it presents certain practical difficulties. If only these rights have to be recognised which promote the social welfare, then the question arises: as to who would decide as to what and wherein the social welfare lies. Then the social welfare theory of rights suffers from all weaknesses as the legal theory of rights suffers.

Conclusion

Various theories with regard to the rights speak about the changing liberal mood from one century to the other. Each theory of rights suffers from its own demerits, but each theory has its own importance. The theory of natural rights is important in so far as it indicates that rights are natural to men as men. The legal theory of rights is important because it sets the state behind the rights, for the protection of rights. The historical theory of rights is important in so far as it gives rights the sanction of the past experience. The social welfare theory of rights is important in so far as it makes rights as socially desirable values.

(v). Rights of a Modern Citizen: Laski's Views

Harold J. Laski (1893-1950), a British political scientist and a leader of the Labour Party, had an eventful career. Starting as a pluralist (1916-20), he turned to be a socialised Benthamite (1920-25), a Fabian (1925-32); a Marxist (1932-42) and finally ended up as a liberal among the socialists and a socialist among the liberals between 1942-1950.

Laski has definite views on rights which speak of his liberal-socialist stances. In his description of what rights are and what their nature is, Laski seems to be a liberal, but when he speaks of specific rights, Laski is, more or less, a socialist.

Definition and Meaning of Rights

Laski's work, *A Grammar of Politics,* first published in 1925 but which had many editions and revisions till his death in 1950, gives an elaborate explanation of rights. According to Laski, "Rights are, in fact, those conditions of social life without which no man can seek, in general, to be himself at his best". Laski does not agree with Hobbes when the latter means by rights as the power to satisfy desires. The rights, according to Laski, are not the means for the satisfaction of one's desires, but they are social conditions necesary for the development of one's desires; they are social conditions necessary for the development of one's personality. The institution of the state, Laski says, maintains rights rather than grants them. Rights are, he continues, given by the society; they exist because society exists. They are prior to the state because society is prior to the state. Laski says that rights are neither natural nor historical: they are not natural because they did not exist in the state of nature as the advocates of the social contract theory claim; they are not historical because they had existed at one time or the other in history. Rights are, Laski argues, social in the sense that they are socially beneficial and socially essential. The state, he says, only recognises rights and ensures them to every citizen. Rights relate, Laski affirms, to the individual, to the development of his personality. It is a right because it helps individual seek what is best in him. Our rights are our rights because of our membership of the society. Rights, Laski emphasises, are not independent of society, but are inherent in it. "We have them", he says, "not only for ourselves but also for the protection of the society we are members". Rights and functions, Laski says, are corelative. Rights exist because there exist functions, duties and responsibilities. We have rights so that we may develop, so that we may contribute something to the society, so that we are useful to others.

Nature of Rights

Laski's discussion on rights reveals certain features which are:

1. *Rights are given by society*

Rights arise in the society. Men have these rights because they are members of the society. One who is not a member of the society, has no rights. That is why that the theory of natural rights is not acceptable to Laski, a theory which is condemned on the grounds that it specifies certain rights before the emergence of society. Rights are, Laski says, prior to the state but they are not prior to the society.

2. *Rights and Man's Personality*

Rights signify our progress. They are signposts of our development and progress. They are facilities which help man's personality to grow and develop. They add to man's values, ways, and quality of life. Without rights, it is difficult for the people to attain the development of their personality.

3. *Rights are Social*

Our rights, Laski says, are social in nature. They are claims which are allowed by the society. There are, thus, no rights against the society. Society does not, and actually would never, grant us any right which is against society itself. There are no rights which destroy the very values on which a society is based. There are no rights that challenge the very existence of society. It is in this sense that our rights are moral in character. The individual has no right of killing or thieving.

4. *State Protects Rights*

Society grants us rights and the state protects them. Laski declares, "A state is known by the rights it maintains". The state, therefore, has a definite role to play in this respect. Certainly, the state, while maintaining rights, neither denies them nor can take away them. What at best, the state can do is that it restricts and suspends them. In no case the state can deny them. The task of the state is to recognise rights, maintain them and protect them.

5. *Rights are Dynamic*

Rights are always changing in their character. They change with the changes in the social conditions. There can, therefore, be no permanent rights for all times to come. As circumstances change, so change our conditions, so also change our claims on the society, and therefore, so would change our rights as well. That is why that Laski emphasises that our rights have a content which changes with time and space.

6. *Rights and Duties* Go *Together*

Laski does not think of rights without duties. We own rights because we owe duties. It is only after the performance of our duties that we have any valid claim on our rights. The relationship between rights and duties is so close that it is difficult to separate the two. Our rights are duties of the others and others' rights are our duties. Indeed, rights imply duties. We have the right to free speech but we have the duty that we use such a right within the framework of the social order and public good.

Citizens' Specific Rights

The meaning and nature of rights given by Laski make him to be a liberal in his thinking. But when he comes to speak of specific rights, he seems to be a socialist, even a Marxist.

1. *Right to Work:* A citizen, Laski says, has a right to work. His asusmption is that a citizen is born in a world where he can live only by the sweat of his brow. Society owes him the occasion to perform his functions. To leave him without access to the means of existence is to deprive him of that which makes possible the realisation of personality.

2. *Right* to *be Paid Adequate Wages:* Closely related to the right to work is the right to be paid an adequate wage. By the work that he performs, he must be able to secure a return capable of purchasing the standard of living without which creative citizenship is impossible. The right to an adequate wage does not mean equality of income, but it does mean that a person should be able to satisfy his basic needs through the wages he gets. It does mean, as Laski says, that there must be a sufficiency for all before there is a superfluity for few.

3. *Right to Reasonable Hours of Labour:* Related to the right to work and right to be paid an adequate wage is right to reasonable hours of labour. A citizen must, Laski says, "so distribute the period of labour that he may have the pleasure for creative tasks. The right to reasonable hours of labour implies right to rest and leisure. It is the right to discover the land of mind". In other words, this right is the key to the intellectual heritage a man can devote himself to.

4. *Right to Education:* The citizen has the right to such education as will fit himself for the task of citizenship. He must be provided, Laski says,

"with the instruments which make possible the understanding of life. He must be able to give expression to his wants". Certainly, in the modern world, the citizen who lacks education is bound to be the slave of others. Such a man would not, if he is uneducated, rise to the full heights of his personality.

5. *Right to Political Power:* From the right to political power, Laski derives three rights: (i) right to franchise for everyone, (ii) right to be chosen as a governor, (iii) right to freedom of speech and expression. Those rights help man attain his citizenship. In a democracy, a citizen is a citizen because he participates in the composition of the government, because he can rise himself to be a part of the government and because he has the freedom to take his rulers to task.

6. *Other Rights:* Laski holds the view that on the foundations of these rights, there can be other rights as well. Freedom of religion, of equality and the like help people develop their personality. As to the right to property, Laski is of the opinion that one can not have property to the extent that he exploits others. So long as property, Laski says, is beneficial for the promotion of man's personality, it is allowed. In fact, he feels that property is essential for man's development, for his initiative to take up challenge, and for making his life more comfortable.

(iv) Concept of Human Rights

Human rights are rights worthy of disparity and worthy of human beings as human beings. S. Ramphal had very rightly stated that the human rights were not born of men but they were born with men. They are not as much a result of the efforts of the United Nations as are the emanations from basic human dignity. They are human rights because they are with the human beings as human beings or atleast they should be their rights as citizens of this world.

(a) What are Human Rights?

Human rights may generally be defined as those rights which are inherent in our nature and without which we can not live as human beings. They are essential because they help us to develop and use our human faculties, talents, intelligence, and seek to satisfy our spiritual and other needs. They base themselves on mankind's increasing demand for a life in which the inherent dignity and worth of each human being will receive respect and protection.

Human rights lay at the roots of all organisations. These permeate the entire UN Charter, In the Preamble of the UN Charter, there is its determination "to affirm faith in fundamental Human Rights, in the dignity and worth of the Human person, in the equal rights of men and women and the nations, large and small".

Apart from the Preamble, the Charter contains a reference to the promotion of universal respect for the Human Rights in Articles 13, 55, 62, 68 and 76. It may be noted that the Charter does not contain any Bill of Rights which was set up by the Economic and Social Council in February, 1946.

The *Commission on Human Rights* was directed to submit proposals, recommendations and reports concerning an international bill of rights, the status of women, freedom of information and similar matters, the protection of minorities, the prevention of discrimination on grounds of race, sex, language or religion.

The Commission divided its work in three stages:

1. Declaration: defining the fundamental rights and freedom;
2. An international convention or treaty setting forth in precise terms the provisions which governments were willing to accept as legally binding; and
3. To ensure observance of Human Rights and to deal with violations.

The Commission after spending two and a half years of labour under the chairmanship of Roosevelt drafted Universal Declaration of Human Rights. This Declaration was to serve as a common standard of achievement for all people and all nations. The Declaration was approved by the General Assembly on December 10, 1948.

The Universal Declaration of Human Rights consists of a Preamble and thirty articles.

(b) Universal Declaration of Human Rights: Certain Rights

The Universal Declaration of Human Rights contains a series of rights. Among these, the following can be stated in particular:

Articles 3 *to* 15

Articles 3 to 15 contain a list of traditional rights which are prevalent in the Western world. These rights are: right to life, liberty, security, freedom from arbitrary arrest, a fair trial, equal protection of law, freedom of movements, right to nationality, right to seek asylum in other states etc. etc.

Article 16, 17, 18, 19, 20 & 21

Article 16 concedes equal rights to men and women, to marry and form, a family: Article 17 gives right to property: Article 18 and 19 concede basic freedoms such as those of thought and expression. Articles 20 and 21 give the right to peaceful assembly and association as well as a share in the government of one's own country.

Articles 22 and 27

Articles 22 and 27 deal with economic, social and educational rights such as right to work, protection against unemployment, just remuneration, right to form trade unions, right to have rest and leisure, right to adequate standards of living, education and also participation in the cultural life of the country.

Articles 28, 29 and 30

Article 28 ensures social and international order under which the rights guaranteed by the Declaration are provided. Article 29 emphasises the duty towards the community in which alone the free and full development of man's personality is possible. Article 30 makes a statement regarding the use of the freedom and provides that nothing in the Declaration shall be interpreted to give any state, group, or individual a basis for destroying any of the rights and freedoms which it defines.

The Universal Declaration of Human Rights is, thus, the first segment of the International bill of Human Rights. It is followed by the International Covanant on Economic, cultural and Social Rights adopted by the General Assembly in 1966, the International Covenant on Civil and Political Rights adopted in 1966, and the Optional Protocol adopted in 1966 to the latter covenant. Both came into force in 1976.

The International Covenant of Economic Social and Cultural Rights lays down the principle that all people have the rights of self-determination which mean, that they have the right freely to determine their political status and freely to pursue their economic, social and cultural development. The Human rights which the Covenant seeks to promote and protect include the right to work, to free choice of jobs, to just and favourable conditions of work, to equal pay for equal work, to safe and healthy working conditions, and to rest and leisure. The right to form and join trade unions, the right to strike and the right to social security, including social insurance, are also recognized. Protection and assistance are to be provided for the family, and special protection accorded to mothers and children. The Covenant states that an adequate standard of living is also everyone's right, and this includes adequate food, clothing and housing. The fundamental right of everyone to be free from hunger is specifically recognized. Everyone has the right to seek the highest attainable standard of physical and metal health and to an education.

The International Covenant on Civil and Political Rights and the *Optional Protocol* to that Covenant guarantee to everyone the right to life. These say that no one would be deprived of his/her life arbitrarily. The death penalty, where it has not been abolished, may be imposed only for most serious crimes in accordance with the law. No one shall be subject to torture or to cruel, inhuman or degrading treatment or punishment; no one. shall be held in slavery; no one shall be subject to arbitrary arrest/ detention.

The Covenant also guarantees that all persons deprived of their liberty should be treated with humanity and that no one shall be imprisoned merely on the ground of inability to fulfil a contractual obligation. The Covenant provides for liberty of movement—including the right to leave a country—and freedom to choose a residence. It places limitations upon the expulsion of aliens lawfully in the territory of a State party. Provisions are made for the equality of all persons before the courts and for guarantees in criminal and civil procedures. Retroactive criminal legislation is prohibited and the right of everyone to recognition as a person before the law is guaranteed. Arbitrary or unlawful interference with an individual's privacy, family, home or correspondence is prohibited.

In addition, the right to freedom of thought, conscience and religion and to freedom of expression—including the right to seek, receive or impart information—are recognized and the Covenant provides for the prohibition by law of any propaganda for war or any advocacy of national, racial or religious hatred that constitutes an incitement of discrimination, hostility or violence. The right of peaceful assembly and the right to freedom of association are recognized.

The right of men and women of marriageable age to marry and to found a family, and the principle of equality of rights and responsibilities of spouses as to marriage, during marriage and at its dissolution are also recognized.

The right of every child, without discrimination, to necesary measures of protection on the part of his family, society and the State, is recognized as is the child's right to acquire a nationality.

The right of every citizen to take part in the conduct of public affairs, to vote and to be elected, and to. have access, on general terms of equality, to public services in his country are recognized. All persons are equal before the law and are entitled to equal protection of the law. Finally, measures for the protection of such ethnic, religious or linguistic minorities as may exist in States parties to the Covenant are called for.

The Covenant obliges each country which is a party to it to ensure that should someone's right be violated, he or she will be given an effective remedy within that country.

(c) Suspension and Limitations of Human Rights

The Universal Declaration of Human Rights affirms that the exercise of a person's rights and freedoms may be limited—the limitations must be determined by law—but only for the purpose of securing due recognition of the rights of others and of meeting the just requirements of morality, public order and the general welfare in a democratic society. Rights may not be exercised contrary to the purposes and principles of the United Nations, or if they are aimed at destroying any of the rights set forth in the Declaration.

The Covenant on Economic, Social and Cultural Rights states that the rights in that document may be limited by law, but only in so far as is compatible with the nature of the rights, and solely to promote the general welfare in a democratic society.

Unlike the Universal Declaration and the Covenant on Economic, Social and Cultural Rights, the Civil and Political Covenant contains no general provision applicable to all the Covenant's rights authorizing restrictions on their exercise. However, several articles in the Covenant provide that the rights being dealt with shall not be subject to any restrictions except those provided by law and those which are necessary to protect national security.

The Covenant on Civil and Political Rights allows a State to limit or suspend the enjoyment of certain rights in cases of officially proclaimed public emergencies which threaten the life of the nation. Such limitations or suspensions are permitted only "to the extent strictly required by the exigencies of the situation" and may never involve discrimination solely on the groun of race, colour, sex, language, religion or social origin. These limitations or suspensions must also be reported to the United Nations.

Certain rights, however, may never be suspended or limited even in emergency situations. These are the rights to life, freedom from torture, freedom from enslavement or servitude, protection from imprisonment for debt, freedom from retroactive penal laws, the right to recognition as a person before the law, and freedom of thought, conscience and religion.

(d) Conclusions

The United Nations and the other international organisations are pledged to promote "Universal respect for our observance of Human Rights and Fundamental Freedoms for all without distinction as to race, sex, language or religion."

Justice P.N. Bhagwati, while evaluating Human Rights, refers to three generation of Human Rights. He says: "It started with civil and political rights which have been termed first generation Human Rights which were followed by economic, social and cultural rights (as also civil and political rights) and which are described as second generation of, Human Rights, We have now reached the third generation of Human Rights namely the Right to Development." Right to Development involves, Justice Bhagwati says, effective access to

- tangible resources to achieve their basic needs of productive and equitably paid work, sufficient nutrition, health care and hygience, shelter, energy resources, clean water and air;
- the necessary intangible resources, especially education and information, to enable them better to utilise resources, and to participate freely in the process of development;
- structures of production and government to assure the fair and equitable allocation of the above resources; and
- facilities and services to organise themselves to participate, monitor, evaluate and review development programmes and processes, and to hold accountable those responsible for their implementation,

The universal as Human Rights are, they are to be extended equally to all persons regardless of any distinction, Accordingly. they are to be upheld by all the states, whatever their ideologies. To that extent, Human Rights make us the citizens of the world. The essence of Human Rights lies in defining the essential moral conditions which ought to be guaranteed to citizens of any social and political order. The significance of Human Rights may briefly be summed up as under:

1. The Declaration and the Covenants of Human Rights were the first of its kind in the history of International Organisation.
2. They are a sort of statement of rights considered as essential for the development of human personality. Indeed, they, though not binding on the members-states, provides a yardstick to know the progress of the states.
3. They have served a very useful purpose. They are often cited in support of Human Rights,
4. They exert a profound influence on the Constitutions of new Nations and regional agreements. Though not vested with any legal force, they serve as useful instrument in defending human dignity.

Because human rights are universal, they are, therefore, abstract. They are in the nature of norms; ideals which ought to be achieved. What they lack are the institutions which could make them operative.

What they have are the ideals, the hopes and the appeals that numerous states could possibly give them some shape or validity. Obviously, they are, because they are abstract, not real. The signatories of the UN Declaration, as we know, are different in more than one way, and as such it is difficult to expect the application of these human rights with equal fervour by all. If examined closely, the human rights do not sound democratic in the sense that they may conflict with the policies determined by a democratically constituted authority.

But this is not to undermine the utility of the UN human rights. In fact, they aim to offer a meta-political moral framework for politics and social interaction among the states; the human rights ensure a just treatment of the individuals and the groups; they help evaluate the activities of numerous governments, and take them to task through world opinion if they violate them .

SUGGESTED READINGS

1 Dahendorf, R., *Class and Class Conflict in Industrial Society,* (London, Routledge and Kegan Paul 1959).
2 Giddens, A., *Central Problems in Social Theory,* (London, Macmillan, 1979).
3 Greaves, H.R.G., *The Foundations of Political Theory,* (London, Bell and Sons. 2nd edition, 1966)
4 Halsey, A.H., *'T.H. Marshall: past and present'. Sociology,* 18(1) 1984.
5 Hindess, B., *Freedom, Equality and the Market,* (London, Tavistock, 1987).
6 Lockwood, D., *'For T.H. Marshall.' Sociology,* 8(s) 1974).
7 Marshall, T.H., *Citizenship and Social Class and Other Essays (Cambridge:* Cambridge University Press, 1950).
8 Marshall, T.H., *Class Citizenship and Social Development,* (Westport, Connecticut, Greenwood Press, 1973 [First published in 1964, this differs from Marshall 1963 only through the addition of an introduction by S.M: Lipset].
9 Poggi, G., *The Development of the Modern State,* (London, Hutchinson, 1978).
10 Turner, B.S., *Citizenship and Capitalism,* (London, Allen and Unwin, 1986).

8

Nature of the Modern State

State, as a concept, and as an institution, is as old as we can go into the history. If the state, in ancient times, was more than a mere form of Government, and was, in fact, a society, an association, a city and government, it went into oblivision in Middle Ages and took a back seat. With Modem age, it attains a re-birth and becomes, with the passage time, an important phenomenon. Vincent rightly says:

"Statehood not only represents a set of institutions but also a body of attitudes, practices and codes of behaviour, in short, civility which we associate correctly the with civilisation."

The nature of modem state, is numerous perspectives, can be discussed as under:

I: The Liberal-Individualist Perspective on the Modern State

The political philosophy of liberalism arose as an ideology of the capitalist class in seventeenth century. Sabine says that "The individualism of all social theory between Locke and John Stuart Mill depended less on logic than on its agreement with the interests of the class that mainly produced it." The Glorious Revolution of 1688 was a triumph for liberalism as it finally gave the dominant position to the rising middle class or the capitalists against the landed aristocracy. Liberlism in the early phase was individualistic as represented in the political ideas of Locke and Bentham which promoted the cause of free market and maximum individual's liberty. Obviously the activities of the state were highly limited. This is also called classical liberalism. The classical liberalism later modified and correspondingly the expansion of state activities took place. This was also called the positive view of state which substituted the theory of negative state that regarded the state as a necessary evil.

A significant development took place when individualistic liberalism got converted -into group liberalism, which resulted in the pluralist theory and then we have different shades of positive libertarian state in neo-pluralists, new libertarian of right and left variety and communitarians. These are all the off-shoots of classical liberalism. No doubt there are significant differences among them, yet they reflect the flexibility of liberal ideology to adjust according to the changing needs of time. Despite the differences, the history of liberal ideology provides a consistency in its ideology in terms of two important postulates. Firstly, the autonomy of the individual and secondly, the concept of a limited state.

(a) The liberal-individualist perspective of state can be understood under the following points:

1. *Individual a centre point.* To liberals, individual is the centre of gravity. The systems are created and aimed at the welfare of the individual. The liberals reject the feudal conception of individual in which men were not equal and there was a hierarchy of people where man had a well-defined place in the social order. They believe in the equality of men and according to them, each person possesses a personality, whose dignity is to be protected. They strongly refute any argument in which the individual's individuality is compromised. They do not accept the divine origin of state and the resultant divine rights of king because it is based on inequality which makes common man a slave. They do not believe in the independent will of the state or the society like the idealists or Fascists because such concepts of will turn man into slave where there is no respect for his dignity and wisdom. Similarly dictatorship and automatic governments find no sympathy from the liberals. Their thesis is: "Man is the only point from which all must issue and to which all must return." Therefore liberals strongly advocate the cause of democracy because it is the only system which guarantees the preservation of man's dignity and offers opportunities to develop his personality. According to liberals, it is perfectly natural for man to have self-interest and pursue it. In short, individual is autonomous, selfish, self-centred and atomised.
2. *Liberals believe in rationalism.* The liberals believe that man is essentially a rational creature. In fact, liberal-individualistic philosophy emerged as a reaction against the divine theory of origin of state which gave all powers to the king and feudal overlords who were said to be chosen by God to govern. According to the divine theory, any violation of law and authority was regarded not only illegal but also sin which could

invite severe punishment from God. The rationalism of liberals refuses to accept any system based on assumptions. Reason, not faith, should be the basis of any political arrangement.

3. *State is a necessary evil.* The early liberals doubt political powers. To them, state is a necessary evil. It is an evil because it controls, and any kind of control is an impediment to human development. Yet the state is necessary because selfishness and rapacity of men would lead to disorder and chaos in society where no development could take place. In fact this was the reason as to why state came into being. Locke gave the individual maximum autonomy and the state, most minimum functions. He says that state was created to protect the property of the people; for all other things, the state was an evil. Adm Smith, an advocate of *Laissez faire* and *Laissez aller,* too regarded the state esentially an evil and existed to perform functions which an individual could not. The Benthamite state was also non-interventionist. But, the nature of the state is that it is an evil institution.
4. *Liberals-individualists stand for a limited state.* the liberal view of the functions of state is aptly concluded by Jefferson, who said 'that government is the best which governs the least'. According to early liberals, the state's functions are confined to protection of individuals against internal and external enemies, and to enforce contracts legally made between the individuals. According to Locke, state should cover only political aspects of man's life. He defined political power thus: "Political power, then, I take to be a right of making laws with penalties of death and, consequently, all less penalties for the regulating and preserving of property, and of employing the force of the community in the execution of such laws and in the defense of the commonwealth from foreign injury; and all this only for the public good." Locke and other liberals distinguished state from society and advocated limited state to political sphere only. The state and government are formed to do specific jobs and Locke refers to this job as preservation of property; property, which, in its broader sense, includes lives, liberties and estates' and in its narrower sense, includes only 'estates' 'possession' or 'goods'. Locke puts four limitations on government very clearly;
   a. Equality of law
   b. Laws should be made for the good of the people
   c. Tax cannot be raised without the consent of the people
   d. The legislature cannot transfer its power of making laws to anybody else.

Bentham, however, will not agree to such a small content of government's functions. It is the duty of the government to promote greatest happiness of the greatest number. To him, state is a legal entity consisting of the rulers and the ruled where the former govern through laws and the latter undertake to obey him. Bentham says, "when a number of persons are supposed to be in the habit of paying obedience to a person or an assemblage of persons of a known and certain descriptions, such persons altogether are said to be in the state of political society." The purpose of such grouping is aimed at achieving the greatest happiness of the greatest number. The only rationale behind legislation is utility. Bentham is very much concerned with legislation which is directed to remove evils and is always in response to specific instances of unhappiness. The legislator only needs to know the desires of people and make laws accordingly. However, Bentham's principle of utility leaves for the state a very insignificant area of operation and the state's sovereignty is limited to that area only. Bentham's object is the individual's interest and the state is merely an agency for the promotion of individual's interest.

5. *Liberals-individualists emphasis on liberty.* The limited state of liberal-individualists is characterised 'by maximum liberty to its citizens. Liberty is defined as absence of restraints. John Stuart Mill is the most vocal supporter of liberty. While he accepted the concept of negative liberty i.e. the absence of restraints, at the same time he held a positive view. of state. Mill defines liberty as 'pursuing our own good in our own way, so long as we do not attempt to deprive others of their's or impede their efforts to obtain it.' So defined liberty is a means to the end of our own good. Mill divided man's actions in two parts. The first is self-regarding actions which concerns him only and secondly, the other-regarding actions which relate to other individuals. Mill says. "The only part of the conduct of anyone for which he is amenable to society is that which concerns others. In the part which merely concerns himself, his independence is, of right, absolute. Over himself, over his own body and mind, the individual is sovereign." According to Mill, individuals' liberty should be curtailed against his will to prevent harms to others. In the self-regarding sphere of individual's action, where state has no authority to interfere include (a) the inward domain of consciousness, the liberty of conscience, of thought and feeling, of opinion and sentiments on all subjects, of expressing and publishing opinion, (b) liberty of tastes and pursuits; the liberty of framing plans of our life, of doing things; and (c) liberty of combinations; freedom to unite etc. Mill holds, '... that the individual is not accountable to society for his actions, in so far as these concerns the interests of no person but himself ... that for such action as are prejudicial to the

interests of others, the individual is accountable, and may be subjected either to social or to legal punishment, if society is of opinion that the one or the other is requisite for its protection.' Mill advocated freedom from tyranny of majority also. He said that political authority cannot silent the people who hold contrary views. "If all mankind," he wrote, "minus one were of one opinion, mankind would be no more justified in silencing that one person than he, if he had the power, would be justified in silencing mankind."

6. *Liberal state is a consent state.* To liberals, state is an artificial institution created by the people for their own well being. Locke says, "Men being, ... by nature all free, equal and independent, no one can be .... subject to the political power of another without his own consent. The only way whereby anyone diverts himself of his natural liberty and puts on the bonds of civil society is by agreeing with other men to join and unite into a community." Locke and other liberals believe in majority rule. Locke's state is a joint stock company in which the board of directors (government) are chosen through a majority vote. They govern the company to promote the interests of shareholders. The government is a trustee government and, as and when it violates the trust, the people have not only a right but also a duty to change or rebel against the government. Locke says, "whenever the legislators endeavour to take away and destroy the property of the people, or to reduce them to slavery under arbitrary power, they put themselves into a state of war with the people, who are thereupon absolved from any further obedience." The government has no right to violate the trust or mandate given to it by the people and in case they do so, the people can change such a government. Bentham also advocates a representative and responsible government, representative in the sense that the government should be periodically elected and convened and responsible in the sense that it should not be despotic. Although Bentham did not give his individual the right to revolt, all the rest, Locke especially have given such power to the individual.

7. Liberals believe in the *concept of competition.* The early liberals believe that 'competition is natural and common good is realised through it. According to liberals, the evolution of nature is characterised by an incessant struggle for survival. Herbert Spencer forcefully advocated the law of organic evolution through natural selection to human society and reached to the conclusion that state should allow the nature to do its work. In the eternal struggle for existence, only the fittest survive and rest perish. Man survived the competition among different species in the nature and hence now is dominating the world. Spencer and other liberals want to implement this concept of competition in human society as well. There should be competition .among individuals in

which only the fittest will survive. The state should not help the poor, and the downtrodden, as it is against the spirit of competition. Liberals advocate competition both at the political as well as economic level.

At the level of politics, liberals stand for democracy which is based on competition. Democracy is characterised by general and rational rules of competition which are free, fair and open. Universal adult franchise stems from this proposition. Individuals are equal, hence everybody has a right to vote. There may be some general restriction on the basis of age and other factors. Similarly the whole concept of election is based on competition. The candidates compete to get maximum votes from the voters. The fittest survives and is elected to legislature where again there is a competition to make government; the party that musters majority of seats in the legislature forms the government. The competition still continues between the government and the opposition. The opposition occupies a pious position in the system and the leader of opposition enjoys the status of a cabinet minister. It is duty of the opposition to criticise government and make it responsible. The people who are vested with popular sovereignty are the ultimate judge and give their mandate in periodical elections.

The rules of the competition are to be extended to the economic field also. The economic theory of liberals is mainly derived from Adam Smith's *'Wealth of Nations'*. Ricardo and Malthus further developed it. This economic theory was also called the theory of *laissez-faire*. It was a theory of free market, free trade and non-interference of the government in economic affairs. The theory assumes that men being self seeking and selfish know their interest best. Therefore, they should be left to themselves. The economic activities should be left to the individuals. This will result in prosperity in trade and commerce and increasing profits. Free trade will also benefit the consumers because of competition among the traders as well as the industrialists. Liberals believe that the market is self regulative and state should not interfere. The state interference kills the initiative and self-reliance of the man. Spencer said that an overgoverned or collective state has monotony and uniformity. The Liberals advocate *lassiez faire* on the basis of practical grounds. The experience shows that state has failed miserably whenever it tried to interfere in economic activities. Whenever there has been state regulation in economic affairs, the result has been chaos and confusion because the state and its structures are not suited for economic activities. By its interference, the state spoils not only the free market system, its own functions also suffers badly.

The liberal-individualistic perspective of state has been criticised by many theorists. *Firstly,* state cannot be considered as a necessary evil. In fact it is the first condition of any civilised existence. The state not only maintains peace and order in the society but it also reconciliates the conflicting interests and protect weak and down trod dens against the strong. Training of good citizens is the responsibility of state and it must discharge this responsibility fully. Garner aptly remarks that 'the state emancipates and promotes as well as restraints.' *Secondly,* the economic theory of liberalism has been proved wrong historically. The policy of *Laissez Faire* leads to exploitation of man by man. Gilchrist rightly states that 'no better argument exists against the theory of individualism than the practical results which followed its adoption in the political and industrial life of England.' It was discovered in the beginning of nineteenth century that the policy of non-interference of state brought miseries and distress to the workers, children and women. Free competition resulted in monopolies in trade and industry. The theory of survival of the fittest is brutal and immoral. *Thirdly,* the state has a duty to protect the weak. The modern state has become a welfare state in which the state looks after the entire personality of individual. The experience of Japan and India proves that the state's regulation of economic activity has resulted in prosperity for the common man. *Lastly,* Marxists have vehemently criticised this theory. According to them, the liberal state is a class state where the state is, used as a means to promote the interests of the capitalists and to exploit the proletariat.

The liberals themselves realized the fallacies of their arguments and made suitable corrections in their theory. The result was positive liberalism and a positive view of the state.

(b) Mill and Green put great emphasis on the fact that state and its political machinery are man-made and the goal of the government is the development of individual's personality. Mill demanded that the intellectual and moral qualities of the citizens should be stimulated and utilised in the service of the society. The government should promote the virtue and intelligence of the people. Green is also interested in man's self-development and the self in the individual is not merely an individual self but a social self also and the membership of the society means participating in its activities, and receiving, in turn from it the right to moral self development. The objective of state is to create social conditions where individual's moral participation in society's life is possible. Sabine rightly says, "Full moral participation in a social life was for Green the highest form of self development and to create the possibility of such participation was the end of a liberal society... Accordingly, for Green, politics was essentially an agency for creating social conditions that make moral development possible." Green defined state as a 'body of persons, recognised by each other as having rights, and possessing certain institutions for the maintenance of those rights.' Thus in his definition of state, rights occupy a dominant position. But to Green rights do not emanate from state. In fact, rights are granted by the society and state maintains and protects them. Thus the state is not the source but a guarantor of rights. Green declared. "It is not, however, supreme coercive power, simply as such, but supreme coercive power exercised in a certain way and for certain ends, that makes a state."

Mill advocated the cause of representative government. According to him, ".... the ideally best form of government is that in which the sovereignty, or supreme controlling power in the last resort, is vested in the entire aggregate of the community, every citizen not only having a voice in the exercise of that ultimate sovereignty, but being, atleast occasionally, called as to take an actual part in the government, by the personal discharge of some public functions, local or general." The representative government is ideal because (i) the rights and interests of people are secured and (ii) the general prosperity attains a greater height. Mill advocated proportional representation so that the minorities are not alienated from the national mainstream. However, Mill remained a reluctant democrat, as he wanted to grant restricted franchise to people who were literate and paid taxes. But the importance of Mill lies in the fact that he regarded man as a consumer and appropriator and also as an exerter and developer and enjoyer. Macpherson rightly states that the society that comes up on Mill's model of man is one which permits and encourages everyone to act as exerter, developer or enjoyer of the exertion and development, of his or her own capacities. Mill's case for the positive state is offered to help create an exerter, developer and enjoyer. The functions of such a state, though limited, are lengthy and heavy. The functions of state according to Mill include preservation of peace and order; laying down laws of inheritance: definitions of property; laws about contract; setting up civil tribunals to settle disputes; registry of birth, marriages, deaths and general statistical data; monopoly of money; presenting standards of weights and measures; paving, lighting and clearing streets; making and improving harbours, lighthouses, surveys, maps etc; fostering exploration, colonization, culture, research and universities etc. Green also stands for a positive state, though it exists to remove obstacles, it is an hinderance of hindrances. The state confines itself to the removal of hindrances. "Under this head, however," Green says "there may be and should be included much that most states have hitherto neglected... " He has not specified such obstacles which state should remove, but does point out the directions like the enforcement of the parent's duties to educate their children, restricting the freedom of contract and the population. Thus the concept of state as developed by Mill and Green was a limited state, but at the same time its nature, functions and perspective were widened manifold to make it a positive state.

(c) The pluralists like MacIver, Laski, Barker and Lindsay further developed this concept of limited and positive state. Like Green, they also accepted that concepts of right and liberty do not have their existence at the mercy of state. Green believed that the various associations are important in so far as they develop moral man's instinct in state and, therefore, he would permit them to work independently. The pluralists go further and regard state as an association although Unique. MacIver defines state as follows: "The state is an association which, acting through law as promulgated by a government endowed to this end with coercive power, maintains within a community territorially demarcated the universal external conditions of social order."

The doctrine of pluralism arose in Europe as a reaction against the state absolutism which was responsible for many wars and which ultimately culminated into the doctrine of Fascism. Mussolini declared, "All within the state, none outside the state, none against the state." The Fascists regarded state or society as end and individuals the means. To them, the state was totalitarian whose control extended over all the spheres of economic, social, political, moral and religious life. The pluralists clearly differentiated the state from the society and regarded state as one of the associations in the society. The associations like the state have their own personality and limited functions. Society consists of many associations like family, church and state, and state cannot be regarded as above the society; in fact it is created for specific functions. "Its chief task" MacIver says, "is to uphold the rule of law, and this implies that it is itself also the subject of law, that it is bound in the system of legal values which it maintains. Its task is incomplete, nay broken, if it seeks exemption from the legality which it also imposes." The state should concentrate on the things that are Caeser's. For the pluralists, since the structure of society is federal, therefore the authority must also be federal. However they also believe that the state should coordinate the activities of different associations. But the state, in any case, cannot monopolise the total loyalty of individual. The state ultimately is the servant of the society and by its very nature, it is a limited state. For a detailed study of pluralism, the readers are requested to refer to chapter six.

II: Contemporary Libertarian theories of the State

The. post-war period (i.e. 1945 onward) witnessed, in the West, a host of shades of opinion, varying but not hostile from one another,

but all these in the broader framework of liberalism. These included, among others, the classical pluralists (Truman, Dahl), the reformed pluralists (Richardson, and Jordon), the plural elitists (McFarland, McConnell, Lowi), the neo-pluralists (Lindblom) on the one hand, and on the other, the advocates of what may be termed as the New Right (Hayek, Nozick), and the New Left (Pateman, Macpherson and Poulantzas) and the communitarians (Sandal, Walzer, Taylor). What is common among them all is their avowed conviction in scienticism, empiricism, positivism, behaviouralism and post-behaviouralism. They are all libertarians in so far as (i) they all demonstrate, in varying degrees, their concern for individual liberty, (ii) autonomous individual with all capabilities, initiative, capacities infact, (iii) and as a consequences of these (i) and (ii) a limited and a restrictive state. To that extent, all are individualists, but their individualism crosses limits of individuation. As these streams developed one after the other, their perspective about the nature of the state kept changing because of the compulsions of the fast changing times.

It is, indeed, difficult to fix all these contemporary libertarian streams into any time-frame, for no particular stream was built, as it were, on its earlier stream. They all grew side by side and some, even, simultaneously, but mostly after the 1970s.

The post-war pluralists (we may call them 'classical' with the emergence of its later forms) were different from those of the pre-war days. The pre-war pluralists, such as Lindsay, Laski, MacIver, Barker, rose to condemn the Austinian legalistic, monistic and the absolutistic sovereignty and in the process, came to recognise the utility of the association in the society, state including. The post-war pluralists, of whatever form, though still backward in theorising what they claim to hold, have, indeed, made inroads in dominating the thinking of the people, especially in the United States of America.

Broadly stated, pluralism holds (a) that the state is neutral: (b) that societal groups are potentially equal in their influence; and (c) that the access to the political system is open to all. All shades of pluralists regard power as dispersed and the state as the regulator of the conflicts in society. The fact remains that the pluralists have no definite theory of state; what they have is the theory of government. Though it is government that does everything in the name of the state, yet it does not include what all the state includes. The pluralist perspective of the state, if at all there is any, regard the state (in fact the government) a set of institutions such as executive, legislature, judiciary and civil service which are distinct from society. For the pluralists, David Marsh

(*Theory and Methods* ill *Political Science,* 1995) says: "The state is often seen as a site of conflict between departments that represent: a range of interest groups. Authority is dispersed even within the government and hence no single interest is able to dominate the state. Yet the state is rarely neutral but reflects the range of groups pressures it faces..... The process of making policy within the state is an attempt to bargain between a range of conflicting interest. Politics is a constant process of negotiation that ensures conflicts are resolved peacefully."

The following is a brief summary of the nature and perspective of the state relating to the different models of pluralism based, largely, on Marsh's description:

(a) The *classical pluralist perspective* of the modem state includes the following features:

- (i) The state is a site of group conflict and, therefor, is highly responsive to group pressures.
- (ii) Groups, with varying resources, while easily formed, they exist in their relations of continual conflicts.
- (iii) Power is an observable and a dispersed phenomenon.
- (iv) Groups are the bases of government, especially the potential groups.
- (v) Society is not only distinct from state, but is also non-political.

(b) The *reformed pluralist perspective* of the modem state includes the following features:

- (i) The state is fragmented and is responsive to groups. But the access to the state (or government) is differential.
- (ii) All the groups are not equal; only privileged groups participate in policy making, but there is a role for excluded groups in forcing policy changes:
- (iii) Power, here as well, is both observable and dispersed.
- (iv) Democracy is threatened by policy-making potential groups, but the excluded groups do have a limited role in protecting the democratic norms.
- (v) Society and the state get integrated into each other through potential groups.

The *plural elitist perspective* of the modem state has the following features:

- (i) The state is, indeed, fragmented with highly resourced potential groups having a degree of access to the state and hence, claiming a corresponding degree of state autonomy.

(ii) The potential elite groups have easy access to the governmental positions, but different groups dominate in different areas.

(iii) Power is both observable as well as unobservable. Though there is a tendency towards the concentration of power, yet it is dispersed atleast in certain policy areas.

(iv) There exist groups, though in segmented policy areas, but they do limit the effectiveness of democracy.

(v) The civil society is distinct from state, but has a limited influence on it.

The characteristic features of *nee-pluralist* perspective of the state are:

(i) The state is biased towards the business interests in economic policy.

(ii) The business interests have a crucial role in policy making, reducing, thus, the importance of group behaviour.

(iii) Power is unobservable-structural and ideological. It is concentrated in primary issues, but dispersed in secondary ones.

(iv) There is no control over power which is concentrated in primary issues, and hence, there is democracy, but it is very little.

(v) Society is distinct from state but has a limited influence on it.

Marsh refers to a still another stream called the *radical democracy*. Its distinctive features are:

(1) The state is dominated by the privileged potential groups.

(2) The privileged potential groups are important but those excluded also play an important role in developing alternative forms of politics.

(3) Power is ideological as well as concentrated, though there exists opportunities for its dispersal through alternative political forms.

(4) There is no room for traditional type of democracy, democracy through numerous political structures. But there is a potential. for developing alternative forms of democratic participation.

(5) The society becomes highly political and also an alternative to the state.

The New Right is the new libertarian right as the New Left is the new libertarian left. The New Right (Hayek and Nozick) arose as a protest against the New Left (broadly a group with socialist sympathies, the feminists, the ecological campaigners, the pacifists) in late 1960s and the early 1970s. The New Right (also called the *neo-liberals* or *neo-conservatives)* are committed, generally, to the following:

(1) That political life, like the economic life, is or ought to be a matter of individual freedom and initiative;

(2) That there has to be accordingly a *laissez faire* market society with a minimal state;

(3) The political programme, David Held says, of the New Right includes:

(i) the extension of the market to more and more areas of life;

(ii) the creation of a state stripped of excessive involvement in economy and in the provision of opportunities;

(iii) the curtailment of the power of certain groups (for instance, the trade unions) to press their aims and goals;

(iv) the construction of a strong government co enforce law and order.

Nozick advocates a minimal state. What is needed is the least instrusive form of political power commensurate with the defence of individual liberty. He says that there is no need of any excessive state, for such a state would violate the rights of the individuals. His perspective of the modem state can be stated as:

(a) that less the state interferes in the lives of individuals, better it is and better for the individuals; (b) that if it attempts to promote equality, it steps beyond its legitimate boundaries; (c) that it is protective agency and, therefore, protects people against force, theft, fraud and the violation of contracts; (d) that it has to sustain a monopoly of force for protecting rights of the people, adjudicating conflicts among them and doing everything that is to be done in the name of defence and foreign relations.

The New Right scholars, as better individualists, seek to establish a minimum state and a maximum individual in the changed conditions of the late 20th century. Hayek says that (i) the citizens enjoy liberty only if the power of the state is circumscribed by law, rules which specify the limits on the scope of state action; (ii) that the law is not what restricts the individual initiative but is one that disallows the state activity of not guaranteeing the life and liberty of the individuals; (iii) that the legislative scope of the state is, and must be, restrained by the rule of law; (iv) that the state should "roll back" in its functions and powers to the level as proclaimed by the early individualists (v) that there has to be effective political leadership or constitutional state with minimization of bureaucratic regulation and of collectivism of all types.

The New Left is reflected in the writings of Pateman, Macpherson,

Poulantzas and is characterised by what Held says "participatory democracy". Pateman feels that within the framework of inequalities of sex, class and race, individuals can neither be free nor equal. She also says that if the state, the capitalist state as such, is inescapably locked into the maintenance and reproduction of inequalities, then its whole claims to be a distinct entity would always be in doubt. Poulantzas, advocating what he calls 'socialist pluralism', urges that the state must be democratized by making parliament, state bureaucracies and political parties more open and accountable while new forms of struggle (as expressed in factory-based politics, women's movement, ecological groups) must ensure that both society and the state are democratized. Macpherson, while giving Mills' ideas a radical twist, strongly feels that liberty and individual development can only be achieved with the direct and continuous involvement of citizens in the regulation of society and state.

The New Left scholars have, in short, sought to combine and refashion insights from both the liberal and the Marxist traditions. Their perspective of the modern state can be stated briefly as under:

(1) That all the key institutions of society, including as large as the state and as small as the work place, should be built on direct participation of the citizens;

(2) That the leaders of the political parties be made accountable to their respective members;

(3) That the open institutional system be maintained to ensure the possibility of making experiments in the system itself;

(4) That the poor be taken care of; unaccountability of bureaucratic power be eradicated; and open information system be ensured so to have an access on decisions made and policies determined.

The communitarian perspective of the modern state, associated with the names of Sandel, Walzer and Taylor, has come up as a reaction against liberal theorists such as Rawls and Dworkin. According to them:

(1) The idea of individual is the idea of liberal-individualism, the idea that eclipses the idea of the community, the idea of society as such.

(2) The source of all values is the community itself. The development of the community depends on the values it cherishes.

(3) Citizens alone, as members of the community, can obtain the higher levels of citizenship only in the state. Sandel, following Aristotle (not surprisingly if the communitarians call themselves as the neo-Aristotleans) says: ".... we cannot conceive of our

personhood without reference to our role as citizens, and as participants in a common life."

(4) Politics is an on-going affair; a sort of business as usual; never ending; and is and around us. Richard Gunn says: "their (communitarians) central, and plausible, contention is that we are in and of politics as the very same moment as we begin to speak or think; Politics is our context.. ... "

(5) Politics is a pre-supposed phenomenon. Before there are rights and duties, there has to be a political order. Such a view is, more or less, a Kantian view. Following such a view, politics tends to presuppose politics; it becomes a circular activity. Sheldon Wolin makes a point on behalf of the communtarians by describing politics both as a source of conflict and a mode of activity that seeks to resolve conflicts and promote adjustments if it succeeds in doing so, then the circle is complete; it is a sort of standing miracle, the role made of activity which can discover its resources within itself."

The communitarians are not the admirers of Marxism, though they value the idea of community; they are not anarchists because they regard politics a necessity. Their tilt is more towards the New Left than towards the New Right.

The perspectives about the modern state in the West have changed from time to time. The anarchist would regard it a worthless institution, the individualists declare it a necessary evil; the later liberals think of it as a positive institution; the pluralists tend to limit its autonomy as much as possible; the New Right feels happy on its being 'rolled back' to the individualistic level; the New Left considers the state an agency for bringing changes provided its mechanism is completely 'participated'; the socialists find in it a potential instrument that helps establish socialism, and the Marxists, regarding it a class institution, give to it the destructive task of destroying the class system and the constructive task of building the classless society.

III: The Modern State: Social-Democratic Perspective

Socialism, after the death of Marx, witnessed various variations, mostly as a reaction against the Marxian Socialism. The basic difference between the Marxian socialism and the other variants was the method by which the present capitalist society would change into a socialist one. While the Marxists thought that the class antagonism, a characteristic of capitalist society, would come to an end through revolution and by the proletariat after it captures power, the non-Marxist socialists hope to have socialism through evolutionary and democratic means, i.e., socialism through state and by democratic means. These new variants of socialism appeared, at the turn of the 20th century, in forms such as evolutionary socialism (Germany), syndicalism (France), Fabianism and later guild socialism (Great Britain) especially. These variants represent a temperate, moderate and non-doctrinal kind of socialism as against revolutionary socialism of the Marxists.

Variants of Socialism: Their Perspective on the Modern State summarized

(a) *German Evolutionary Socialism:* The German evolutionary socialism, called by the Marxists as revisionists, was represented mainly in the writings of Bernstein (1850-1932). As a reaction to Marx's theory of class struggle, he propounded a theory of class permeation drawn largely from Fabianism. According to Bernstein, capitalism is not going to go so soon as Marx had visualised and as it has to stay, and became stronger than before, the possibility of transformation to socialism through revolution is most minimum. He said: "I confess openly, I have extra-ordinary little interest or taste for what is generally called the final goal of socialism. This aim, whatever it be, is nothing to me, the movement is everything." What it means, in Bernstein's opinion, (i) that socialism is a matter of evolution; (ii) that it has to come through gradual and successive stages of movement and not through any revolution; (iii) that socialism has a long journey to reach its destination and that it can cover the distance through regulations of the state passed from time to time; (iv) that capitalism has to be struck through trade unionism engineered by the workers' movement; (v) that socialism can be built not on the ruins of democracy but through its essence.

Thus for Bernstein in particular and German evolutionary socialism in general, the state is or can be, an agency for bringing about socialism and that socialism, at its any mature stage would always need the state rather its abolition. Obviously, the evolutionary socialists do not regard the state as non-entity, for if it can serve the interests of the capitalists, it can also serve the interests of the workers, and if all the sections of society get represented in the state, it can serve as an agency of social welfare.

(b) *Syndicalism:* Tilted towards Marxism-anarchism combine, syndicalism is a trade union movement regarding it as the basis of the new industrial structure which would replace capitalism. Like the Marxists, the syndicalists (Georges Sorel: 1847-1922, *General du Travail)* regard the state as a class institution, presently dominated by the capitalists and an institution that is an instrument of capitalist exploitation. As such, echoing the anarchist view, all the states are, according to the syndicalists, power states and that only their abolition (the abolition of the state as an institution) can hopefully make the situation better, for workers in particular. The syndicalists are not the admirers of democracy, for they believe that democracy, in any form, is a bourgeois system sustained only by unresponsive and absolute bureaucracy. They are socialists in- so far as they advocate a free, self-regulating and self-evolving workers' society. In fact, they are a combination of Marxism (seeking workers' amelioration) and anarchism (immediate abolition of state and that too through violence).

(c) *Fabianism and Guild Socialism:* There is hardly any line of. demarcation between Fabianism and Guild Socialism for their advocates are found in both: Shaw, Webbs, Olivier, Bland, Wallas and others. All these Fabians built the ground on which later, Guild Socialism and thereafter the Labour Party, emerged with Richard Tawney, Harold Laski and others as their champions. These British variants of socialism are usually referred to as democratic socialism. Fabianism or Guild Socialism attempts (a) to organise the society afresh by emancipating land and industrial capital form individual and class ownership to the community as a whole, (b) to abolish private property in land and of rent, (c) to utilise the surplus wealth for the service of the people through a democratically-constituted state; (d) to propagate socialist opinions so to aim at social and political changes leading to effective and responsible citizenship.

(a) Characteristics of Democratic Socialism

Before describing the characteristics of democratic socialism, one may clarify a point of distinction. When we use the term 'social democratic', we are more close to democratic socialism than to 'social democracy'. The term 'social democracy' owes its genesis to Marxism (initially, the Marxist parties were called the social democracies) and as such 'social democracy' is a Marxist phenomenon, and therefore, contains, in it, a deference towards the concept of democracy and the institution of state. Democratic socialism, like social democratic concept, is a socialism with democracy, and/ or a democracy with socialism.

The following are, in brief, the characteristic features of social democratism or democratic socialism:

(1) The complete abandonment of the idea of revolutionary methods and violence as a means to power; and the complete acceptance of parliamentary means.
(2) The transformation of the socialist parties who speak only for the interests of the working class to peoples' parties which seek to establish general welfare.
(3) The recognition that the definition of socialism as a social and economic ideal was inseparable from the idea of democracy, both as a means and as an end. As a means, socialism has to be attained through democratic means or democratic polity has to bring about legislation relating to social justice. As an end, socialism has to establish democratic norms and democracy has to attain the ideal of socialism.
(4) *Respect for human freedom and human personality.* The acceptance of the state to the extent it is necessary.
(5) The surrender of the idea of nationalisation or state ownership of the means of production as a 'first principle' of socialism, and the substitution of public control of enterprise and planning as the means of achieving economic growth and equitable incomes.
(6) A complete opposition to all types of totalitarianism and authoritarianism and the establishment of polity, democratically constituted, which is responsible for what it does and responsive to what it ought to do. It is as much a democratic state with the ideals of socialism as is a socialist state with the ideas of democracy.

(b) Harold J. Laski: The Social Democrat/Democratic Socialist

Harold J. Laski (1893-1950), while holding a chair in the London School of Economics and Political Science was a dynamic and pragmatic personality and the one who went very well with the fast changing times of ours. He began with as a pluralist while attacking the monistic theory of sovereignty as propounded by John Austin. This was a period of World War I. During the days of reconstruction (say 1923 and onwards), he turned to become a social Benthamite, regarding the state as an agency necessary for the welfare of the people. The failure of capitalism, as evidenced in the Great Depression of 1929 particularly, made Laski a Marxist, considering the state as a class institution which exists to promote the interests of the capitalists and exploit the workers. A little before the World War II. Laski, disappointed as he was with the way Marxism was being practised in Soviet Russia, settled down to democratic socialism, making his position as if he were a Marxist among the liberals, and a liberal among the Marxists. George Catlin describes three Laskis: (i) the mauve with a lot of blue in it followed by (ii) red, and (iii) then pink phase.

(i) *The State: Not more than an Association:* As a pluralist, Laski had condemned the Austinian monolithic state. He had never entertained the idea of a state with absolute and unlimited powers. In fact, he found no justification of a state that was Hobbesian in nature. For him, the state was an association, an association like any other, and at times, serving in a rather limited way than associations like the family (much before the establishment of the institution of the state) and the Church (commanding more obedience than the state). It was on this ground that he insisted on allegiance to other associations. His famous argument can be summed up in his own saying: "Because the society is. federal, the authority should also be federal." Because the state was an association like any other, it has, he would argue, no right to seek the monopoly of peoples' obedience. The state has no special moral claim over the individuals and has, as such, no special power to control them. Like any other pluralist of his times, Laski was at best when he was to demolish the Austinian absolute sovereignty, but was most weak in building a case for pluralism: in theory, it is all fine to talk of corresponding power to every association for what it does, but in practice, it is no easy task to build pluralism.

(ii) *State as a Co-ordinator and as an Agency of Peoples' Welfare:* Laski soon realised the limitations inherent in abstract pluralism. He was soon to realise that the state as an association is much different than the other associations; it may not have any superior power or claim, but it certainly has a superior position to the other associations. Pointing to the difference between the state and other associations, Laski says: "It (the state) is an association like others: churches, trade unions, and the rest. It differs from them in that membership, is compulsory upon all that live within its territorial ambit, and that it can, in the last resort, enforce its obligations upon its subjects." But, despite these differences, the state does more than any other association does or all the other associations together can do. It is the state that establishes social order, provides security, prepares a ground in which the people and all the organisations can function smoothly and peacefully. Indeed, it does not control other associations as it does not interfere in their internal functioning, but it does coordinate their efforts. He says: "Above all, it may be suggested, it will make, and for the first time, the co-ordinating work of the state a matter of principle".

For Laski, the state is much more than a coordinator. During the phase when Laski was a social Benthamite, he, almost like any collectivist, advocated the idea that the state can do a lot for the individual and that, as a fellowship of men, it aims at the enrichment of the common life. According to Laski, "It (the state) is the association to protect the interests of men as citizens" and its job, therefore, is "to secure common needs at the level which the society as a whole deems essential to the fulfilment of its general end."

(iii) *State as a Class Institution:* During the phase when Laski had embraced Marxism, owing to the ever-increasing inconsistencies in the capitalist mode of life, he rose to declare the state as a class organisation which is dominated by the capitalist. He began viewing the state as an agency of exploitation whose only job was the oppression of the working class. It was during this phase of Laski as a Marxist that he was much allured by the material development made in Soviet Russia, admiring in the process, the dictatorship of the proletariat as quantitatively and qualitatively better than the bourgeois state as Lenin actually felt and had declared so.

(iv) *Laski's Socialism:* Laski's love for Marxism was short-lived. He soon discovered fallacies in theory and even practice of Marxism. Around the W orld War II, Laski was more or less a socialist, more of English orientation than of Marxian. His socialist philosophy relating to the concept of the Modem State can be summed up briefly as under:

(i) A peaceful change, and not a revolution, can bring about changes in socio-economic structure of the society. Such a change can be made possible through laws passed by a democratic state;

(ii) Capitalism has outlived its life; and therefore it has to go, sooner or later. The socialist idea is the idea of the future.

(iii) The victory of political democracy with its universal adult franchise can help the exit of capitalism as also the entry of socialism.

(iv) With the advancement of industrial and technological development, capitalism has became anachronistic and lost its validity in the present context. In his view, the forces of production, accordingly, have become incompatible with the relations of production;

(v) Laski's socialism brings about a polity where there is a rational and equitable distribution of wealth.

(vi) The conception of democratic socialism which Laski visualises is one where there is a harmonization of social control of economic processes with the liberty of the individual.

(vii) In Laski's social democratism, the state exists to fulfil the promise of socialism through a structure democratically established.

(viii) Laski's state is an instrument that exists for the individual. However important a state may be, it tends to exist for the protection of peoples' rights and for the promotion of a conducive atmosphere where the people can unfold their inner capacities so to be able to touch their possible heights.

IV: The Modern State-The Marxist Perspective

Marxism is the name of a coherent system of ideas which gives us a new form of reasoning or method for understanding nature, society and the entire human history. This coherence was achieved by Marx who preferred to call his ideology as 'Scientific Socialism, Besides Marx, Engles, Lenin, Stalin, Mao and Gramsci have been other theoreticians of Marxism.

The ideology of Marxism arose as a reaction against liberalism as liberalism was a reaction against feudalism. Feudalism represented autocratic rule; liberalism advocated liberty. Liberalism though gives freedom, human rights and constitutional government, yet it lands up in inequality, exploitation and alienation. Marxism came as a corrective that advocates equality and a classless and stateless society.

The Marxian theory is based on the concept of historical materialism or the economic interpretation of history. According to this theory, the economic or material factor is the sole guiding force in the history. The modes of production create productive forces i.e. relation between men. Marx said, "The social relations are intimately attached to the productive forces. In acquiring new productive forces, men change their mode of production and in changing their mode of production, their manner of gaining a living, they change all their social relations. The windmill gives you society with the feudal lord; the steam-mill, society with the industrial capitalist.," The relations between. mer, so created by the modes of production are indispensable and independent of their wills and they correspond to a definite state of development and their material forces of production. The sum total of there relations of production constitute the economic structure of society, the foundation on which various super structures are created and state is one of them. The change in the economic structure correspondingly change the super structure. Thus the state is not static; its form changes according to changed environment. Simultaneous changes also occur in other superstructures like religion, ethics morality and culture. Infact the whole social, political, cultural and intellectual life is determined by the modes of production. Marx said "It is not the consciousness of men that determines their existence, but on the contrary, their social existence determines their consciousness." The Marxists regard state and society as distinct realities, the former being dependent on the latter. The type of society dictates the type of state.

The Marxist view of state can be summarized as under;

(i) *State as a class Institution:* The Marxists regard state as a class Institution. State is the product of a class society. There was a historical period of primitive communism when there were no classes and hence no state. Engel writes, "The state ... did not exist from all eternity. There have been societies without it, that had no idea of any state or public power." The classes appeared in the slave-owing society and soon the state appeared. In each succeeding class society that followed the slave-owing society, there was a state. In the socialist society which unlike the slave-owing, feudal and capitalist societies, is a class-less society (in socialism, only the remnants of capitalist society remain) the institution of state in the transitional form of dictatorship of the proletariat would be there, but as all the remains of capitalism are destroyed and as socialism is completed and marches into a communist society, which is classless, the state automatically withers away. State exists with the classes and without the classes, it has no existence.

(ii) *State a man made institution.* The Marxists believe that state is a man made institution created at a particular historical period. State cannot be held as a natural institution; it is an artificial institution. It carne into existence when it was needed in the slave-owning society, which was divided into slaves and slave-owners. The slave owners who owed the means of production exploited the slaves. Lenin says that.... "the fundamental fact is that the slaves were not regarded as human beings—they were not only not regarded as citizens, but not even as human beings." When the exploitation of slave-owners crossed the limits, the slaves revolted. In this struggle between the two, slave-owners being less in number created a number of institutions including the state to keep slaves under their control and perpetuate their exploitation. The state, so created, was not very developed, yet it had the required capacity to coerce slaves into submission. The early states had different forms of government system, ranging from monarchy, autocracy to democracy but their nature was the same. The Marxists believe that man, though, is a social animal by nature, is a political animal by compulsion. He was made to adopt the state. Engel writes: "The state, then, is by no means a power forced on society from outside; 'neither it is the realisation of the ethical idea', the image and the realisation of reason; as Hegel maintains. It is simply a product of society at a certain age of evolution. It is the confession that this society has become hopelessly divided among itself and has entangled itself in irreconciliable contradictions which it is powerless to banish. In order that these contradictions, these classes with conflicting economic interests, may not annihilate themselves and society in a useless struggle, a power becomes necessary that stands apparently above society and has the functions of keeping the conflicts and maintaining 'order'. And this power, the outgrowth of society, but assuming supremacy over it, and becoming more and more divorced from it, is the state."

(iii) *The state belongs* to *economically dominant class:* The Marxists believe that the state is and has been the state of economically dominant class. In the slave owing society, when the state came into existence, it was the state of the master, a class that owned the means of production. Similarly, in the feudal society, the state belonged to the feudal class. In the capitalist society, the capitalist class controls the state and the political machinery. Marx declared, "The executive of the modem state is but a committee for managing the common affairs of the whole bourgeoisie." Engels also said, "Because the state arose from the need to hold class antagonism in check, but because it arose, at the sametime, in the midst of the conflict of these classes, it is, as a rule, the state of the most powerful economically dominant class, which through the medium of state, becomes also the politically dominant class... " He further argues, "The possessing classes ... keep the working people in servitude not only by the might of their wealth, by the simple exploitation of labour by capital but also by the power of the state, by the army, the bureaucracy, the courts."

(iv) *The state is a means.* It is the instrument in the hands of those who control it. "According to Marx", Lenin says, "the state is the organ of class domination, the organ of oppression of one class by another." The government through which the state expresses itself cannot be a creative force, in fact, it is an destructive force through which the ruling class imposes its will upon the subject classes and maintains its privileged position in economic matters. In, such an environment, the objective of state cannot be common good of all. To Marx, the modern state is nothing more than the form of organisation which the bourgeoisie necessarily adopt both for internal and external purposes for the mutual guarantee of their property and interests." Therefore, the concept of democratic government in capitalism is contradiction in terms, as 'democracy cannot exist in any society which is divided into two antagonistic and irreconciliable groups.' Engels also held the same view when he said, "The antique state was ... the state of the slave-owners for the purpose of holding the slaves in check. The feudal state was the organ of the nobility for the oppression of the serfs and dependent farmers. The modern representative state is the tool of the capitalist exploiters of wage labor." It is only in exceptional cases that the state can pose as the mediator between the conflicting classes. The state is always a means and the capitalist state is no exception to it. The highest purpose of the state remains to be the protection of private property. Engels said, "In reality the state is nothing but a machine for the oppression of one class by another and indeed in the democratic republic no less than in monarchy. In the democratic USA, Engels saw two great bands of political speculators who alternately take possession of the state power and exploit with the most corrupt means and for the most corrupt purposes and the nation is impotent against these two great cartels of politicians who are allegedly in its service, but who, in reality dominate and plunder it." The purpose of such a regime is, as Marx said, 'to perpetuate the rule of capital and the slavery of labor,' The repressive functions of state increases with the progress of industry, because it widens and intensifies the class antagonism between capital and labour and the state power assumes the 'character of national power over labor, of a public force organised for social enslavement, of an engine of class despotism,' Even when the state becomes a welfare state, its character does not change. It facilitates and increases the oppression and exploitation of the proletariat by the bourgeoisie. Laski aptly puts it, "The capitalists identify social good with their own preservation. Attack upon them, they will punish as sedition. Education, justice, religions teachings are tempered to serve their interests."

(v) *State-A coercive institution:* The Marxists believe that the basis of state is force and not the will of the people. The idea of state as a coercive institution is significant in Marxian theory for two reasons; Firstly this power of coercion is connected intrinsically with the existence of classes; it is an instrument in the hands of ruling class. Secondly it is the essence of state. In the pre-state times, the whole tribal community constituted self organised and armed population but with the emergence of state, its coercive power got separated from the people. As Engles said, "the state presupposes a public power of coercion separated from the aggregate body of its members." Thus the state and state power become one and the same. Marx said, "The government comprises the tolls of repression, the organs of authority, the army, the police, the officials, the Ministers, the priests". The state power to Marx is "the concentrated and organised force of society." The force does not remain same in all the times; its intensity grow as the class struggle increases. It may be less in societies where class struggle is not much intensive. In modem Europe Engles saw otherwise "where the class struggles and wars of conquest have nursed the public power to such a size that it threatens to swallow the whole society and the state itself." Engles also calls the state as 'a special repressive force' which has a right to levy taxes and contracting public debts, a feature which was unknown in tribal society. The taxes are necessary for the maintenance of coercive power of the state. Engels further asserts, "As civilization makes further progress, these taxes are no longer sufficient to cover public expenses, the state makes drafts on the future, contracts, loans, public debts." Another aspect of coercive aspect of state is the privileged position of the state officials. They stand above the society and get 'respect by exceptional laws which render them specially sacred and inviolable.' A police constable enjoys more power than all the organs of early tribal communities combined.

(vi) *State as a temporary institution.* Since the state arose with the emergence of classes and since it remains class state no matter what its form, it is destined to its doom with the disappearance of classes in the society. The Marxists view state simply as a parasite feeding upon, and dogging the free movement of society, with the abolition of classes this parasite will cease to function. Engels wrote, "We are now rapidly approaching a stage of evolution in production, in which the existence of classes has not only ceased to be a necessity, but becomes a positive fetter on production. Hence, these classes must fall as inevitably as they once arose. The state must irrevocably fall with them. The society that is to reorganise production on the basis of a free and equal association of the producers will transfer the machinery of state where it will then belong, into the Museum of Antiquities by the side of spinning wheel and the bronze axe." The abolition of the state is carried on through three stages. Firstly, the overthrow of the bourgeois state by revolution; secondly the establishment of the dictatorship of the proletariat; and finally the withering away of the proletarian state. Marx wrote, "Between capitalist and communist society lies the period of the revolutionary transformation of the one into other." There corresponds to this also a political transition period in which the state can be nothing but the revolutionary dictatorship of the proletariat. The dictatorship of the proletariat will be as ruthless and oppressive as were the dictatorship of preceding dominant classes. The only difference being where as the earlier dictatorship was aimed at maintaining and promoting class relationships, the dictatorship of the proletariat aims at the destruction of remnants of capitalism in socialism and abolition of classes. By doing so, it prepares the grounds for a communist society where there is an absence of classes and therefore, no exploitation and oppression and hence no need of the state.

(vii) *Functions of modern capitalist state:* According to the Marxists, the state broadly performs two main functions in any society. These are the destructive functions and the constructive functions. Both the functions are performed simultaneously. While on the one hand, the state destroys the old order, it also creates the new order on the other hand. The state in the slave owning society destroyed the old order of the primitive communist society while at the same time it created the new order of the slave-owing society. Similarly it did so when the feudal and capitalist societies came into existence. In socialism also the working class after capturing the power, would abolish the capitalist order and after establishing socialism would create condition for the state to wither away. Following Ralph Miliband, we can safely assume the following four functions of a modern capitalist state:

A. *Repressive functions:* The state through its army, police, judiciary and other instruments repress. In the class struggles of capitalist society, the state is a major participant. It is in one way or another, permanently and pervasively present in the encounter between conflicting classes. It is biased and always involved, even where it is not invoked, if only because it defines the terms on which the encounter occurs by way of legal norms and sanctions.

B. *Economic functions:* State intervention in economic life has always been a decisive feature in the history of capitalism, so much so that, its history cannot begin to be understood without reference to state action. The constantly increasing importance which the state must assume under capitalism was well recognised in classical Marxist writings. Engels wrote, "The modem state, no matter what its form, is essentially a capitalist machine, the state of the capitalists, the idea of personification of the total national capital. The more it proceeds to the taking over of the productive forces, the more does it actually become the national capitalist, the more citizens does it exploit. The workers remain wage-earners—Proletariat. The capitalist relation is not done away with. It is rather brought to a head." The state intervenes in the life of the people under advanced capitalism, and, to a great extent sustains it in a multitude of different ways which cannot all be labelled 'economic'. The state regulates and controls the economic and other functions for the desired ends.

C. *Ideological-Cultural or Persuasive functions:* The state has to maintain its legitimacy. It cannot project itself openly as a class state, therefore, it has to perform certain ideological-cultural or persuasive functions so as to enlist the confidence of the people. In other words this is a function which legalises the system as perfect. The strength of the capitalist system derives from institution like church, family, school and from the communication industry like radio, television, press and other mass media. They are protected by the state as they perform tremendous job of persuading people to blindly accept whatever is fed into their minds.

D. *International Functions:* The international functions of the state is to protect and promote the national interests. The capitalist states have indeed attained a world wide development; expansion has been to a point of creating a world which was never so dose, as it is today. However, the capitalist state serves the interests of the capitalist class : either by going alone or collaboration with other states.

We may sum up the Marxian perspective of modem state, as follows:

a. The economic factor is the sole guiding factor in the development and understanding of history and the modern state.

b. Society and state are two distinct realities, the type of society explains the type of state, the society thus furnishes the basis over which is constructed the superstructure of the state.
c. The state is not independent of society.
d. The state is a means for the fulfilment of the ends of those who control the society. The slave-owing society serves the masters; the feudal state serve's the feudal lords and the capitalist state serves the capitalists.
e. The class society produces a state that serves the economically dominant class -in order to exploit the weaker class.
f. The state thus is an instrument of class oppression and plays dual rule of destruction and recreation in any society.
g. The abolition of private property is necessary for a classless society.
h. The dictatorship of the proletariat is not the abolition of state. The state is used for the welfare of the proletariat and preparation for a classless society.
i. The state withers away in the communist society.

The basis of Marxian perspective of state is historical materialism, which is an inadequate analysis of history. In history changes take place not only because of economic factor but there are also factors like human passions, sentiments, emotions, religion, personality that shape history. Engels later clarified when he wrote, "According to the materialistic conception of history the factor which is in the last instance decisive is the production and reproduction of actual life. More than this neither Marx nor I have ever asserted. But when anyone distorts this so as to read that the economic factor is the sole element, he converts the statement into a meaningless, abstract, absurd phrase." Secondly, Marxian theory of class struggle is not true. It is more a piece of propaganda than the reality. Thirdly state is neither a class institution nor it is a means of perpetuating the class interests, The state belongs to all. It creates conditions in the society in which the individual can develop his personality. The purpose of modern state is to achieve the common good. It reconciliates the divergent interests and thus creates harmony in the society. The failure of the socialist state in Soviet Union and in different parts of the world proves that the Marxian theory of state is untenable to some extent atleast. The concept of a stateless communist society is only a romantic imagination distant from the realities of the world and its development.

V: The Gandhian Perspective

M.K. Gandhi (1869-1948), popularly known as 'Gandhiji' and with respects as 'Mahatma Gandhi', was a human being *par excellence.* He was much more than a name; he was a great *soul.* He was more than the great; the greatest among the greats. His contribution to the world in general and to India in particular was, indeed, unparalleled. To the world, he gave a new strategy, the strategy of *Ahimsa* through which *Satya,* the highest religion, the God incarnated, could be attained. To India, he gave a *mass* organisation, a movement in the name of the Congress, a *Swarajya* which, by the standards of the slave India meant independence for the country, and a direction which could help the people of India, the lowliest included, to build an ideal society as well as an ideal polity in what he termed as 'Ramrajya'.

Gandhiji was an all-in-one sort of man. To describe his one aspect means neglecting all the others. To say that he was a political figure is to conceal much that was in him. He was religious in his convictions; political, by compulsions; a reformer, by temperament.

Among the anarchists, he was an individualist; among the individualists, he was a liberal; among the liberals, he was a socialist; among the socialists, he was a Marxist, among the Marxists, he was a spiritualist. His personality was an embodiment of numerous facets, each incorporated in the other. There is a bit of every 'ism' in him. This is what is reflected in every act that he did and on every phenomenon he chose to ponder, perspective on the state including:

(a) Gandhiji's Distrust of Political Power

Like all anarchists, Gandhiji nurtured a distrust for all types of power, including the political power. Power, by its very nature, is coercive, impulsive and compulsive; it imposes, obstructs, and spies, its existence means the absence of free will, of inner self and all that is eternal in the individual. This is true about political power which is expressed through the state. Echoing almost what an anarchist would say, Gandhiji used to say: "The state represents violence in concentrated and organised form. The individual has a soul, but the state is a soulless machine; it can never weaned from violence to which it owes its very existence." So, for Gandhiji, the state was an instrument of organised violence; the state means the use of violence; the greater it is, there is the use of violence at a larger scale. Gandhi, the anarchist, is obvious when he says: "I look upon an increase in the power of the state with the greatest fear because, although while apparently going good by minimizing exploitation, it does the greatest harm to mankind by destroying individuality, which lies at the root of all progress." Thus, Gandhiji was no admirer of the theory of absolute power of the state.

Like Leo Tolstoy *(The Kingdom of God is Within You),* Gandhiji categorically rejected both the absolute state and the individual property. Like all anarchists, Gandhiji held the view that force tends to degrade those who possess it and those on whom it is excercised. But he was no anarchist who would abolish the institution of the state altogether. Like any anarchist, he was a critic of the state and of property (both exploitive in nature), but he had never advocated anarchy. That is where he departs from the anarchists: He thought, like any individual, that the state, though an oppressive instrument, had utility for the individual; that it was a necessary institution, though evil as well.

(b) The Least State

Like the classical liberals, i.e., the individualists and the New Right advocates of our times, Gandhiji favoured a state with the least functions. He was of the opinion that until society becomes self-regulative and self-evolving and until the individual becomes perfect, the state, so long, would be necessary. Notwithstanding his opposition to the coercive and absolute state, Gandhiji never advocated its abolition lock, stock and barrel. Knowing fully well the limitations of human nature as also the non-realisation of the stateless society in any near future, he permitted the institution of the state as minimum as possible. He fully ascribed to what Thoreau had advocated that the government ought to rule the most minimum. Less are the functions of the state, less would be its powers, but until the time the society does not attain its self-evolving character. What he visualises is the absence of the state coercive apparatus in his *Ram Rajya* until then, the state exists. Paul Power says: "Unlike Tolstoy, Gandhi did not endorse a stateless society for the temporal world... His approach to the ethical nature of the state agrees with Max Weber's view that the state is a technical tool rather than something of intrinsic worth."

Gandhiji was an individualist in another sense as well. The focus of his study was the individual; the state existed for the individual and not the vice versa. He advocated not only a minimum state, he also propounded a maximum individual. He was of the view that all political institutions were means for attaining individual welfare. It is in this sense that Gandhiji was liberal in so far as he respected the personality of the individual and had always valued human liberty. If to be a libertarian means passion for liberty, and individual liberty, Gandhiji was a libertarian.

(c) Gandhiji's Socialism

Gandhiji was not a socialist of either Fabian type or of Marxian one, If socialism means work for all and service for humanity, Gandhiji was a socialist, Obviously, what Gandhiji greatly hated was exploitation of man by either the state or the other man. Gandhiji had often declared himself as the servant of the people, for he believed in the saying that service of man is service of God. His socialism was not the socialism of the workers, but was of the poor, the deprived, the low. Basically, he was a reformer and had entered politics, so to help achieve maximum good of the people. He once wrote: "my work of social reform was in no way less or subordinate to political work. The fact is that when I saw that to a certain extent my social work would be impossible without the help of political work. I took to the latter and only to the extent that it helped the former." Gandhiji's ideal was *Ramrajya,* the rule more for all than of all. In so far as socialism means a state that serves the people, Gandhiji was certainly a socialist. His sarvodaya concept was more than socialism.

(d) Gandhiji's Ramrajya

Gandhiji was close to Marxism in so tar as he propounded a type of society which is stateless in character. Like any Marxist, Gandhiji opposed the institution of the state as an instrument of oppression and exploitation; like any Marxist,. he found all evils in individual property; like any Marxist, he condemned the partisan state; and like any Marxist he visualised in his *Ramrajya* a society without coercion and without force.

But Gandhiji was more than a Marxist. he did not feel content with material advancement. In fact, material progress did not concern him as much as moral progress. By conviction, Gandhiji was a spiritualist, an ethical being and this is where he rose above Marxism. He transformed his views on the individual property into a trusteeship, a concept which ate away all types of exploitation. His concept of Ramrajya was more of a state that would be than the state as it is.

Real Swarajya was not merely the attainment of political freedom, but was much more that. According to him, Swarajya begins from the individual, it is the rule of the self; it is a matter of self-evolution and self-regulation. In the concept of swarajya, power rests with the individual, with the self; such a power flows from bottom to top; it is power that is decentralised. More the power advances up, more does it become decentralised. From the individual to the top the system works itself, without any imposition and without any compulsion. Thus *Ramrajya* is a state without coercion; hence stateless, it is a state without exploitation, hence free.

(e) Conclusion

Gandhiji's perspective of the state was a polity, more moral than physical. He viewed it as an ethical institution, a spiritual institution at that. Gandhiji was not anti-political; in fact, he was immensely political. This was so because politics, for him, was one method of seeking one part of the whole truth. The political activity therefore, for Gandhiji, was an activity that would take people to *Ramrajya.* At heart, he was for an autonomous individual. According to Richards:

"His (Gandhiji's) concern for individual liberty is such that he thinks we should be prepared to die rather than live in slavery and his lifelong struggle for self-government in India seems to bear out his passionate belief in the value and importance of freedom." To quote Gandhiji himself. "We must be content to die if we cannot live as free men and women". Freedom of the individual rather than the absolutism of the state was Gandhiji's essence of political philosophy.

SUGGESTED READINGS

1. Barry, Norman P., *On Classical Liberalism and Liberatarianism* (New York: St. Martins Press, 1987)
2. Bottomore, Tom., *Dictionary of Marxist Philosophy* (Oxford: Basil Blackwell, 1985)
3. Brown, Alan., *Modern Political Philosophy* (London, Penguin, 1986)
4. Callinicos, Alex; (ed) *Marxist Theory* (Oxford: OUP, 1989)
5. Dahl, Robert., *Dilemma of Pluralist Democracy* (New Haven: Yale University Press, 1982)
6. Dunleavy, Patwick and Brendan, O'Leary., *Theories of the State* (London: Macmillan Education, 1987)
7. Dyson, Kenneth, H.F., *The State Tradition in Western Europe* (Oxford: Martin Robertson, 1980).
8. Girvetz, Henry K., *The Evolution of Liberalism* {New York. Collier Books, 1966)
9. Gray, [ohn., *Liberalism* (Oxford: OUP, 1986)
10. Green, David G., *The New Right* (Sussex: Wheatsheaf Books, 1987)
11. Hall, John H., and Ikenberry, G. [ohn., *The State* (Minneapolis: University of Minnesota Press, 1989)
12. Holmer, Leslie, *Withering Away of the State* (London: Sage, 1981)
13. Kothari, Rajni, *State Against Democracy: In Search of Humane Governance* (Delhi: Ajanta, 1988)
14. Mises, L. Von., *Socialism* (Indianapolis: Liberty Classics, 1981; first published in 1921)
15. Parekh, B., *Gandhi's Political Philosophy: A Critical Examination* (Hound mills, Macmillan, 1989)
16. Sarangi, Prakash., *Liberal Theories of State: Contemporary Perspectives* (New Delhi: Sterling, 1996)

9

Liberty

Liberty and its synonym freedom are one of the most discussed concepts in Political Science. Liberty has also been an ideal for which thousands of people have sacrificed their lives. For these people, liberty or freedom has a romantic connotation, to achieve it at any cost and not to surrender it, come what may. Liberty has also been used in the national sense, i.e., national liberty which means to achieve freedom from foreign rule as India achieved on 15th of August 1947. But this chapter does not deal with national freedom, we are only concerned with liberty as a concept.

Historically speaking, liberty is a modern concept. The Greek city states gave liberty only to citizens; the slaves had no liberty. Even the Athenian ideals of liberty had no sympathy for slaves. The famous Greek statesman Pericles said that freedom meant advancement and political activity for full citizen. The Stoics believed that liberty is necessary for the development of individual's personality. Thus the idea of liberty certainly existed in old times but none of them except the Stoics could define it in modern sense. In the medieval times freedom was considered a privilege. It meant an exemption from tax, toll, duty or jurisdiction of a lord. Those so exempted and privileged joined the ranks of the noble and the honourable. In fact, till the end of sixteenth century freedom was synonymous with gentle birth or breeding, nobility, generosity, magnanimity and all the traits which were claimed by the nobles as the reason of their superiority over others. The inauguration of modern age saw the rise of middle class. or capitalist class which invoked the slogan of liberty against the feudal society. John Locke declared that man has a natural right to life, liberty and property. The U.S. Declaration of Independence (1776) viewed life, liberty and pursuit of happiness as inalienable right of man given by the God. The French Declaration of the Rights of Man and Citizen (1789) says that "Men are born and remain free and equal in rights" and that

"The aim of every political association is the preservation of the natural and imprescriptible rights of man. These rights are liberty, property, security and resistance to oppression." It also declared that "liberty consists in the power to do anything that does not injure others; accordingly, the exercise of the natural rights of each man has no limits except those that secure to the other members of society the enjoyment of these same rights. These limits can be determined only by law ... "

I: Meaning of Liberty

There is a tendency to take freedom for granted. This is primarily because a precise and generally acceptable definition of liberty is very difficult. Freedom has been defined in terms of particular political purpose and political ideology. Let us briefly understand some of these interpretation of liberty. Firstly, freedom is defined as social relation or social freedom. As Zygmunt Bauman says, "For one to be free there must be atleast two. Freedom as social relation means social difference and social division. I am free means that there is a form of dependence from which I want to escape." Freedom of movement means that there are people whose movement is not free. If being free means acting without restriction, it implies that actions of some others are constrained. Hobbes said liberty depends on the silence of law; Locke said that 'where there is no law there is no freedom.' Liberty as social relation does not find any inconsistency in both definitions because we are socially free to act in a certain way if there is no law prohibiting, that act and if this is the case then others are unfree to hinder me from doing so. In brief, liberty as social freedom means freedom of one person against others who are unfree to hinder his enjoyment of freedom. Freedom also refers to freedom of choice. Hume defines liberty in this sense. According to him liberty is the power of acting or not acting, according to the determinations of the will. Freedom of choice means there are many alternative actions and the individual is free to choose them. Sometimes freedom refers to free will. Freedom as free will has been advocated by the religious preachers like Pelagins, St. Augustinc, St. Thomas Aquinas and John Calvin. According to them, God has made human beings free and human beings are free to choose between good and bad according to their will. They are free to work towards salvation or doom and they are responsible for their deeds. Freedom has also been interpreted as free actions. It means that freedom consists in voluntary action which is not motivated by fear of punishment. Freedom in this sense also refers to actions which are determined by a man himself without any influence of others. J.S. Mill said, "the only freedom which deserves the name is that of pursuing our own good in our own way". Freedom has also been defined as free persons. Here freedom refers to a characteristic of persons. A person is free to the extent he is able to develop his capacities to the fullest. Freedom here means self realisation, Laski uses liberty in this sense. He says, "By liberty I mean the eager maintenance of that atmosphere in which men have the opportunity to be their best selves." Marx also talked in the similar way when he discussed the communist society "in which the free development of each is the condition for the free development of all". Freedom also means feeling free. It means doing, what one desires. A person feels free to the extent that he does what he wants. Here freedom is the state of mind. It can also be state of affairs. We derive a feeling of freedom when we are free to choose one of the several alternatives. Still there are people who feel free when they escape from freedom and submit themselves to others and act according to their will. Often freedom is identified with a free society. Here freedom is a characteristic of a group. A society in which liberties are evenly distributed is called a free society. This means democracy. Freedom is considered as synonym to democracy. These different interpretations of liberty give a descriptive meaning of it. Liberty also has valuational meanings which means freedom is a value which can be estimated.

Freedom is also defined as protection of basic rights. Classical liberalism advocated this kind of freedom. It believed that a free society is based on *laissez faire*. Individuals have rights and liberties and the individuals who are enjoying such rights are free. The government can restrict a person's freedom only when necessary to protect other person's freedom. This view does not take into consideration the poverty or other factors which hinder the enjoyment of rights. Another interpretation of freedom takes care of this aspect which advocates freedom as satisfaction of basic needs. According to Sidney and Beatrice Webb, "Personal freedom means, in fact, the power of the individual to buy sufficient food, shelter and clothing." This concept of freedom requires restriction on individuals freedom for the common good of the society. It means state regulation concerning public health, education and welfare. Here freedom includes desirable social unfreedom and excludes undesirable social freedom. Freedom is also defined as government by consent. This persuasive definition of freedom says that the government should be representative of the people, who have given their consent to be governed by the government. Rousseau took this argument to another extreme. He said individual may be forced to be free. The individual is free when he obeys the laws reflecting the will of the majority or the "General will." His concept of freedom gives individual no choice but only to act according to the wishes of the authority.

Liberty or freedom means different things to different people. By way of conclusion, some such meanings may be summed up as under:

(i) Freedom means freedom of choice when an individual has to choose between a series of alternatives.

(ii) Freedom means free will, the actual choice of an individual despite or irrespective of available alternatives.

(iii) Freedom means free action, the voluntary actions which an individual performs.

(iv) Freedom means free persons, unslaved, a quality of self-realisation as Marx would like to put.

(v) Freedom means feeling free, when a person does what he desires to do without any hesitation or compulsion.

(vi) Freedom means a free society when the people make their own destiny, independent of any external control.

II: Definitions of Liberty

We have mentioned above some of the definitions of liberty. Other definitions of liberty are as follows:

Liberty consist in 'absence of restraints'. – *Hobbes*

Liberty is 'the opposite of over government.' – *Seeley*

"Freedom consists in a positive power or capacity of doing or enjoying something worth doing or enjoying". – *T.H. Green*

"Liberty is the freedom of individual to express, without external hindrance, his personality." – *G.D.H. Cole*

"Liberty means to secure enjoyment by the individuals and by the association of the power to think their own way under the shelter of the law, provided they do not impair the corresponding rights of others." -*Ramsay Muir*

Liberty is "the absence of restraint upon the existence of those social conditions which in modem civilization are the necessary guarantee of individual happiness" – *Laski*

"Freedom is not the absence of all restraints but rather the substitution of rational ones for irrational". -*McKechnie*

Liberty means, "that the state treats each and every moral person as a free agent, capable of developing his own capacities in his own way and therefore, capable of enjoying and exercising the rights which are the conditions of such development". -*Barker*

A careful study of the above definitions on liberty reveals two concepts of liberty. First is the negative view of liberty which defines it as absence of restraints and the second being a positive conception of liberty which advocates liberty for all. Liberty here is defined as necessary for the development of individual's personality. We shall study both the negative as well as positive concepts of liberty in details. But before that let us study forms of liberty.

III: Forms of Liberty

There are three forms of Liberty:

1. Civil Liberty
2. Political Liberty
3. Economic Liberty

1. *Civil Liberty:* Civil Liberty refers to such liberties which are available to a man in society. *Firstly,* it means right to life. Appadorai aptly puts it, "The most fundamental. of all rights is the right to life, the foundation on which the superstructure of other rights can be built up." Therefore, all the Constitutions recognise this as a fundamental right. The assumption is that man is basic to nature; without him the world has no meaning, therefore, his life is sacrosant. Any attempt to kill any individual or murder is taken very seriously and law provides rigorous punishment in many countries even capital punishment. Man has no right to take away his own life also. Suicide is also a crime and accordingly dealt with by law. *Secondly* is private liberty. Laski says, "By private liberty, ... I mean the opportunity to exercise freedom of choice in those areas of life where the results of my efforts mainly affect me in that isolation by which, atleast ultimately, I am always surrounded". The right to follow one's religion comes under private liberty. There should neither be penalty nor any advantage in following one particular religion. *Thirdly,* individual has a right to privacy. This is the right to be left alone and it means protection from governmental authority or any private individual to intrude into one's home, correspondence, or thoughts. Individual has a right to protect his abode, communications, even his free time from unauthorised intrusion. A major complaint of citizens of socialist countries has been that they are not left alone by the government. *Fourthly,* civil liberty also include freedom of speech and expression, The democratic principle believes that you may not like my views, but I have a right to be heard. This means right to criticise and oppose governmental policies. It also means a free press, which is the most important platform, for the expression of ideas. *Fifthly,* civil liberties

include right to form association. Ii, modem pluralist society, the individual can develop his personality and contribute to the common good through associations only. *Sixthly,* right to assemble peacefully and without arms. *Seventhly,* freedom of movement. In fact a list of civil liberties would be very long and would depend upon specific political conditions in different countries. To Blackstone, civil liberty consists in three articles—personal security, especially of movement; and personal property, or the free use, enjoyment, and disposal of all acquisitions. However, we will still describe one more important type of civil liberty which is right to equality. As we know, equality does not mean complete equality in an egalitarian society; it only means elimination of discrimination based on colour, caste, creed, religion, belief, sex and other factors. We may conclude civil liberty with Barker. According to him, "Civil liberty consists in three differently expressed articles: physical freedom from injury or threat to the life, health and the movement of the body; intellectual freedom for the expression of thought and belief, and practical freedom for the play of will and the exercise of choice in the general field of contractual actions and relations with other person." Civil liberties are generally available to all persons living in the state, irrespective of whether they are the citizens or aliens.

(ii) ***Political Liberty:*** Political liberty is available to man in his capacity as a citizen of the state. To Blackstone, it is a negative liberty which means the power of curbing government. Blackstone viewed government as something external to man, which is not true. As Barker says, "Government is not external; it is in us, or springs from us." Therefore, Laski is correct when he says, "Political liberty means the power to be active in affairs of state." The universal adult franchise stems from this assumption. Right to vote is a valuable right with which people elect their government. Individual also has a right to get elected, subject to limitations imposed by the provision of the constitution. Political liberty also means right to political dissent through peaceful means. It also means that the powers of the government are limited. The government is responsible to the people who are sovereign and are the very source of governmental authority. People have a right to participate in governmental activities and have access to the. positions of authority. People elect their government on the basis of election and control it. As Barker aptly puts it, "by a general and continuous process of discussion, in which we all freely share according to our capacities." Gladstone, therefore, identifies political liberty as synonymous to democracy. According to Laski, two conditions are essential for the political liberty to become real. First is education. "I must be educated to the point where I can express what I want in a way that is intelligible to others." Our education system is defective which trains the children of the rich to habits of authority and the children of the poor, habits of submission. Such a division of attitude can never produce political freedom because 'a class trained to govern will exert its power' (as it is conscious of it) while the other class will 'not fulfil its wants because it does not know how to formulate its demands.' "It is only when men have learned that they themselves make and work institutions that they can learn to adjust them to their needs'." The second condition of a real political liberty is the free flow of information and news. Laski says, "A people without reliable news is, sooner or later, a people without the basis of freedom." Therefore, the mass media, press, radio and television should be free and give impartial and reliable news.

(iii) ***Economic Liberty:*** The whole idea of civil and political liberties become superfluous and futile if they are not accompanied with economic liberty. A poor man can never be a responsible citizen as deprivation makes him incapable of enjoying his liberties. Therefore, individual must be free from poverty. This means that the minimum economic requirements of food, clothing and shelter must be available to all. Right to work must be given to all. Individual should also be entitled to a decent wage. In modem times, in almost all the countries, the governments fix a minimum wage for both the skilled and unskilled workers. This does not mean that there should not be private property. It certainly exists but highly regulated. Economic liberty also does not assume equality of income. It definitely stands for the elimination of wide economic disparities. A state with wide economic disparities becomes two states: of the rich and poor in which stability and democracy will never acquire permanence.

Laski advocates democracy in industry for economic liberty. The' worker cannot be treated like commodity who can be bought and sold in market like coal, tools and chairs. He should have a respectable place in the industry. He must not live at the mercy of capitalists.

He must have a role both in setting up of the standards and application of standards by which his contribution is to be judged. Otherwise he will work only under fear, the fear of being thrown out of job and the resultant starvation. Laski rightly states, "A system built upon fear is always fatal to the release of the creative faculties and it is, therefore, incompatible with liberty." The best course is the worker's participation in the management of industry.

The three forms of liberty may conflict with each other and the experience proves that so is the case. The enjoyment of civil liberty of expression sometimes conflict with the democratic state which in the name of political liberty ban expression on the plea that it might give rise to hostility towards the government or promote hostility between castes or classes. Similarly, the workers demand for more wages restricts the employers freedom of contract. The reservation of seats in legislative assemblies and jobs restrict other's liberties. In some cases political liberty has to rescue economic liberty like in the case of conflict of interest between the employers and employee. In some cases political liberty is to be curtailed for economic liberty. Barker rightly states that liberty is a complex notion, which at once unites men in allegiance and divides them by its division. Here the principle of justice is to be introduced. Liberty should be taken as one of the principles of justice. Justice demand that law should not only reconcile the liberty of one man with that of others, but it should also bring about a reconciliation between different forms of liberty.

IV. The Concept of Negative Liberty

The early liberals advocated the negative concept of liberty. The important thinkers in the category are Hobbes, Locke, Jefferson, Burke, Adam Smith and J.S. Mill. Here we will discuss some of these thinkers.

To Locke, life, liberty and property are the natural rights. They are pre-state as they existed even before the creation of state. The state was created by people because their natural rights were in danger. Therefore, the state and government are subservient to the natural rights. Government is a trust and remains in power till the people's wishes. Locke advocated a limited government and maximum liberties to the people.

Hobbes and Locke belonged to the era of possessive individualism of seventeenth century which comprised of following seven propositions according to Macpherson:

- (i) What makes a mail human is freedom from dependence on the wills of others.
- (ii) Freedom from dependence on others means freedom from any relations with others except those relations which the individual enters voluntarily to further his own interest.
- (iii) The individual is the master of his own person and capacities, for which he owes nothing to society.
- (iv) The individual cannot alienate the whole of his property in his own person, he may alienate his capacity to labour.
- (v) Human society consists of a series of market relations.
- (vi) The freedom of an individual can only be limited to secure the same freedom for others.

(vii) Political society is a human management for the protection of individual's property and, therefore, for the maintenance of orderly relations of exchange between individuals.

Adam Smith advocated a policy of *laissez faire* in which he stood for non-interference of government in economic activity. The market is self-regulative and the law of demand and supply takes care of both the capitalists and the labourers. The worker is at liberty to sell his labour and the capitalists is free in his economic ventures. Thus a free market ensures maximum liberty to both capitalists as well as the workers. The state has no role to interfere and protect the weak. Here liberals advocated the theories of struggle for existence and the survival of the fittest. In nature there is a struggle for existence and in this struggle only the fittest survive, rest perish. In society also there should be struggle for existence in which the fittest will survive. The state has no business to protect the weak and poor who cannot survive the struggle.

The negative view of liberty regards state as a necessary evil. It is an evil because it restraints and all restraints are evils. It is necessary because of the selfishness and rapacity of individual. Without state, there cannot be peace and order in the society and this constitutes state activity. The state should not undertake welfare activities because it is not meant for these purposes. The state should concentrate only on its political functions for which it is created. The functions of state according to liberals are three: (i) maintenance of law and order to protect individual; (ii) to protect society from outside aggression and (iii) to maintain the sanctity of contract between the individuals. Thus the state is a highly limited state, the object being maximum liberty to the individuals. Bentham too favoured an individualist state.

(a) J.S. Mill on Liberty

John Stuart Mill is one of the greatest exponents of negative liberty. He lived at a time when the functions of state were increasing manifold. Mill saw this expansion with suspicion and a threat to the freedom of individuals. The importance of Mill lies in his refusal to compromise with individual's liberty.

According to Mill, individual's activities are divided into two parts—self-regarding and other—regarding. Self-regarding activities are exclusive his concern which do not affect others, while in other-regarding activities individual has to interact with others. In the self-regarding sphere like choosing a career there should not be any control. He says, "In the part which merely concerns himself, his independence is of right, absolute Over himself, over his own body and mind, the individual is sovereign." The individual's liberty cannot be curtailed on the basis of physical and moral goodness. He cannot be compelled to do certain act because it is better for him or it will make him happier or it is wise or even right for him. Individual himself is the sole judge as to what constitutes right or wise or happiness and what is better for him. One may reason with him or persuade him not to do a particular act but he cannot be compelled. Only when his conduct harms others, his liberty can be curtailed. Mill aptly remarks. "That 'the only purpose for which power can be rightfully exercised over any member of a civilized community, against his will, is to prevent harm to others."

The objective of individual in his life is to develop his personality, which is possible only when he has complete freedom in self regarding activities. Any restraint here will hamper the development of individual's personality. Therefore, restraint is evil. However, in other regarding activities, Mill does not mind restraints because liberty is to be enjoyed by each and every person of the society and, therefore, it may be limited and restricted.

Mill also defined the contents of liberty. It comprises *firstly,* the inward domain of consciousness, which means liberty of conscience, thought and feeling, absolute freedom of opinion and sentiments on all subjects practical or speculative, scientific, moral or theological. *Secondly,* the principle of liberty requires liberty of tastes and pursuits; one should be free to plan one's life; of doing all actions as one likes without harming others even if others think that such action is foolish, pervert or wrong. *Thirdly,* freedom of association for any purpose which does not involve harming others.

Mill stands for an absolute liberty of expression. The government has no right to suppress it. He asserts, "If all mankind minus one were of one opinion, mankind would be no more justified in silencing that opinion than he, if he had the power, would be justified in silencing mankind." Mill reminds us of Socrates and Jesus Christ whose freedom of opinions were suppressed. He says, "Mankind can hardly be too often reminded that there was once a man named Socrates between whom and the legal authorities there took place a memorable collision." An opinion is not to be suppressed because it may be voicing truth as was the case with the opinions of Socrates and Christ. If the opinion is right, we lose the opportunity of correcting the false opinion that we hold and if wrong, we lose the benefit of viewing a cleverer perception and livelier impression of truth produced by its collusion with a wrong opinion. Mill further says, "Those who want to suppress it, of course, deny its truth; but they are not infallible. They have no authority to decide the question for all mankind and exclude every other person from the means of judging, To refuse a hearing to an opinion because they are sure that it is false is to assume that their certainty is the something as absolute certainty. All silencing of discussion is an assumption of infallibility."

Mill is also aware of tyranny of majority and society. Though he favours democracy, he is also very clear that the majority may become as tyrannical as the despotic rulers and tyrants were in the past. Liberty may be threatened by the exercise of powers by the majority. Therefore government's powers in a democracy should also be limited for the sake of liberty. He says, "The people who exercise power in a self-soverning state are not always the same people with those over whom it is exercised... The limitation, therefore, of the power of government over individuals loses none of its importance when the holders of power are regularly accountable to the community...." In political speculations, the tyranny of the majority is now generally included among the evils against which society requires to be on its guard.' Liberty is to be protected not only from the tyranny of majority but also from that of the society. Society tries to impose its own ideas and practices on individual. It restricts those who do not obey the social order. The objective is "to fetter the development and, if possible, prevent the formation of any individuality not in harmony with its ways, and compel all characters to fashion themselves upon the model of its own." Mill stands for the autonomy of individual, who is not responsible or his actions to the society, so far his self-regarding actions are concerned. Individual is to be given a free atmosphere to develop his different faculties.

Mill also advocates certain limitations on individual's liberty. We have already mentioned the first limitation i.e. liberty is subjected to the condition of not harming others. In case of self regarding functions also in some circumstances, the liberty may be curtailed. Nobody can be allowed to commit suicide. Individual can be prevented from consuming poisonous food. Secondly, Mill justifies these interventions because in such cases, individual does not know his interest well while the society knows it better. Thirdly, the children are exempted from the enjoyment of liberty because liberty is available only to human beings in the maturity of their faculties'. Fourthly the backward people or races cannot have liberty. Mill advocated a despotic government for them. Needless to say that this is the objectionable assumption liable to be used by imperialism to justify despotic rule over the colonies.

(b) Negative Liberty and Modern Libertarians

In modern times, the concept of negative freedom has been propagated by many writers from the West. They defend liberty as the absence of restraints. Among its forceful advocates are Isaiah Berlin, Rawls, Pennock and Milton Friedman.

According to Berlin, liberty counts in doing what one desires to do without interference from other persons. He says, "You lack political liberty or freedom only if you are prevented from attaining a goal by human beings. Mere incapacity to attain a goal is not lack of political freedom." Thus there is no lack of liberty, if a person is not able to use his rights because of poverty or ignorance. On the contrary, Berlin says there is an absolute loss of liberty if my liberty rests on some one's misery and my liberty is curtailed to relieve him of his misery and there is no increase in other person's liberty. The relief of misery cannot be termed as increase in liberty. According to Berlin, the concept of negative liberty has historically, justified tyranny, in which state stands outside the actual individual human being and that is dangerous. He says, "I wish my life and decisions to depend on myself, not on external forces of whatever kind. I wish to be the instrument of my own, not of other men's acts of will." Berlin's definition of a free man is of a man who is not in irons, not imprisoned in a jail nor terrorised like a slave by the fear of punishment; it is not lack of freedom not to fly like an eagle or swim like a whale. Freedom means non-interference by others. "The wider the area of non-interference, the wider my freedom." Says Berlin.

Berlin sees no particular connection between negative liberty and democracy. An individual may have more negative liberty under an easy-going despot than in an intolerant democracy. Berlin, here, is reminding us of Mill's views on the tyranny of majority. The sovereignty of the people can destroy the sovereignty of the individual because democracy does not guarantee a minimal individual liberty. It does not involve any logical commitment to 'some frontiers of freedom which nobody should be- permitted to cross.' Berlin believes in the autonomy of individuals and "if the essence of men is that they are autonomous being ... then nothing is worse than to treat them as if they were not autonomous, but natural objects." The reformers do exactly that. They treat the men as objects who have no wills of their own. Thus they degrade men. Berlin also finds no relation between liberty and the conditions required for the realisation of liberty. When we try to create necessary socio-economic conditions of real freedom, we forget freedom itself. In fact absence of necessary socio-economic conditions for the realisation of liberty does not mean absence of liberty. Liberty is present even there, where there is no justice and equality.

Lastly it is to be remembered that Berlin stands for what Graham Wallas calls two spheres view of liberty. It means man's life can be divided into two spheres; in one sphere man should be completely free, where there should not be any control or coercion. There is still the second sphere where control and interference in man's life is necessary. The liberty may be curtailed here. Berlin in fact is advocating Mill's division of man's actions—self-regarding and other regarding. Like Mill, the negative liberty is available in self regarding activities of an individual, while restraints may be necessary in other regarding activities, so that the others are not harmed.

Rawls and Pennock have followed Berlin in their conceptions of liberty. Pennock says, "Liberty is the opportunity for spontaneous and deliberate self-direction in the formation and accomplishment of one's purposes." Opportunity, to Pennock, means 'the absence of external control of threats, physical impediments or moral or legal obligations.' Therefore if I am not able to enjoy liberty because of social circumstances, it does not mean absence of liberty. Rawls is more concerned with the relative value of different liberties. He is not concerned with negative or positive liberty. Like Berlin and Pennock, he also refuses to count poverty or social reasons as factors restraining liberty. They do affect the worth of liberty, its value to an individual but do not determine whether that individual has liberty. Rawls bases his argument on the basis of twin principles of justice. The first principle is that everyone is to enjoy the most extensive liberty which is to co-exist with similar liberty for others and secondly that socio-economic inequalities must work to everyone's advantage. These two principles divide the society into two spheres-the political sphere, as a citizen where liberty is inviolable and equal, and socio-economic sphere where considerable inequality may prevail.

Milton Friedman also supports the concept of negative liberty. Liberty means, according to Friedman, "the absence of coercion of a man by his fellowmen." Further he asserts, 'Freedom .... has nothing to say about what an individual does with his freedom; it is not all embracing ethic.' To Friedman-economic freedom is a necessary condition of political freedom. He praises competitive capitalism, which alone can guarantee civil liberties. The restrictions on economic freedom constraints political freedom because they are not wholly distinct. Decisions made in one also affects the other. Friedman advocates free economy; there should not be any constraint in the operation of free market and state should not undertake pension schemes and exchange control. To Friedman, capitalism is a necessary condition for political freedom and only times when there were no tyranny, servitude and misery were the times of free market economies like in Athens and early Roman period and in certain nineteenth and, twentieth century societies. The operations of a free market economy disperse the concentration of political power. He is against positive view of liberty because it does not accept a free market society. He is also against socialist state on the same ground. He criticises the concept of democratic socialism because any form of socialism is incompatible with individual liberty. Friedman says, "A society which is socialist cannot also be democratic in the sense of guaranteeing individual freedom."

The modem libertarians advocate freedom of speech, assembly and association and liberty of thought and conscience very vehemently. These liberties should be protected from the interference by other individuals through political or legal provisions. Thus modern libertarians regard. civil liberties as sacrosant. But why civil liberties be given more importance than other socio-economic rights? Modem libertarians have advanced three arguments in this respect.

1. The civil liberties are basic. They are key to other liberties. If they are lost, others will also be unsecured.
2. These civil liberties do not harm others who also enjoy the same liberties. Thus they can be widely distributed among the people.
3. The civil liberties are connected with rationality. Men make decisions and it is not necessary that every decision may be right. Therefore we should be open to criticisms. Hence freedom to express one's views and criticise those of others is absolutely necessary.

The concept of negative liberty can be summed up in following points:

(i) Liberty means absence of restraints.
(ii) Liberty is necessary for the development of individuals' personality.
(iii) Man's activity can be divided into two spheres—self regarding and other regarding. In self-regarding activity, man should be given full freedom, which include freedom to expression, and thought, to assemble and to form association.
(iv) The state should have a very limited function, as it is a necessary evil.
(v) Liberty is to be protected from the tyranny 'of majority.
(vi) Political and civil liberties are to be protected at any cost. They cannot be sacrificed in the name of equality and justice.
(vii) Mere incapacity to use liberty does not mean absence of liberty.

(c) Criticism

The concept of negative liberty was in vogue in eighteen in eighteenth and first half of nineteenth centuries in England and other parts of the Europe. There is no doubt that it brought prosperity in the society.

However, very shortly its ill effects were also noticed. The concept of negative liberty furthered the liberties of propertied class at the expense of the liberties of the weak, who virtually became slaves. Macpherson aptly states that a formulation of negative liberty which takes little or no account of class-imposed impediments, deliberate or unintentional, is not entirely adequate. Secondly, Mill's division of human activities into two—self regarding and other regarding, is questionable. Human activities cannot be divided in such a manner. Mill himself put drinking and gambling in self-regarding activity of a man. But a little understanding of effects of drinking and gambling will make it other-regarding activity. A worker wastes his money in drinking and gambling. Consequently, he cannot look after his family and children who live a life of misery and poverty. Besides there are other social effects of drinking and gambling like crime. Thus, all talks of self-regarding activities are but nonsense. This mistake has also been committed by Berlin, Pennock and Rawls. Mill (and his followers) as Barker puts it, separate the inseparable. "The conduct of any man is a single whole; there can be nothing in it that concerns himself only, and does not concern other man; whatever he is, and whatever he does, affects others and, therefore, concerns him". Therefore, Barker calls Mill as the prophet of an empty liberty and an abstract individual. Same is true of ,concept of negative liberty as advocated by modern libertarians.

V: The Concept of Positive Liberty

Historically speaking, the concept of positive liberty emerged as a reaction to excesses committed by the concept of negative liberty. It was realised that the negative liberty which defined liberty as absence of restraints led to a social situation in which only a few were able to enjoy it while the majority in a cesspool of misery and deprivation had no relations with liberty. The later half of the nineteenth century saw the end of negative liberty and a new era of positive liberty was heralded. T.H. Green, Bosanquet, Barker and Laski are the principle architects of positive liberty. Here we shall study some of them.

(a) Views of Green

According to T.H. Green, positive freedom means, "a positive power or capacity of doing or enjoying something worth doing or enjoying, and that, too, something that we do or enjoy in common with other". It means that freedom possesses two qualities. Firstly, it is the freedom. to do or enjoy what is worth doing or enjoying along with others. Freedom is to be enjoyed not in isolation but in common with others. To

Green 'it is the liberation of all the powers of man for the social good.' It means a power of the individual by which he has a share in the goods that society produces and an ability to contribute in the common good. Secondly, freedom is determinate or definite. Freedom is not licence, to do anything as one wishes. On the contrary it is the power to pursue those objects which make our lives better. It is the quality of doing what is worth-doing. To Green, freedom means self-perfection which a man does by contributing to the welfare of social whole. It is a moral freedom.

Green is highly critical of the policy of *laissez faire* and its effects on the social system. Real freedom cannot exist where there is ignorance, poverty and moral depravity. He said, "To an Athenian slave who might be used to gratify a master's lust, it would have been a mockery to speak of the state as the realisation of freedom; and perhaps it would not be much less so to speak of it as such to an untaught and underfed citizen of a London yard, with gin shops on the right hand and on the left." In other place, he says, "If the ideal of true freedom is the maximum of power for all members of a human society alike to make the best of themselves, we are rightful in refusing to ascribe the glory of freedom to a state in which the apparent elevation of the few is founded upon the degradation of the many, and in ranking modem society, founded as it is on free industry with all its confusion and ignorant license and waste of effort above the most splendid of ancient republics." Thus Green's effort is, in the words of Barker, to reintegrate the individual into those socially created values which the unhistorical Benthamites had ignored." He demonstrated that, if the source of all spiritual values is the individual, the individual should be considered in his universality that is, in those aspects that join him to other individuals.

The object of state, according to Green, is to remove hindrances to freedom. Here he emphasises a wide role for state. Ignorance, drinking and poverty are hindrances to good life and he wants state to remove these evils. He also advocates state action in housing and labour welfare. He, in fact, wants all the hindrances to good life be removed by state action. Yet the state remains a negative state, whose functions are limited. Wayper says, "The negative form in which Green speaks of state is nevertheless significant. It is a reminder that in the final analysis what matters most in life must remain within the province of the individual-the development of his moral nature." Green belongs to the idealist tradition which regards state as a natural institution necessary for the moral realisation of the individual. The state creates conditions necessary for good life.' But it cannot be an absolute state.

(b) Views of Laski on Positive Liberty

Defining liberty Laski says, "By liberty I mean the eager maintenance of that atmosphere in which men have the opportunity to be their best selves. Liberty; therefore, is a product of rights. Without rights there cannot be liberty, because without rights, men are the subjects of law unrelated to the needs of personality." To Laski, liberty is a positive thing. It is not just absence of restraint. It means certain action or conduct of individual can be prohibited in common interest .and such prohibition do not constitute an invasion of liberty. Thus liberty is not in danger if some one is refused permission to commit murder or if some one is asked to obey traffic rules. But the problem is that sometimes the government claims that it is acting on common interest and invades liberty. No prohibition is justified just because government has made it. For example, the restriction of the franchise to the owners of property was an invasion of liberty. Laski wants that all the prohibitions imposed by the state 'should be built upon the wills of those whom they affect.' To Laski, all such restraints are evil which stop a person doing something which he thinks worthwhile to do. Similarly, we have a life of spiritual enrichment and any restraint is evil when it frustrates such life. We also have a right to personal initiative in the things that add to our moral stature and this cannot be restrained. Laski wants liberty of thought, expression, will and conscience.

Laski does not agree with Mill's division of human action into two spheres-self regarding and other regarding. He says, "All conduct is social conduct in the sense that whatever I do has results upon me as a member of society." Liberty involves, in its nature, restraints. One cannot enjoy liberty at the expense of other's liberty.

To Laski, liberty means presence of opportunity. We can create channels; we cannot force men to take advantage of those channels. Laski cites an example to prove his point, "A man may feel that all that he cares for in life depends upon success in love; we can remove the barriers of caste or race or religion which, in the past, have barred his access to that love. But we cannot guarantee to him that his plea will be successful."

Laski has discussed three aspects of liberty-private, political and economic. These rights we have covered in forms of liberty in this chapter.

According to Laski there are three conditions of liberty without which it cannot be secured for the general masses. They are as follows:

i. *Absence of special privileges – The* presence of special privileges lead to frustration and kill the habit of creativeness. They give a life of deprivation to those who do not possess special privileges. They lose the ability to realise their own good. Laski declares, "Special privilege is incompatible with freedom because the latter quality belongs to all alike in their character as human beings." The common good can only begin by the abolition of special privileges.

ii. *Universality of rights – Laski* says that there cannot be liberty, where the rights of some depend upon the pleasure of others. Here he advocates state control for the protection of political and economic freedom. My rights as a citizen should not be encroached upon. Similarly he wants state regulation in the distribution of wealth, in matters of livelihood and other welfare measures.

iii. *The state should be impartial-State* action should be aimed at securing benefits to all. However, it is very difficult because state is compelled to support the interest of a small section. Therefore, we must try to seek that system which will minimise the bias involved. Rights are, therefore, important because they are the guarantee of a minimum bias. A citizen today should guard the rights of man and must react whenever he sees that the state is acting in a biased manner for the secret of liberty is courage.

However, later on Laski changed his views. In his preface to the second edition of *A Grammar of Politics* he says; "In 1925 I thought that liberty could most usefully be regarded as more than a negative thing. I am now convinced that this was a mistake and that the old view of it as an absence of restraint can alone safeguard the personality of the citizen."

The concept of positive liberty can be summed up as follows:

i. Liberty is not merely absence of restraints. It is more than that.
ii. Liberty includes private, political and economic liberty.
iii. Liberty cannot be realised where there is existence of special privileges, where there is no equality of rights and when state action is biased.
iv. Rights are necessary for liberty.
v. The state activity should be extended to include welfare of the individuals. For the purpose, individual liberty may be curtailed.

VI: The Marxist Concept of Freedom

In order to understand Marxian view of freedom it is necessary to know Marx's views on man and his essence. Marx refuses to accept liberal view of atomistic man. An isolated self-seeking man to Marx is a fiction. Man is intrinsically connected with other fellow-beings. Human essence is the totality of social relations. Therefore, man's purpose is not to seek his self interest. Man, in Marxism, is defined by his capacity to work and is distinguished from other creatures by his ability to produce freely. Man is a creator and has the ability to enjoy his creation. Being social, his creative activities are directed not only for himself, but for the development of all the members of the society. Man can thus be understood in terms of human values of love, sympathy, art, culture, music, games, literature, knowledge of philosophy and sciences.

Freedom follows from such a comprehensive understanding of man and his essence. Marxism has no intention of getting involved in the liberal's understanding of liberty in terms of negative and positive freedom. The Marxists take freedom in a wider context. Freedom means living life to the fullest. Not only individual's minimum economic requirements are to be realised, but he should also be able to cultivate human values and be creative and develop his personality. Petrosyan rightly remarks, "Marx's understanding of freedom implies activity aimed at creating real conditions for the free all-round development and flowering of man's individuality. " True freedom can be found only in a free society. The problem is that the free society does not exist in a class-divided society. It only existed in primitive communism, where there was no private property. With the origins of private property, a class. divided society came into being, which is still continuing. Marx wants to eliminate the root cause of class-divisions which is private property. Only with the elimination of private property, classes will disappear and a free society will emerge in the form of communism, where the individual will really be free. A detailed analysis of Marxist notion of freedom can be done under following heads:

(i) Freedom as recognition of necessity
(ii) Freedom as social action
(iii) Freedom in a capitalist society
(iv) Freedom in a socialist society
(v) Freedom in communist society

(i) *Freedom as recognition of necessity:* According to Marxists, man is governed by certain objective laws which he does not create. They emerge independent of his wilL Freedom consists in understanding these laws and using them for his benefits. That is what Engels means when he says "Freedom is the recognition of necessity." These objective laws consists of two types—one works at the level of nature like laws of gravitation and the other being the laws of social development. The objective laws of nature are determined by the nature itself while the objective laws of society are determined by the means of production. In both cases man can not change them. But he can study them and in their study he is free. Initially when man came on to this earth, he was highly ignorant. He was a slave of the nature. Slowly he learnt many things about the nature and used them to his benefit and became free to that extent. Engels writes, "Freedom does not consist in an imaginary independence from natural laws, but in the knowledge of these laws and in the possibility which is thus given of systematically making them work towards definite ends ... Freedom of wills, therefore, means nothing but the capacity to make decisions with knowledge of the facts ... Freedom therefore consists in command over ourselves and over external nature, a command founded on knowledge of natural necessity; It is therefore, necessarily a product of historical development. The first men who separated themselves from the animal kingdom were in all essentials as unfree as the animals themselves but each step forward in the field of culture was a step towards freedom." By understanding of the objective laws, man becomes the master of nature and society ana gets benefits out of them. Thus by understanding rules of water, one swims in a river or by understanding the rules of air one flies in a plane or by understanding the natural cycle of rains, the farmer organises his agricultural activities. Similarly man has to understand the social laws of development which will make him clear that the property creates classes which are antagonistic to each other; a class divided society only results in exploitation and obviously where there is exploitation there can be no freedom. These conclusions are based on objective laws of society which cannot be changed by man. In this context freedom lies in understanding these objective laws and use them to benefit us. Marx declared, "The true realm of freedom ... can blossom forth only with this realm of necessity as its basis."

(ii) *Freedom as social Action:* The existence of objective laws which are free from man's control does not mean that there is no role for man. Marx declared, "Man makes his own history, but he does not make it out of the whole; he does not make it out of conditions chosen by himself, but out of such as he finds close at hand." Philosophers have only interpreted the world, but the point is to change it. The freedom comes when man after understanding the objective laws involves himself in revolutionary activity. There is no doubt that the ultimate cause of revolution is the conflict between forces of production and relations of production, a conflict which is outside of human will. But once this conflict emerges it creates man's consciousness of it and also the will to revolt. The human will is the immediate cause of revolution. Engels said, "Freedom of the will consists in nothing but the ability to come to a decision when one is in possession of a knowledge of facts." Antonio Labrida declared that volitions are a result of necessities. To Marx, revolutionary activity itself constitutes freedom because as Cornforth puts it. "A passive slave is simply a slave but slave in revolt is acting as a freeman even though he still wears his chains. Such people are pioneers of human freedom" Man is not merely a slave in the hands of material circumstances, he can also alter them.

(iii) *Freedom in a capitalist society:* In a class-divided society freedom is always a relative concept. it means different things to different classes. In a capitalist society freedom to capitalists means freedom to exploit the workers, while workers starve. Freedom to them means freedom to be exploited. In fact, in the capitalist society freedom is limited to a small section of population while the majority is always unfree. However in another significant manner neither the worker nor the capitalists are free. This Marx explained in his theory of alienation. To Marx human essence lies in the pursuit of human values. Man is a creator and wants to enjoy his creation, but in capitalist society he cannot do so because he is suffering from alienation. According to Marx the roots of alienation lies in the private ownership of means of production, where the profit motive dominates. The capitalist becomes a machine whose purpose is to make more and more money. M o n e y , a dead thing, dominates the living thing. The capitalist feels alienated from the production. The workers also suffered from alienation. Marx writes, "The bourgeoisie .... has converted the physician, the lawyer, the priest, the poet, the man of science into its paid wage labourers. It is tom away from the family its sentimental veil, and has reduced the family relation to a mere money relation .... The labourers must sell themselves piecemeal, have been reduced to mere commodity, like any other article of commerce ... Owing to extensive use of machinery ... the worker becomes an appendage of the machine. Not only the workers are the slaves of the bourgeois class, and of the bourgeois state; they are daily and heavily enslaved by the machine, by the individual bourgeois manufacturer himself." Marx finds man's alienation in capitalist society in four ways—(a) from his product, (b) from nature; (c) from his species and (d) from himself. A detailed study of Marx's theory of alienation has been made in the Marxist concept of property. An alienated being cannot be free. Hence, Marx advocates elimination of private property.

(iv) *Freedom in a socialist society:* Socialist society is, to Marx, the first phase of communism. Trotsky termed it as the most ruthless form of state. It is also called the dictatorship of the proletariat. Lenin said, "The purpose of the dictatorship is to establish socialism, to put an end to the division of society into classes, to make all the members of society workers, to make the exploitation of one human being by another for ever impossible. This end cannot be achieved at one stride ... The reorganisation of production is a difficult matter. Time is requisite for the radical transformation of all departments of life." Lenin claimed that dictatorship of the proletariat is better than the bourgeois democracy because here the majority rules over the minority. The workers are free while the remnants of capitalism are unfree, All the means of productions are nationalised and become government property. But what about the freedom? Marx and Engels viewed socialism as a transitory phase and they did not give much thought to freedom. Moreover socialism was not achieved in any state during their life time. However the experiences of socialist states in twentieth century proved that the political system provided political, social and economic rights but it could not provide freedom. The political rights were available for only those who were the yes-men of the regime. The people always felt the loss of freedom. The economic performance was also less than satisfactory. This all led to the death of these socialist states with the exception of Cuba and China.

(v) *Freedom in a communist society:* According to the Marxists, the communist society will be a free society where man will be able to develop his personality in all its multi-dimensional form. The production will be for consumption and not for profit. The state shall wither away and the society will be a vast association for production and all work will be performed as a habit. There will be no landowners, no capitalists, no wage workers but only human beings. Classes will disappear as there will not be private property. Thus there will be no exploitation, no oppression and no alienation. The communist society will be characterised by abundance of wealth, where each will contribute according to his ability and will receive according to his needs. Engels said, "On the one hand, no single individual will be able to shift his share in productive labour, in providing the essentials of human existence, upon another, and on the other hand productive labour instead of being a means of slavery will be a means towards human freedom, in that it offers an opportunity to everyone to develop his full powers, physical and intellectual, in every direction and to exercise them so that it makes a pleasure out of a burden." This is a society, as Marx prophesied, "in which the free development of each is the condition for the free development of all." Man will be able to develop both as a person and as an individual. The human energy, which hitherto was being wasted in class struggle, will be devoted to social purposes. Man will really become creative and will enjoy his creation. Engels asserts, "Then for the first time, man, in a certain sense, is finally marked off from the rest of the animal kingdom, and emerges from mere animal conditions of existence into really human ones. The whole sphere of the conditions of life which environ, and which have hitherto ruled man, now comes under the domination and control of man, who for the first time becomes the real conscious lord of Nature, because he has now become master of his own social organisation. The laws of his own social action, hitherto standing face to face with man as laws of nature foreign to, and dominating him, will then be used with full understanding, and so mastered by man. Man's own social organisation, hitherto confronting him as a necessity imposed by Nature and history, now become the result of his own free action. The extraneous objective forces that have hitherto governed history, pass under the control of man himself. Only from that time will man himself, more and more consciously, make his own history—only from that time will the social causes set in movement by him have, in the main, and in a constant growing measure, the results intended by him. It is the ascent of man from the kingdom of necessity to the kingdom of freedom." It is this freedom of man which is the objective of Marxian ideology.

The main points of Marxian view of freedom is as follows:

(i) Freedom is a comprehensive concept which is to be seen in-terms of man's essence, purpose and values.

(ii) Freedom means all around development of human personality.

(iii) Freedom means the understanding of objective laws of Nature and society and to use them for man's benefits.

(iv) Freedom also means involving oneself in revolutionary activity.

(v) In a class-divided society, freedom is impossible. Freedom cannot exist where there is exploitation, oppression and alienation.

(vi) Elimination of private property is necessary for the achievement of freedom.

(v) Freedom does not exist in a socialist society.

(vi) Freedom can only exist in a communist society.

VII: Safeguards of Liberty

Liberty is the condition for any civilized existence. Without liberty, the individual loses his potentiality. to development his personality. Therefore liberty has a sacrosanct value which is to be protected at any cost. The government, social and individual attitudes are some of the factors which may encroach upon and limit liberty. Hence the question before us is-how to protect liberty from various encroachments? Following are some of the safeguards of liberty:

(i) *Rule of Law* – As we have seen earlier that the early liberals believed that state is a necessary evil because it restrains and every restraint, constitutes a limitation upon liberty. Anarchists dismiss state as an unnecessary evil. According to them all laws are bad and, a free people and a free society can only exist when all the laws are abolished. But these views are negative and cannot be accepted. Liberty cannot be a licence to do anything. If liberty becomes synonymous with licence then the law of jungle will prevail in the society where crude physical force, deceit and fraud will rule the social order. In such a situation, 'there can not be liberty, only chaos and confusion will be the characteristics of human organisation. Montesquieu rightly suggested that it is principally by the nature and preparation of punishments imposed by law that liberty is established or destroyed. The purpose of law is to put restraints on one person's liberty so that others can also enjoy liberty. There cannot be absolute liberty, only a limited liberty. The limitations imposed should be for a fair social order in which each and every person is allowed to develop his faculties.

(ii) *Democracy* – The only system that can guarantee a free and fair opportunity to develop individual's personality is democracy. Lincoln rightly defined democracy as a government by the people, of the people and for the people. It is the people's welfare which is supreme because people are sovereign. A rule by dictator or a monarch gives freedom only to a person and his henchmen. Oligarchy gives freedom to a particular section of the people. Only in democracy the entire population enjoys the high principles of liberty. No doubt, democracy has loopholes. There cannot be perfect democracy but then the human beings are also imperfect. Perfections is an ideal which cannot be accomplished in the imperfect world. Given the imperfect world, democracy is the most perfect system of government, which has no alternative. This does not follow that democracy does not need any safeguards for liberty. In democracy also there are innumerable dangers to liberty which must be checked.

(iii) *Independent Judiciary*—The independence of judiciary is absolutely necessary for the protection of liberty. The judges must be free from the executive control because they have to protect individual's liberty from any invasion caused not only from other individuals but also from the government. Therefore they have to act fearless and impartial. This means only person of high integrity should be appointed as judges. Their salaries should be protected by adequate constitutional provision. Their dismissal and terms of office should be subjected to extreme care. Therefore all the democratic constitutions provide a cumbersome procedure for their removal. In India judges of Supreme Court and High Courts can be removed only on the grounds of proven misbehaviour or incapacity by a special majority of both the Houses of the Parliament. Similar provisions we find in U.S.A. and other countries. J. Kent rightly says, "To give the judges the courage and the firmness to do their duty fearlessly, they ought to be confident of the security of their salaries and station."

(iv) *A bill of rights*—A bill of rights is also essential for the safeguard of liberty. A detailed and written bill of rights helps citizens in understanding their rights. It also puts specific limitations on governmental authority. In U.S.A., individual's rights were incorporated through constitutional amendment. The Indian Constitution also provides a detailed list of fundamental rights of the citizens. These rights can be modified only by a special procedure provided in the constitution.

(v) *A democratic social order*—Dne of the important safeguards of liberty is a democratic social order. It means that democracy should prevail ill society as well. It means existence of the attitude of tolerance and a fellow feeling for each other. It means that every person has a dignity which has to be respected. A society divided in terms of class and caste prohibit the development of such conditions as are necessary for the enjoyment of liberty. There should not be any discrimination on the basis of caste, class, creed, religion or sex. Similarly, liberty cannot be enjoyed in a society which has, widespread economic disparities. The minimum economic requirements of food, cloth and shelter should be, available to every person in the society.

(vi) *Vigilance* – Eternal vigilance is the price of liberty. One can be free only when he wants to be free and is ready to pay price for it. The people should protect their liberties. They should carefully watch the programmes and action of government and voice their protest whenever they feel their liberties being threatened. The existence of such a people will deter a government from undue interference in liberty.

Conclusion

Liberty, it may be noted, is the essence of democratic life. Both the liberals and the Marxists lay emphasis on the importance of man's life: the liberals, limiting it to the individual's political life; the Marxists, extending it to the entire universe: individual, society, nature. Nevertheless, liberty constitutes an important ideal worth cherishing. Its quality lies in strengthening democratic polity, and man's endeavour to lead a rich life.

SUGGESTED READINGS

1. Adler, Mortimer J., *The Idea of Freedom,* 2 vols (Garden City, N.Y. Doubleday, 1958-61)
2. Bay, C, *The Structure of Freedom* (Stanford, California: California University Press, 1958)
3. Berlin I, *Two Concepts of Liberty* (Oxford: OUP, 1988)
   ________*Four Essays on Liberty,* (Oxford OUP 1969).
4. Cranston, Maurice, *Freedom: A New Analysis* (London: Longmans, 2nd Edition, 1955)
5. Friedrick, Carl J., (ed.) *Liberty* (New York: Atherton, 1962)
6. Laski, Herald J., *Liberty in the Modern State.* (London, George Allen & Unwin Ltd.)
   ________"Liberty" in *Enclopaedia of Social Services,* Vol 9, (New York: Macmillan, 1933)
7. Mill, J.5., *On Liberty* (London, Watt & Co, 1948).
8. Marx, Karl, *Economic and Philosophic Mansucripts of* 1844 (Moscow: Progress Publisher, 1970).
9. Muller; Herbart J., *Issues of Freedom: Paradoxes and Promises* (New York: Harper, 1960).
10. Oppenheim, Felix E., *Dimensions of Freedom:* All *Analysis* (New York: St. Martins, 1961)

10

Equality

The U.S. Declaration of Independence declares, "We hold these Truths to be self-evident, that all men are created equal." The French Declaration of the Rights of Man and Citizen explicitly recognised that men are born and remain free and equal in rights. Article 1 of the Universal Declaration of Human Rights also accepts that 'all human beings are born free and equal in dignity and rights.' The Preamble of the Indian Constitution talks about equality of status and opportunity. The concept of equality is a fundamental basis of modem democratic state.

However, it is very difficult to define equality. Laski aptly puts it, "No idea is more difficult in the whole realm of political science." The concept of equality has such varied facets and a multitude of implications, that even after an exhaustive study on the subject, one really feels of not having mastered it. Let us understand the various meanings of equality.

I: Meaning of Equality

An important difficulty in understanding equality stems from the fact that the nature has created man as unequal. This inequality can. be very obviously observed in terms of physical and intellectual strength, capacity and beauty. The human society has further accelerated inequality including caste, colour, creed, property sex and many other factors. Appadorai, therefore says, "The statement that all men are equal is, then, as erroneous as that the surface of the earth is level." Burke condemns equality as a monstrous fiction', Coleridge as a infeasible proposition', Bentham as 'an anarchic fallacy' and Carlyle as a 'palpable incredibility and delirious absurdity.' Still we talk of equality of men and it constitutes the foundation of modern democracy.

Equality is sometimes referred to as equality of characteristics in men. The obvious inequality among men in terms of intellectual and physical strength, sex, colour, character traits, natural endowments, religion, age, social rank, property and other factors do exist. But the task is to identify certain properties that are similar in men. The men are equal means that men share certain qualities which must be specified. Hobbes said that the nature has made men so equal, in the faculties of the body and mind that even the weakest can kill the strongest and no one can outwit the other. He postulated two kinds of equality between men, equality of ability and equality of expectation of satisfying their wants, Understanding equality in terms of equality of characteristics means that the resemblances among men are more significant than the obvious differences.

Equality is also understood as equality of treatment. This means that men irrespective of their differences are of equal worth and dignity Therefore they are entitled to be treated equally. Locke argued in this fashion. According to Locke, men are equal because every man has equal right to his natural freedom. But to Laski, "Equality does not mean equality of treatment." A mathemati1an and a brick layer cannot be given equal treatment. It cannot be identity of rewards also.

According to Barker, "the principle of equality means that whatever conditions are guaranteed to me, in the form of rights, shall also and in the same measure, be guaranteed to others, and that whatever rights are given to others shall also be given to me." This notion of equality is essentially a legal notion which demands equality before law. However even today, Barker rightly states, this is a 'notion difficult to grasp and hold in its own true shape and form'. In the past, the powerful sections of the community have stated their claim of superiority before law on the basis of their standing in terms of wealth or social rank. We are different in general capacity; our wealth means a larger stake in the country, and our culture a great grasp of affairs; it is only fair that our superiority in general capacity should be accompanied by superiority in legal capacity, and that we should have something more than an equal standing before the law.' In modem times principle of legal equality has been accepted and the less wealthy and other less powerful sections, to quote Barker again say, "We are now equal to you in legal capacity; it is therefore fair that we should also be equal in general capacity—in wealth and the opportunities it brings; in the general equipment and endowment of our faculties—and that legal equality should thus be crowned by social equality." The result has been class conflicts in many political systems.

According to Laski, equality is a coherence of ideas and it implies a certain levelling process. "It means that no man shall be so placed in society that he can overreach his neighbour to the extent which constitutes a denial of the latter's citizenship." In simple words equality means men should be treated equal socially, economically and politically. According to Laski equality means the following:

(i) "the absence of special privileges. There should not be any individual or class who have special privileges. Politically nobody enjoys a superior position and no body can be denied access to the avenues and authority.

(ii) adequate opportunities are available to all. It does not mean equal opportunities because that is not possible in modern societies which are characterised by so many disparities. Children who come hungry to school cannot, on average, profit by education in like degree to those who are well fed." Further 'the native endowments of men are by no means equal'. Some people are in better position in their lives because of the atmosphere in which they are porn. Laski says: "Children who are brought up in an atmosphere where things and the mind are accounted highly are bound to start the race of life with advantages no legislation .can secure. Parental character will inevitably affect profoundly the quality of children whom it touches. So long, therefore, as the family endures—and there seems little reason to anticipate or to desire its disappearance—the varying environments its will create make the notion of equal opportunities a fantastic one."

Bryan Turner, in his book, *Equality*, gives a comprehensive meaning of equality by highlighting its following characteristics:

(1) That all men are fundamentally equal in persons.
(2) That all must have equal opportunities.
(3) Equality of conditions, for all social groups.
(4) Equality of outcome and/or results

Equality means both negative and positive equality. Negative equality means absence of discrimination on the basis of birth, caste, creed, colour or religion; positively, it means creation of circumstances in which men are really free. It means as Laski says that talent do not perish for want of encouragement. It means, "one man is not entitled to a house of twenty rooms until all people are adequately housed. It also means that minimum economic requirements of food, shelter. and cloth be guaranteed to each and every member of the society. In fact the claim for equality is a protest against unjust, undeserved and unjustified inequalities. Therefore on the one hand it means that all people are not the same; inequalities are obvious but on the other hand it also means that weaker should be protected from various types of exploitation; he should be promoted as he also posses a right to decent living. But the basis of discrimination should be reasonable. The Indian constitution is the best example of the modern concept of equality, the characteristics of which are as follows:

(a) The state cannot deny to its citizen 'equality before law and 'equal protection of law'.
(b) State has also been prohibited from discrimination on grounds of religion, race, caste, sex or place of birth.
(c) Equality of opportunity in matters of public employment and no discrimination on grounds of religion, race, caste, sex, descent, place of birth, residence or any of them.
(d) Abolition of untouchability and prohibition of its practice in any form.
(e) Abolition of titles, except those of military and academic distinctions.

At the same time reasonable restrictions have been placed, which provide for special provisions for women, children and, scheduled caste and tribes, and backward classes. The Constitution also provides directive principles of state policy in which state has been directed to work in such a way so as the citizens of India really become equal and the objective of socio-economic justice is attained.

The Constitution of India treats all alike, but it treats some specially. These some are unlike the rest-backward socially, politically, economically, intellectually. The Constitution regards them the weaker sections of society and declares legal and constitutional discrimination in their favour so to help them rise so high that they become equal to all the rest.

The above discuss on 'equality' brings further its following major themes:

(i) *Impartiality:* this means impartial allocation of some benefits as also impartial application of laws" ..
(ii) *Equal shares to all:* this means that the same benefits/rights be given to all irrespective of any distinction.
(iii) *Equal shares to equals:* this means that equals should be treated equally.
(iv) *Proportional equality:* this means that the treatment be given in proportion to men's in equality
(v) *Unequal shares corresponding to relauani differences:* This means that the state must discriminate so to benefit those who need benefits.

Equality is, thus, not perfect or absolute equality. It is equality of treatment, thus legal equality; it is equal satisfaction of basic needs, thus economic equality in so far as it fulfills the basic necessities of life; it is 'to each according to his merit', this is proportionate equality; it is 'to each according to his need',. this is economic equality in so far as it speaks of sufficiency for all before it is superfluity for few.

II: The Concept of Equality-An Historical Analysis

The Marxists believe that the origin of inequalities are to be found in the rise of private property. This view was also held by Rousseau. In the primitive society, there was a complete equality as there was no discrimination on any ground. Man for his survival was dependent upon the nature which provided for in plenty. But with the rise of private property, the society was divided into haves and havenots and thus inequality entered into the human society. The Marxists, therefore, believe that real equality can be achieved only with the eradication of private property. We tend to agree with the Marxists that man has practised inequality, though we also witness in history theorists and different movements advocating the objective of equality. Both Plato and Aristotle accepted and promoted inequality as a basis of. their ideal states. Aristotle even justified the institution of slavery. The Greek city-states were based on inequality, the slaves had no political or social rights. Generally the slaves were not even regarded as human beings. They were one of the forms of property. However, in the same Greek tradition we find the Stoics and other philosophers who supported the idea of equality among men. Stoics opposed slavery and advocated universal brotherhood and citizenship. Spartacus who was the leader of slaves, asserted that the blood of all men belong to the same colour. He waged a war for the purpose which did not succeed. Another leader of slaves Aristonicus did the same thing with similar fate. The Roman juristic construction of *Jus Jentium* was a great step forward towards the conception of equality of people. However, the Romans also practised inequality especially in their attitude towards the non-Romans. The medieval feudal order was totally based on inequality. The society was divided into three groups—the clergy, the nobles and :the common people; the first two groups only enjoyed the rights while the third was supposed to be inequal. The Christian vision of universal brotherhood clearly proclaimed the idea of equality to be realised in heaven, not in this world. In modern times the concept of equality was given special emphasis by the bourgeoisie in their struggle against the theory of divine rights of the kings. Hobbes declared that men are equal. Locke wrote, "To understand political power a right, and derive it from its original, we must consider.... A state also of equality, where in all the power and jurisdiction is reciprocal, no one having more than others." Rousseau differentiated between two kinds of inequality—natural inequality and conventional inequality. Natural inequality like intellectual and physical strength, age, health, beauty etc. are the creation of nature and therefore unalterable. However, conventional inequality i.e. discrimination based on caste, creed, colour, sex, property etc. is man-made and therefore alterable. The liberal tradition raised the slogan of equality, and practised inequality at the same time. After demolishing the absolutist powers of the king and achieving democracy, they created a negative state with the objective of maintaining law and order for the benefit of property-owners. The ideology of Marxism arose against this trend; it stood for the emancipation of proletariat. Marxism emerged as a powerful movement; it also became official ideology of the Soviet Union and other socialist states. However this experiment failed. But what is important is that even the so-called socialist states failed to move towards the concept of equality. As a result of onslaught of Marxism, the liberal state modified and became a positive state. But it is still far away from the ideals of equality. The teeming millions of people in the various parts of world live under the poverty line, devoid of minimum basis of survival, while a few prosper.

III: Dimensions of Equality

There are three dimensions of equality:

(i) Political Equality
(ii) Economic Equality
(iii) Social Equality

(i) ***Political Equality:*** The dimension of political equality stands for democracy and universal adult franchise. There have been various forms of government. However democracy is the only form of government which believes and promotes equality among the people. Therefore we have no alternative to democracy despite its obvious weakness. This democracy has to be based on universal adult franchise. There should not be any electoral qualification based on caste, colour, creed, sex, or property for a voter. It should be based on general rules which must be applied to every body. Viewed in this context, the concept of political equality is a phenomenon of this century. In England and other Western countries, the universal adult franchise was gradually achieved; the women in England got the right to vote as late as 1918. Political equality also means absence of special privileges and no man or a body of men should be excluded from access to the avenues of authority. In other words, it means right to participation in the governmental affairs. The terms of such participation must be universal and reasonable. Political equality also includes legal equality which means all the citizens are equal in the eyes of law and enjoy what Barker calls "an equal degree of legal personality". However political and legal equality is still a dream, as Barker aptly remarks, "All may possess equal rights; but all have not an equal power of vindicating rights, so long as the vindication demands expenditure, and so long as the same are more able than others to meet the expenditure demanded. In the actual operation of the courts, as distinct from the rule of the law of the land, inequality still remains, though it is steadily being diminished by reforms in their operation."

(ii) *Economic Equality:* Laski also agrees with Barker when he says that 'political equality' is never real unless it is accompanied by virtual economic equality; political power, otherwise, is bound to be the hand-maid of economic power." Historically speaking, the political power has always been monopolised by those who possessed economic power. Aristotle pointed out the equation between democracy and the rule of the rich. In modern times, Karl Marx gave an economic interpretation of history which powerfully suggested that political power has always been owned and controlled by' the propertied class. Bryce, however, holds a different view, He remarks in his *Modern Democracies* that since democracy "is merely a form of government, not a consideration of the purpose to which overnment may be turned, (it) has nothing to do with Economic Equality.... Political Equality can exist either along with or apart from Equality in property." But we cannot agree with Bryce. The fact is that political power is intrinsically related with economic power even in democracies. According to Laski, "A state divided into a small number of rich and a large number of poor will always develop a government manipulated by the rich to protect the amenities represented by their property."

The principle of *economic equality,* according to Laski, means that "The urgent claims of all must be met before we can meet the particular claims of some one. The differences in the social or economic position can only be admitted after a minimum basis of civilisation is attained by the community as a whole." It means the fulfilment of minimum economic requirements of food, cloth and shelter. For the purpose the weak are to be protected and power of the strong be limited because the common welfare includes the welfare of the weak as well as of the strong. The quality of any state depends upon the extent to which it is able to achieve the minimum economic requirements of its people. Secondly economic equality means approximate equality of wealth. This does not mean equal pay to all. It only means, as Laski suggests, none should by virtue of differences in rates of payment exert undue pressure upon the fabric of institutions. 'Where there are great inequalities of fortunes, there is always inequality of treatment." Unfortunately this is happening today. The people who have nothing but their labour to sell are being victimised. Laski notes that the desire of the great iron masters of France to dominate the heavy industries of Europe may well send the next generation to die on the battlefield. Similarly in the expansion of imperialism, thousand of soldiers have died to protect or secure the markets for the capitalists. Laski says that the great inequalities of wealth make impossible the attainment of freedom. It means that the rich will always manipulate the state machinery for their own benefits and to the disadvantage of the poor. Therefore, monopolisation of wealth in few hands should be done away with. Thirdly, Laski advocates democracy in the industrial world. The decision should be rational which can be explained. 'It means the abrogation of unfettered and irresponsible will in the industrial world'. There should be workers' participation in the management of industry. The problem is that the employer always thinks in terms of self interest. He may dismiss a worker who refuses to adulterate or falsify his accounts. Fourthly Laski wants key industries like coal and electric power, transport and banking, the supply of meat and the provision of houses should be controlled by the government. If left to the private enterprise, they should work under the rules which should be very strict.

According to Barker, the modem state faces two-fold problems in relation to economic equality. It is partly a matter of status and partly a matter of property and income. The matter of status means whether it is possible for the state to create a system in which workers and capitalists stand on more equal footing. In the matter of property and income the issue is as to what extent the state corrects inequality in their distribution. The state has imposed taxes on riches and increased the wages of the workers. However, much has to be done in this field for the sake of economic equality.

(iii) ***Social Equality:*** The dimension of social equality wants the extension of equality into society in general. Here also it does not mean the uniformity in social status because as Barker opines, equality is 'a derivative value', it being derived from the supreme value of the development of human personality—'in each alike and equally'. But then every personality has its own system and therefore uniformity, if imposed, will defeat the spontaneous development of all the varieties of human personality. Social equality means that there should be absence of discrimination in terms of caste, creed, colour, religion and descent. It means social harmony in which all the individuals have equal opportunities to develop their personality. It also means absence of special privileges in the society. The segregation of a people from the general population in terms of untouchability is a big blot on the Indian society. The concept of social equality would demand emancipation of women, children, untouchables and other economically and socially backward communities. However, the social inequalities cannot be eradicated in a short time. It takes a fairly considerable time. A combination of legal, economic and persuasive factors can be a good direction. However, the fact remains that no society till—todate has been able to achieve complete social equality.

IV: Liberty and Equality: Relationship

Regarding the relationship between liberty and equality, there are two views. The first view regards liberty and equality as incompatible while the other view regards them compatible to each other. Let us examine the first view first.

The first view regards liberty and equality as opposed to each other. De Tocqueville, Lord Acton, Bagehot, Hayek, Friedman, Mosca, Lucas and Pareto are some such writers who believe the two concepts as anti-thetical, The basis of their argument is that liberty and inequality are natural. Therefore by nature liberty and equality are contradictory to each other. Secondly, every advance in equality diminishes freedom; every protection of freedom effectively hinders the promotion of equality. For achieving the objective of equality would mean curtailing the freedom. Lord Acton said "The passion for equality has made vain the hope for freedom." In order to develop the poor, the government not only taxes the rich but also puts constraints on their freedom to develop further. Therefore whenever there is a state legislation on equality, freedom of others become restricted. The early liberals also believed that liberty is absence of restraints. They advocated total freedom to individuals which cannot be restricted in the interests of equality. According to Friedman, liberty means maintenance of capitalism because historically speaking the rise of capitalism restricted ,the absolute powers of the kings. Thus capitalism checks the power of state whereas the ideals of equality presupposes overthrow of capitalism. Thus liberty and equality cannot go together. Keith Dixon points out that there have been many governments which deliberately pursued anti-egalitarian policies and justified their actions on the basis of the argument .that long-time inequalities of reward and status increase efficiency and raise the standards of those lower in hierarchy. But this argument cannot be accepted as Dixon himself has rejected it. The interest of the poor can never be enhanced by giving economic freedom to the rich. There are certain writers like Scruton who attempt to bring about reconciliation between liberty and equality. Scruton is a pluralist and argues that no person should be dominant in one sphere of social life by virtue of his dominance in another. To him priority of freedom over equality would be determined within relatively distinct spheres of the human good. Thus security and welfare would be governed by the concern for equality, while reward and punishment is the area where liberty should rein. But this view of dividing human activities and identifying certain autonomous areas for liberty is highly complicated and difficult to put into practice.

The fact of the matter is that liberty and equality are not opposed to each other. The objective of both is the same i.e. development of individual's personality. Dixon rightly puts it, "Inequalities themselves are a form of constraint. If I am denied access to education, for example, by virtue of my class origins, my sex, or the colour of my skin, my choices are thereby diminished. If I live my life continuously subject to hierarchial authority I am denied a sense of personal autonomy and control. My wants and needs become subject to definition by others and hence my freedom is restricted." In a society of unequals, the freedom only exist for the property owners, while the rest are denied the fruits of liberty. Liberty can only be useful in the society when there is equality; atleast where the minimum economic requirements are guaranteed to individuals. This view demonstrates the relationship between the two. Its advocates are Laski, Tawney, Pollard, Barker and the like. According to Laski, "There cannot, in a word, be democratic government without equality; and without democratic government there cannot be freedom." He further says, "Political equality, therefore, is never real unless it is accompanied by virtual economic equality; political power, otherwise is bound to be the handmaid of economic power ... the state must dominate property, or property will dominate the state." This takes us to another aspect of relationship between liberty and equality. A society, where liberty is devoid of equality will be a society of strife and class conflicts. Laski quotes Madison who wrote. "the only durable source of faction is property." But it is obvious that to base the differences between men on a contest for economic wealth is to destroy the possibility of a well ordered commonwealth. It is to incite all the qualities in men-envy, arrogance, hatred, vanity which prevents the emergence of social unity. In fact both the concepts of equality and liberty demand check on property. Equality that aims to end gross economic inequalities is the true basis of liberty. Tawney is right when he says, "A large measure of equality, so far being inimical to liberty is essential to it." Pollard aptly puts it, "There is only one solution of the problem of liberty. It lies in equality." According to Barker we should dismiss any general policy of economic equality because in such a situation we lose the diversity and the dynamic process of movement which are necessary conditions of the best society in which each of us can-be at his best. A static and immobile society of economic equality is not the environment in which the greatest number of persons can achieve the greatest possible development of the capacities of personality. Such achievement is a dynamic process which involves a dynamic society, with a rich variety of stations and functions and an easy movement of coming and going among those stations and functions." Therefore, our effort should be in the direction of progressive correction of economic inequality.

In conclusion, we may say that equality and liberty are not incompatible to each other. Both are essential for a harmonious development of individual and society. The concept of liberty, as Dixon says, should be committed to the principle that 'other things being equal individuals have the right to define and pursue their own wants satisfactions unhindered by authority or by the tyranny of orthodox opinions:

V: Equality and Justice

Justice is derived from *Jus* which means bond or tie. Justice is a social system in which men are bound together. However, justice is also a very complicated concept like equality in Political Science. In ancient times, Plato defined justice as doing one's duty and non-interference in other's affairs. He divided people on the basis of reason, spirit and appetite, as the rulers, soldiers and the producing classes and justice concerned with the observance of duties related to one's station of life. However in modern times we cannot accept such a view of justice. According to Barker, "The end of any legal association or State ... is to assemble and establish the external conditions required by every citizen for the development of his capacities; and this end is the justice." According to Robert Tucker, "The idea of justice connotes a rightful balance in a situation where two or more parties or principles are in conflict." According to Benn and Peters, "To act justly, then, is to treat all men alike except where there are relevant differences between them."Merriam says, "Justice consists in a system of understandings and procedures through which each is accorded what is agreed upon as fair." To Rees, justice 'requires that if two persons are equal they should have equal shares; if they are unequal they should have unequal shares' in proportion to their inequality.' This is the concept of distributive justice based on proportionate equality. However, the Marxists do not agree with this explanation. To them, private property is an evil and should be eliminated, then only a truely just society will be obtained.

Thus justice is a relative concept which means differently to different people depending upon their view of society. However, in a general sense it means a just society which provides opportunities to the individuals to develop their faculties. Viewed in this context, equality and justice are intrinsically related. Real justice can be available in a society of equals. But a complete equality is impossible. It is not needed also as we have explained earlier. In a society of unequals, as we have in modern times, justice in the context of equality would mean following things:

1. Absence of special privileges
2. Equality of opportunities.
3. Equality before law and equal protection of law.
4. Provision for political, social and economic rights.
5. Fulfilment of minimum basic requirements of food, shelter and clothing and negation of wide economic disparities.
6. Absence of discrimination in terms of descent, age, caste, creed, colour, sex, property religion etc.
7. Protection of the weak and for the purpose the rich may be

restrained. Socially and economically backward be given special consideration in politics and economy.

8. A balanced view of industry and economy where interests of labour and capital are subject to a just reconciliation.
9. The purpose is not to achieve complete equality but equity.

To conclude, justice stands for a harmonious development in the society in which the modern objectives of equality are to be realised. Thus both the concepts are inter-related and together they satisfy the ideals of modern polity.

SUGGESTED READINGS

1. Benn, S.I., and Peters, R.S., *Social Principles and the Democratic State* (London: Allen and Unwin, 1959)
2. Berlin, 1., *"Equality as an Ideal"* in Olfanso, F.A. (ed.) *Justice and Social Policy: A Collection of Essays* (Engleswood Cliffs, N.]: Prentice-Halls, 1961).
3. Lakoff, S.A., *Equalify in Political Philosophy,* (Cambridge: Harvard University Press, 1964)
4. Sartori, G., *Democratic Theory* (Detroit Mich: Wayne State University Press, 1962)
5. Tawney, R.H. *Equality* (New York: Barnes and Nobles, 1931)
6. Williams, Bernard., *"The Idea of Equality* in Laslett, P., Runciman, W.G. (eds), *Philosophy, Politics and Society* (New York: Barnes and Noble, 1963)

11

The Concept of Property

The concept of property has been a major issue in Political Science. It has affected all the ideologies and the ideologies in turn have affected it, the reason being that property constitutes the most important factor upon which the foundations of any ideology is to be built. At the same time, property also becomes a very difficult and controversial . concept.

I: Meaning of the Concept

The word property is derived from the Latin 'propriates' which means one's own. Defined in this sense, property is the ownership of material things to the exclusion of others. The Supreme Court of India defined property thus; "The word property must be understood in a corporal sense as having reference to all those specific things that are susceptible of appropriate appropriation and enjoyment as well as in its judicial or legal sense of a bundle of rights which the owner can exercise under the municipal law with respect to the use and enjoyment of those things to the exclusion of all others."

According to Frank Snare, in ordinary language, property and ownership are interchangeable. Following him, we can include the following in the concept of property.

1. It is a right to use things in any way which is not prohibited. Things could be immovable like land and buildings and movable like money, jewellery and livestocks.
2. It is an exclusive right to use and to the exclusions of others.
3. It also means a right to sell, dispose of or transfer to others.
4. The use of that thing by other, without the consent of its owner is unlawful and liable to be punished. The owner too cannot misuse it.

5. The unlawful use i.e. using property without its owner's consent, would invite damages to be paid to the owner.
6. The owner is responsible for any damage that his property causes to others.

Property cannot, and in fact, should not be an absolute ownership. Every legal system enunciates various restrictions on property. There is also a social and legal sanction behind property. Property cannot be conceived without state and society. it is only through state laws that property becomes a matter of right. Further, property also involves liabilities and obligations. Till now we have talked about private property. We also have public property. The public property is available for the people to use it. But that does not mean that the user becomes the owner. Those who use a public garden or public transport do not become a collective owner by virtue of its use. The title of the land vests with the local authority or state, who can sell it. Such properties are called public because (i) they are not privately owned; (ii) the local authority or state is accountable to the public; and (iii) the purpose of the property is to provide benefits to the public. Thus, in case of public property, the public is supposed to be the owner, but the state may dispose it of in public interest. Besides private and public property, we also have community property, also called common property. In India it is called panchayat's property. This property is not a public property, because its use is restricted to a specific people who live in that village, who are entitled to use, for example, land to graze animals. Thus a variety of property exists in a liberal state. The socialist states, however, do not believe in private property. They stand for its total abolition. In a socialist state, all property is owned by state and the entire economic structure is controlled and owned by the state. In developing countries, property is viewed from the angle of socio-economic justice which means the following:

(i) The citizens have a right to own, sell and dispose of property;
(ii) Property cannot be used for exploitation.
(iii) Minimum economic requirements of food, clothing and shelter should be guaranteed to all the citizens and for the purpose, the rights of the property owners may be restricted. Usually a ceiling is fixed on property with a view to avoid its monopolisation in few hands. The objective is to reduce economic disparities.

II: Development and Growth

The concept of private property is a modern concept and its systematic development can be found at the end of seventeenth and early eighteenth century, because the particular set of economic conditions to which private property refers was not present before the arrival and consolidation of capitalism. Yet the private property in some form or the other is present from time immemorial. The description of society in the Old Testament amply proves that it possessed some of the characteristics of modem capitalism. This ancient society had private property, division of labour, market exchange and money.

Man began his life on earth in a very simple manner. The primitive societies were characterised by the simplicity of wants and their satisfaction. Human society was food-gathering pastoral society. Everything was owned by the tribe jointly. But once the tribe settled down, it came to possess land and at a later stage some dwelling units as well. The communal ownership of all the properties continued. Gradually it was accepted that the hutment in which a family was staying belonged to that family. Private property also existed in the form of consumable products like foodstuff. But as the techniques of production developed and wants became more complex, a stage arrived where new arrangements became necessary to incorporate the changing requirements of the society. The result was the extension of private property from consumable to productive goods. The Old Testament describes a conflict between the tribal society with its communal property and primitive economic activity, and a more developed society characterised by class and caste divisions based on private property. Soon the primitive society disintegrated and the scope of private property grew to include land, but the individuals right over property was highly limited.

Development of private property led to domestic and foreign trade and accumulation of wealth. The Hebrew monarchy grew in this period which is marked by sharpening of class divisions between the rich and the poor. The luxury of courts was based on evergrowing enslavement and impoverishment of the masses. During this period, we also find spiritual revolt by the prophets who castigated the unjust order of the new commercial classes of traders, usurers and the land robbers. They also demanded limitations on private property. However in their protest, they could not understand the forces which were responsible for that exploitative order: Their protests remained utopian—either expecting God's wrath or arrival of some messiah who would deliver mankind from the life of sin and restore the old partriarchial society.

In Greek city states, Plato had understood the evils of private property. Therefore he deprived the rulers from having private property. He idealised a state in which the rulers had no motive for economic exploitation; communism of property and wives followed from this assumption. Later on, his disciple, Aristotle attacked the concept of communism of property. His attack was based on incentive argument that communal property will not be looked after as carefully as private property. Aristotle also realised that conflicts are bound to take place, when men, unequal by nature in skill and industry are not differentiated by varying opportunities of enjoyment. Aristotle also believed that private property is necessary for the development of individual personality, yet he was aware of danger of economic disparities and their contribution in revolution. However he never advocated abolition of property. He only wanted its more enlightened and liberal use. Aristotle also justified the inhuman slavery system, which was the basis of socio-economic progress of his times.

The Roman Empire that followed the Greek City states upheld the right of private property almost without any limit and guaranteed freedom of contract. The society further witnessed the growing poverty of the general masses.

The medieval society was sharply divided in terms of social classes and groups. The society was also highly dominated by the Church. The Church sometimes condemned those economic ideas which increased exploitation and inequality and sometimes was indifferent to the miseries of the world. Trade and profits were usually condemned by the religious philosophers. However, they could not stop the organisation of society on the basis of a solid economic system which rested on private property and flourishing trade. The Church reacted by prohibiting usury. The religious philosophers also criticised it. The feudal lords rented out their landed property to tenants who would not only pay rents but also provide military services to them. Later on, the peasants were tied to their land, a new system of bondage that replaced slavery: The flourishing trade crated a new middle class or bourgeoise who were the authors of capitalism. Thus, capitalism was clearly based on the institution of private property which remains its foundation even today.

III: The Liberal Theory of Property

We have seen earlier that liberalism is a political philosophy of autonomy of individuals. State and society are presumed to be nothing more than a collection of individuals. The objective of state is the betterment of individual. State, by creating an order, creates conditions in the society in which individual can develop his various faculties. Therefore they wanted the state to be hindrance to hindrances which curtail the development of individual's personality. Property, to them, is very important because without it, the individual will have no basis or incentive to develop. Men have a natural love for their property. Machiavelli, therefore, said that men will sooner forgive the death of their father than the confiscation of their property. Initially the early liberals stood for a right to unlimited property like Locke and to a great extent Bentham. To them, state was a necessary evil which restraints the individual. With John Stuart Mill, we find the inauguration of the concept of positive state, which was a reaction to the miseries brought about by the negative state. This period also saw the rise and consolidation of socialist movement which condemned, and stood for the abolition of, property. The Marxian view of property suffers from extremity which was not welcome by the people in general, because nobody wants to lose property. It was felt that elimination of property was neither practical nor necessary. But there cannot be a right to accumulate unlimited property. What was desirable was a synthesis between the two and the democratic socialist principle sought to do the same. Yet we do have modern libertarians who, despite the accumulation of experiences by the mankind to the contrary, still believe that there should not be any restriction on property. We will take all these views one by one. First we discuss the liberal theory of property with reference to John Locke, Bentham and J.S. Mill.

(i) John Locke's views on Property

John Locke is the most vocal supporter of private property. He wrote his famous work *'Two Treaties of Government,* in the seventeenth century, in which he expounded his views on property.

To Locke, property existed even in a pre-state environment i.e. what he calls state of nature. The institution of state was absent and people were living peacefully. But unfortunately this peace could not remain for ever and consequently people's property was in danger. Therefore, people decided to make a contract by which the state and the government were created. Thus the state and government came into existence for the sake of preservation of property. The property is a natural right and the government has no right to abrogate it. In fact it is the aim of the government to protect and preserve property.

Locke has used the term property in both narrow and broad sense. In broad sense, property means life, liberty and estate, while its narrow sense is restricted to land and goods. However both constitute a limitation on the government.

According to Locke every individual has a right to life. For his survival and comforts, nature or God has given him the earth and its produce, which is a common stock for all mankind. Man also has a property in his own person. He says, "The Labour of his Body, and the work of his Hands, we may say, are property his." When he mixes his labour in the common stock given by the nature, he makes it his property. A flower in the plant or a fruit on a tree is the commonstock, but when I pluck them they become my property. Similarly a piece of land becomes my property when I till it or use it in any other way. And for this appropriation I need no permission or consent from anybody. Such an appropriation has, however, three limitations:

(i) Enough should be left for others, because every man has a right to life;
(ii) Right to appropriation does not mean right to spoil. A man can remove from the nature only as much which he can use because as Locke says, "Nothing was made by God to spoil or destroy.";
(iii) The right to appropriation is justified only when it has been accomplished by man's own labour. Only that share of common stock belongs to me and becomes my property which I have procured through my labour.

It may seem that Locke stands for a limited right to property. But this is not the case. He very cleverly removes all the three limitations and argue for an unlimited right to property. The first limitation is removed by Locke when he says that 'he who appropriates land to himself by his labour, does not lessen but increase the common stock of mankind.' This means that the production from the acquired land is partly consumed by the man himself and the rest is left for the others to consume. Macpherson rightly points out, "Thus, although more land than leaves enough and as good for others may be appropriated, the greater productivity of the appropriated land more than makes up for the lack of land available for others." Locke now justifies unlimited accumulation of land by individual. This unlimited accumulation of property also provides to the labourer who does not own property, a living. He is better than those people who live in areas where the land has not been properly utilised; 'he lives, lodged and is clad better than the king of an Indian tribe in the empty wastes of inland America.'

The second limitation is the spoilage limitation. Nobody has a right to spoil. He can possess as much as he can consume and the rest is for others. This limitation is transcended by the introduction of money.

Gold and silver do not spoil and man has, therefore, a right to their unlimited accumulation. Thus one can sell the surplus production of his land and the money that he receives is rightfully his because it cannot spoil. The resultant economic disparity came into existence even before the state came into being. To Locke, both land as well as money is capital and the purpose of capital is to make more and more capital by profitable investment.

The third limitation on property i.e. one can have as much property as he can by using his own labour is also done away with. Every man has a property in his person which he can sell. Thus one can sell his labour and whatever he produces is the property of that person who has bought his labour. This means I can acquire property through the doings of my servants. Locke justified the wage relationship of modem capitalist society, where labour is purchased to make more and more capital.

Locke's views on property can be summed up in following points;

(i) Right to property existed even before the state came into being.

(ii) The purpose of state and government is to protect and preserve property.

(iii) Right to property is a natural right given by God and it constitutes a limitation on state and government.

(iv) Economic disparities are also natural and pre-state. They are good for the society.

(v) Wage relationship is equally natural and property earned through it is equally justified.

(ii) *Bentham's Views on Property*

Bentham made modifications to Locke's concept of property. He does not accept the natural right to property. To him the entire concept of natural right is non-sense. Natural property rights would mean bankruptcy of the government because then the government could not impose taxes on the people. It will have to depend upon the voluntary contributions of the individuals. To Bentham, property is the product of law.

According to Bentham, property gives a sense of satisfaction. In property, we see something of ourselves. The things we have made, the house in which we have lived, the fields we have farmed, all of them are some part of ourselves. There is a personal attachment to the possessions and therefore people are so much concerned about the security of their property.

Bentham defends property on the basis of general utility. The individual's happiness can be achieved in four things—subsistence, abundance, equality and security. The state does not have to interfere in man's work to subsistence because he has a natural desire to live and hence he takes care of procuring his means of remaining alive. But the state should see that the individuals are rewarded the result of their efforts. Otherwise they will have no incentive to work. Bentham felt that abundance was meant for a small portion of population. The labourers would never be able to achieve abundance. But then there is nothing wrong in the abundance of wealthy. The abundance of wealthy is necessary because it provides resources to the community in times of natural calamity. No doubt abundance creates inequality. But then it is the result of the security of property. Without security, there will be no property and without property there cannot be general guarantee of subsistence.

For Bentham security of property is a major condition of achieving the greatest happiness of the greatest number. Therefore, he advocated legal protection to the distribution of property that exist in any given time. Bentham also justifies the sanctity of contract on the basis of its contribution to the maintenance and reliability of commercial transactions. Bentham is against the acquisition of property without adequate compensation. The state must respect the law of inheritance. But if an owner dies without heir then his property should be taken over by the state for redistribution. Bentham dislikes slavery, but if there are slaves already and have been bought by their masters in good faith, the masters must not suffer the loss by the abolition of slavery. The slavery should be abolished only after the death of the masters.

Bentham defended usury and was against state regulation of economic activity. Bentham wants individuals to be left alone. That government is best which governs the least. The property right is no natural right. They are created by the state and the state should create it with a view to maximise utility. The utility is maximised, according to Bentham, when the goods and services are bought and sold at prices mutually agreed upon between the buyers and sellers and the system of property rights should facilitate such a commerce. Thus he stood for a laissez fa ire policy or free trade against state regulation in economic activity.

However Bentham also advocates state welfare for the weak, The policy of law should be to achieve a comparatively equal distribution of property. Atleast arbitrary inequalities should be avoided, because the greatest happiness of the greatest number cannot be achieved by unequal distribution of wealth. He also wants protection for old age people against destitution. Bentham also advocates taxing property for the unemployed and weaker people. But these taxes should be reasonable. Lastly, Bentham never believed that the property rights are absolute. Property does not mean to use it as one pleases. 'My knife is mine, it means that I can put it where I like, but not in your chest'. He believes in the maintenance of balance between equality and security in practice. But if there is a conflict between the two, security of property is to be given prime importance.

To sum up, Bentham's concept of property has following features:

- (i) Property is not pre-state or a natural right but created by state.
- (ii) Possession of property gives a feeling of personal attachment.
- (iii) Bentham justifies inequality of property.
- (iv) The property may be acquired only after paying adequate compensation to its owner.
- (v) Bentham stands for sanctity of contract.
- (vi) Law of inheritance is justified.
- (vii) If there is any evil like slavery, it should be remedied without loss to the owners.
- (viii) Bentham stands for non-interference of state in economic matters.
- (ix) The state should help the weak.

(iii) J.S. Mill's Views on Property

John Stuart Mill was a follower of Bentham, yet he was a product of his times which had changed. He was the product of transition in which classical liberalism was being challenged by the philosophy of socialism. Initially he accepted Bentham's idea with, ofcourse, his own modification but later on he became influenced by socialism. He himself became a member of Parliament with the help of his working-class followers. As a politician, he became a radical and social reformer. He became a liberal with a sharp leaning towards the later Fabian school of socialism. His objective was to remove the evils of capitalism without sacrificing its essential principles. As a result, we find a lot of inconsistencies in his views on property. The practical politician in him gave an expression that completed one epoch of early capitalism of Locke and Bentham, and inaugurated the other, the other being the epoch of socialism. To that extent, he still remains the mouthpiece of modern English liberalism. His view on property can be summed up as follows:

- (i) *Defence of Laissez Faire:* Mill stood for autonomy of economic activity. He was a great champion of liberty of individual and there was no question of compromise. But the doctrine of liberty has nothing to do with the defence of free trade or laissez faire. Mill wants no restriction on trade because restrictions on trade are restraints and all restraints are evil In fact to Mill, restraint on trade is harmful because they do not produce the results which are desired from them. Therefore, the market should be free and it should be left to the buyers and sellers to organise it. There should be free competition in the sphere of production and exchange.

Mill defended the right to form trade union on the basis of *laissez faire.* State cannot deny the workers their trade unions because it is their right based on the general rule of freedom of contract. Mill also defends competition. He did not agree that competition always lowers wages. Competition among employees can lead to higher wages. He related competition with justice which demands that the worker should understand the role of the market and he should demand neither more nor less than the worth of his work. He rejected communism because of its hostility to competition. He said, "I utterly dissent from the most conspicuous and vehement part of their (communist's) teaching, their declamations against competition."

(ii) *Mill plea for state action:* Mill stands for reforms which would redistribute property and income. He believes that distribution of human race into employers and employed cannot be permanently maintained. This, he thinks, would ultimately be superseded by partnership in the form of 'association of labourers with the capitalists' and perhaps finally in 'association of labours among themselves.' According to him, attack on the institution of property would continue 'until the laws of property are freed from whatever portion of injustice they contain'. He also makes it clear that if the choice were to be made between communism with all its chances, and the present state of society with all its sufferings and injustices; if the institution of private property necessarily carried with it as a consequence, that the produce of labour should be apportioned...., almost in an inverse ratio' then communism is to be preferred.

To Mill ownership of land is a trust. Property rights are not natural rights. They are social privileges, given by the law. Trade is also a social act. Therefore property in general demands interference from state and society. Mill advocated a theory of special taxation of 'unearned increment' and socially created values. The value of property increases as the society advances and constitutes 'unearned increment'; the owners of the property have no role in this increase and therefore state may take over or tax the increased portion of the property. If the state does so, it is doing no injustice. to the owners because it is an unearned income created by the society and therefore should be used for the benefit of all. For this Mill says, "The first step should be a valuation of all land in the country. The present value of land should be exempted from the tax, but after an interval had elapsed, during which society had increased in population and capital, rough estimate might be made of the spontaneous increase which had accrued to rent since the valuation was made." Thus Mill increased the state's role in economic activity.

Mill was dissatisfied with the workers' conditions in industry. They were working in pathetic circumstances where long hours of work coupled with low wages was the rule. During his times, it was suggested that wage levels in economy reflected the size of the 'employer's wage fund' and the number of workers seeking employment and the average wage could be calculated by dividing the first by the second. The workers can improve their lot by having small families. Mill advocated for the restriction on the growing population. But then it is difficult to expect workers to restrict the size of their families because of poverty and their ignorance. However still if the workers have to take up the responsibility of improving their lots themselves, a change in social attitudes and organisation would be needed as an incentive for them. For the purpose, Mill advocates worker's management in industry. He says that self-management in industry is a complement to self control in domestic life.

Mill deplored the employers' attitude towards their workers as feudalistic. He was sure that this could not exist for long. Once self government in industry is attained by the workers, this feudalism will go away. Mill was confident that workers would not remain content as wage earners for long. They would only be contented by being associated in the management of industry.

Mill advocated state legislation to increase wages and low working hours for the workers. He wanted justice for workers. Their reward should be in proportion to the efforts they make. He wanted protection of public health, insurance against illness, industrial accidents and indigence in old age. Mill also wanted state to take up education for all children. This, however, does not mean state control over education. The competition from private enterprises must also be there. State should also restrict monopolisation of economic activity.

But this does not mean that the state should interfere in every economic activity. Mill shared with Bentham that habit of putting more and more matters in the hands of the state was inimical to progress. Excessive state interference also means loss of freedom. Mill says, "If the roads, the railways, the banks, the insurance offices, the great joint stock companies were all of them branches of government....... if the employees of all these different enterprises were appointed and paid by the government, every rise in life, not all the freedom of press and popular constitution of the legislative would make this or any other country free otherwise than in name." More power to the state means more and more 'powerful bureaucracy. Mill is highly critical of bureaucracy which encourages an uncommendable type of ambition and it gets so entrenched that "nothing to which the bureaucracy is really adverse can be done at all ... the more perfect that organisation ... the more complete is the bondage of all.... " Mill was very correct here. The rule of bureaucracy means the rule of file and procedures, red-tapism and corruption. As the members of bureaucracy belong to the rich class, they have no sympathies for the poor and their welfare. Mill says, "Even an insurrection or revolution whatever else it might do, does not disturb the bureaucracy. Since there is no one else capable of taking their place." Thus Mill is against the bureaucratic control of state which is not responsible to the people.

(iii) *Private property justified:* Mill only wants state intervention in the distribution of property. He does not want its abolition. He also accepted the liberal emphasis on competition in economic life. He had sympathies with socialist doctrine, but he never accepted communism. He said that communism should not be compared with the existing capitalist societies where the private property is not regenerative. It should be compared with a social order which contains' only the best features of capitalism. In other words, as Eric Roll suggests, 'he envisaged a state of society in which the existing distribution of property, caused by past conquest and violence, had been corrected in which inequality of opportunity had been reduced to a minimum, in which legislation was designed to favour the diffusion of wealth, in which there was universal education and in which population was limited.'. In such a society the principle of private property, Mill confidently declares, will have no necessary connection with the physical and social evils which almost all socialist writers assume to be inseparable from it." He had no objection in the accumulation of private property as a result of a person's own efforts. But he disliked the unrestricted right of inheritance. No body should be able to begin life at too great an advantage over everyone else.

Mill also believed that we are heading towards a stationary state. A time will come when there will be no increase in wealth. In fact there will be decline in profits. This will be due to improvements in the techniques, the law of diminishing returns, the accumulation of capital and the working of competition. Then the conditions of working class will improve. Only thing is that the rise in population should be controlled. In such a stationary state, wealth will be more evenly divided and that will be the ideal state of private property.

To conclude, Mill's views on property are the following:

1. Mill stands for the policy of *laissez faire* and competition which is favourable to workers also.
2. He wants state action in distribution of wealth.
3. Property is not a pre-state right but cleated by law.
4. Unearned increment on property should be used for public benefits.
5. He wants state regulation in working conditions and workers.
6. Mill justifies private property. He only wants its evil to be removed.
7. He believes that society is heading towards a stationary state where wealth would be evenly divided.

(iv) The Modern Libertarians and Property

However we have modem libertarians who are highly critical of increasing state role in property.

Ayn Rand has given a moral justification of capitalism. She believes that the free market economy is the only economic system that can guarantee the dignity of man and his freedom. To Rand, ideal man is engineer, scientist and industrialist. She says "Since my purpose is the presentation of an ideal man. I had to present the kind of social system that makes. it possible for ideal men to exist and to function—a free, productive, rational system, which demands and rewards the best in every man; great or average, and which is obviously, *laissez jaire* capitalism." Rand's man is a rational being who is guided by his thinking and not by, feelings and desires and who sees his interests in terms of a life time and selects his goals accordingly". A rational man acts according to his self-interest and capitalism is the only system that provides him the basis for working. She says, "In a capitalist system, all human relationships are voluntary. Men are free to cooperate or not, as their own individual judgements, convictions, and interests dictate." Rand is highly critical of state interference in economic matters.

She does not see any difference between socialism, fascism and welfare state. All of them interfere in the market activity, arid are specific variants of 'statism'. Statism is "the principle or policy of concentrating extensive economic, political and related controls in the state at the cost of individual liberty." The socialist doctrine negates private property and makes the state as the owner of property while fascism gives control of the property to the government though ownership remains in the hands of private individuals. The welfare state to Rand is also fascist because it stands for the preservation of private property with governmental control of its use and disposal. She also says, "A mixed economy is merely semi-socialised economy—which means: a semi-enslaved society."

However, Rand believes that 'a pure unregulated *laissez faire* never existed anywhere in the world. The political systems of the nineteenth century were not pure capitalism, but mixed economies: at the most they were close to capitalism and of course there was more freedom. According to Rand, "Freedom is the fundamental requirement of man's mind" Man should be free from physical compulsions and only political power is the power of physical coercion and that freedom, in a political contest, has only one meaning; the absence of physical coercion."

Rand is against the welfare activities of the state. The state has no business to help the unemployed, aged and the weak. She declares, "Only individual men have the right to decide when or whether they wish to help others; society as an organised political system has no rights in the matter at all." She wants welfare and charity to be left to voluntary associations. She wants no restriction on right to property. She is against any limitations on inheritance. The only economic rights are 'property rights, and the right of free trade' and there cannot be such things like 'an economic bill of rights,' a right to a job or, right to a fair wage or a fair price. 'She also denies the existence of public interest.'

According to Rand the basis of the government is the consent of governed' and the governmental function is limited to three broad categories—(i) the police to protect men from criminals, (ii) the armed services to protect men from foreign invaders; (iii) the law courts, to settle disputes among men according to objective laws.

Rand advocates free trade from international point of view. The peace in world can be maintained only by a free trade. According to her, "... the major wars of history were started by more controlled economies of the time against free countries." A statist economy logically leads to war because wealth is publically owned and a citizen has no economic stakes in peace, while war holds out the prospects of larger handouts from the government. The capitalist society, on the other hand, does not need war because (i) the principle of individual rights does not permit a man to rob another inside or outside his country, (ii) the private citizens have a stake in peace because they will have to meet the cost of war in the form of taxes. They will also suffer due to business dislocations and property destructions. Therefore they are against war. Thus the only way of elimination of war is to free the market and free trade among different countries. The operation of free trade would result in international division of labour, would bring people together and would make them prosperous.

Robert Nozick is another writer who favours existing inequalities in terms of property. People are justified in having property if it is not a stolen property and no fraud is involved. He dismisses all talks of egalitarianism because 'whatever is held is prima facie, justifiably held.' The existing inequalities in terms of property are the result of a long historical process and therefore justified. The people who talk of unequal distribution in society give us a feeling that these inequalities have been deliberately created from the resources according to some specified criterion, which is not true. Further, he says, "we are not in the position of children who have been given portions of pie by some one who now makes last minute adjustments to rectify careless cuttings." Therefore any talk of egalitarianism means paternalism at the best or at worst dictatorship. Nozick says that why should we assume that people should be treated equally and given equal shares in the common stock. Nozick wants people to keep whatever they have and it is the responsibility of the egalitarians to prove that these people should be debarred from keeping their property. However Nozick is not convinced with any argument given against property. Therefore he is against governmental interference with existing property rights.

(v) Liberals' justification of Private Property:

The above study of liberal views on property with reference to Locke, Bentham, Mill and Nozick demonstrates that right to private property is well justified. To Locke, private property is a natural right, while Bentham and Mill accept it as a right guaranteed by the law. However, all of them regard property imperative for individuals. Other important liberals who justify private property are Adam Smith, Malthus and Herbert Spencer. The justification of private property therefore constitutes an essential principle of liberalism. This also justifies the inequalities in the society which are consequences of property rights. In *Coppage vs Kansas* (1915) case, the US Supreme Court said the following:

"No doubt, wherever the right. to private property exists, there must and will be inequalities of fortune ... And since it is self-evident that, unless things are held in common, some persons must have more property than others, it is from the nature of things impossible to uphold the freedom of contract and the right of private property without at the sametime recognizing as legitimate those inequalities of fortune that are the necessary result of the exercise of these rights."

The liberals have justified private property on following grounds;

(i) Property is a *natural right;* some liberals like Locke believe that property is a natural right. By his birth, an individual acquires this right. Locke says that God has put man on this earth and given him reason to use the resources of the earth therefore man has a right to property so that the earth is turned into a usable commodity. He himself possesses property in his person and when he mixes his labour in the common property of earth given by God, it becomes his property. As much land a man, Locke argues, "tills, plants, improves, cultivates and can use the product, so much is his property." The liberals believe that property is a natural and inalienable right and it is the duty of the government to protect it. The U.S. constitution also accepts this position. But all the liberals do not accept the theory of natural right. Like Bentham and Mill, they believe it is a social privilege, authorised by law.

(ii) *Psychological basis:* Liberals believe that individual is governed by his self interest and there is nothing wrong in it. He knows his interest better than others and even government, and he can do better than the government in satisfying his interest. Therefore, as Appadorai puts it, "Self-help is the best help. Psychologically, property provides incentive to individual to work. Without property there will not be any incentive to work. Further property gives him a sense of satisfaction of his living. In property he sees his achievements of life."

(iii) *Moral basis:* Morally, property is justified because it is a reward for one's ability and capacity, which he has earned by his efforts. It is only because of private property that man uses his initiative and efforts to develop his personality and he has a moral claim to the property so acquired.

(iv) *Social basis:* According to Adam Smith, "the Providence has made society into a system in which natural order prevails. Human conduct is naturally actuated by six motives-self-help, sympathy, the desire to be free, a sense of propriety, a habit of labour, and the tendency to truck, barter and exchange one thing for another. There the individual is the best judge of his own and therefore be left alone." Further the different motives of human action are so balanced that the benefit of one does not conflict with the good of all. Self-help is accompanied by sympathy and therefore whatever the individual does for his development, it also helps the society. It is primarily due to natural balance of human motives. Adam Smith says, that in pursuing his own advantage each individual is 'led by an invisible hand to promote an end which was no part of his intention.' In simple words, it means that individual's development leads to common good in the society. The property is a source of social virtues like love towards family, generosity and charity. Property gives man a status in society which ultimately leads to his happiness and contentment, and only such persons can be of any benefits to the society.

(v) *Economic basis:* Liberal believes that the system of private property give better efficiency and production. Therefore there should be *laissez faire* and free trade. There should not be any restriction and the state should be no more than a referee in the economic world. As a referee, it should see that the participants in the economic activity should follow the rules of the market and there is no fraud and treachery. Liberals believe that market is sel-regulative and state has no role to play in economic activity. The individual should be left alone and in such a situation, a capitalist will invest his capital to his best advantage. Likewise the labourer will also find out his job where he can get maximum wages. Thus a free market operates on competition and it helps both the capitalists as well as the workers. Free competitions among the producers benefit the consumers. A consumer gets cheap goods, as the producers compete to sell their goods. The right to property thus brings general happiness and common good in the economic field.

(vi) *Biological basis:* The right to property has also been justified on biological basis. Nature is characterised by a struggle for existence. In this struggle only the fittest survive. Nature has witnessed a struggle between different species for existence, and man emerged victorious because he was the fittest. The liberals have extended this argument in human society also. The government should not interfere in economic field. The natural law of struggle for existence and survival of the fittest should be the fundamental rules of the economic activity. Only the fittest will survive and the property they achieve is justified. The weak may be allowed to 'perish and the government should not help them because this is against nature's justice.

(vii) *Historical basis:* The institution of private property is an old system. It has existed from time immemorial, that itself proves its justification. Further history also proves that the Western society which was based on property developed fast in contrast to the Eastern societies which were based on collective property. Now they are dominating the world.

(viii) *Pragmatic basis:* State is a man made institution created for the specific purposes of maintaining law and order. Therefore, by its very nature, it is limited. It is not designed to perform economic activities. History provides ample example when state has tried to infiltrate into economic matters and failure has been the result. In India most of the public enterprises are incurring huge losses. In late 1960s, the Indian Government introduced rationing system which also failed. In fact, it encouraged hoardings and other evils with regard to the distribution of food stuff. Thus experience shows that governmental interference in economic matters produces bad results. Therefore the state should remain aloof from the economy; the demand and supply rule of the economic system is sufficient for its working. The property should be independent of state's interference.

This concept of private property and its logical conclusion of the policy of *laissez faire* or free trade was implemented in England and other parts of Europe in eighteenth and nineteenth centuries. This resulted in flourishing market and prosperity. However, it soon became apparent that right to unrestricted property and the state non-interference lead to exploitation of man by man. It also resulted in poverty for the millions. The socialist movement grew out of this phenomenon. The liberals were quick to understandthis defect in liberal theory. Therefore they modified their doctrine and accepted state regulation of property and economy.

IV: The M arxian Concept of Property

In Marxism, the concept of private property finds a pivotal position. It is the property which is responsible for development and progress in human society. However this development has not been healthy because the property divides the society into two classes—the property owners and those who do not possess property, in other words haves and have-nots, These two classes struggle with each other as their interest in terms of property clash with each other. In this struggle, the state is always biased. It is on the side of property-owners, as they control it and use it as a means to further their interests. Property owners not only control the state apparatus, they also create or control other institutions like religion, ethics, family through their ideology. Thus the history of mankind is a history of domination of the property owners over the have-nots. Therefore, Marxism is highly critical of private property and wants to abolish it, so that a new society is created in which there is no exploitation. In fact with the abolition of private property, there won't be any private interest and clash of interest, therefore no class and no class struggle. An ideal stateless society will follow which will be based on perfect harmony and equality.

Thus, to the Marxists, property is a hindrance to the real development of society. This position is in contrast to the liberal theory of property which believes that property is essential for the development of man and society.

Marx differentiates two kinds of property. The first is consumable or personal property which means a property which is meant for consumption by the man. It includes food stuff, house, utensils, car etc. Marx has no obsession to their possession by the individuals: What he objects to is the producable or private property which includes land, rent, profit, cash in banks etc.. Private property is a property which is used for making more and more property. The Marxists believe that it is this kind of property which is responsible for all the evils in society and therefore it must be abolished.

The question is how the private property came into existence? Marx's friend Engels attempted to explain the origins of property in his *The Origin of the Family, Private property and the State.* Initially there was no private property. Man was food gatherer which he used to achieve by collecting vegetables and fruits and by hunting the animals. This is also called by Marxists as the stage of primitive communism. But this stage did not continue forever. Man soon started domesticating the animals like cows and buffaloes. Later on agricultural activities also commenced. According to Engels, the domestication of animals had three effects i.e. the emergence of patriarchical family, slavery and private property. Once the private property came into existence, it changed the whole structure of the society.

According to the Marxists, the society is always divided into two classes on the basis of property ownership. The people who own property or means of production constitute one class and who don't own them constitute another class. In the work of production, people enter into definite relations and these relations of productions are the relations of property. When the property or the means of production is the land, we have the classes of feudal lords, the owners and the serfs, the non-owners, In capitalism, the machine is the new means of production, we have capitalists who are the owners of the machine and non-owners are the wage labourers or working class or as Marxists call them the proletariat. Thus property creates relation between the people, 'the wind-mill gives you the society with the feudal lord; the steam-mill, society with the industrial capitalists.'

Property relations create not only classes but also class conflict. The reason is that the interests of property owners and property non-owners are antagonistic to each- other. The property-owner's want to expand their property and this can only be achieved when they pay less to the labour while the labour demands more for its subsistence. Thus a class-struggle is unavoidable. To the Marxists, history is nothing but the history of class-struggle.

Property is also responsible for changes in the society. In the development of society a stage comes when new mode of production arises. They come into direct conflict with the existing relations of production or property relations. For example the rise of machinery as a mode of production was in direct contradiction to the then existing property relations of landlords and serfs. In such circumstances, revolution becomes inevitable. This is because property constitutes the basics of the society. The argument is very simple in Marxism. The mode of production determines the social relations of production i.e. relationship between men. This is economic relations and these economic relations in turn determine the legal, political and other social relations. Engels says, "...that in every society that has appeared in history the manner in which wealth is distributed and society divided into classes or orders, is dependent upon what is produced, how it is produced, and how the products are exchanged. From this point of view the final causes of all social changes and political revolutions are to be sought, not in men's brains, not in man's better insight into eternal truth and justice, but in changes in the modes of production and exchange. They are to be sought, not in the philosophy, but in the economics of each particular epoch." The introduction of machinery as a mode of production resulted in the death of feudalism and creation of capitalism.

According to the Marxists, property is also responsible for the creation of state. Engels says, "The state .... did not exist from all eternity. There have been societies without it, that had no idea of any state or public power. At a certain stage of economic development which was of necessity accompanied by a division of society into classes, the state became the inevitable result of this division." This stage of economic development was that of the beginning of private property whose protection gave rise to the state. Property creates classes and class conflict, and the class conflict creates the state. The highest purpose of the state is the protection of private property. Historically the state came into being when the property of the masters was being threatened by the revolt of the slaves: the purpose was to maintain the hegemony of the masters over the slaves. Thus the state is a class organisation, an organisation of the particular class which is the exploiting class. It is merely the organised power of one class for oppressing another. Thus in ancient times, as Engels puts it, the state is "the state of slave-owning citizens, in the middle ages, the feudal lords; in our own the bourgeoise." The ancient state checked the slaves, the feudal state oppressed the serfs and dependent farmers and the modem state is the tool of the capitalist exploiters of the wage labour. Thus the state came into existence when the division of society into classes was brought about by a mode of production based on private property.

According to the Marxists, property is responsible for all the evils, therefore Marxism stands for its total abolition. Marx and Engels declared in the *Communist Manifesto* that the theory of communism may be summed up in a single sentence-the abolition of private property. The Marxists are critical of capitalism because it is based upon the institution of private property. Let us now study the Marxian critique of capitalism.

(i) Marxian Critique of Capitalism

Modem capitalist society is a democratic society which means political power is exercised and controlled by the people for their own benefits. The Marxists do not accept this. According to them, the liberal state is just like any other state designed to protect and promote the private property and oppress the working class. However Marx's most important contribution is his analysis of capitalist society in terms of theory of alienation.

According to Marx, men are defined by their capacity to work, and are different from all other creatures by their ability to produce freely. Man is not only a creator, he is also aesthetic and enjoys his work. But in capitalism with its basis on private property, both the work and enjoyment are dehumanised. To Marx, property is a form of failed. appropriation because we only acquire the external non-human aspect of things, and fail to acquire their richer substance. We do not enjoy it. The richer we become in conventional terms, the poorer we really are. Marx finds man's alienation in capitalist society in four ways: (i) from nature (ii) from his product, (iii) from his species being and (iv) from himself. In other words man's alienation is to be viewed and understood from four different perspectives such as in relation of the workers to the product of his labour, in relation to the activity of production in terms of its impact on the worker, in relation to himself and in the context of his social life to other men. This alienation is the result of private property.

Private ownership of the means of production leads to man's alienation from his labour. Marx says "The more the worker produces, the less he has to consume; the more value he creates, the more valueless, the more unworthy he becomes; the better formed his produce the more deformed the worker, the more civilized his object, the more . barbarous becomes the worker; more powerful labour becomes, the more powerless becomes the worker, the more ingenius becomes the worker and more he becomes nature's servant." The problem is that the worker himself becomes a commodity like labour; more the commodities he creates, he becomes more cheaper. Whatever he creates is not controlled by him but it is independent of him. His work becomes his enemy, as an alien power confronting him. Marx says, "Thus all the process of civilisation or in other words every increase in the powers of social production .... in the productive powers. of the labour itself such as results from science, inventions, division and combination of labour, improved means of communication, creation of world market, machinery etc enriches not the labour but rather capital, hence it only magnifies again the power dominating over labour; increases only the productive power of the capital. Since capital is the anti-thesis of the worker, this merely increases the objective power standing over labour." Thus the capital is the cause for man's alienation. The worker does not enjoy the work or the creation that he does. Marx aptly puts it." The worker, therefore, only feels himself outside his work and in his work feels outside himself. His labour is therefore not voluntary, but coerced, it is forced labour.... As a result, therefore, man only feels himself freely active in the animal function-eating, drinking, procreating, or atmost in his dwelling and in dressing up and in his human function he no longer feels himself to be anything but an animal. What is animal becomes human and what is human becomes animal." All the human values are also dominated by the consideration of private property and money, and thus the basis of honesty, gentleness, beauty, powers, and wisdom is money. You are judged by your ability to amass more and more property. The capitalist is no way better than the workers. He also becomes a machine which produces money. He is forced to maximise profits otherwise he loses in the competition. He is the instrument of the power of capital in dehumanising the workers, not an independent agent. Money is a dead thing, yet it dominates the living beings. The workers and the capitalists—both think about the money always, and the object of life becomes its, more and more, accumulation. Thus, according to Marx, the ·alienation is not limited to worker alone. The capitalist also suffers from the same kind of alienation. Capitalism is thus condemned both from the worker as well as capitalist point of view. None of them control its operations and enjoy its product.

Marx believed that alienation is due to the surplus value and the division of power which creates classes in the society. The division of power increases the wealth by raising the productive power of the labour; it also leads to inequality and private property. Alienation, automatically follows. Marx explained inequality in terms of surplus value. The capitalists wants to have more and more profit. He must get more than what he pays as wages to the workers. For the purpose he pays less to the workers and the surplus that the capitalists gets as a result is used further for the creation of private property. Thus the surplus belongs to the labour which the capitalist usurp and create further property. Marx concludes that property is responsible for political, economic and social evils and only remedy is its abolition, only way of its abolition is the overthrow of the capitalist system.

(ii) Property Under Socialism and Communism

The overthrow of capitalism is followed by the establishment of socialist democracy or dictatorship of the proletariat. The institution of private property will be done away with. People will be rewarded according to their efforts. Nobody will receive any income without earning it. The labour will get its due and there will not be any capitalist to appropriate the surplus. This socialist society will pave way for communism, where each will get according to his needs. In communism man will really be a freeman. He will be unalienated man, which to Marx is a total man. He will be free "to hunt in the morning, fish in the afternoon, rear cattle in the evening and criticize after dinner .... without ever becoming hunter, fisherman, shepherd or critic." In communism, there is no private property, no classes, no class exploitation, no class conflicts and hence no government or state. People are happy and unalienated. It is really a heaven on the earth.

The Marxian plea of abolition of private property has been a revolutionary idea. It also alarmed the capitalists about socialism and communism. However, even during the times of Marx .and Engels and also after, a different brand or shade of socialism developed which did not share many of Marxist's views including his views on private property. The evolutionary socialists, the Fabians, the guild socialists and the democratic socialists do not want the abolition of property. They shared the liberal idea of property which justifies its existence and view it necessary for the development of individual's personality. What they desired is the regulation of property, so that it is not used for exploitation. It should be used, on the contrary, for common good.

V: Laski's Views on Property

To Laski there are certain advantages in having property. Property gives security; it is a safeguard against the want of the tomorrow. "The man of property has a stake in the country. He is protected from the fear of starvation. He need not accept the work he does not desire. He can take the leisure in which most men now find the opportunity of significance. He can, if he so wills, surround himself with that environment which makes life an artistic thing. He can avoid the grim routine, and become an explorer in that intellectual hinterland where the creative faculties most readily discover their channels of self-expression. He can protect his children against the dread of want."

But the problem is that the number of property-owners is always less than those who do not possess property. The people devoid of property have no meaningful life. The political system is dominated by the owners of property. Nodoubt there have been major state legislation like fixing the minimum wages, yet the concept of private property perpetuates the division into the rich and the poor and separates the poor from the conditions which make possible their effective citizenship.

Laski's views of property can be understood under the following heads:

1. Criticism of capitalism.
2. Criticism of basis of private property
3. Laski's views on functionless property.
4. Laski on theories of reward.
5. Laski's theory of industrial organisation.

1. Criticism of Capitalism:

Laski is a critic of capitalism and its political ideology of liberalism. According to him, the liberal theory of state assumed a sovereign state to avoid anarchy and it was based on three functions of state. First it secured order; secondly it provided a technique of peaceful change and lastly it enabled demands to be satisfied on the widest possible scale. The state definitely secures order but the problem is that it does not provide a technique of peaceful change and does not permit demands to be satisfied on the largest possible scale. This is because of the institution of private property. The supreme coercive power of state is used to protect and promote the interests of those who own instruments of production. Some concessions may be granted to those who do not possess property, but the last two functions of state cannot be achieved so long as the instruments of production are privately owned. Theoretically, peaceful change in a liberal state is possible through the Constitution but in practice the owners of the property who possess the state power always resist the change. The liberal state also fails to satisfy demands on the largest possible scale because capitalism is based on profit and therefore it cannot satisfy the demands of those who do not possess property. In other words the distributive process in a liberal state is defective and 'the coercive power of the state is used to promote the differences in relation to the satisfaction of demand...'

Laski is against economic disparities which are the inevitable result of capitalism. To him, capital is social labour and therefore the whole society has a right over it. A small minority of capitalists cannot monopolise it.

Laski agreed with those that the state and government operate in favour of the propertied class. There is ample evidence regarding this in history. "The Greek city was biased against the slave. The Roman Empire was biased against the slave and the poor. States in the medieval world were biased in favour of the owners of landed property. Since the Industrial Revolution, the state has been biased in favour of the owners of the instruments of production as against those who have nothing but their labour power to sell." He accepts the Marxian concept of economic interpretation of history. He says, "Changes in the methods of economic production appear to be the most vital factor in the making of change in all the other social patterns we know." The law, the culture, the religion, the education system, styles of architecture, the character of our science, the basic framework of all that we call civilisation is, at bottom, determined by these productive relations."

A major defect in capitalism, according to Laski, is lack of planning in production. 'Production is carried on wastefully and without adequate plan'. Preferences are not based on social utility." We build picturesque palaces when we need houses. We spend on battleships what is wanted for schools. The rich can spend the weekly wage of a workman on a single dinner, while the workman cannot send his children adequately fed to school. Goods and services are produced, 'not for use', but to acquire more and more profit. To become more and more rich is the ideal and therefore production is done 'not to satisfy useful demands, but demands which can be made to pay.'

The profit motive dominates the scene and for this end, all means-moral and immoral are justified. For this objective, Laski says, "They will ruin natural resources. They will adulterate commodities. They will float dishonest enterprises. They will corrupt legislatures. They will prevent the source of knowledge. They will artificially combine to increase the cost of their commodities to the public. They will exploit sometimes with hideous cruelty, the backward races of mankind. They infect with their poison those who work for the wages they offer. They compel strikes which result in serious damage to the community ... They may destroy the quality of political life. They may even pervert religious institutions to the protection of their ideas." However, they cannot secure a well ordered state' because it is 'historically obvious that a community divided into rich and poor is, when the latter are numerous, built upon foundations of sand.'

To Laski, capitalism and democracy are contradictory. While the economic basis of power is narrow and capitalism stands for its protection and promotion, the citizens in a democracy use the political power at their disposal to increase their material well being. Yet this union of economic oligarchy and political democracy worked well so long as the capitalism was in its phase of expansion. However after the first world war, the capitalism entered into the phase of contraction which not only limited the profits of the capitalists but also increased unemployment resulting in lower standards of life. The dissatisfied people revolted and used their political power. Their political power became a challenge to the economic power of the owning, class. In such a situation arose Fascism which to Laski is nothing but simply the expedient adopted by capitalism in distress to defeat the democratic political foundation.... ' This analysis explains the widespread attack on principles like freedom of speech, due process in political offence (which was remarkably illustrated by Hitlerite legislation and activities) and right of labour to strike. Laski attacks capitalism from international point of view. Capitalism is organised on national basis and the capitalists use their state to further their economic interests. They also want to capture foreign markets and to them state becomes a means for protecting and extending their investments abroad. This results in competiting 'economic imperialism where, arms *are used* to secure gains, 'Fear, suspicion and hatred are born of this atmosphere. The interest of *world* community has to give way before the interests of powerful states. For example the Japanese occupation of Manchuria before the second world war, where Japan preferred to sacrifice the hope of peace and international security to the imperial ambitions of her governing class. The failure of world Economic Conference in 1933 and the Disarmament Conference in 1934 is also because of this reason. Laski declares, "Capitalism, in a word, is, rooted in a system which makes power the criterion of right and war the ultimate expression of power." There can not be peace m the world in such an atmosphere.

2. *Criticism of the Basis of Private Property:*

The liberals have justified the concept of private property on various grounds. Laski criticises all the grounds as follows:

(i) *Psychological basis:* The first justification of private property has been psychological. Psychologically, the people need some incentive to work and private property provides such incentive. The desire to make property makes people work and in the process good of the community is also achieved. Laski criticises this justification on two grounds. Firstly, the good of the society is achieved only when the goods produced also brings about good for the society. But this is not the case always. For example, the people dealing in harmful drugs and narcotics may become very rich, but their goods are not for the good of the community. Secondly, people who acquire property by means of heredity may not have any incentive to work. In fact, psychologically the private property was based on fear and any system based on fear cannot survive for long.

(ii) *Ethical Basis:* Liberals have justified private property ethically. The property is the result of individual's effort and hardwork and therefore he has a moral right over it. But there are many people who work very hard, yet they cannot make property. The fact of the matter, Laski says, is that property actually is a reward for a particular kind of ability which consists in the capacity to make more and more profit. The profit motive cannot contribute to social well-being in any way. Private property is morally inadequate because it confers rights to those who have done nothing to earn it. Thus it creates parasites in the society who deprive others the opportunity to live a decent life.

(iii) *Private Property a source of virtues:* The liberals also believe that it is the private property which provides a man such virtues like love of one's family, generosity, inventiveness and energy. But this means that the majority of people who do not have property lack these virtues, which to Laski, is not a correct statement of fact, for these virtures have been present in persons who have never amassed property at all. People do not work just to amass property. For example, Newton's inventiveness was not due to the desire to make more property. The poor also love their family and this love has no relation with property.

(iv) *Property as the result of supplying effective demands:* The property has also been viewed as the result of supplying effective demand. Laski does not appreciate this view because it has no social utility. There may be unjust demand for example. for obscene literature or prostitutes and property made by such efforts cannot be justified.

(v) *The historical argument:* Private property has also been justified on the basis of history. The developed societies of the West have been based on private property while the backward societies on a collective basis. The developed societies are more progressive and there is more freedom. for individuals. But, according to Laski, this does not mean that they provide more happiness to individuals. The reason is that we cannot say much about the backward peoples on the basis of available knowledge which is very less. Further historically speaking the concept of private property has always been subjected to control. At no time in history, it was regarded as absolute. People have been aware of danger of private state property and both politically and philosophically attempts made to mininlise this danger by putting control over it. Plato in fact rejected the notion of private property. The modem liberal state started with an unlimited right to property and it became a negative state. But soon it had to change its colour and become a positive state in which right to property became limited and subject to state regulation. The state saw the expansion of its operation to economic field where its obligation was to achieve common good and reduce economic disparities. According to Laski, the right to property should be related to the social needs.

3. *Laski* is *against Functionless Property*

Laski is a critic of functionless property. To him, functions are related to duties and no man has a 'moral right to property except as a return for function performed. He has no right to live unless he pays for his living: To him, people who owe functionless property, are parasites upon the society. Therefore he is critical of inherited property. According to Laski, hereditary wealth involves two things: (1) There is a class freed from the legal obligation to labour. (2) So freed, it is able to utilise its leisure in a way that taxes the productive effort of the remaining members of society. In fact such people misuse their leisure. They devote to aimless pleasure. They dominate institution and set standards of. taste. They provide employments and form the habits and ideals of the class which attains wealth by its own efforts. Their economic position involves a definite social predominance. They are able, by their prestige, to set the perspective of the state. However, this does not mean that a 'man is not entitled to provide for his immediate descendants.' Laski says security should be provided to children. Children should be given adequate education and support to enable them to enter the battle of life. "Inheritance is always justified," Laski comments, "where it means the provision of an income for widowhood, on the one hand, and the education of children on the other". Beyond that there cannot be any inheritance. Man can have a right to that property which is the result of his own personal efforts. However Laski advocates compensation to the property in the form of annual pension. Otherwise it may result in conflicts in the polity, as Machiavelli said, men will sooner forgive the death of their fathers than the confiscation of their property.

4. Laski on Theory of Reward:

How much a man is entitled to is the basic question before Laski. Laski discusses various theories of reward and finds them unsuitable. The first theory is the communist doctrine of equality of income. Laski says that it is not justified to reward equally where needs are unequal. A bachelor cannot be entitled to the same income as the parents who have five or six children to maintain. There can not be equal reward for unequal effort also. The second doctrine advocates the fixation of remuneration by the haggling of the market.' The operation of supply and demand fixes the reward for the labour. Laski does not agree with this theory, because such a system is based upon competition, which is unfair to labour. It leaves one-third of the average industrial community on the verge of starvation. For them it means poor health, undeveloped intelligence, miserable homes, and work in which, broadly speaking, the majority can find no source of human interest.' Therefore the state has to pass laws such as minimum wages acts to protect the labour. The theory of supply and demand is essentially a capitalist norm which Laski abhors. Capitalism has failed to deliver goods to the society. Here the motive is profit and for the purpose the demands are created irrespective of their social utility. The third theory of reward is quite attractive. 'It demands that each contribute to society according to his powers, and be rewarded by society according to his needs.' To Laski, this theory is very simple and unrelated to reality. It is difficult to measure both the 'power' of individual and his 'needs'.

According to Laski, the reward must be determined on the basis of two conditions; Firstly, it should enable the individual to develop his personality and secondly, it should preserve and develop the necessary function of society. For the purpose he advocates following things:

(i) Minimum economic requirements should be provided to all citizens. Laski calls it a common civic minimum.

(ii) The demands of weaker classes, children, old people, disabled and defective persons should be met.

(iii) Only socially useful work should be paid.

(iv) The common civic minimum or minimum economic requirements is not the same for all the members of the community. The human wants are not identical. An agricultural worker or a minor needs a more costly diet than a clerk. The minimum is to be decided according to the nature of job.

(v) The wages are to be fixed keeping in view the fact that each socially necessary occupation attracts a sufficient talent to run them adequately. Therefore there cannot be equality of wages. A judge or a doctor should be entitled for more than a worker or minor.

(vi) The reward in terms of economic gains should not be given overemphasis. The great artist pursues his end for its own sake and not for financial gain. Similarly scientists like Newton were not after economic gains. Laski says, "The great soldier finds his reward not in the income he receives, but in the public esteem that is the measure of his repute. The average high civil servant could earn far more than his salary in the business world; but the consciousness that he has his hands on a great machine more than compensates for a comparatively modest income." Even those businessmen who have the aim of making more and more wealth do so because they want more standing and power in the commercial world.

(vii) In every society, there are people who are adventurous, and who take risk. Then there are also people who go for long training and preparations to get good positions. Laski justifies such efforts and therefore payment by achievement is also allowed.

(viii) The social control should be in the realm of production and not in consumption. If a worker wants to buy a piano which he cannot play, it is his business. Similarly if a businessman wishes to have a house with endless bedrooms, it is his business and there should not be any restraint. In consumption also, class-standards should be avoided. rules should be implemented equally to all the classes and individuals.

5. Laski's theory of Industrial Organisation

Laski wants the rights of property to be well-founded in a theory of industrial organisation, There should be discipline in industries but at the sametime its aim should be general well-being of the product and the methods by which that product is attained. Laski's theory of industrial organisation can be summed up as follows:

(1) The ownership of industry on the basis of inheritance is to be abolished.

(2) Industry must be made a profession. The object of every profession is service. Thus industry is also a public service, where the object should not be profit. The industry must serve the community and the personal interest of the industrialists be subordinate to this. end:

(3) Laski suggests three changes for the industry to be professionalised. Firstly, the owner of the industry must not have a control over it. The owner renders his services by the loan of his capital to the industry and he should be paid for this service and no more. He cannot usurp the profits. Secondly, once the function-less owner is removed, the rules of the industry be made by its working force, upon the basis of functions performed. This means workers' participation and control in the management of the industry. Thirdly, Laski wants to include more social aspects in the industry. This also means three things; (a) the profits earned must be for the benefit of the community and not for the private undertaker. The production of essential commodities may be done under cooperative production or consumer's cooperation or under state. They cannot be left in the hands of private enterprises. The socialised production may also involve nationalisation. However other methods will also be adopted; (b) Industries whether public or private must have a constitution. There must be standard hours

and standard rates of pay. Industry must be democratically managed and there must be absence of arbitrary and whimsical powers in relation to hiring and dismissal of employees. Similarly the promotion to a foreman must be based upon his ability, with the approval of those, the particular foreman is to control; (c) There must not be any chance or nepotism in industry. The head of the factory must possess required qualification. There must not be any secrecy in the matters like cost of production and rates of profit.

Thus, Laski stands for a scientific reorganisation of industry. The reorganisation should take place piecemeal and by stages, so that community learn by experience. He also wants various experiments to be undertaken in regard to the operation of industry. There may be mistakes "But, Laski declares, "there is no birth without pain; and those who would comfort the prospect of a better life must not turn aside because there are dangers on the road."

SUGGESTED READINGS

1. Cranston, M., *What are Human Rights?* (Lond,on; Bodley Head, 1974).
2. Laski H.J. *A Grammar of Politics,* (London, George Allen & Unwin Ltd.) 1973, 3d print.)
3. Locke, J., *Two Treatises of Government* (Cambridge, Cambridge University Press, 1960 print)
4. Macpherson C. B. *The Political Theory of Possessive Individualism* (London: OUP, 1962)

   ____ *Property: Mainstream and Critical Positions* (Toronto: Toronto University Press, n.d.)
5. Mount, F. *Property and Poverty: An Agenda for the Mid-80s* (London: Centre for Policy Studies, 1984)
6. Shapiro, 1., *The Evolution of Rights in Liberal Theory* (Cambridge: Cambridge University Press, 1986)
7. Suvorova, M and Romanov, B., *What* is *Property?* (Moscow: Progress Publishers, 1986)
8. Tawney, R.H. *The Acquisitive Society* (Bombay: Orient Longmans, 1955)
9. Tully, J., *A Discourse* 011 *Property: John Locke and His Adversaries* (Cambridge: Cambridge University Press, 1980)

12

The Concept of Justice

The word "justice" is, indeed, baffling. It is so not because of what it includes, but what it excludes. So, with numerous shades of people, it has a different connotation. Ask a man of law, he would say that justice means the judgement pronounced by a judge; ask a man of religion, he would say that justice means a set of morals and values which we should follow: ask a poor man, he would say that justice means abolition of poverty; ask a Cephal us, he would say that justice means keeping one's word; ask a Polemarchus, he would say that justice means helping a friend and harming the enemy; ask a Thrasymachus, he would say that justice means the will of the stronger to De imposed on the weaker; ask a Glaucon, he would say that justice means the protection of the weak. The list can be still extended. What it means is that the meaning of the word 'justice' depends on our view of society and its various aspects as also where do we find ourselves in the society. For a worker, justice would include, among other things adequate wages; for a subaltern, it would include absence of outrages committed on him; for a feminist, it would include abolition of masculinist repression.

Let us make an attempt to understand the concept of justice as it has developed over the ages, especially in the West.

I: Etymology and Development

Derived from the Latin word 'jus' and also included 'justus' and 'justitia', and connected with the word 'jungere', again a Latin word, justice means, what Professor Barker says 'primarily a joining or fitting, a bond or a tie,' gliding into a sense of binding or obliging." Defining the word 'jus' Professor Barker remarks that in its original form, it means something" what is fitting and therefore, also. binding".

Elaborating the etymological meaning, he says that the word 'jus' conveys "the idea of valid custom to which any citizen can appeal, and which is recognised and can be enforced by a human authority." It is clear that Professor Barker, while largely drawing from the original Latin word, goes on to give justice a legal connotation. So, he says, the word 'jus' in its developed form, would mean, "a body of binding or obliging rules which-the courts recognize as binding, and not only recognize but also enforce." But for Professor Barker himself, justice is not merely a relationship between man and man (as about law and as in courts), but is a relationship between value and value. He, therefore, concludes. "....the function of justice may be said to be that of adjusting, joining or fitting the different political values. Justice is the reconciler and the synthesis of political values: it is their union in an adjusted and integrated whole."

The meaning given to the word 'justice' has been different in different times. With the Sophists of ancient Greece, justice meant the interest of the stronger ... of the social group which is militarily stronger and economically rich to impose its will on the other groups. As against this, Plato emphasised on the moral and ethical element in justice by saying that it means performing one's duties with all abilities and capacities towards the social whole. Aristotle, on the other hand, holds the view that justice means equal share to the equals and unequal to the unequals, distributing power and position proportionately to the worth or contribution of the individual: flutes to be distributed among those who know flute-playing as Aristotle had once put it. The Romans, known for their contribution of law to the Western political thought, used 'jus' therefore, justice so to denote the body of laws. and the courts which enforce them, laws emanating from customs, legislative declarations and judicial pronouncements. During the medieval period, owing to the dominance of Christianity and the institution of the Church, the idea of justice came to be related to the idea of the rule of right, the idea of morality, the idea of righteousness, the idea of justness. It is interesting to note four categories of law in the hierarchical form in the writings of St. Thomas Acquinas. St Thomas talks of the *lex aeterna,* the eternal law, the supreme and the one that exists in God; the *lex divina,* the divine law which is below the eternal law and one that exists in the Scriptures; the *lex naturalis,* the natural law which is at number three below the eternal law and the divine law and the one that exists in the reason implanted in man by God. And below the natural law, is the *lex humana,* the human law which expresses itself in accordance with all the higher types of law, is made and imposed by human authority. Justice, during most of the medieval period, meant a body of ethical rules emanating from the scriptures, man's sense of morality and those made by man conforming to the principles of eternal, divine and natural law.

The natural rights theorists of the early modem period thought of justice as the rule of reason, a bridge between the medieval religious notion of justice and the ethical notion of justice as developed by a modem rationalist being. Locke and his followers held on to this concept of justice. That law is the expression and embodiment of justice was the meaning given to the word 'justice' by theorists in most part of the eighteenth-nineteenth centuries, declaring law as the declared will of the state and as the most obvious dimension of justice. With the development of democracy and democratic processes and institutions, justice came to be understood as equal participation of all the sections of society in political and public matters. The liberals, till date, identify justice with legal and political equality, including in it the rule of law, equality before law, equal protection of laws, one person-one vote. Again, with the development of industry, economic dimension of justice began to be advanced by socialists, syndicalists and anarchists with whom justice meant the establishment of a just social order, an order without economic exploitation and without political enslavement. Later, the Marxists developed the idea of socio-economic justice in which there were to be not only just laws, but also a just society. Social justice, a recent phenomenon, is associated with an egalitarian order with social ownership of major means of production if possible and without private property if necessary. Justice, in the Marxist sense, means distribution of burden according to our capacity, and of benefit according to our needs. It, in the contemporary liberal and libertarian sense, means sufficiency for all and thereafter competition for greater benefits.

II: Justice-Its Dimensions

Numerous dimensions of justice include: legal, political, social, economic and socio-economic. The *legal* dimension of justice assumes (a) that law is the declared will of the state; (b) that it includes both the customary and statutory law; (c) that it is issued by a defined authority and is enforced and imposed by the court; (d) that if violated, it is accompanied by a corresponding punishment; (e) that it is limited by the provisions of the Constitution or the conventions; (f) that the Constitution is its supreme form, regulating the activities of the government and prescribing the rights and duties of the people. The *political* dimension of justice is an extension of the legal dimension for both, the legal and political dimensions, are advocated by the liberals, both of yester years and modern. its features include; (a) establishment of a democratic order without any discrimination; (b) political equality; (c) one person-one vote; (d) rule of law and not rule by peoples' whims; (e) enactment of-the Constitutional provisions; (f) free press and democratic rights, (g) fair and impartial periodic elections. .The *social* dimension of justice reflects a just social society; its peculiarities would include: (a) elimination of all kinds of discrimination; (b) abolition of privileges based on birth, race, caste, creed, or sex; (c) social roles to be determined by capacity; (d) social mobility to be an alternative to rigid stratification; (e) equality of each with each and of each with all; (f) universal brotherhood. The *economic* dimension of justice attempts to discover justice in the. economic structure of the society; its features, as expressed in the writings of socialists, anarchists, syndicalists, are: (a) establishment of a social order as the principle of mutual cooperation; (b) attainment of maximum production achieved through voluntary and independent economic enterprises; (c) equitable distribution of commodities so produced; (d) abolition of exploitation of man by man; (e) social security in the event of accident, illness and old-age; (f) prohibition of concentration of material resources in the hands of the few. The *socio-economic* dimension of justice is, by and large, a Marxist connotation of justice. Its features include: (a) a classless society, (b) abilities be matched to work; (c) work to be matched with needs; (d) an exploitation-free and oppression-free social order.

III: Justice and its relation with Liberty and Equality

Justice is a unifying force, a force that unites person to person, and value to value. It is as Professor Barker rightly says, a synthesis, a final principle that regulates the general distribution of rights, as his share in the whole system, and it thus 'adjusts' person to person. Adding to his argument, he continues: "...it (justice) gives to each principle of distribution (liberty, equality and cooperation) its share of weight in determining the distribution actually made, and it thus 'adjusts' principle to principle."

The idea of justice is the general right ordering of human relations or the final adjustment of persons and principles. It resides in all minds and as such is no abstract conception but is a social reality. It is neither morality nor ethics, for it relates itself to the outward life. But that outward life needs a set of conditions as also a set of norms which only are provided by morality. Professor Barker, thus, concludes: "If justice is not morality, it is based upon it. If its code is not that of ethics, it is a code which-is ultimately derived from ethics."

Explaining the relationship of justice with liberty and equality, Professor Barker points out: "Justice is a joining or fitting together not only of persons, but also of principles. It joins and knits together the claims of the principle of liberty with those of the principle of equality; it adjusts them to one another in a right order of their relations." Equality may quarrel with liberty; for if its application be pushed to the length of what is called a 'classless' society; with absolute equality of possessions, it is at once brought into conflict with the liberty of each to try himself out in the effort of acquiring for himself some individual equipment."

The job of justice is to adjust, balance and reconcile person to person, principle to principle, value to value, and claim to claim. Professor Barker rightly regards justice as the holder of balance, saying that justice holds in the balance both the claims of persons to rights and the claims of different principles to. determine the distribution of rights," measuring them by the standard of the maximum development of the capacities of personality in the maximum number of persons".

IV: Socialist Theories of Justice: Marxist, Anarchist, Democratic-. Socialist

There is a point in bringing the anarchists, the Marxists, and the democratic socialists together and clubbing them all as socialists (we are slipping out syndicalism, utopian socialism, radical socialism, evolutionary socialism, fabianism, guild socialism and the like, for each is either a variant of one or of two or more). Though all of them are not socialists of the same shade, yet they are *the socialists* in their own right. Hence, there is something common among them so far as some aspects of socialism are concerned. What is important to note is what exists in each that is related to the other and that is what makes them the socialists. If socialism, in its essence, means, as it really is, not a very favourable attitude towards capitalism, all of them are the socialists; the anarchists, for example condemn capitalism as a charter of economic exploitation; the Marxists provide a severe critique of capitalist mode of production; the democratic socialists see, in capitalism, the worst form of moral degradation. If socialism is the political philosophy of the working class or a doctrine that claims to fight for the cause of the workers, then all of them—the anarchists, the Marxists and the democratic socialists—are socialists. If socialism regards exploitation as the consequence of uneven distribution of social wealth, then all of them can, and in fact should have, claim to be socialists. If socialism means justice for the worker, the poor, the lowly, the downtrodden, then all are, indeed, socialists. If socialism means equal opportunities for all and a system without discrimination then all of them are socialists in the sense we use the term. There is, thus, some degree of socialism in each—anarchism, Marxism and democratic socialism.

This is not to say that anarchism, Marxism, democratic socialism have nothing in uncommon. There are very important differences among them; differences about the objectives; differences about the strategy to be adopted in the realisation of those objectives. An anarchist would like to abolish state first and capitalism thereafter; a Marxist would, on the contrary, abolish capitalism first and state thereafter; a democratic socialist would neither at any point in future, abolish state nor capitalism. With regard to the means to be adopted for the attainment of the stated objectives, the anarchists would not mind using violence; the Marxists would adopt peaceful methods if possible and violent, if necessary; the democratic socialists would seek to bring about socialism through peaceful democratic means and with the help of the state.

On the right-hand side of democratic socialism stand anarchism and its variants, those which want to abolish the institution of the state as in one go and those that accept socialism willy-nilly. On its left are Marxism and its variants, those which wish to abolish capitalism lock, stock and barrel and those which believe in the indispensability of socialism as a higher, though not the highest, state of society's material development. Democratic socialism with its variants hold the view that capitalism can be regulated, workers' cause can be taken care of, socialism can serve to be an end in itself.

With socialists of all shades, justice exists where there is no injustice. This commonly understood meaning of justice does not explain much, but it is from where all the socialists start. The chief concern of all the socialists has been injustice meted out to the workers, peasants, poor, unemployed, the lowly and so on in the system that exists in the society in general, and the capitalistic one in particular. That is why the socialists are more vocal, and even furious, in explaining what is unjust than in describing what justice really is. So, the socialist idea of justice springs from the realms of injustice which exists in the society. Because the presence of law kills the liberty of the individual, the anarchists regard such a situation as a situation of injustice, and therefore, justice, according to them, would exist where the individuals are free. For the Marxists, justice in the class societies is always a class justice, justice for the capitalist and conversely injustice for the workers. Hence the Marxists find justice only in a classless society. The democratic socialists are both socialists as well as democratic, and therefore, for them, justice exists in a just order and in a just society.

(a) ***Tile Marxist Theory of Justice:*** The Marxists are vocal about uneven distribution of income as an example of injustice. While advocating their theory of justice (to be more specific as something that is opposed to injustice), the Marxists go much beyond the anarchists. Proudhan rightly remarked once that all property is theft, but Marx and his followers relate property, to class society, class society of antagonistic classes—one owning the means of production, the exploiters and another without the means of production, the exploited, and antagonistic classes into a class concept of justice—justice for the rich. For the Marxists, justice is not merely just laws, but also just laws emanating from just society; it is not merely economic or social in nature, but also socio-economic in its ramifications.

According to the Marxists, justice is, more or less, a relative term; it is different for the rich and different for the poor; different for man, and different for woman; different for the capitalist and different for the worker. For the Marxists, justice like property and law and politics, is a reflection of commodity relations, especially under capitalism. They say that under a communist society, justice would reflect different relations than those in a capitalist system. The bourgeois justice, the Marxists would declare, is bourgeois in the sense that it protects them and exploits the workers; it legitimises the capitalist's profit on the one hand, and the labourer's wages on the other; it legalises inequality. But in a communist society; because of the social ownership of the means of production, justice would mean equality of all and equality for all. It would mean absence of all discrimination, all exploitation and all oppression. It would mean work for all in accordance with their abilities as also fulfilment of all the needs of all the persons in return to what each of them does. Hence the idea of justice, in the Marxian scheme, is associated with the nature of the society itself. In a slave-owning society, justice would highlight something that is most impracticable—the ethical ruler; the medieval European society saw justice in Christianity; the capitalist Western society seeks to find justice in the justification of private property system. In a communist society, justice is just society and its corresponding just rules—a justice without coercion, without repressive state machinery, a justice where people obey laws as a matter of habit rather than any threat of punishment. The Marxian justice is one which springs from within the socialistic and cooperative relations among the people.

The Marxists do not believe that the idea of justice is the idea coming from the sky, hence eternal; sprouting from the deep sea, so hidden. It, they say, exists in the system it finds itself; it is the system that gives it a meaning; it would mean different things in different systems of relations of production. If in the capitalist system, the Marxists seem telling us, the principle of justice would and in fact, is "take as much from the society as you can," in the Marxian society, if it could really be built, the principle of justice would mean: "give as much to the society as you can". In the capitalist justice, rights have an edge over the duties whereas in the Marxian justice, duties override the rights. The capitalist notion of justice is more close to liberty than equality while the Marxian idea of justice is more close to the idea of equality than that of liberty.

(b) ***The Anarchist Theory of Justice:*** Even the anarchists are of various types, mention may particular be made about William Godwin (1756-1836—*An Enquiry Concerning Political Justice and its Influence on General Welfare and Happiness),* Pierre Joseph Proudhon (1809-1865—*What* is *Property?)* and with them the Russian Bakunin (1814-1876), Kropotkin (1842-1921) and Tolstoy (1828-1910). One may, however, be tempted to include, among the anarchists, Mahatma Gandhi and Bertrand Russell. All these anarchists regard the state as a negative institution, some to the extent of abolishing it altogether. All of them take the disdainful view of the present capitalist society and dub it most exploitative, oppressive and unjust. They see justice in the absence of political coercion: political authority, in its any form, is all evil, and therefore not only unnecessary but also undesirable. They, therefore declare that the only way to establish justice is to abolish the state completely and replace it by an entirely "free organisation of society." For the anarchists, justice is not to be found in the presence of the government, but in its absence; not in the submission to any political authority above, but in the existence of free individuals with their independently arrived agreements; not in their natural quarrelsomeness, but in their natural cooperativeness.

Regarding individual as essentially good and immensely social, anarchism depends mainly on the natural tendencies of human soul, as led by reason and justice, or the establishment of free, autonomous and just social order. According to William Godwin, neither laws nor law courts ensure any justice, for they are the products of people's passions, jealousies, timidities and ambitions over the ages. Proudhon found in property negation of social justice, and therefore he was opposed to it—property that creates further property. He found in state a supporter of property and therefore he was against all types of political authority. Proudhan's anarchist society is a free society where freedom is united with order, order with reason, and reason with justice. Bakunin finds injustice in the framework of private property, political authority, and religion: where these exist, there exists injustice; where they are absent, there alone we have justice. Kropotkin was a naturalist, and therefore, believed that if people are left to themselves to work out for their way of life, they would develop a number of voluntary associations to make social existence possible, maintain peace, practise mutual aid and create, in the last analysis, justness. Unlike Godwin and Proudhan who were individualistic anarchists, Bakunin and Kroptokin who were communistic anarchists, Tolstoy was a Christian anarchist; Mahatma Gandhi, a spiritual and a moral anarchist; and Russell is a humane anarchist.

For the anarchists, justice lies where there is no state, no property and no religion, and where there is free individual, voluntarily willingness and the reign of liberty. Justice finds expression not in bondage, but in freedom. It is a sense of liberty and not of slavery, of emancipation and not of exploitation, and of acting in accordance with free will, and not of the will dictated by any external force.

(c) ***Democratic Socialist Theory of Justice:*** The democratic socialist justice neither touches the extremes of the Marxian variants nor those of the anarchist ones. It is a mid-way concept of justice: unlike the Marxists, the democratic socialists find justice in a regulated, restrictive and controlled system of capitalism: capitalism need not be thrown out; unlike the anarchists, they find justice through the state and its laws. Indeed, like the Marxists and the anarchists, the democratic socialists believe, rather equally strongly, that justice and exploitation do not go together and that the idea of justice must incorporate in itself the idea of equality.

The democratic socialists do not regard, as the Marxists and the anarchists do, all laws as bad and all state as an instrument of class exploitation. On the contrary, the democratic socialists, like all the liberals and the libertarians, hold the view that justice exists where the law exists, but the kind. of law that is an embodiment of 'social service' and not, of awful majesty. Indeed, they think that police is necessary but it need not be extensively armed; that law, as an expression of justice, must regulate the conduct of the people, but it need not be more than enough; that courts have to dispense justice, but they need not be subject to those who hold political power. The democratic socialists find the idea of justice in the idea of rule of law and hence, they provide for the courts a heavy agenda such as diffusion, decentralisation, federalisation of political and economic power. They regard justice as a frame, as a system, as a goal to be set and attained by laws, and laws which have to be made by the state democratically structured. Hence, the democratic socialists do not throw the baby (of justice) along with the bath-tub (of liberal-capitalism). Justice exists as does liberalism-capitalism: what does not exist in the bathwater is the filth and the dirt. For the democratic socialists, justice cleans the dirt, shines as gold in the society, reconciles man with man, principle with principle, value with value. They believe that justice exists in a democratic order, for undemocratic system is always unjust; it exists in the framework of equality, for inequality is never just. Where people participate more, there is more equality and where there is more equality, there we find the idea of justice.

But for the democratic socialists, justice is not merely a matter of equality, it is also a matter of liberty—liberty which is not licence to do anything, but an atmosphere in which one grows without impeding the liberty of any other. The democratic socialist theory of justice reconciles, rather adjusts, the two extremes as are provided by the liberals and the Marxists. They are liberals in so far as they see—Justice in some infrastructure—laws, courts; they are Marxists in so far as they see it in a system which is exploitation-free.

In conclusion, we may that the Marxist view of justice is : "Share the burden according to your capacity; and benefits, according to your needs." The anarchists, on the other, regard justice as a principle which says: "Share at will, take as you can." And the democratic socialist view of justice is: "Take in proportion to what you give."

V: Libertarian Justice: Hayek, Rawls and Nozick

The notion of justice, as has developed over the ages, is really very old. It has moved in its nature say, from Plato's ethical to Aristotle's distributive, then religious, utilitarian, socialist and down to the libertarians—F.A. Hayek *(The Constitution of Liberty: 1960)*, J. Rawls *(A Theory of Justice:* 1972), Robert Nozick *(Anarchy, State and Utopia:* 1974) to name a few among them. The libertarian justice stands opposite to any and every socialist view of justice, and hence is an argument against social justice. It has nothing to do with any moral, ethical, intrinsic, eternal, natural values. It is individualistic, for it revolves around individual; libertarian, for it follows the notion of liberty. In economic terms, the libertarian justice demands: "no more redistribution"; in political terms, it asks for a minimal state; in social terms, it admits the claims of inequality.

(a) Hayek-Fallacies of Social Justice

Friedrich Hayek, (1899-1992) an Austrian-born British economist, is a philosopher of freedom. He feels that the freedom of individual has been reduced by an activist state. His answer to the onslaughts of ever-increasingly powerful state is a limited state based on spontaneous order in society, a state providing essential conditions for the preservation of an overall order. Freedom, as the condition of man in which coercion is most minimum, Hayek says, goes well along the limited state.

For Hayek, justice, in its nature, seeks to attain individual good, rather than the one that is called the social good. He argues that social justice does not secure liberties for the individual through which he/she can pursue his/her own good. He also says that as social justice stands for a particular purpose (of distribution of goods, or / and services to be given to the individuals in society), it is concerned more with the procedure than with the result—patterning the norms of distribution so that people share goods/services equitably, forgetting as to what an individual should get in return and as reward to what he/she gives to the society. So, for Hayek, justice seeks, not this or that purpose but a spontaneous order that helps develop rules of conduct, in short, the rule of law generally. His theory of justice, therefore, is a procedural justice: Justice must be sought in a rule of law, treating individuals equal disregarding their position, if any; all state-directed policies are incompatible with the principle of rule of law. The Hayekian justice is freedom, all freedom for the individual, all that he/she wants to obtain for his/her good. Conversely, for Hayek, injustice occurs when an individual interferes with the domain of freedom of another person when this is secured by just and universally observed rules, injustice meaning the existence of coercion. Condemning social justice, Hayek offers two adverse consequences of the idea of distributive social justice: Firstly, to seek to secure a particular pattern of justice will mean that one set of values related to human purposes will be given a preference to others in a society and this is incompatible with a liberal and free society in which the diversity of ends is recognised. Secondly, because there will be a lack of clarity and precision about these values reflecting social and moral diversity, to attempt to distribute goods and income and services according to one or the other of these criteria will be a very indefinite enterprise and will have a very great deal of power in the hands of the officials who will, of necessity, have to exercise power in a discretionary way. He, therefore, concludes that the claims of social justice would ultimately lead to the arbitrariness of government. In the name of the government's responsibility of securing just rewards for the individuals, it would usher in an era where the government would act unjustly and would ultimately yield before the interest groups that stand for private and not for public interest.

The idea of social justice does not only, in practice, end up in a sort of civil war among the numerous interest groups where the government itself becomes a party, it also helps transform a free society into a totalitarian one. His solution, therefore, is:

(i) a state that acts neutrally between the competing interests of numerous groups;

(ii) a set of abstract laws which will secure the maximum amount of individual freedom from minimum coercion;

(iii) a free market unconstrained by the distributive principles of social justice.

Hayek's views, on the subject, can not be accepted in toto. His over-dependence on the free market and its rules do not prevent, and in fact, cannot prevent the economically strong groups to act in their own interests. Such a situation would ultimately demand some norms of distribution and this would not indeed be, unjust. Furthermore, it can not be predicted in a free market as to what would be the economic benefits for an individual as also for a group which is relatively weak. It is also difficult to accept Hayek's arguments that the state seeking social justice is illegitimate and that the market is always legitimate, for the state is not always wrong, and the market, not always right.

(b) Rawls—the Contractarian Justice

John Rawls, (born 1921) is an American philosopher. His work *A Theory of Justice* has been regarded as a significant contribution to liberal political theory. His interest in the liberal state and in the concept of justice has led him to formulate and reformulate his theory of justice for about four decades. In 1958, justice, for him, is fairness, one that became the part and parcel of Rawlsian vocabulary on justice. A revised version of Rawls's theory was published in "Distributing Justice" (1967). The most elaborate and comprehensive argument of his theory was presented in *A Theory of Justice* (1971).

John Rawls' views on justice can best be summed up in his own words by highlighting the following:

"First Principle"

Each person is to have an equal right to the most extensive total system of equal basic liberties compatible with a similar system of liberty for all.

"Second Principle"

Social and economic inequalities are to be arranged so that they are both:

(a) to the greatest benefit of the least advantaged—and
(b) attached to offices and positions open to all under conditions of fair equality of opportunity.

First Priority Rule *(The Priority of Liberty)*

The principles of justice are to be ranked in lexical order and therefore liberty can be restricted only for the sake of liberty. There are two cases:

(a) a less extensive liberty must strengthen the total system of liberty shared by all;

(b) a less than equal liberty must be acceptable to those with the lesser liberty.

Second Priority Rule ***(The Priority of Justice over Efficiency and Welfare)***

The second principle of justice is lexically prior to the principle of efficiency and to that of maximising the sum of advantages; and fair opportunity is prior to the difference principle ... "

Stated simply, Rawls' conception of justice demands;

(i) the maximisation of liberty subject only to such constraints as are essential for the protection of liberty itself;

(ii) equality for all, both in the basic liberties of social life and also in the distribution of all other forms of social goods, subject only to the exception that inequalities may be permitted if they produce the greatest possible benefit for those least well off in a given scheme of inequality ("the difference principle");

(iii) "fair equality of opportunity" and the elimination of all inequalities of opportunity based on birth or wealth.

Rawls' contractarianism is not essentially of Hobbes, Locke or Rousseau. It is so only to show that certain moral principles are binding upon us because they would be acceptable by rational beings like us in the "original position". Justice, for him, is not law of nature or something based on reason, but is fair distribution on fair procedure This is what justice, for Rawls is: Justice as fairness.

Rawls admits that all individuals are not equal: say, equal in knowledge; all do not live in similar conditions: say, in similar social and economic conditions. There are some, Rawls declares, who are subject to what he calls "a veil of ignorance" and this veil excludes them not only from others, but also from themselves—the least advantaged members of society. Justice demands, so far as Rawls is concerned, due care for the least advantaged members of the society as well. It is the distribution of benefits among all the members of the society not in proportion to what he does, but in such a manner that the weakest of the weak is duly benefitted. Such a distribution of benefits, Rawls feels, is not only fair, but is also in accordance with the norms of justice.

Thus we may conclude with summing up Rawls' notion of justice as under:

(a) Justice, for Rawls, is fairness.

(b) It assumes a view of society as a fair system of cooperation between free and equal persons.

(c) Its object is to find out appropriate principles which help realise liberty and equality.
(d) These appropriate principles, attempting to seek liberty and equality are the result of an agreement among the people concerned in the light of their mutual advantage.
(e) As the people see themselves free and equal, they soon realize that they need the same primary goods so to pursue their own conception of good.
(f) These primary goods include, among others, the basic rights, liberties, opportunities, income, wealth, self-respect.
(g) Justice would mean that all the primary goods are to be distributed equally unless an unequal distribution of any or all of these goods, is to the advantage of the least favoured. To put it the other way, justice exists to the greatest benefit of the least advantaged-within the framework of established inequalities.

Rawl's theory of justice was well-timed. It was presented at a time (1971) when liberalism was becoming infashionable and was facing serious challenges. In his own country (USA), dominant values and political institutions were being questioned by various movements led by students, black and anti-Vietnam war activists. The utilitarian tradition, till then so popular, seemed an inadequate basis for the protection of minorities. Sarangi writes: "There were questions about proper use of political power and just distribution of liberties and other social goods. Perhaps Rawls was responding to these historical developments and trying to present a persuasive theoretical alternative to utilitarianism."

Rawls' theory of justice is, indeed, important atleast in (a) providing, as Chantal Mouffe says, a defence of political liberalism which establishes its autonomy from economic liberalism; (b) providing an alternative to utilitarian thought. One of Rawls' important contributions, as Bhiku Parkash says, consists in giving liberalism a new foundation and a new vitality. He gives liberalism a moral depth which it has always lacked. Parekh writes: "He (Rawls) shows that men are not only materially but also morally and ontologically interdependent, that they grow together and complete one another and that the full development of each is inseparable from the full development of all within a just society. In taking this view, Rawls is able to relate liberty, equality and justice and to elucidate the radical dimension of liberalism."

And yet, the *shortcomings* in Rawl's theory, cannot be overlooked (i) His account of the original position is far from clear: why people who are not in the original position should adopt principles chosen by those who were? If there is a bias in the original position and if, as a consequence .of that bias, the principles chosen do not respond to the norms of fairness. Sandel says that Rawls' notion of original position "contains a strong individualistic bias... —The original position seems to presuppose not just a neutral theory of the good, but a liberal, individualistic conception—...". (ii) His difference principle' is not without some demerit. Admitting the differences, i.e., inequalities, Rawls believes that an agreement would be reached between people. But will the wealthy share, and cooperate? (iii) Rawls gives priority to liberty and this, in itself, is another attack on him. Rawls says that a person in the original position will choose "the basic liberties" in priority to any distribution of income, wealth and power because by so doing he would have better chances of obtaining primary goods. If that is so, what would happen if the basic liberties conflict or how, at all, can they be restricted? Rawls has no answer to such questions except that he assumes a state of cooperation among them. (iv) There is a clear contradiction between the first principle which demands equal liberty, liberties for all and the second principle which justifies inequalities-inequalities between the most favoured on the one hand and the least advantaged on the other. (v) It is difficult to assume, as Rawls wants us to assume, liberty for all in a system of inequalities: Liberty among the unequals is liberty of the stronger, his power to control the weak. (vi) Rawls' argument is more favouring the principle of liberty, whatever tall claims he may insist with regard to the principle of equality. The fact that Rawls' first principle relates to the principle of liberty demonstrates his choice for this principle: Liberty comes first, everything else follows it (vii) Rawls' theory of justice is largely individualistic and libertarian. It is social in a very limited sense in so far as it does not exclude the weaker sections of society in his arrangement of justice.

(c) Nozick—the Entitlement theory of Justice

I Like John Rawl, Robert Nozick (born 1938) is an American libertarian political pholosopher, known for his restatement of classical liberal case for a minimal state and his rejection of both economic management and social welfare. He is for a state which is like a "night-watchman", one which is limited to the narrow functions of protection against force, theft, fraud, enforcement of contracts, and so on.

Nozick's theory of justice stands opposite to that of Rawls in an important respect. Whereas in Rawls' theory, justice is seen as particular pattern of social arrangements adjusting entitlements and resources in as neutral and fair manner as is possible, in Nozick, it is a view that individuals have rights and that those rights be respected at ail costs and in all circumstances. According to Nozick, justice is not a matter of attempting to organise or reorganise society and its institutions to achieve some distributive pattern, but is one of respecting basic rights which limit what may be done to someone without consent and the entitlements which such rights yield. For Nozick, rights are so fundamental and the constraints upon others' actions are so strong that only one can justify a minimal state: a minimal state means most minimum laws and conversely most maximum liberties and rights of the individual as individual. This is a position which takes Nozick close to Hayek, and farther back to Locke.

We may briefly outline Nozick's theory of justice which is 'entitlement' theory as against the distributive theory. His argument is that if the state does something against the individual for which he is entitled, it is a case of injustice: individual is entitled to certain " rights, already with him, and if the state takes them away, it does something which is not just. Nozick's assumption is that individual's rights are with the individual because he is an individual, no state had ever given these rights to him and no state through any arrangement can ever take them away from him. Justice, for Nozick, lies in not disrupting individual's entitlements; any thing that disrupts them through any patterned device is illegitimate and unjust. As against the Marxian principles: 'from each according to his ability to each according to his need' which, for Nozick, is a patterned device, he offers justice as one 'from each as they choose, to each as they are chosen.'

Nozick's entitlement theory of justice has the following characteristics:

(a) There is no social entity with a good that undergoes some sacrifices for its own good. There are only the individual people, different individual people with their own individual lives.

(b) Individuals have rights, and there are things no person or group may do to them. So strong and far reaching are these rights that they raise the question of what, and if anything, the state and its officials may do.

(c) The fact that there are different individuals with separate lives means that no one may be sacrificed for others.

(d) The idea of basic rights implies their enjoyment by the individual and also constraints on the others not to coerce the rights of the fellow-individual.

(e) Justice has historical essence in that it came about in course of time and not through any set formula or pattern.

(f) Justice seeks to protect the rights of the individual, rights which individual has because he/she is an individual "Things come," Nozick says, "into the world already attached to people having entitlements over them". Individuals have rights because, as individuals, they are entitled to them.

(g) All and any type of interference in the entitlements or rights of the individual are illegitimate. Nozick's justification of property right is based on the principle that it is an entitlement of an individual. In this context, the buying and selling of property, in the market, is merely the transformation of property rights.

(h) Following Locke, Nozick believes that person is inviolable, that he/she has an absolute property right in his/her own person, powers and capacities that he/she comes to possess unquestionable property right in unowned things (extending Locke's argument), and that no one else has the right to question or coerce an individual's rights, property right including.

In Nozick's view, justice is not a matter of how the distribution should be made. If it means so, then it becomes a type of patterned distributive justice which, according to Nozick, would "involve appropriating the actions of other persons". It is a matter of how the distribution has come about; it is a matter of what one is entitled to; and finally, it is a matter of protection of one's entitlements. Such a type of justice is compatible with a minimal, and not with an extensive, state.

There is much that separates Nozick from Rawls. Rawls favours distributive scheme; Nozick opposes it; Rawls' argument begins with social obligation; Nozick, with individual rights; Rawls' state is relatively more than a minimal', Nozick's merely minimal; Rawls is a defender of liberal-democratic and to some extent, a welfare state; Nozick, on the other, argues in favour of a libertarian minimal state; for Rawls, justice is always distributive; for Nozick, it is not justice if it is distributive and he says that a society is just so long as its members possess which they have a right to.

Nozick's entitlement theory of justice is more a theory of rights, especially that of property than a theory of justice. He extols the virtues of eighteenth-century individualism on the one hand, and the nineteenth-century *laissez-faire* capitalism. He isolates individual from other individuals, forgetting that individual does possess sociality howsoever lone he may be. There is, above individual private interest, a social interest as well. Indeed, individual rights are inviolable, but Nozick goes on to make them absolute. His concept of minimal state and his passion for individual's basic rights make him a defender of Locke's theory in the present century. His notion of justice is vague, if not abstract. He throws away all the norms and principles normally associated with the idea of justice and brings it to mean the protection of status quo.

VI: Justice: Subaltern and Feminist Perspectives

The idea of what constitutes justice is always different for different people. In fact, it goes with the status or position of the individual. If, for a ruler, it denotes the maintenance of law and order, it would mean, from the point of view of the ruled, the existence of certain rights and their protection. The liberals find justice in the existing system of things; the socialists, in the absence of exploitation and discrimination; the anarchists, in anarchy; the libertarians, in liberties and rights; the communitarians, in public good. The unemployed would see justice in the provision for employment; the subalterns, in the elimination of deprivations; the women, in the abrogation of men's dominance.

(a) Subaltern Perspective on Justice

The dictionary meaning of subaltern is 'subordinate' 'lower in rank', particularly 'below the rank of captain'. In social sciences, it would, broadly speaking, mean an individual or a group standing lower in the social pyramid: the poor, the lowly, the downtrodden, in short, the weaker sections of the society. In broad sense, subaltern would include the tillers, the tribals, the agricultural labourers, the scavengers, the leather workers, in Gandhiji's terminology, 'the Harijan', the Dalits, the weakest of the weak.

The fact of social inequality is the fact of high and low; the rich and the poor; men of higher castes and those of lower; the socially favoured and the socially boycotted; in Marx's terms: the master and the slave, the lord and the serf, the bourgeoisie and the proletariat, the exploiter and the exploited.

History provides ample evidences of discrimination, deprivation, degradation of the people belonging to the lower strata of society. In the name of justice, injustice is inflicted on them; the law, as the incarnation of justice, is made by and exists to serve the interests of the superior; conversely, the law denies justice to the inferior.

It is interesting to note differences between the Marxian notion of opposing classes at different stages of history and the subaltern groupings. Whereas in the Marxian thesis, these antagonistic classes are economically determined groups, in the subaltern connotation, the groupings- are socially and culturally determined as well. That is why that we talk of the Dalits in the Indian caste system and of the tribals in the context of regionally backward tribes of India. But in both cases (Marxian and the subaltern), the disadvantaged are always exploited, discriminated, denied. The subaltern as also the exploited classes are denied the benefits of the basic necessities of life, are looked down upon as out-castes, are never given opportunities to better their conditions. Each type of society, at any given time, throws up the exploited lot as mere slaves. Obviously, for the deprived, justice is not what it is for the comfortable.

For the subaltern, justice is not the rule of law, much less a code of morals. For the tiller of the land, grant of land is justice: for a socially boycotted individual, social equality is justice; for a culturally underdeveloped, elimination of all impositions is justice; for a slave, emancipation is justice. If the subalterns rise in arms, it is understandable, for their revolt is the expression of their outrages against the system itself, their non-conformity speaks of their alienation.

The subaltern perspective on justice demands social justice for the disadvantaged. It demands two-fold objective at the same time: (i) elimination of all types of discrimination; and to provision for special care so to attain social equality. The subaltern perspective of justice is not merely economic, but is also social, cultural, educational, and even psychological. The subaltern has not to be developed, but is made to feel that he/she is developing. The subaltern perspective of justice would, among other things, seek to remove traditional disabilities, eliminate exploitation in all forms, reserve positions in all public sector enterprises as in legislatures, make available all facilities required for social development. It would be unjust if the law does not protect the weaker, if the society does not embrace the lowly, if the government denies the deprived, basic necessities of life. The subaltern perspective on justice does not content itself with a job for the unemployed, an assistance for the aged, medicine for the sick, but goes further to include a complete transformation of society into one that can rightfully claim to be equalitarian. The subaltern justice is not libertarian and therefore, does not sacrifice equality for liberty. It is rather a phenomenon of protective discrimination, a discrimination in favour of the weak for purposes of not only raising the quality of life, but also taking advantages of the fruits of equality. It is heartening to note that the subaltern studies are being taken up both at macro-level and micro-level, in India as well as elsewhere.

(b) Feminist Perspective on Justice

The feminist philosophy, including its political theory, speaks of man's domination of woman as a curse inflicted on her by a socially-structured-male society. What is actually a natural sex-inequality is made a social gender inequality and then follows all sorts of values (if at all' they, really, are) associated with masculinity. The female, feminism believes, is regarded inferior to male in all qualities. Physically she is dubbed as dull and dud; intellectually, as a being with less or no wisdom; socially, she has a place lower than man. She is considered ineligible for all public activities; her life is confined to the private life of the family-mothering the babies. Even in the family, she is not only second, but is always secondary. All her miseries, the feminists say, are the result of man's atrocities. Because she is physically weaker than man, she is made to lead a subordinate life. Almost half of humanity lives and has, in the past, lived in servitude, dependent always, at one or the other time, on man: be he a father, brother, husband or the son. Until recently, public or political life had been an area out of her bound. This is the situation in ,most part of the world to-day for most of the female folks. The rise and development of feminism have helped in not only understanding women's woes but also in bettering their conditions-social, economic, familial. Indeed, there have been cases of dowry deaths, brides' burning and of Sati, yet the woman, to-day is no more a commodity to be bought and sold at man's whims. Worth quoting are the few lines from a femnist icon Simone de Beanvoir to Chicago writer Nelson Algren: "I'll be good. I'll do the dishes. I'll sweep and I'll go buy eggs and rum cake myself. I won't touch your hair, your cheeks or your shoulder without permission."

The basis on which feminism lies is the idea of equality. Feminism abhors inequality between man and woman, and conversely demands equality as the very core of society. Because woman is regarded unequal to man, she is made to suffer throughout her life: her subordination, powerlessness and oppression are the consequences of male dominance. Justice, in feminist perspective, demands escapism from woman's internalisation of female gender, and the low self-esteem, apathy and sense of helplessness that goes with it. What is needed, the feminists say, is not merely equal rights which man possesses, but also, as the socialist feminists insist, communalisation of domestic and childcare functions: the male superiority would have to be abolished; patriarchal culture would have to be demolished; gender socialisation would have to be imbibed; women's liberation from male oppression would have to be fought out. The feminists do not regard law to be neutral in disputes between man and woman; the idea of justice is, by its very nature, male-structured. Mackinnon says: "When law (in the male-structured society) is made ruthlessly neutral, it will be most male." It is as Mill rightly thought, foolish to think that a woman's interests can be incorporated in her husband's and that is why that he insisted on exposing the myth of male protection. Most feminist scholars felt, very strongly indeed, that women are as rational as men are, and therefore, they are entitled to the same legal and political rights. The feminist perspective on justice means, among others, elimination of all male domination, equality of rights, bridging the public and the private spheres, and creation of society, culture and politics in new, rather non-patriarchal forms.

Janet Radcliffe Richards, in her remarkable essay, *The Sceptical Feminist* (1982), provides a thought provoking feminist perspective on justice. She says that justice is bound up with individual's freedom to pursue I his own destiny and this is what women are, currently, denied systematically. Drawing largely from Rawls' *A Theory of Justice* (1971), she like Susan Moller akin (*Justice, Gender and the Family:* 1990), uses the idea of a model of the just society in which women would be as free to explore their own potential as men. She argues that a sexually just society would require a radical restructuring of work, increase the choices available to women, and ensure that the benefits and the burdens of having children were shared more equally between the sexes. Equally convincing is akin's argument. She says, and with this we may conclude the feminist perspective on justice that at present, women are systematically disadvantaged in all areas of life; that her ideal is a society in which child-rearing and domestic work are shared equally; that this equality within the home would make possible gender equality in all other areas of life; that a just society would be one without gender. Arguing akin's case, Valerie Bryson says. "...it is within the home that children learn the values on which they will base their adult life," and that such values of democratic citizenship cannot be learned in a family based on domination and inequality" as the present male-constructed society, really is.

SUGGESTED READINGS

1. Ackerman, B., *Social Justice in the Liberal State* (New Haven: Yale University Press, 1980).
2. Barry, B., *The Liberal Theory of Justice* (Oxford: The Clarendon Press, 1973).
3. Engels, F., *Anti-Dubrlng* (Moscow: Foreign Languages Publishing House, 1954).
4. Galstan, W.N., *Justice and Human Good* (Chicago: University of Chicago Press, 1981).
5. Goldman, A., 'The Entitlement Theory of Justice', *Journal of Philosophy*, 73, 1976.
6. Hayek, FA., *The Constitution of Liberty* (London: Routledge, 1960).
7. __________*The Mirage of Social Justice* (London: Routledge and Kegan Paul, 1976).
8. Miller, D., *Social Justice* (Oxford: The Clarendon Press, 1976).
9. Nozick, R., *Anarchy, State and Utopia* (Oxford: Blackwell, 1974).
10. Okin, S.M., *Justice, Gender and the Family* (New York: Basic Books, 1990).

11. Rawls, J., *A Theory of Justice* (Oxford: The Clarendon Press, 1972).
12. Richards, J.R., *The Sceptical Feminist* (Harmandsworth: Penguin, 1982).
13. Sankhdhar, M.M. and Mukherjee, Subrata (eds) Essays *on Fabian Socialism* (New Delhi: Deep and Deep Publications, 1991).
14. Stammler, Rudolf, *The Theory of Justice* (New York: Macmillan, 1925).
15. Jucker, Robert C, "Marx and Distributive Justice" in Fredrik Carl J. and Chapman, J.W. (eds.) *Justice* (New York: Atherton, 1963).
16. Walzer, M., *Spheres of Justice* (Oxford: Martin Robertson, 1983).
17. Wollheim, R., "Crime, Sin and Mr. Justice Davton". *Encounter* 13, 1959.

13

The Notion of Common Good

The common good is an attractive idea, but at the same time, is difficult in so far as it means different things to different people. It is also difficult in so far as its meaning and the related connotations are concerned. The liberals and the Marxists, opposed as they are, view the idea of common good in diametrically different senses; for the former, common good lies in the good of the individual while for the latter, it lies in a classless society. The communtarians, as against the neo-liberals, see common good in the good of the community, and the Gandhians, in a moral and just society. The different ideologies, keeping on to their respective poles, give different meanings, looking at the concept of common good from their own angles, and hence, refer to partial, restrictive and inadequately limited views. The good of the individual may not necessarily mean the common good, for it may seek good for one, and deny it to the other; the common good may not necessarily seek good of all, and may confine good common to all; the common good may not mean good of the many, for it is bound to exclude the good of the few; obviously, good of a minority cannot be called as the good of all, for ignoring the good of the majority never takes us to the goal of common good. And if we take Rousseau's theory of General Will as the starting pointing of understanding the notion of common good, we may succeed in finding out common good in Rousseau General Will as the *will for all* but only at the cost of sacrificing the claims of quality. The idea of common good is, indeed, bewildering.

I: What is Common Good?

Common good as a goal is different from common good as a procedural norm. This is not to say that we are giving common good a meaning in relation to its goal. Nor does it mean that we are considering common good as merely a norm. Our tentative meaning of common good has the characteristics of both: as a goal, it seeks good of all and good for all; as a norm; it means acting justly in a just manner already fixed and prescribed.

Common Good as a Goal: Common good is not individual good at the cost of social good, nor it is social good at the cost of the good of a single individual. It is as much private good as is public: it seeks the good of an individual as much as of the whole community. A good that does not aim at the good of the individual can not be called common good. Likewise a good that does not seek the interest of all can not be said to mean common good. When attempts are made to attain the interests of others, it would mean the dominance of sectional interest over the social interest. Obviously, the attainment of such a good is not be the attainment of common good. As a sectional good is not the common good, so is the majoritarian interest, not a public interest, and therefore, is not what we mean as common good. Common good is as much the good of one as it is the good of all.

The idea of common good implies the performance of certain functions, functions which serve the people. Defence, order, transportation, roads and the like are 'common' functions required by all, nearly all. But would the performance of such 'common' functions mean the attainment of common good? It is, but the idea of common good is more an idea associated with services than with the obligations. 'Defence' is a matter of obligation; hospitalisation, of service. The emphasis, in the idea of common good, is on the provision and extension of services, and thereafter, on preservation of peace and order. Common good, in its essence, contains an element of welfarism.

Though common good contains a measure of welfareism, all welfare activities may not result in the attainment of common good. Common good may demand a rocket range for stalling an aggression, but it may seek the uprooting of a hundred families which is certainly not a welfare act. Common good is not a victory of one claim on the other, it is the adjustment of all the claims, their harmonisation. If common good is the meeting point of numerous claims, sometimes, conflicting, it includes, essentially, everything which is good in each of such claim-minimum common good. Opinions may differ about what percentage of unemployment is consistent with 'full employment', but-it certainly includes some measure, though minimum, of unemployment. Differences and contrasts among the claims do not mean that there can be no mutually agreed common claim. There is! Common good is what is common in all claims; what is good for each, and therefore, for all. It is a goal in the sense that it is a common factor, a balancing device, a sort of compromise, a point in which all see their good, inherent in it.

Common good, as a goal, then, has .the following features:

(i) Common good is not the good of one or the other; it is the good of both, good of all.

(ii) Common good, as the good of all, means good common to all, and common for all.

(iii) Common good is a matter more of a service than of an order; it gives more than it takes.

(iv) Common good, being the good of all, means a meeting point of all the claims: a give-and-take point; it adjusts and reconciles what is common in all.

Common Good as a Procedural Norm: Common good is seen as a procedure as well. Common good is a device of doing things justly rather than a goal, minimum as it may be, to be achieved. The argument is offered: Common good is found not in what we do, but in how we do. To repeat, one may quote Benn and Peters: "... the common good is not an objective in which all particular objectives are somehow reconciled and in which everyone shares... Neither is the common good merely the good of the majority; for we often think it right, for example, to tax the majority to relieve a needy minority; and we should condemn majority action if we took no account of suffering, inflicted on the few merely because they were a few. On our interpretation, 'to seek the common good' means to try to act justly in the sense of justice'.... ". So, common good, as a procedure, means a norm, a just norm, a just norm of doing things.

We may, thus, conclude that common good is to be understood both as a goal, i.e. a goal to be achieved so to serve the good of each and all; as a procedure, i.e., achieving the prescribed goal in such a just manner as does not discriminate against anyone.

II: Notion of Common Good-the Liberal Perspective

The idea of common good is an old one. It is old in the sense that its dimensions, one or the other, are found in the writings of a host of philosophers in the West. Plato thought that common good lies in the ideal state and that the ideal state is one where everyone contributes to the good of the society in accordance with the best one has in terms of abilities and capacities. According to Aristotle, it is the state through which the ideal of common good or what he called the "good of life" could be achieved. The Romans found common good in laws as issued, by the sovereign. During the medieval age when religion-dominated European society, common good meant the observance of the Christian teachings. In most part of the European history, until the end of medieval age, the idea of common good was the idea. of a norm, an ideal and an ethical end. As the western tradition, until the beginning of the late modem age starting with the French Revolution, was non-democratic, the idea of common good was confined to the writings of the philosophers or to the teachings of Christianity.

Even in the early liberal period, individualistic as it was, the idea of common good was almost exterior. Thomas Hobbes, as Macpherson tells us) thought of individual as the proprietor of his own person who owes nothing to others or the society. John Locke, the forerunner of classical liberalism, thought of individual as the end: his philosophy begins and ends with the individual. Jeremy Bentham had never accepted the argument of a society as a social whole: for him, the only reality is the individual, his interests and that, there is nothing which can, if properly, be called the common good or the social good. John Stuart Mill, despite his concerns for the representative government and also community could not leave his individual-liberal ground: he used to say that it is liberty which is individual's greatest asset and that liberty consists in pursuing one's own good in one's own way, without. harming the like liberties of others.

From the classical liberals—Locke, Bentham, Smith—down to the present-day nee-liberals, either of the right (Hayek, Nozick) or of the left (Rawls)—there has hardly been any substantial change in their conception of what they thought, if really they did, of 'common good'. The liberal's commitments to the ideal of liberty, and to the autonomous individual, have never been in doubt. So, for the liberals, the idea of common good has meaning only within the framework of the individual good: common good lies, their argument is, in the good of the individual; the fulfilment of the individual's interests ultimately results in or leads to the fulfilment of the interests of the whole society.

The liberal assumptions can be best summed up in what Bill Jordan (*The Common Good*, 1989) says, as under:

(1) Each person is the best judge of what is good for him or self. It is, in the fitness of things that everyone be allowed to take his/her own decisions, follow his or her own plan of action, and conversely, not to be forced to do things for the good of society. as a whole or for the good of others, unless and until it is the only option that remains in hand.

(2) As individuals compete, among themselves, for their limited resources, they are bound to have different interests. The only way, for yielding best results, is to coordinate the conflicting interests through the mechanism of market.

(3) As the individuals know what is good or bad for themselves and as a consequence of this, they possess their varying interests, they have to have freedom to choose from whatever alternatives are available to them. Accordingly, the freedom to choose implies a responsibility, responsibility about what has been decided. The people may, with others, share a measure of responsibility and hence, they are responsible only to what they commit, partly.

(4) Individuals have their interests; they have the right to make decisions about what they desire. Obviously, they would seek their own good, through their own efforts. Accordingly, no one has a general right to help others or be helped by others.

(5) After having employed their efforts, individuals seek fulfilment of their interests, partly or wholly. As to what they earn through competition or cooperation within the frame of market system, they have the obvious right to keep that earning to themselves. Individuals, having earned through their efforts, are entitled to what they earn, possess, acquire, dispose and hence, have legal right to property.

(6) Under circumstances of market system, the government has very little to do, minimum as is possible: leave individuals as free as possible, and control them if it is necessary in the interest of individual freedom and fair competition.

How does the idea of common good arise? Where does it lie? What are its implications? These are some of the questions which have been answered by Bill Jordan, with a relatively better case of the liberal view of common good, he presumes a situation of ship, sailing on sea with dangers of sinking, and with people unknown to one another.

(1) "*The Common good arose from a shared situation:* In this stance, all 'the people on the ferry, though they came from different backgrounds and cultures, were literally in the same boat'. Because all were in mortal danger, all had a need to escape from the ship."

Thus, the idea of common good is the result of a situation, a situation of mortal danger. This means that if the situation would not have arisen, there would have been no need for common good as such.

(2) *The situation created common interests:* Although each passenger had an individual interest in preserving his or her own life, all had a common interest in cooperating to help each other to escape. What I mean by a common interest is that each could quickly assess that an orderly, concerted, combined effort to survive

would be more likely to succeed than a free-for-all, in which everyone tried to save themselves ... ".

Thus, common good is, more or less, the preservation of one's own good and cooperation does not amount to any unity but to escapism: cooperation so to avoid a free-for-all situation.

(3) *All cooperated with each other for the sake of the common good:* Concerted cooperation did not imply that everyone tried to rescue everyone else, as this would have been equally chaotic. Nor did it mean that everyone stood back, saying to each other, "After you, Cecil; no, after you, Claude'. It meant that all were active in a joint effort to get out, which it was in the interests of all to achieve by cooperation".

Thus, common good is not welfare of all. It lies not as much in preservation as, in avoiding the situation of potential destruction. Common good is not a positive situation of obtaining something, it is a situation of avoiding something: people cooperate, with all efforts available, not so much to reach a goal as is to save themselves from a fall.

(4) *Those with special abilities played key roles:* The fact that all played an active role did not imply that everyone did the same thing. Very fit and strong people built ladders out of furniture, carried small children up them, broke windows, and so on. A very tall man acted as a 'human bridge' over a watery chasm, allowing others to pass over his body to safety".

Thus, common food demands active role of all if they have to escape from virtual destruction. But this does not mean that all do the same task, much less receive the same reward. Common good is neither common activity nor does it mean common reward.

(5) *Those with special needs received extra help:* For example, children and disabled people, who were in no position to save themselves, were given physical assistance by stronger passengers. It was reported that one passenger carried a baby in his teeth, and that another held a small child above his head' as the water rose to engulf him".

Thus, common good lies in assisting those who are needy, weak or helpless. It does not mean helping everybody, but only those who, by virtue of their physical disabilities, are unable to escape from the death-trap.

(6) *Existing commitments were recognised:* Although everyone cooperated for mutual safety, individuals gave priority to helping members of their families. Some intuitive balance was struck between

concern for the good of all and concern for closest relatives".

Thus, common good is confined to the limits of mutual safety and security and does not extend beyond. It does not mean mutual benefit, benefit of all. What it means is discriminatory benefit—benefit for the nearer prior to the benefit for the farther.

(7) *All shared responsibility for the good of all:* Everyone was included in the common good, without regard for their status or origin. Until the official rescuers arrived, and unless a trained member of the crew was at hand, all took part as equals, with equal responsibility."

Common good is not the concern of the related few and as such, not the obligation of the few. It is the responsibility to contribute one's share equally.

(8) No *one was compelled to act against his* or *her will:* Although some people behaved heroically, no one was forced to do so. No individual was sacrificed for the good of others, or used as a means of other's safety without consenting to this role."

Thus, common good and its attainment depend on the free will of the individual. We can not compel a person to forget his own good and care only for the good of others.

The liberal notion of good is more a notion of individual good than a social good. The liberals see common good only in the individual good, see individuals as discrete, see discreteness as the embodiment of personal, private and individualised interests, interests as they come straight from individual's desires, desires which are absolute and unlimited. Hence, the liberal notion of common good is what is commonly required by all, and good so far as it does not harm anybody. The liberals' notion of common good revolves around the individuals, free individuals, libertarian individuals. Their concern for the common good is marginally public and is predominantly private.

III: Notion of Common Good—the Communitarian Perspective

The "common good" theory, if one likes to put the record straight, is a reaction against the liberal individual notion of what constitutes as common good. The communitarians, be they 'left', 'pluralist', 'socialist', 'conservative', appeal to the idea of community as an inescapable ideal. Their emphasis is on the existence of community, more on the community of ends than on the individual's private ends—on the common good. They characterise society less as an aggregate of individuals and more in terms of its constituting a community. They see society as a system of shared values and commonly subscribed practices and institutions. The emphasis is on the values, practices, institutions as integral part of the society. Common good springs, indeed, *from the individuals,* but only when they think themselves as part of the larger whole—the society. The freedom of the individual is enlarged or becomes meaningful only when it responds to the good of the society. Thus, unlike the foundationalists (meaning the individualists, the liberals and the neo-liberals) who prefer "right" to "good", the communitariana prefer "good" to "right". Richard Bellamy holds the view: "Whereas foundationalists seek to separate the right from the good and come up with a set of human rights valid for the societies, communitarian situate rights within the context of a certain kind of community that promotes a particular conception of the individual and his or her relations with others". From the communitarian perspective, rights emerge in their true character as secondary rather than primary principles. So, they declare that community, instead of diminishing liberty, freedom or rights, helps enlarge them.

The communitarians do not agree with the view that we can develop cogent views of the good through abstract philosophical reasoning. They says that the notion of the good is not the product of individual preference or emotional attitude. Rather, it is, they declare, embodied in the ways of life of particular communities. It is impossible to give the idea of good by any external rational foundation: it is given in particular forms of life. No philosopher creates the idea of good; he only reclaims! it. For the communitarians, the community is the basis of practical reason and political judgement; individual is important in so far as it is influenced by the values of the community.

Arguing against the liberal point of view which finds social good, if at all it is there, only after the individual good has been attained, the communitarians say that the flourishing of the society has to trade; not on agreements (Rawl's theories) but on values implicit in the existing way of life in society as it exists.

The communitarian notion of common good can be summed up by highlighting the following features:

(i) Community, and not the individual, is the source of all values.
(ii) Common good lies within the ambit of the community itself.
(iii) Community is more than the aggregate of discrete individuals; it is rather the sum-total of values combined together,
(iv) The values go on to make what common good really is.
(v) Individual is not merely a part of community, but is its constitutive organ: born in it, nurtured by it, and developed by it—the community, its values.

So understood, communitarianism is a reaction, developed by diverse notions from philosophers like Hegel, Green, Bosanquet, Tawney,

Williams, Wolff and many others, against individualism, subjectivism, atomism, the alienation, the instrumentalism, the contract-based and market-oriented character of liberalism.

The communitarian perspective of common good is closely associated with the ends clear to community. It is, therefore, rightly argued that such a community-based idea of common good is or has to be linked with the idea of democratic participation. The underlying idea is: more is the participation of the individuals, better are the chances of attaining common good, conversely, lesser the participation, fewer are the possibilities of the state achieving the ideal of common good.

The communitarian notion of common good is subject to criticism, especially the following:

(1) Common good rests on the idea of community as the basic truth. What it means is that the idea of common good is the idea coming, as it is, from the community itself. The common good theory, while emphasising the significance of community *derecognises the importance of individuality.* It may not regard individuals as aggregate constituting society, but it has to recognise that the individuals constitute society, and as such, play a definite role in the society.

(2) The common good theory is unrealistic. Though one may imagine some desirable ideal of a harmonious community, the realities of actual politics do not allow its realisation. Common good remains, in its essence, utopian.

(3) The communitarian notion of common good smacks of being ideological, and hence pre-conceived, partisan and prejudiced.

(4) The realisation of common good has the danger of bureaucratisation. The idea of common good implies a vast range of public-service functions to be performed by the state and its machinery, obviously through officials. There is a danger in common-good state turning into a bureaucratic state. In such a situation, the common good turns out to reflect the bureaucratic rationality rather than the values for which a community stands.

IV: Notion of Common Good-the Marxian Perspective

The Marxian perspective on the notion of common good has its cognisance only in a system which is classless, without exploitation, without alienation, without oppression, without injustice. A just society, according to the Marxists, is one that is classless. In a class society, what is called justice or what is called common good, is, in reality, justice for the rich, and only his good: in the name of the common good, the economically dominant group usurp the hard-earned material benefits unto itself: the masters did it in the slave-owning society; the feudal lords did it in the feudal society; the capitalists do it in the bourgeois society—the haves do it in all types of class societies. Common good, according to the Marxists, does not lie in a class (say, capitalist) society, for in such a society, the capitalists eat away what is earned by the labour; nor does it lie in a classless society (say, socialist) where the principle is: "from each according to his ability, to each according to his work", because in such a society, one's ability is recognised and one's work is assured, but one's needs are not fully met. Common good, therefore, in the Marxian view, lies in a system which is without class-antagonism and without state's coercion (a classless and a stateless society) and where the principle accepted and adopted is: "From each according to his work to each according to his needs."

From the above, it is clear that the Marxian common good presupposes: (i) an equal society; (ii) work for each and work for all in accordance with one's abilities and capacities; (iii) production so planned that it meets the requirements of all the people; (iv) state of plenty and prosperity. Obviously, the Marxist perspective on common good is closely related to the highest stage of material development. This means that in all class societies, the realities of common good are only empty words, and if at all there is any good, it is the good of the haves. The socialist society, though classless, and also a transitional one between the capitalist and the communist society, does not guarantee common good, but it does prepare ground for it. As Marx writes, "... after labour has become not merely a means to live, but has become itself the primary necessity of life; after the productive forces have also increased with the all-round development of the individual, and all the springs of cooperative wealth flow more abundantly—only then can the narrow horizon of bourgeois right be fully left behind, and society inscribe on its banners: "From each. according to his work to each according to his needs."

The Marxian perspective, unlike the liberal's, does not regard individuals as discrete, separate and isolated beings, fighting for their respective interests and seeking common good so long as it does not go against their individual and private good. Nor does it, like the communitarians, regard social good exclusively prior to the individual one. The Marxists are neither individualists nor idealists. They do not see individual and society separate from each other, as the individualists and the idealists do. They do not regard individual and society as opposed and therefore, antagonistic to each other. They say that there is an inescapable relationship between the individual and society and that the interest of each lies in the interest of the other: the individual's interest is not common interest if it ignores the social interest; the social interest is not common interest if it goes against the interest of any single individual.

The Marxist highlight a very important point of individual—society relationship. It is that the individuals are not lone entities, they are born in the society—in the already existing/society. The society makes them what they become. And in turn, they make the society, different from the one they were born in.

If the interests of all the individuals have to constitute common good, it has to presuppose *all individuals as equal.* Inequality and common good do not go together: it is only within the framework of equality that common good could be realizable. This is why the Marxists argue that in each class society, which by its very nature is an unequal society, the common good is not the good of all, but is the good of the few. As in a capitalist society, for example, the interests of the capitalists and those of the proletariat do not coincide, all talk of common good is a mere sham and all efforts towards attaining it an exercise in futility. Equality, which helps attain common good, is equality in terms of (i) social ownership of means of production and distribution, (ii) equitable adequate rewards, (iii) equal opportunities, (iv) absence of all discrimination: social, economic, political religious, casteist and so on.

The idea of common good, the Marxists argue, is not the idea of empty words. It means the realisation of the needs of the people so to improve the quality of life. It, therefore, presupposes a state of plenty and prosperity, and hence development of the highest order:

Communism, and with it the common good, is no utopia in so far as it assures the highest stage of material development and the benefits reaching the-common people and making their life rich in real terms. V, Afanasyev (*Marxist Philosophy,* n.d.) points out, rather, rightly: "All members of communist society, by virtue of their equal relation to the means of production will be in the same position, enjoy equal conditions of work and distribution and actively participate in administering society's affairs. Harmonious relations between the individual and society will become the rule because social and personal interests will be fully combined". Thus, common good, in the Marxist thought, is not the reconciliation of 'the social good within the ambit of individual good; it is also not the reconciliation of individual good within the framework of social good; it is the amalgamation of both in each other. To imagine individual good without social good is as absurd as is to think social good without individual good.

It may, however, be said that the Marxists view common good as an objective which not only makes it almost a norm to be realizable, but also obliterates, common good as a just procedure, a just way of doing a thing. The Marxian common good confines itself to the materialistic development and presumes, rightly or wrongly, that common good would be achieved if material development were to be achieved. The material benefit and its distribution, Jordan argues, would not be "moral in nature, nor would they necessarily try to give all citizens an interest in the common good". His fear is that the distribution of common good benefits "might involve the dictatorship of the proletariat', and the deliberate exclusion of certain groups from any share of power or any benefit of membership."

V: Notion of Common Good-the Gandhian Perspective

Mahatma Gandhi (1869-1948) was a many-sided personality. "He was", C. Ramachandran says, "at once a saint and a revolutionary, a politician and a social reformer, an economist and a man of religion, an educationist and a satyagrahi; devotee alike of faith and reason, a man of action and a dreamer of dreams." "He was", he continues, "a great reconciler of opposites and he was that without any strain or artificiality. He loved greatly but without sentimentality. He unreservedly accepted the fact that truth can reside in opposites."

His notion of common good was not that of a philosopher, for he never claimed to be so. He thought of common good as any man would. This notion of common good would not be of a state with all coercive powers flowing from above, but would be one rising from an autonomous individual—decentralised to the core. It would not spring from a state without morals, but from a state with morality, one that cares more for the means than for the end, based on the ideals of truth and non-violence. It would not be an economy which is capitalist-oriented or socialist one, but would be one where the principle of trusteeship would reign. His notion of common good would not admit any discrimination or distinction, but would be one where the lowly would be respected as would be the one highly placed. His conception of Ramrajya approximates closely to his notion of common good. His appropriate order, Professor Ramashray Roy says, "must be based on ahimsa, harmony, service, duty, Swadeshi, self-restraint, and self-sufficient autonomous local communities that emphasize non-possessiveness, equality, non-exploitation, and decentralization of decision-making." He quotes Gandhi: "In this structure, composed of innumerable villages, there will be ever-widening never ascending circles. Life will not be a pyramid with the apex sustained by the bottom. But, it will be an oceanic circle whose centre will be the individual always ready to perish for the villages, the latter ready to perish for the circle of villages, till at last becomes one life composed of individuals, never aggressive in their arrogance but ever humble, sharing the majesty of the oceanic circle of which they are integral units. Therefore, the outermost circumference will not wield power to crush the inner circle but will give strength to all within and derive its own strength from it... No one ... (will) be the first and none the last."

Gandhiji's just order seeks to achieve common good or what may be called in the Gandhian terminology, *Sarvodaya.* The word 'Sarvodaya' literally means good of all, welfare for all, upliftment, somewhat leading to the betterment of the last or the lowly. Gandhi takes the word Sarvodaya from Ruskin's *Unto the Last,* from antyodaya. His notion of common good (Sarvodaya) demands that the needs of the neediest deserve our attention. What it means. is the service of humanity including the service to be done for the most needy. Common good, according to Gandhi, is the good of each and good of all, the greatest good of all. Sarvodaya, therefore, means "the general good" or "the common good of mankind".

It may, however, be noted that Gandhiji's notion of Sarvodaya is different from the utilitarian principle of "greatest happiness of the greatest number". The greatest material, and at the cost of spiritual or moral, happiness, may not necessarily lead to the greatest good. Moreover, the idea of the greatest happiness is the happiness of the greatest majority, the good of the greatest number. Gandhi observes: "... as the object is the happiness of the greatest number, people in the West do not believe it to be wrong if it is secured at the cost of the minority.... The exclusive quest for the physical and material happiness of the majority has no sanction in divine law", and he declares: "... the true solution ... lay in the application of the maxim, 'the greatest good for the greatest number'."

Sarvodaya, as common good, is socialism so long as it aims at the welfare of all. It is not socialism if it seeks to establish materialism or what the Marxists say the highest stage of materialism. It is not socialism if it believes in the antagonism of the opposing classes and in class struggle. It is not socialism if it adopts violent and revolutionary methods for attaining good of all. It is not socialism if it propagates a class rule, may be of the proletariat. The Gandhian socialism is a moral kind of socialism which seeks the development of all in all fields of life. His conception of Sarvodaya, or the common good, is socialist in so far as it aims at 'good of all', anarchist in so far as it abolishes all kinds of coercion, individualist in so far aa it believes in the essential goodness of man.

The Gandhian perspective of common good, it may be argued, has the numerous features, especially the following:

(1) Common good, or *Saroodaya,* is the good of the individual as found in the good of all. It does neither want the individual to make sacrifice for the society, nor the society, for the individual. It is the good of each with the good of all.

(2) It is the good of each and good of all, but it is good in its greatest number and for all aspects of life.

(3) It is not merely material, but is. moral and spiritual as well.

(4) It is the amalgamation of almost all ideologies in so far as they seek to attain the good of all.

To conclude, one may say with Vinobha Bhave that Sarvodaya or the Gandhian notion of common good "does not want the rise of the few; not even of the many, or for that matter, the rise of the greatest number. We are not satisfied with the greatest good of the greatest number. We can be satisfied only with the good of one and all, of the high and the low, of the strong and the weak, the intelligent as well as the dull ... "

SUGGESTED READINGS

1. Acton, H.B., *The Morals of Markets: an Ethical Exploration;* (Longman, 1971)
2. Afanasyev, V., *Marxist Philosophy* (Moscow: Foreign Languages Publishing House. n.d.)
3. Barker, E., *Principles of Social and Political Theory* (Oxford: Oxford University Press, 1961)
4. Benn, S.I. and Peters, R.S., *Social Principles and the Democratic State* (London: George Allen and Unwin Ltd., 1975)
5. Jordan, Bill., *Common Good* (New York: Rasil Black-well Ltd., 1989)
6. Kumarappa, Bharatan (ed) *Sarvodaya* (Ahmedabad: Navajivan Publishing House, 1954)
7. Margolis, H., *Selfishness, Altruism and Rationality: a theory of Social Choice* (Cambridge: Cambridge University Press, 1982)
8. Miller, D., *Social Justice* (Oxford: The Clarendon Press, 1976)
9. Radhakrishnan, S., *Mahatma Gandhi: 100 years* (New Delhi: Gandhi Peace Foundation, 1968)
10. Roy, Ramashray., *Gandhi: Soundings in Political Philosophv* (Delhi: Chanakaya Publications, 1984).

14

Democracy

Democracy is a very difficult word to understand. Its numerous connotations have so vastly been stated that there could hardly be a definition of democracy containing all that it possesses. As a system of government, to some, it is a form of government while for others, it is a way of life. It is government of the people for a member of the ruling class; but a narrow and indefensible oligarchy for the poor. As a form of government, as Burns tells us, democracy is another name for self-government, Lecky on the other, considers it as the government of the poorest, the most ignorant, the most incapable, And yet it is, by far, a better system of government as compared to monarchy, as the rule of one; oligarchy as the rule of the few, howsoever able they may be; dictatorship, either of one person or one party. As compared to the other forms of non-democratic systems, democracy is more educative, more responsive, more responsible, caring more for the people, and less prone to revolution and violence. Its chief plus point is its basis: it is based on equality, liberty and welfareism.

I: Meaning of Democracy

For so multi-faceted a word like democracy, it is likely that one may leave out one or the other aspect while giving it a meaning. The political aspect of democracy emphasises everyone's share in the government; its economic aspect demands abolition of exploitation; its social aspect seeks elimination of all distinctions. A rather conservative definition of democracy is given. by Professor Dicey: "Democracy is a form of government in which the governing body is comparatively a large fraction of the entire nation." Professor Bryce hints at a more liberal definition of democracy: "Democracy is that form of government in which the ruling power of the state is vested not in a particular class or classes but in the members of the community as a whole". Maclver's definition of democracy, highlighting the representative system, says that it is not as much the way of governing as is "a way determining who shall rule and how".

The word 'democracy' has a Greek ancestry, *demos,* meaning a form of rule by a section of the populace as opposed to the rich or the aristocrats. The Greek meaning implies the rule of the commoners, the poor, the least intelligent. That is one reason that democracy, as Aristotle thought, was a perverted form of government, the rule of the mob. The Greeks, it may be noted, did not include in the ruling populace, the aliens, the women, the children, and the slaves.

The dictionary meaning, given to democracy, says that it is the rule of the people. But this does not make things clear unless we know what or who constitutes the people. If by people, we mean all the adults without any other qualification attached to it, we may not have the rule of the people, because all the people do not rule, and in fact, can not rule. If by people we mean those who participate in decision -making or administering or legislating, then such a system would be rule of the few, and not of all the people. So considered, the rule of the majority would also be not democratic (rule of the people) for it would exclude the few—minority. Any meaning of democracy must include the people, directly or indirectly, constituting the government. The role of the people in the composition of the government makes the government, the government of the people, but it would be a democracy if it is controlled by the people. What it means is that government of the people is one constituent of its being a democracy, its another constituent is that it has to be a government *by* the people, i.e., people must have control over what the government does. This would mean that the people should have freedoms and liberties and rights so to check the dictatorial tendencies, if any, of the government. There is yet another constituent of democracy, and perhaps an important aspect and that is: that the government has to be a government *for* the people, i.e., it exists for the welfare of the people. It is, in this context, that Abrahim Lincoln's oft-quoted definition of democracy has any significance: democracy is the government *of* the people, *by* the people, and *for* the people.

A despot may rule in the interest of the people but nobody would call such a government democracy; a people's rule, either themselves or through their representatives, may not grant substantial freedoms, much less care for their comforts, would hardly be a democracy. An oligarchical rule, howsoever popular in terms of service for the people, would not be democratic unless it guarantees liberties to the people. The idea of democracy is the idea of participation, of representation, of control, of accountability, of self-development. Professor Lively (*Democracy,* 1975) summarizes the following *characteristics* in a democracy:

(1) That all should govern in the sense that all should be involved in legislating, in deciding on general policy, in applying laws and in governmental administration.
(2) That all should be personally involved in crucial decision-making, that is to say, in deciding general laws and matters of general policy.
(3) That rulers should be accountable to the ruled; they should, in other words, be obliged to justify their actions to the ruled and be removable by the ruled.
(4) That the rulers should be accountable to the representatives of the ruled.
(5) That rulers should be chosen by the ruled.
(6) That rulers should be chosen by the representatives of the ruled.
(7) That rulers should act in the interests of the ruled.

II: Democracy — Its Development

The Western idea of democracy has its roots in ancient Greece. But the idea, then, was considered a perverted idea. Plato and Aristotle had no word of praise for democracy. As Laski says: "It (democracy) was of course a limited democracy based on slavery; and in no Greek community (Athens including) did free citizens constitute the majority of the inhabitants." Aristotle's notions of citizenship, emphasising the virtues of being a legislator and a judge, and of polity, as the government of all in the interest of all, were not even labelled as democracy', for he had used the term in a perverted sense. During the period of ancient Roman empire, the ideas of good government and sound administration were important but the democratic element, then, was nominal in the republican period and non-existent in imperial. The idea of plebians never had any democratic character, much less the power of legislation, the Senate, (or the patricians) had power and authority together with the emperors, but they were no commoners in the sense we use the term in democracy. Cicero, Seneca, Gaius and Ulpian expressed shadowy democratic ideas by pointing out equality of men at the time of their birth.

The Middle Ages had no conception of democracy. The dominance of faith over politics, of Christiandom over the kings and the feudal lords, of birth over merit, of extinct equality over dead liberty made democracy and the democratic institution a far cry in the whole period of the medieval age, It was only during the late Middle Ages when the two swords (authority: ecclesiastical and temporal) came to be separated from each other that the ideas of benevolent rule representation, contract appeared which prepared the basis for democracy that the West was to follow.

With renaissance, reformation and enlightenment grew the present form of democracy in the West. Way back, the Magna Carta (1215) had voiced some freedoms; the Petition of Rights (1628) curtailed the absolute powers of the king, the Glorious Revolution (1688) followed by the Bill of Rights (1689) cut short the unlimited powers of the rulers on the one hand and made them accountable for their action (execution of Charles I and the fleeing of James II in highlighted England, for example). All these developments how the idea that government has to be a government *by* the people. The American War of Independence (1776) and the French Revolution (1789), emphasising on the Rights of Man and on "Liberty, Equality, Fraternity" and the revolutions of 1848 in most of the non-Anglo-French countries of Europe and later winning of the suffrage rights brought in focus that the government has to be government *of* the people. The introduction of the welfare state, following the proletarian revolution, filled up the vacuum of the idea that democracy has to be government *for* the people.

This, in short, was the rise and growth of the democratic idea: non-democratic in most part of the Western tradition; liberal before it was democratic. From here evolved representative democracy: elitist, pluralist, participatory and peoples'.

III: Democracy—Thematic Models of its Growth

For having a clearer idea of the growth of democracy, it would be instructive, if not informative, to give a summary of different models of democracy as stated by David Held *(Models of Democracy, 1987)*.

1. *Classical Democracy:* In a small city-state arid in slave economy, citizens, though limited, enjoy equality among themselves and participate directly in legislative and judicial functions. There is a provision for open assemblies with executive directly elected, by lot or by rotation-assembly's powers include all common affairs.
2. *Protective Democracy:* Politically better organised and existing in a society of patriarchal chiefs, citizens need protection from the rulers and from one another. It is a system where the rulers rule in the interests of the citizens generally, maintain private ownership of the means of production and also market economy; it is a system which, though speaks in the name of people, represents

interests rather than the people and where the emphasis is on accountability of what the rulers do; and the rulers, while remaining in their respective sphere, act independent of one another: law-making with the legislature, law-executing with the executive, and justice with judiciary. The model is protective because it protects the ruled from the arbitrariness of the rulers, protects the rulers from the infringement in one-another's sphere, protects the whole legal system from those who violate the rules.

3. (i) *Radical Model of Developmental Democracy:* The system visualises small non-industrial communities with a society of independent producers where men are made free from work and politics. The citizens, in this model, enjoy political and economic equality; no one masters the other; all enjoy equal freedoms; legislative powers with directly elected legislative, bodies, executive with 'magistrates', either appointed, or elected directly or chosen by lot.

   (ii). *Developmental Democracy:* The system visualises an independent civil society with a *laissez faire* state supported by competitive market economy; private ownership of means of production exists alongside the community or cooperative forms of ownership. In this model, participation in political life is regarded necessary for (1) protection of individual interests, (2) development of informed, committed and developing citizenry. There is popular sovereignty with universal franchise alongwith proportional system of representation; the government is representative; the system of checks and balances exist so to avoid absolutism.

4. *Direct Democracy and the End of Politics:* The system visualises classless society with the working class coming victorious against the bourgeoisie where private property is abolished and market economy is destroyed. In this model, the attempt is made to achieve free development of all with the freedom of each; there is no exploitation, and hence, there is complete political and economic equality; each receives what he needs by putting in his/her abilities. Public affairs are regulated by communes, all officials are elected and, therefore, can be recalled, economy is planned, and public affairs are collectively governed.

5. *Competitive Elitist Democracy:* The system visualises industrial society with competitive groups competing with one another for power and benefit; the electorate is poorly informed, and, therefore, is politically almost apathetic; there is the freedom of opinion and, therefore, differences of opinion are allowed. In this model,

the elite is reelected because it is skilled and is, therefore, capable of making decisions: political, and non-political. The essential features of such a model of democracy are: (a) parliamentary government with a strong executive or presidential government with an alert legislature; (b) competition between groups and political parties; (c) dominance of party politics; (d) well-trained bureaucracy.

6. *Pluralist Democracy:* The system visualises the existence of numerous communities in the society with their own culture, basis, strength and objectives and each attempting to achieve something for its own group. There exists active citizenry alongwith numerous passive body of citizens; full political participation is impossible because of unequal involvement in politics. This model encourages government by minorities generally, prevents the development of powerful factions and hence, has almost unresponsive state. The essential features of such a model are: (a) freedoms and liberties are available; (b) the device of checks and balances so to, keep legislatue, executive, judiciary in their respective domains; (c) the presence of competitive electoral system; (d) the existence of diverse range of and sometimes overlapping interest groups seeking political influence; (e) the law and the Constitution are respected; (f) the state, instead of being impartial, seeks to attain its own sectional interests.
7. *Legal Democracy:* The system visualises effective political leadership, guided by liberal principles; bureaucratic role and that of the interest groups are minimised. This model considers the majority principle as an effective means of protecting people from the absolutism of the rulers; political life, like economic life, becomes a matter of individual freedom and initiative; there is the majority rule so to function justly and wisely; the rule of law prevails. The essential features of such a model are: (a) a state that works on the basis of Constitution; (b) rule of law prevails over rule of men; (c) free-market society; (d) a state with minimal functions and maximal individual autonomy.
8. *Participatory Democracy:* The system visualises a perfect and just society with material resources available to everyone and also an open order where informed decisions are ensured to each. This model (i) ensures an equal right to self-development; (ii) fosters a sense of political efficacy; (iii) nurtures a concern for collective problems; (iv) contributes to the formation of a knowledgeable citizenry. The essential features of such a model are: (a) direct participation of citizens in each institution of society; (b) party leadership is made accountable to party membership; (c) an open institutional system is maintained so to ensure the

possibility of experimenting all political forms.

9. *Democratic Autonomy:* The system visualises the availability of an open information, ensuring informed decisions in all public affairs, setting of the government's priorities with extensive market regulation of goods and labour, minimization of unaccountable power centres in public and private life. This model expects individuals to be free and equal in the determination of the conditions of their own life; guarantees equal rights and demands equal obligations. The essential features of this model in respect of the institution of state are: (a) autonomy enshrined in the Constitution; (b) competitive party system; (c) central and local administrative services internally organised according to the principle of direct participation. In respect of society, the key features of such a model are: (a) existence of diverse institutions and groups; (b) self-managed enterprises; (c) community services (education, health etc. etc.) are internally organised on the principle of direct participation; (d) private and voluntary enterprises to help promote diversity and innovation.

IV: Democracy-Direct and Indirect

The traditional forms of democracy are described as direct and indirect. In direct democracy, people are themselves the rulers; in indirect democracy, the people are the electorate and they rule through their representatives, who are periodically elected. In direct democracy, there is no distinction between the ruler and the ruled: the ruled is the ruler, and the ruler is the ruled; in indirect democracy, between the ruler and the ruled, there stands the representative.

Direct democracy is possible only in countries, small in population and not very large in territory. That is why it was there in city-states like Athens in ancient Greece and that is why it is found in small town-like cantons in Switzerland, though there are devices like initiative and referendum and recall in most of the other cantons and in some states of the U.S.A. *Initiative* is the device through which the people make proposals for legislation or initiate proposals for amendment in the Constitution. It is, therefore, the first word with the people and a sort of sword through which people can attack to ward off any challenge to democracy. *Referendum* is the device through which the people approve or disapprove any legislation or proposed amendment. It is, therefore, the last or the final word with the people, and a sort of shield through which people can defend themselves in case democracy is threatened. *Plebscite* literally means 'decree' of the people. It is a device, as Professor C.F. Strong says, to obtain a direct popular vote on a matter of political importance. *Recall* is a device by which elected representative can be recalled if the majority of the electorate so decide.

Indirect democracy is also known as representative democracy. It is this type of democracy which is usually in vogue in most of the countries today. In such a form of democracy, the electorate elect their representatives from constituencies: single or multiple through ballot system: open or secret. Representative democracy is expressed through devices: territorial representing constituencies, functional representing interests, or proportional representation of minorities.

In non-socialist countries, democracy is known as liberal democracy as has come to be understood in elitist, pluralist or participatory form, to mention a few among many, and in socialist countries, the kind of democracy that prevails has come to be known as peoples' democracy. Democracy, whether direct or indirect, ensures a form of government better than any other; educative, responsive, responsible; seeks welfare of all; abhors violence and revolution, guarantees reforms and obedience of the laws; upholds both equality and liberty. But it is also regarded as the government of the incompetent, of irresponsible multitude, which turns into petty party politics, which corrupts both the rulers and the ruled, which is generally unstable, and usually imaginary. And yet, democracy, as a form of government, has been admired -by all. Bums concludes, rather rightly: "No one denies that existing representative assemblies are defective, but even if an automobile does not work well, it is foolish to go back to a farm cart, howsoever romantic it may be."

Democracy, indeed, is the best of all the forms of government, and yet it is the most difficult. It needs a conducive atmosphere for its sustenance, survival and success. Socially, there must be social justice, elimination of discrimination, and a sense of unity among the people. Economically, there has to be economic equality and economic security. Politically, there should be liberty, law and order, local institutions, judicious majority and cooperative minority, rule of law, free press, impartial periodic elections and so on. Equally, there has to be politically alert citizenry in whom duty-abidingness, common interest, sense of fair judgement and the like virtues are deep-rooted.

V: The Elitist Theory of Democracy

1. Background of the Theory

The elitist theory of democracy is an amalgamation of two opposing, rather conflicting strands: elitism and democracy. Elitism implies the rule of the few whereas democracy, in its direct form, means the rule of all. The elitist theory of democracy is not elitist in so far as it claims to be democratic; it is not democratic in so far as it traces its roots in elitism. The elitists, notably Vilfredo Pareto and Gaetano Mosca (both Italians) and Robert Michels (Swiss), never found democracy as a viable proposition. Their argument is: democracy in the sense of popular exercise of power and peoples' participation in society's public affairs can not be, in practice, realized; power is, and has always remained the privilege of the dominating few; democratic system is impossible and impracticable. The elitists, therefore, accept the view that democracy is a device that marks the harsh reality of elite rule and that history is nothing but the graveyard of oligarchies—or what Michels declared as "the iron law of oligarchy."

The classical elite theorists such as Pareto, Mosca, Michels together with the present-day elitists such as C. Wright Mills, Schumpeter Mannheims, Sartori oppose the classical form of democracy as the direct rule of the people themselves. Mosca's words still serve an authoritative statement of the elite theory. "In all societies—two classes of people appear: a class that rules and a class that is ruled. The first class, always the less numerous, performs all political functions, monopolises power and enjoys the advantages that power brings, whereas the second, the more numerous class, is directed and controlled by the first.....". In other words, the elitists hold the view that it is always the few who have ruled the many; the elite that rules the masses. Michels puts forth the elite argument by speaking about "the political immaturity of the mass', 'the organic weakness of the mass', 'the need which the mass feels for guidance', 'the apathy of the masses and their need for guidance'. The elitist conclusion is: as the masses are incompetent, so there arises the need of the leaders; as the masses are politically immature, so the idea of mass sovereignty is always a myth; as the masses are apathetic, so they are not political; as the masses are disorganised, so they are irrational; and as the masses are irrational and manipulable, so there are possibilities of demagogic leaders destroying democracy and then turning to fascism.

The elitist argument of the rule of the few over many never found favour with the exponents of democracy. The 'democracy' theorists, while lauding the will of the people, keep singing, with Rousseau, the chorus of the will of the people as the will of God. They are convinced that the people as a whole, have a will of their own, separate from and independent of the will of the individuals, whether individually or severally. The revolutionaries of the American War of Independence and of the French Revolution, as also the idealists (Hegel, Green and others) who followed them, kept alive the notions of 'Rights of Man' or of 'people' in the hearts of the theorists of democracy.

The 'democracy' theorists have been sceptical about elitism as have been the elitists, about classical democracy. Each knows its merits as also its weaknesses. The elitists know how practical they are, and how undemocratic they are at the same time. Similarly, the 'democracy' theorists know how great servants of the people they are, and how impracticable they are at the same time. The fusion of one into the other produces a form of government which is called 'elitist theory of democracy', 'democratic elitism', 'competitive theory of democracy', 'plebscitary elitism' as Max Weber would have called it. The necessity of the growing industrial society during the 18th-19th centuries necessitated the need of one by the other. The industrial society had thrown up diverse economic, industrial and other social groups wanting to have an edge in public affairs and hence competition among themselves. Elitism had to turn towards democracy as democracy, towards elitism. Michels' 'iron law of oligarchy' comes to be accepted in the sense that direct democracy is considered not a possible practicable system; 'democracy' comes to be accepted in the sense that the people make a choice among the elites available and the system makes them democratic in so far as the elites are made responsive and responsible to the masses. Summing up the idea of democratic elitism, Schwarzmantel (*Structures of Power,* 1987) says; "The fact that masses have a choice between different elites satisfies all the requirements of a democratic system. Organisation implies oligarchy, as Michels asserted; democracy needs leadership. In this sense, the elite-mass distinction is preserved and the analysis remains in the elitist tradition. On the other hand, it is a necessary and sufficient condition for a democratic system that, at stated intervals. the masses decide which elite is to rule".

2. *The Elitist Democratic Theory Explained*

Joseph Schumpeter (*Capitalism, Socialism and Democracy,* 1943) may rightly be called the most influential proponent of the elitist theory of democracy. He attacks democracy by saying that there is no such thing as 'the will of the people', that the masses, being ill-informed, do not formulate the agenda of politics, that the political issues are always raised, articulated and debated by the leaders, that initiative, in politics, travels from top to bottom and not from bottom to top. When the masses elect the leaders or a particular elite, the government is formed. In such a situation, Schumpeter says, the leaders should be free and autonomous to formulate and carry out policies of the government as composed by the people. The democratic element, in a situation like this, is preserved in (a) periodic election of the leaders by the masses, and (b) in the accountability of the leaders towards the electorate. The elitist elment is preserved in (a) enough autonomy of the leaders to formulate the policies, (b) enough freedom to execute them. The elitist view of democracy may be summed up as Weber once described in a situation like this: "In a democracy, people choose a leader in whom they trust. Then the chosen leader says, 'Now shut up and obey me'. People and party are then no longer free to interfere with his business.... Later the people can sit in judgement. If the leader has made mistakes-to the gallows with him."

If one likes to put democratic elitism in a historical situation, one would presume an order where there exists a host of social and economic groups, hence, of an industrial society, an order where there is an active strata, though small, on the one hand, and a poorly informed and politically apathetic electorate on the other, an order where competition among the groups, say the elites is regarded natural,' and an order where differences of opinion are not only allowed to exist, but are also tolerated.

For an order of democratic elitism, Schumpeter insists on the following conditions:

1. The calibre of politicians must be high.
2. Competition between rival leaders (and parties) must take place but within the prescribed norms.
3. There has to be a well-trained independent bureaucracy to aid and advise politicians.
4. Excessive criticism of government on all issues be permitted.
5. A political culture capable of tolerating differences of opinion be guaranteed.

In democratic elitism, the following features should constitute a broad framework of the elitist theory of democracy:

1. The elite's unflinching faith in democratic norms. It needs to realise that it possesses power as long as the electorate wants it.
2. The establishment of the elite-masses contact is the only basis of the elitist democracy.
3. Non-interference of the masses in elite's business: formulation of policies and in the conduct of administration.
4. The elite's capabilities and experiences in political and public matters is a matter beyond any doubt.
5. Effective and active competition among the groups—constant and always continuing.
6. Circulation of elite from among the masses.

3. ***Assessment of the Elitist Theory of Democracy***

The elite theory of democracy has some inherent limitations:

(i) *The theory* is no *longer* democratic, *if* by democracy *we* mean a system where there is a substantial amount of popular power and citizens' involvement. In this sort of democracy, the masses only produce a government, they do not sustain it.

(ii) The elite theory of democracy does ensure a measure of responsiveness by the leaders to the led, but democracy, in its essence, is not just confined to responsiveness, nor is it limited to checking and controlling the executive. Democracy implies *involvement of the people at each level* of governance, from initiating a legislative proposal to vetoing the other.

(iii) The elitist thesis that the masses, in general, need not interfere in elite's public affairs and the insistence that the politicians may keep 'get on with the job' are not compatible with classical democracy and is, in fact, a surrender of sovereignty. Indeed, democracy does mean citizens' participation in politics, but it also means right of the citizens to judge or pass judgement on their rulers. Real democracy is *not only descriptive in* the sense of being a way of electing the governors, *but is normative* in the sense of being a way of judging the rulers and the existing power system.

(iv) Democratic elitism *cuts out from democratic theory its very heart*—the idea of participation. Schwarzmentel writes: "It (democratic elitism) takes a purely static view accepting the features of present-day mass society fixed for ever instead of envisaging a process that would. transcend the elite-mass dichotomy. The stability of the existing order is thus made the chief value, and democratic involvement then appears to threaten that value."

(v) The democratic elitism *alienates the ruled from the rulers*. Despite the fact that the ruled can exercise control over the rulers it does not imply that the ruled control the rulers. All the agencies and devices through which the masses can possibly control the rulers remain under the control of the ruled. The distance between the ruled and the rulers keep widening.

(vi) Democratic elitism is *more elitist* than democratic. The fact remains that the rulers—the elite—remain a class in themselves. As such the theory is more elite-oriented, and its democratic convictions are both formal and imaginary.

(vii) The elitist theory of democracy is *anti-liberal,* for it does not recognise the individual a rational being. It is *anti-socialist,* for it has a theory of political democracy and has, in fact, no theory of socio-economic democracy.

(viii) The elitist theory limits democracy only to "*governance*" level.

(ix) In terms of progress, the elite theory of democracy is *a step backward.* It has removed from its essence the moral content of democracy, a feature the classical theory of democracy had possessed. What was the heart of the classical theory of dernocracy—democratic humanism—was replaced by the elitists with what they made—democratic mechanism. The elitist theory of democracy is retrogressive. Macpherson writes: ".... democracy is reduced from a humanist aspiration to a market equilibrium society. And although the new orthodox theory claims scientific neutrality, its value judgement is clear enough: whatever works, is right."

The strength of the elitist theory of democracy lies in the fact that effective political power has always, in all societies and in all ages, remained in the hands of the few—a select minority. It also lies in the fact that such a system of democracy has, in reality, worked effectively well in Western political systems, that any other alternative of democracy could .not and has, in fact, not worked, and that the socialist model as against the elitist one, has proved infeasible.

VI: The Pluralist Theory of Democracy

(i) Elitism, Pluralism and Nee-pluralism

There is much that separate elitism, pluralism and neo-pluralism from each other, though they are parts of the larger frame of liberalism of either yesterday or today (a) To an extent, pluralism, as it developed especially in the United States of America in 1940s, 1950s or later, was a reaction against elitist theory of democracy. While the 'elitist democracy advocated the exercise of power by a dominant and relatively united group,' one or strictly very few (C. Wright Mills, *The Power Elite,* 1956), the pluralist had an absolutely opposite thesis, saying that power is held not by one or the other group, but by groups; (b) Within the framework of liberalism, pluralism demonstrated a more democratic orientation than elitism. The elitist theory had a very poor view of the masses and were convinced that only the elite (thc ruling class, the governing class, hence, only political) had the aptitudes and capabilities to rule, The pluralist democratic theory admits numerous groups of all shades, competing to obtain power of the state; (c) The pluralists are more democratic than the elitists in so far as the former do not allow the state to act arbitrarily: for there is a network of parties, groups, associations, in the pluralist frame, exercising their democratic rights to check the absolutism of the state; (d) The elitists do presume a fragmented society, but not the one in which numerous groups are equally powerful, but the one where there is the monopoly control of the more powerful. In pluralism, on the other, the state is highly responsive to numerous groups. In elitism, there is no group conflict; in pluralism, there is; (e) In pluralist democracy, the people, though non-political, are not a polotical, but in elitist theory, the people are regarded apolitical, and, therefore, made to act as non-political; (f) elitism is a matter of containment; pluralism, of democratization.

There is also much that separates neo-pluralism from pluralism. (a) Neo-pluralism is an extension of pluralism, but the one in which the role of the business groups is relatively crucial; (b) in a pluralist democracy, groups are powerful, more or less, equally, whereas in a neo-pluralist arrangement, dominant groups are seen distinct from secondary weak groups; (c) Power is an observable phenomenon and is relatively dispersed in pluralism whereas in neo-pluralism, power is unobservable, hidden structurally and ideologically, and, therefore, is concentrated in big issues but dispersed in secondary ones; (d) In the pluralist theory, democracy exists through conflictual groups whereas in neo-pluralist theory, it exists, but very little; (e) In pluralism, society is distinct and in a way, non-political; in neo-pluralism, society is distinct, but with limited influence.

2. *Development and Growth*

Pluralism, in the initial stages of its beginning, began as a reaction to the concentration of sovereignty in the nation-state. Its advocates, mostly Englishmen, argued that the state sovereignty in the sense John Austin used the term is merely a legal fiction, that its monopoly of individual's allegiance is untenable, that the 'intermediate institutions such as churches, universities, economic organisations and the like are as important as the state on the one hand and the primary groups like the family on the other, that these other groups, including also the intermediatiaries, play important role in the life of the individuals, and that they should be allowed to exist independent of the state. The English pluralism, fearful as it was of the state powers, urged for assurance that the state would not interfere in the functioning of these groups. That was, indeed, the message one gets from the writings of Figgis, Maitland, G.D.H. Cole, Robson, Lindsay, Barker, Laski and Maclver.

Pluralism, as it grew and developed in the United States, was largely the result of the writings of Truman, Bentley, Dahl, Lindblom, though its ancestry is related to Schumpeter, Weber, Madison, and others. It has, in the Western political system, travelled through various phases and assumed the names of 'empirical democratic theory' 'a descriptive-explanatory account of democratic politics. With the changing times, pluralism has passed through its classical stage to reformed and then to nee-pluralist ones. Each subsequent stage of pluralism was a variant of the preceding one. To explain the point, one may examine the position of the groups in the changing pluralist variations, for pluralist democracy is, essentially, group democracy. With the classical pluralist theory, groups are easily formed in a society and they exist because they compete; in the reformed pluralist theory certain groups gain privileged access over the ones, excluded in nee-pluralism, the role of the business interests becomes more crucial as compared to others, of mostly secondary importance. Furthermore, in the classical pluralist theory, the task of the government tends to mediate and adjudicate between the demands of the numerous conflictual groups; in the reformed phase, it responds to the groups, not equally but differentially; in nee-pluralist phase, it becomes almost a tool in the hands of the business interests.

3. Pluralist Democracy: Features

Though there are numerous variations of pluralism, yet it is possible to state some recognizable features common in all. Pluralism is a process, a process of political action, and a process which, in Lasswell's phrase, settles who gets what, when and how. It assumes a multiplicy of groups/actors competing for power, influence, job, status and so on in a variety of political arenas. It minimizes the connections between the different arenas and maximizes the openness of the contests. In it, democracy is competitive rather than consensual and where politics is pragmatically focussed upon "the here and now" situation.

The characteristic features of pluralist democracy, common to all shades of pluralism, as summed by Schwarzmantel, are:

(1) There is no single group which is able to exercise systematic and pervasive control over more than one range of issues. What it means is the existence of numerous groups in the society and the fact that each group is dominant in its own area—all trying in varying degrees, to influence the government. More the issues, more the groups and more dispersed and varying is the influence.

(2) The idea of countervailing power (as used by J.K. Galbraith) exists. in pluralist scheme. Galbraith explains that in an advanced economy, there exists a balance between the capital and the labour with no one having an in-built advantage over the other. Both exist not in a situation of perfect competition, but in one that is imperfect where both hold power and both can influence and

restraint governmental action.

(3) Though the pluralists do not have any coherent theory of state, yet it asks for a state which is neutral. Indeed, the role of the dominant business groups is growing fast, yet the pluralist democracy envisages a state which acts as an umpire, impartially controlling the conflicts of groups, supervising and regulating social antagonisms.

(4) As the pluralist democracy survives in a multiplicity of groups with their own interests and demands, pluralism is not committed to any ideology. There is, thus, the plurality of ideas and, therefore, no uniformity of belief, any belief, "a society of publics" as C. Wright Mills would have used the phrase.

(5) The pluralist democracy is a democracy of competition, consent and accountability. It is a democracy of competition because it allows competition among the numerous groups; it is a democracy of consent because it is run by a group which has a considerable support and consent, and it is a democracy of accountability because the elected representatives have to be responsible to the electorate for what they do.

(6) The pluralist democracy is a democracy in the sense that it prevents the concentration of political power in the hands of few. It is also a democracy in the sense that it permits the numerous groups and all citizens their democratic right of participation in politics.

4. *Assessment of the Pluralist Theory of Democracy*

The pluralist theory of democracy remains within the ambit of the Western political systems: systems which allow economic inequality and political democracy, separation of powers, rule of law, constitutionalism, competitive society, citizenship rights, a system of freedoms and liberties, a talented bureaucracy. Its strength lies in its effective application in the Western society, in whatever form it suits a system.

And yet its weaknesses can be highlighted:

(1) The assumptions that a society has numerous groups and that the groups play a significant role are not empty assumptions. But it is *too much to assume that the numerous groups are powerful equally*. Indeed, certain groups, mostly the economically dominant groups, have more resources and more means, and, therefore, hold more powers in · the society at the cost of others. This makes the whole pluralist assumption undemocratic.

(2) The pluralist theory of democracy while making group as a

political unit, *ignores the emphasis on individual* which was the hallmark of the classical democratic theory. The pluralists have reduced individual to a rhetorical sovereign: making him almost a slave to the, groups around him and submerging his identity in that of the group.

(3) As the pluralist democracy is a group democracy, it is always likely that politics may not be able to receive the attention of the problems and issues concerned with the average citizen or an ordinary group. To put the point the other way, *power may prevent certain issues to come before open discussion.* Bachrach and Baratz rightly point out that a group may be powerful enough to determine the "agenda" of politics, and to make sure that certain items are never put on that agenda. This kind of process may make the pluralist democracy as democracy or the dominant.

(4) The pluralist view of the democratic state as neutral arbiter is countered by (a) ever-increasing power of the state, and (b) imposing and influential business groups in the society. As the state assumes more powers, it becomes more bureaucratic and hence, *less democratic.* As the economically powerful groups exert influence on the state, they make the state as their instrument. And if in a situation like neo-pluralism where the state comes to forge its own interests, it hardly remains neutral then.

(5) In an unequal and market sort of society where the power is captured through competition, the emerging victorious group not only holds the power but attempts to I retain it. Power, in the hands of the small cohesive group dominating the society, *fades the pluralist vision of dispersion of power* and thus makes the whole politics, *oligarchical.*

But up to a point, pluralism has a value and an appeal to those who believe in liberty and in democracy. To those who hate tyranny and concentration of powers and to those who favour dispersion of power, to them, pluralism must provide a workable system and to that extent, it may appear to be democratic.

VII: Theory of Participatory Democracy

Democracy has, indeed, been a puzzling concept. Its theoretical implications and its practical applications keep throwing up newer problems day after day. The recent rethinking on the terms of reference relating to democracy has been put forth by Carole Pateman *(Participation and Democratic Theory, 1970; The Problem of Political Obligation: a Critique of Liberal Theory,* 1985), C.B. Macpherson *(The Life and Times of Liberal Democracy,* 1977), and N. Poulantzas *(State; Power, Socialism, 1980)*. They all represent what may be called as 'participatory democracy'. Professor Held tells us: "'Participatory democracy' is the main counter-model on the left to the 'legal democracy' of the right",— counter model on the left so far as it condemns closed society of the socialist societies, and a critique of the right in so far as it exposes the so-called 'equalities' which the Western societies claim to have won. Pateman questions the idea of 'free and equal' citizens and says that the existing inequalities of class, Sex and race have gone to denounce the equalities among the citizens. She even challenges the impartiality of the state and goes on to say that the state, instead of removing inequalities, sustain and reproduce them. Poulantzas holds the view that the socialist democratic model has failed to train citizens in the art of democratic administration. Macpherson, while declaring the Western societies as liberal democratic—liberal first and democratic later—doubts if liberalism would succeed in shouldering the weight of democracy as seen in direct participation of the people in administration.

1. Participatory democracy—Explanation of the Theory

The theory of participatory democracy, as advocated by Pateman, Macpherson and Pouluntzas, can be, briefly, stated asunder:

- (a) Democratization of parliaments, bureaucracies, political parties and the like is the first condition of participatory democracy so to make them all more open and more accountable.
- (b) Drastic decentralization of powers, both vertically and horizontally, so to enable the formulation of policies and decision-making run from bottom to the top.
- (c) Reorganisation of political parties, while making them less hierarchical, on the principles and procedures of participatory democracy.
- (d) Accountability of the political administrators and managers to the people they represent.
- (e) Direct participation of citizens in the regulation of the key institutions of society, including the workplace and the local community.
- (f) Maintenance of an open institutional system to ensure the possibility of experimentation with political forms.

So understood, participatory democracy envisages an equal right to self-development; a type of society which fosters a sense of political efficacy, nurtures for collective problems and contributes to the formation of a knowledgeable citizenry capable of taking a sustained interest in the governing process (Held: *Models of Democracy, 1987).* Birch offers rather a relatively negative meaning of participatory democracy. He says in his work, *(The Concepts and Theories of Modern Democracy,* 1993): participatory democracy "means a system in which small local units, informally organised, would have a veto power over national decisions." Dahl *(A Preface to Economic Democracy,* 1985) goes on to give a list of conditions so to meet the criterion of collective decision-making and extensive involvement:

1. *Equal votes:* The rule for determining outcomes ... must take into account, and take equally into account, the expressed preferences of each citizen as to the outcome; that is, votes must be allocated equally among citizens.
2. *Effective participation:* Throughout the process of making collective decisions, each citizen must have an adequate and equal opportunity for expressing a preference as to the final outcome.
3. *Enlightened understanding:* In order to express preferences accurately, each citizen must have adequate and equal opportunities ... for discovering and validating his preferences on the matter to be decided.
4. *Final control of the agenda by the demos:* The demos must have the exclusive opportunity to make decisions that determine what matters are and are not to be decided by processes that satisfy the first three criteria.
5. *Inclusiveness:* The demos must include all adult members except transients and persons proved to be mentally defective.

The demands of the participatory democracy are, indeed, numerous. Among them, notable inclusions are: a constitution enshrining the principle of autonomy, and therefore, equal rights, equal rights to cast a vote, and equal rights to enjoy the conditions for effective participation, enlightening understanding and the setting of the political agenda. Participatory democracy has to have a broad scheme of rights—political, to ensure effective participation; economic, to have an access to adequate economic and financial resources; social, to include childcare, health, education. Obviously, such a scheme of rights would specify obligations of the citizens towards one another and also the responsibilities of the state towards the citizens and their groups.

2. *Participatory Democracy—An Assessment*

The idea of participatory democracy is an attractive idea. But attraction is nothing more than a fantasy, and therefore, falls short of practical application. As an idea, participatory democracy is an advance over all other strands of democracy—elitist, pluralist, socialist, but there are certain limitations which this theory of participatory democracy suffers from.

(1) Participatory model of democracy *fails to specify the conditions* necessary for such a democracy, as also the means of securing such conditions.

(2) Indeed, there is no better method of learning than practising what we want to learn. Accordingly, we learn to participate by participating, but there is no evidence to show that participation would help, as Professor Held says, 'to trigger a new renaissance in human development.' It would be *unwise* to *think that participation would make people cooperative and dedicated;* it would, rather, be wise to presuppose that participation would not make people morally or intellectually better than what they are.

(3) To count much on participation is to *demand more than what* is *possible.* It is questionable whether participation would lead to desirable political outcomes and would reduce tensions resulting from distributional questions of social justice and democratic decisions.

(4) Participatory democracy *attacks the principles of liberalism* (i.e., citizens are free and equal and so on) on the one hand, but does not leave out the means through which liberalism works; it accepts competitive political parties, representative system, periodic elections, and so on. It is, thus, a theory which builds itself on bases which it chooses to attack.

(5) The crux of participatory democracy is the availability of specialised information and expertise to those who make decisions. In such a situation, groups of amateur politicians, Birch says, "may lend themselves to manipulation by demagogues or by ideological factions: "Open participation", he continues "may mean *domination* by those with strong ideological motivations who are willing to give their time to it, but who would not necessarily be able to win a competitive election."

(6) Participatory democracy envisages substantive involvement in all spheres and at all levels. The important question is as to how these spheres and levels are to be connected with each other, and how the different aspects of these spheres and levels would come together. The participation theorists never thought that such problems would ever be there. To that extent, the terms of references with regard to participation theory have been *too narrowly drawn.*

(7) Participatory theory is too demanding. It makes a politician out

> of each citizen. A chemist may not like to indulge in politicking; an astronomer may not find time for politics; a businessman may not have an aptitude to know as to what goes on in the debates of the municipal committee. Why demand so much from the people? Why seek so large changes in the lives of the common people? Why not leave politics to the politicians? Such are the questions, some even valid, of the critics of the participation theorists ...

All that the critics of participation theorists say is not valid. Indeed, a chemist may not have a liking for politics, but it is too much to say that a chemist is only a chemist, and not a father, a resident, a cricketer, a citizen, a voter, and not a being because he keeps his shop open for twenty-four hours a day. True also, participatory democracy anticipates an alert citizen-body and a host of institutions of all sorts, but this does not mean that we should abandon the project because it is too expensive, too time-consuming, too demanding.

The merit of the theory of participatory democracy lies in the fact that (i) it focuses on the individual not in isolation, but in the context of co-operative effort, with others; (ii) it engages in finding out the means for achieving the ideal of self-rule, (iii) it provides, or atleast attempts to provide suggestions for remedying the ills of the existing societies, and (iv) it helps us to know or discover the limitations of the existing systems and thereafter, to envisage changes in the political, economic, social conditions of the people.

VIII: The Concept of Peoples' Democracy

'Peoples' democracy' is associated with the Marxian theory of democracy. The Marxists do not think bourgeois democracy as the real democracy. For them, it is the dictatorship of the capitalists: rule of the capitalists, by them and for them; it is a class democracy, i.e., democracy of a class, a dominant class, an economically dominant class; the rule of minority over majority. For that matter, no class society can ever claim to be democratic. A class system, the Marxists say, is conflictive in nature, and therefore, is exploitative. In a situation of inequality and exploitation, there can be democracy only for the rich, the possessing class. Professor Held says: "Marx believed that democratic government was essentially unviable in a capitalist society; the democratic regulation 01 life could not be realized under the constraints imposed by the capitalist relations of production". Giving the Leninist account of Western democracy, Neil Harding says: "Western-style representative democracy was no more than a sometimes convenient constitutional form through which the real economic dominance of the capitalist class was exercised. In the epoch of monopoly or finance capitalism, it had become redundant and potentially destabilizing for the maintenance of the cycle of production and reproduction of capital. During the war, it had finally become discredited and had been displaced by the direct rule of finance capital that unabashedly utilized the state to maintain and extend its own power." "From all this," Harding continues, "it followed that representative democracy, with its elaborate division of power and its attendant separate jurisdictions for legislative, executive, judiciary, army, and police could not possibly serve as the political form of the realization of socialism. Liberal democracy had not merely preserved, it had refined-and sanctified the age-old and basic division of society into governors and governed."

(1) *Explanation of the concept of Peoples' Democracy*

For the Marxists, democracy and its full form can only be found in a classless society, beginning from the socialist society onward. Revolutionary as Marx was, he saw in a revolution an engine of history, pushing history ahead to unfold an era of real human freedom. "The political instrument of their enslavement cannot serve as the political instrument of their emancipation", for 'a master of society' will not become 'a servant' on request, "so writes Marx *(The Civil War* in *France,* 1870). Once the bourgeois democracy is abolished by the working class, there would usher, the Marxists say, a transitional period of the dictatorship of proletariat which would eventually pave way for a classless and a stateless society—the real permanent democratic society. Lenin believed that though the dictatorship of proletariat would be a bourgeois state without the bourgeoisie, yet it would be, as compared to the dictatorship of the capitalists under capitalism, democratic in so far as it would be the rule of majority (therefore by them and for them) over the minority, both quantitatively and qualitatively rule of the working class over the capitalists who would constitute minority: rule of the exploited over the erstwhile exploiters

The socialist state would be qualitatively different from the bourgeois state, for socialism would mean rule not of the rich, the capitalists, the few, but would mean rule of the common man, the workers, the people. Under socialism, after adopting the socialist economy, the power of the state would be reclaimed by the people; the people would debate, discuss and finally decide all public issues; they would implement what they decide and would adjudicate all their disputes themselves. Under socialism, the power of the people, as it really was under Bolshevism, for example, would be direct, immediate and unrestricted. Marx and Engels had stated, *(The Communist Manifesto,* 1848) that socialism would be "an association in which the free development of each is the condition for the free development of all".

Marx had thought that the discovery of the Commune (1871) was the political form under which the economic emancipation of labour could be worked. The commune, it was argued, was to make a reality of democracy by involving all citizens in all aspects of the governmental process and it was to retain control over all its functionaries by electing them all. Under socialism, in the Bolshevik view, as Harding says: "Democracy was to be direct, participatory and transformative. Its purpose was to transform people from passive objectives of the purposes of the others into conscious and active subjects."

So considered, the features of the peoples' democracy, as stated by Professor Held, may be summed up briefly asunder:

(1) Regulation of public affairs by councils organised pyramidically in the socialist era, and leading ultimately to self-regulation under communism.

(2) Election and recall of all the officials of the state under socialism while governance of the public affairs by the people collectively under communism.

(3) People's militia to sustain the socialist society, leading to a system without coercion and with self-evolving norms under communism.

(4) Defeat of the bourgeoisie, unity of the working classes and elimination of all class privileges of the socialist era to be followed by abolition of private property, scarcity, market system, and the establishment of a society of all for all.

(5) Beginning with the free development of each, and ending with the free development of all would make way for a free society where each and all would have all freedoms, end of exploitation, and ultimately the achievement of complete political, social and economic equality.

(6) Peoples' democracy rests on the principle of what 'each can give' to the one that is extendable to 'receive what you need'.

The concept of peoples' democracy, as suggested, by Professor Held, would make somewhat a picture like this: "The machinery of the state would be replaced by the commune structure. All aspects of 'government' would then be fully accountable: the general will of the people would prevail The smallest communities would administer their own affairs, elect delegates to larger administrative units, and these would, in turn, elect candidates to still larger areas of administration. This arrangement is known as the 'pyramid' structure of direct democracy; all delegates are revocable, bound by the instructions of their constituency and organised into a 'pyramid' of directly elected committees."

(2) *Assessment of Peoples' Democratic Theory*

One may be tempted to say that the concept of peoples' democracy, as has developed through the writings of Marx, Engels, Lenin and through its application in some of the socialist countries, reflects the characteristics of elitist democracy on the one hand, and participatory theory on the other. What the concept and practice of peoples' democracy shares with elitist democracy is the fact that the power of decision-making lies in the · hands of the few—the elite in the case of elitist theory of democracy and the communist party or what may be called in Lenin's vanguardism. Both, somewhat realistically, believe that there is always an unequal influence of all the people over the decision-making. But this is not to say that the Marxian democracy shares with the elitists the idea that ordinary citizen is apolitical and illiterate in shouldering the responsibilities of managing the public affairs.

What the concept as well as the practice of peoples' democracy shares with the participatory theory is an aspiration to a much fuller participation (i.e., self-rule in all respects) by the whole populace in decision-making. But it is wider and more ambitious, to the extent of impracticability, in scope than participatory theory.

Peoples' democratic theory is the democracy of Marxism-Leninism, Marxian in theoretical terms and Leninist in practice. To that extent, the concept of peoples' democracy is more democratic if viewed from the eyes of Marx; less democratic if viewed from Lenin's point of view. Marx was, indeed, a theoretician *par excellence:* his analysis of fraudulent democracy was unparalleled; his description of the socialist society first and the communist society later as the society of the whole people was fairly democratic. But as the concept came to be handled from Marx's times of capitalism to Lenin's days of socialist revolution, there came up the institution of a new type of party, the party as the vanguard of the people. With that the people came to be eclipsed by the workers; workers, by the party; the party, by the leaders; the leaders, by the chief. Marx had created a democratic ideal, Lenin substituted it by a group and Stalin made it dictatorial, the personality cult. Plamenatz says that when one moves from German Marxism to Russian Communism, one moves from horses to mules.

This, of course, does not mean that the concept of peoples' democracy is flawless. One may identify some of weaknesses as under:

(1) If what Marx thinks and in what Lenin modifies, there is, in such a classless society, a *propensity of an authoritian form of politics*

when it is led by a vanguard and that too in the name of the people. In such a society of the whole of the people, there is, Professor Held argues, "no longer a place of systematically encouraging and tolerating disagreement and debate about public matters ... There is no longer scope for the mobilization of competing political views."

(2) The society of the whole people or what may be called 'the Commune structure', where there is no public discourse, and the procedure to protect peoples' autonomy, there is no guarantee that those elected by the people into high offices would like their action to be scrutinized or their behaviour checked. The limitless powers with the Communes would generate and foster *dictatorship.*

(3) The Marxian picture of the communist society as "an association of free men, working with the means of production held in common and expanding .... in full self-awareness as one single labour force; ....an association in which the free development of each is the condition for the free development of all" are all good, good democratic words, but without practical application, only *blueprints* of the new society.

(4) Numerous difficulties arise when the ideals of government of the people are replaced by 'the government of things', 'self-regulating' and 'self-evolving system'. Things do not and in fact, are not as simple as are viewed. There has to be some one to - initiate a proposal, for the proposal would not be born out of nothing; there has to be some one to suggest as to where a steel plant is to be built; there has to be someone to make a beginning. To say that things would begin themselves is a position which is *untenable.*

(5) There are severe limitations of smooth functioning of institutions in a classless society. The idea that the executive tasks can be spread amongst the population, that the delegates act under and within instructions, and that the representatives are recallable—are all very attractive, but at the same time *unworkable.*

(6) The classless society of the Marxist-Leninist type expects a citizen body which is highly political, highly social, highly effective, ready to accept all the responsibilities related to its status or position. The citizen of the peoples' democracy has to be a part of a larger part and at the same time, has to be a part connected with another. Given the differences of mental and physical differences as of cultural gaps, it is, indeed, *impossible* and even *undesirable* to assume that a person would do all his different roles equally well, and that all the people, do so. And then, it is really impossible to

assume that the people would become accustomed to observing the elementary conditions of social life.

(7) The assumption that a person can be trained to become active through Lenin's vanguardism is a position which stands in direct opposition to what Marx and Engels, repeatedly, held: "We can not ally ourselves, therefore, with people who openly declare that the workers are too *uneducated* to free themselves ... "

(8) Marx did not, Professor Held thinks, produce an adequate theory of institutional structures of the classless society. He reduces political institutions to an undifferentiated type, to a complex of organisations which are not dearly separated, makes power conceal in a hierarchical form and then, assumes the new system would be transparent, open and accessible to all. All this is a gamble, "a gigantic gamble". A.J, Polan *(Lenin and the End of Politics, 1984)* says, "the gamble that it will be possible to set about constructing the state 'in the best of all possible words'. The odds against the gamble are astronomic.... It demands, in short, ...an absence of politics."

SUGGESTED READINGS

1. Burnheim, J., Is *Democracy Possible?* (Cambridge: Polity Press, 1985).
2. Cohen, J., and Rogers, J., *On Democracy* (New York: Penguin 1983).
3. Duncan, G., (ed.) *Democratic Theory and Practice* (Cambridge: Cambridge University Press, 1983).
4. Held, David, *Models of Democracy* (Oxford: Polity Press, 1987).
5. Held, D., and Pollitt, C, (eds.), *New Forms of Democracy* (London: Sage, 1986).
6. Lively, J., *Democracy* (Oxford: Basil Blackwell, 1975).
7. Macpherson, C.B., *The Real World of Democracy* (Oxford: Oxford University Press, 1966).
8. ________, *The Life and Times of Liberal Democracy* (Oxford: Oxford University Press, 1977).
9. Pateman, Carole, *Participation and Democratic Theory* (Cambridge: Cambridge University Press, 1970).
10. ________, *The Problem of Political Obligation: a Critique of Liberal Theory* (Cambridge: Polity Press, 1985).
11. Rodewald, C, (ed.) *Democracy: Ideas and Realities* (London: Dent, 1974).
12. Schumpeter, J., *Capitalism, Socialism and Democracy* (London: Allen and Unwin, 1976).

15

The Concept of Change

The concept of change is of primary importance in the life of man and society because they are not static. However, Western political thinkers and sociologists do not attach much significance to the concept of social change. For them, changes in the society are riot fundamental social changes but are changes merely in social institutions, in their forms and in their structures. McClung Lee writes that social changes are not essential changes in life, they alter not the essence of social life, but its forms and the functions and structures of various social institutions. These thinkers, in Marxist phrase, stand for the maintenance of status quo. According to them, the society may suffer from maladjustments or disharmony which are the results of individual's pathological conditions. Social evils are due to individual's vices. These social evils should be corrected slowly and gradually through social reforms. Obviously, the reforms can take place only in a peaceful manner, for violence is no solution to any conflict. Violence is contrary to any civilized existence. In any case, any fundamental change or upheaval is ruled out strongly. This view of change has been challenged by the Marxists. The conflicts in the society, they argue, occur not because of pathological conditions of man but because of material conditions. These material conditions are created by the modes of production and man has little or no control over them. Thus social conflicts are the result of material or economic factors of the given society and the solution to them lies not in gradual, reforms; only a 'revolution can bring about the desired change. Thus revolution is violent and changes not merely the forms, functions and structures of various social institutions, but also the entire society; it alters the essence of social life and hence every aspect of man and society is directly affected. This revolution has to be violent barring few exceptional cases like in England and America where Marx saw the possibilities of a peaceful revolution. Revolution means the overthrow of the established social order and those who benefit from the said social order would always be interested in maintaining the status quo and use all the forces at their command to resist the overthrow. Role of violence thus becomes absolutely essential in affecting the revolution.

However within the socialist circle, there have been thinkers who do not share the Marxist dogmatism. They want socialism without class war and violence. They also repudiate many Marxist views. They want socialism through incremental changes. The Marxists call them revisionists, but they themselves call them by different brands like evolutionary socialists, Fabians, syndicalists, Guild socialists or democratic socialists.

The present chapter deals with all the three views of social change. Firstly, we deal with the Marxist theory of historical change followed by the theory of incremental change advocated by the so-called revisionists and finally we study Karl Popper's theory of piecemeal social engineering which in fact is the liberal theory of peaceful and gradual changes.

I. Historical Materialism as a Theory of Revolutionary Change

Marx called his theory of communism as Scientific Socialism because it is not based on any utopia or imagination, as the socialists theories before him were. On the contrary, Marx did a deep-penetrating study of history and historical processes and evolved ideas which were close to reality. At Marx's graveside, his greatest friend, Engels, declared, "Just as Darwin discovered the law of development of organic nature, . so Marx discovered the law of development of human history...." And this law is his theory of Historical Materialism. The Marxian theory of Historical Materialism is based on his theory of Dialectical Materialism. Thus it is necessary to study Dialectical Materialism before we study Historical Materialism.

(1) *Dialectical Materialism – Dialectical* Materialism is the philosophical basis of Marxism. It is composed of two words—dialectics and materialism, the first, dialectics refer to the law of social development while materialism, denotes the ultimate reality. Let us first understand materialism followed by dialectics.

The doctrine of materialism is opposed to spiritualism which view God. as the ultimate reality. According to spiritualism, God created the world and whatever happens in the world is God's wish. But the Marxists do not believe in the existence of God. Marxism, in fact, is a radical rejection of religion. Religion is nothing but opium of the people under whose influence they cannot understand themselves and their surroundings rationally. To Marx, the ultimate reality is matter. The whole world-living and non-living is made of matter. Man, animal, stone, wood-everything we find in the nature is made of matter. This matter possesses three characteristcs which have their implications in society. These three characteristics are as follows:

(i) Matter is always in *motion*. Matter is dynamic and not static. By its very nature it moves on. So is the case of world is which is always moving. The earth is not constant. It moves around. its axis. All the living and non-living are moving. Thus everything in this world is changing. It may not be obvious while seeing from naked eyes. But the science definitely believes this. From this, the Marxists conclude that everything in the world is changing either rising and developing or declining and dying away.

(ii) *Unity of Opposites:* The Marxists also call this as interpenetration of opposites. The second characteristic of matter is that it is composed of two mutually opposite elements. A magnet, for example, has two aspects—north pole and south pole. Both the poles are inseparable from each other. You break thc magnet to the last, both the poles will still exist. Thus by its very nature, the matter is composed of two opposites. The society is also composed of two mutually opposing classes and it develops as a result of the conflict between them.

(iii) *Quantitative as well as Qualitative Change:* The third characteristic of matter is that it is subject to change—both quantitative as well as qualitative. The Marxists call it as the law of transformation from quantity to quality and quality to quantity. Quantitative change produce qualitative change and vice versa. Quantitative changes are slow and gradual changes while qualitative change is a sudden change in which the matter changes its form or character. For example, when you heat water, it is slowly and gradually heated. The temperature is rising but water remains water, only the amount of heat is raising. This is quantitative change. However, a boiling point comes when the water is converted into steam. The conversion of water into steam is a qualitative change. Similarly, when the water is cooled, a point comes when it becomes ice. The conversion of water into ice is qualitative change, where the matter has changed its form from water to ice. In human society also, both quantitative as well as qualitative changes take place. Quantitative changes are slow and gradual changes. These gradual changes takes place over a period of time without any fundamental change in the character of s o c i e t y .

> But then a point comes where there is total break and the qualitative change takes place in the form of revolution, in which the old form of society is completely destroyed and a new form comes into existence and begins its own process of development. For example, in a feudal society where the production is made for local consumption, gradually development takes place and the buying and selling of surplus production leads to the production of things for the market beyond the local area. This is the slow beginning of capitalism and capitalist production. This was a gradual or quantitative development. However, a point came when the rising capitalist class came into direct conflict with the feudal order and the latter was overthrown and replaced by capitalism. The replacement of capitalism in place of feudalism was a qualitative change. The qualitative change is revolution in which the whole social system is destroyed and a new social order emerges.

Thus materialism, to Marx, explains the nature of human society and its development. The material world is primary and mind or thought is secondary. The spiritual life, for that matter any aspect of life, is the reflection of this reality which is the matter. Marx declared that it is not the consciousness of men that determines their being, but, on the contrary, their social being, that determines their consciousness. It is the development of matter or material development which produces people's habits, attitudes, thinking and the entire social order.

If materialism depicts the reality of this world, dialectics shows the exact evolution of history. According to the Marxists, the development of society is dialectical. The society develops as a result of contradiction and conflict and this development is through three stages: thesis, anti-thesis and synthesis. The history goes by opposites and the seeds of destruction are contained within each historical period. Thesis is the established order while those who challenge it constitutes anti-thesis. As a result of clash between the thesis and anti-thesis, synthesis arises which is the combination of good things of both the thesis and anti-thesis. Thus synthesis is a higher stage of development. For example, when we sow a seed of wheat we have only one seed. This is thesis. After sometime a plant grows out of seed, it develops and flowers. This is anti-thesis. Ultimately the plant dries and get destroyed, and then we have many seeds of wheat. This is synthesis. In thesis, we have one seed while in synthesis we have many. The synthesis is definitely better and higher than the thesis. Later on, the synthesis becomes thesis, again challenged by anti-thesis, the clash leading to synthesis. This is how the development takes place. The slave owning society was the thesis, which was challenged by the slaves, the resulting conflicting led to the establishment of feudalism as synthesis. Later on, synthesis became the thesis. The feudal order was established. It developed to its fullest extent till it was challenged by the farmers and the rising capitalist class as anti-thesis. The conflict between the two led to the destruction of feudal society and creation of a capitalist society, which is synthesis. The capitalist society has also its own contradictions. The workers as anti-thesis will eventually challenge the capitalists and the conflict between the two will destroy the capitalist society and a new socialist society will emerge out of the ashes of capitalist society. The feudal society was a higher society than the preceding slave owning society as capitalism is a higher form of social order than the feudal and similarly socialism will be a more developed form of social order. The concept of dialectic was Hegel's concept which Marx adopted. However, to Hegel, idea or spirit of God was the ultimate reality; to Marx, matter is the ultimate reality. Marx had said that the Hegelian dialectics was standing on its head; he turned it up-side down. This is also called the law of negation which means one thing grows out of another and then battles with it.

Dialectical Materialism is the basis on which the entire Marxist philosophy rests. For the Marxists, it is the key to the understanding and solution of any social problem.

(2) *Historical Materialism or Economic Interpretation of History:* On the basis of the philosophy of dialectical materialism, Marx goes on to explain and analyse history. The basic assumption from which the theory of historical materialism begins is that man, in order to survive, has to eat and to eat, he has to produce, to work. This is man's basic activity and all others activities follow thereafter. Thus the economic activity is the most important activity and it influences and controls man's other activities. It is also the basis of social order. Engels said, "The materialist conception of history starts from the principle that production, and with production the exchange of its products, is the basis of every social order; that in every society which has appeared in history, the distribution of the products, and with it the division of society into classes or estates, is determined by what is produced and how it is produced, and how the product is exchanged." The Marxists believe that the economic basis of the society determines its social structure as a whole and also the psychology of the people of the society. The economic base means the modes of production, the economic foundation or structure which determines the rest of the society called the superstructure or institutional and ideological forms. The people's attitude, behaviour, religion, ethics, morality, culture, social

and political institutions come under the category of superstructure. The economic base includes both the modes of production and relations of production.

The modes of production include land, minerals and physical equipment such as tools, machines, technology. The relations of production are relations between men based on means of production. Under capitalism, for example, machine is the mode of production and the relations of production are the relations between men which are based on the ownership of machine. This means the relationship between the capitalist who own the machine and the workers who do not own the machine. Similarly, in a slave-owing society, relations of production are slave owners and the slaves. In a feudal society, feudal lord and the serfs or peasants. Marx said, "In the social production which men carryon they enter into definite relations that are indispensable and independent of their will; these relations of production correspond to a definite stage of development of their material process of production. The sum total of these relations of production constitute the economic structure of society—the real foundation, on which rises legal political superstructures and to which correspond definite forms of social consciousness. The mode of production in material life determines the general character of the social, political and spiritual processes of life. It is not the consciousness of men that determines their existence, but, on the contrary, their social existence determines their consciousness."

According to the Marxists, as the modes of production change, not only the relations between men change, but the whole character of society changes. The whole superstructure also changes. Initially the relations of production facilitate the development of the forces of production. But the time comes where the relation of production do not develop the forces of production, in fact it fetters them. Here comes the contradiction, which is a fundamental contradiction because new mode of production has emerged and eager to replace the existing mode of production. This fundamental contradiction can only be resolved through revolution. The revolution results in a better developed mode of production, a higher stage of society in the progressive development of man.

Social change, the Marxists insist, signifies social development. It implies a qualitative change in the material relations of human beings; it means the developed shape of production forces, a newer form of mode of production. If the society has to live, it has to develop and if it has to develop it has to change. The productive forces of a given society set the processes of change into motion and the whole process gets completed when a newer mode of production replaces the order one, thus changing the whole fabric of material relations of the old system. A social change comes into effect with the changes in the modes of production. Therefore, the ultimate causes of all social change are to be sought as Marx and Engels said not in men's brains, not in men's better insight into eternal truth and justice, but in the changes of modes of production and exchange. They are to be sought not in the philosophy but in the economics of each particular epoch.

Thus the change in the economic foundation leads sooner or later to the transformation of the whole super-structure. However, no social order is ever destroyed before all the productive forces for which it is sufficient have been developed and new superior relations of production never replace older ones before the material conditions for their existence have matured within the framework of the old society. This means feudalism had to develop to its fullest, only after that capitalism arrives and it is able to replace feudalism only when the conditions for it are ripe within feudalism. After replacing the slave-owing society, feudalism develops for a long time. But then, as a result of development in trade and commerce, the capitalist class comes into existence. The capitalist does not take over immediately. It also develops and then a stage comes when it is able to challenge feudalism which is on decline. Feudalism is destroyed and capitalism takes over. Thus social change is social revolution—an object of achievement. It marks a movement towards progress. It implies the beginning of the newer order.

Marx has divided history into numerous phases as per his theory of historical materialism. The first stage is primitive communism. This was the period where man was dependent on nature for his survival. He was a food gatherer and a hunter. There was no mode of production, and therefore, no relations of production. There was no exploitation because everybody was working to satisfy his basic needs. However, this situation did not remain forever. This primitive communism was threatened because man started domesticating animals followed by agricultural activities: Thus the concept of private property came into being. Mode of production arrived and soon the primitive society was replaced by slave-owning society, in which there were slaves and slave-owners. The slaves were highly exploited. They were considered as forms of property. They started rebelling against their masters. In order to put down their revolt, a series of political and social institutions were created like state, religion, ethics and culture. The third stage of evolution was feudalism where we had feudal lords and serfs or half-slaves. In feudal society, the feudal lords got their living from some form of tribute from the serfs who actually produced things on land. Their conditions were better than the slaves but they were also in chains. They were subjected to harsh treatment from the lords. In feudal society, production was for local consumption. But then, whatever was not consumed locally, that is the surplus was sold to merchants who would sell them in other regions or countries. With the development in trade and commerce, these merchants began to need more than the surplus of the serfs. These merchants would provide raw-material to the serfs who would process them into finished goods.

The finished goods were taken away by the merchants, after paying labour charges, to the market. Slowly and gradually, this merchant class developed into capitalist class. This capitalist class ultimately overthrew feudalism. Capitalism is the fourth stage, where the society is divided into capitalists and the workers. Here production is carried out through the machines and it is for the market. The purpose is to accumulate more and more capital. In such a system the workers are highly oppressed. They will revolt and as a result of their revolt and when the conditions are ripe, capitalism will be overthrown and replaced by socialism. This socialism is transitory in nature, in which the remnants of capitalism will be done away with and its purpose is to create communism, the last stage of evolution where there will not exist any private property, no classes, therefore no state. The production will be for the needs of the people and not for the market. From here, the real history of man would begin.

These changes in the history take place as a result of change in modes of production. The slave-owning society came when the private property in the form of animals and land came which created slaves and slave owners. The windmill gives you a society with the feudal lords and serfs; the steam-mill a society with industrial capitalists and workers.

The concept of historical materialism is intrinsically related to the Marxist theory of classes. Engels referred to historical materialism as "that view of the cause of history, which seeks the ultimate cause and the great-moving power of all important historic events in the economic development of society, in the changes in the modes of production and exchange, in the consequent division of society into distinct classes and in the struggles of these classes against one another." To the Marxists, history is nothing but the history of class struggle. A class is defined as a group of men having the same economic interest. Thus slaves, slave-owners, feudal lords, serfs, capitalists, workers are different classes. These classes are the products of the modes of production and of exchange. Explaining the origin of classes in modern age of capitalism, Engels says, "The bourgeoisie and the proletariat both arose as results of a change in economic conditions, or, strictly speaking, in methods of production. The transition first from hand labour, controlled by the guilds, to manufacture and thence from manufacture to the greater industry with steam and machine force, has developed these two classes." In other words, it is the property which makes two classes, one which own property and the other does not own it. The development and social change in history is brought about by the classes, as a result of their conflicts. These classes conflict because their interests are mutually contradictory. In feudalism, the feudal lords want to get as much as possible out of the labour of their serfs, while the serfs want their production for themselves and their families. They also want freedom to work for themselves. Thus the interests of feudal lords and serfs were in conflict to each other. Similarly in a capitalist society, the capitalist wants to make more and more profit, while the worker needs more and more wages. Therefore, there is a class struggle between the two. Revolution is the result of class conflicts. It occurred in the past when feudalism came because of the class struggle between the slave and slave owner; it led to the establishment of capitalism as a result of the class struggle between the feudal lords and the serfs. Socialism will come as a result of class struggle between the capitalists and the workers. In socialist society the remnants of the capitalists will be destroyed and the property will be owned and controlled by the state for the general benefit of the workers or proletariat. The classes and class struggles are brought about by the property relations and by abolishing property, there will not be any classes or class war. Therefore, the theory of communism has been summed up by Marx and Engels *in The Communist Manifesto,* in the single sentence: abolition of property.

(3) *Historical Materialism and Human Will:* Thus to the Marxists, social change in the form of revolution occurs due to property or modes of production. The new modes of production create new societies. And this is independent of man's will. Whenever the material forces of production come into conflict with the existing relations and production, the society becomes pregnant with revolution. Then what is the role of man? Marx believed that ultimately it is the conflict between material forces of production and the existing relations of production that is the cause of revolution. Thus man's role is limited: According to Marx, man must play his part to hasten it when its material conditions are ripe. He says, "Man makes his own history, but he does not make it out of the whole cloth; he does not make it out of conditions chosen by himself, but out of such as he finds close at hand." Marx's objective is not to interpret the world but to change it. And man definitely has to play an important role in changing it. But finally it is the modes of production which will have final say. The human will at the most,

can simply be the immediate cause of revolution. Further this will itself is created by the mode of production.

According to the Marxists, the revolution is always conducted by the class which is coming to power in the new mode of production. But it is not the only class which wages war against the existing relations of production. The others also take part, because they are highly exploited and oppressed in the existing order. For example, in the overthrow of feudalism, the capitalists were helped by the serfs and peasants, which formed the producing class of feudalism. They were against the feudal order because of its oppression and exploitation and to remain under it meant continued oppression and exploitation.

(4) *Violent versus Peaceful Change:* Revolution, for the Marxists, is inevitable. It takes place in different stages of society because of emergence of new modes of production. But whether it has to be violent or peaceful? Marx admitted the possibility of a revolution through peaceful means. He said in Amsterdam in 1872, "We know that the institutions, customs and traditions of the separate countries have to be taken into account; and we do not deny that there are countries like America and Britain and if I knew your institutions better, I might add Holland to them in which the workers can achieve their goal by peaceful means." Engels also said that in countries like Britain and America it is conceivable that there may be a peaceful development towards the new society. Engels held peaceful methods to achieve revolution as desirable. But on the whole, Marxism believes that a peaceful revolution is not possible. Engels said, "It is desirable that the abolition of private property be brought peacefully, and the communists surely are the lost ones who would object to this method. The communists know too well that all conspiracies are not only useless but even harmful. They know too well that revolutions are not made intentionally and willfully, but that they are everywhere and at all times the necessary results of circumstances which are entirely independent of the will and direction of individual parties and the whole classes. But at the same time the communists see that the development of the proletariat in almost all civilized countries is violently suppressed and that thus the opponents of the communists are working with all power towards making a (violent) revolution necessary. When the suppressed proletariat is finally driven into a (violent) revolution, then the communists shall defend the cause of the proletariat with their deeds as well as with words." The *Communist Manifesto* openly declares, "The communist disdain to conceal their views and aims. They openly declare that their ends can be attained only by the forcible overthrow of all existing social conditions. Let the ruling classes tremble at a communistic revolution. The proletarians

have nothing to lose but their chains. They have a world to win." Marx also said, "Force is the mid-wife of every old society pregnant with a new one." Thus the Marxists believe that non-violent peaceful change is desirable, though it is impossible. It is impossible because the classes whose interests are threatened as a result of revolution will not allow a peaceful revolution. They will resist any attempt to overthrow the existing order non-violently. Therefore, revolution has to be violent.

(5) Thus the theory of historical materialism gives us a different account of history and its development. Traditionally history has been presented as a record of wars between nations and achievements of individual kings and warriors. "Sometimes", as Emile Burns says, "the motive of these individuals are described in a purely personal way—their ambitions led them to conquer territory, or their moral or immoral outlook caused them to adopt certain policies. Sometimes they are described as acting for the sake of the country's honour or prestige, or from some motive of religion." The Marxists, on the other hand, have presented history which is the result of interplay of economic or materialist factor.

To sum up, the theory of historical materialism means the following:

(i) The basis of the theory of historical materialism is dialectical materialism. According to dialectical materialism, the society moves on the basis of certain definite laws.

(ii) Economic activity is an important activity of the individual.

(iii) The materialist or economic factor constitutes the base on which the superstructure exists. Super-structure means people's habits, attitudes, religion, ethics, morality, culture, social and political institutions.

(iv) The modes of production are responsible for social changes in history.

(v) Mankind has passed through numerous stages of evolution—primitive society, slave-owning society, feudal society and capitalist society. Two more stages are to follow—socialist and communist societies. The economic factor is dominant for all the changes in history.

(vi) The theory of class struggle is related to historical materialism. Changes in history take place as a result of class struggle.

(vii) Human will is highly limited in the occurrence of revolution. In fact the will is also the result of the modes of production.

(viii) Social change or revolution cannot be brought about through peaceful means. It has to be violent, much to the disliking of the workers.

Criticism: The Marxian theory of historical materialism has been I criticised from many angles. *Firstly,* the theory of dialectical materialism on which the theory of historical materialism is based is mere a matter of expediency. Marx and Engel never tried to explain it in details. John Plemenatz says that "Dialectical materialism is not really a theory at all; it means very little and implies very little; it is a kind of preliminary pattern to prepare the mind for historical materialism, which no more rests upon it than a slip does on its own reflection in the water." Marx and the Marxists are more interested in historical materialism. *Secondly,* the economic factor has been given undue emphasis. Engels was very much aware of it. He said, "Marx and I are partly responsible for the fact that at times our disciples have laid more weight upon the economic factor than belongs to it. We were compelled to emphasise its central character in opposition to our opponents, who denied it, and there was not always time, place and occasion to do justice to the other factors in the reciprocal interactions of the historical processes." *Thirdly,* the doctrine of class struggle is a myth. In modem times we have the existence of a powerful middle class which the Marxists accepted unwillingly. History is not the history of class struggle but of class cooperation and collaboration. Marx's analysis of capitalism is true to the extent of his times, in which the workers were really oppressed and exploited. But with the advent of modern welfare state, the workers' conditions have improved manifoldly. Therefore, now people have started talking about social change than revolution. The failures of socialist regimes in different countries in recent years have further weakened the Marxist theory of revolution. *Last,* but not the least, the communist society is a utopia.

II: Theory of Incremental Changes

(1) The Marxian theory of change which means a revolutionary change has not been shared by many thinkers. To them it is too sweeping. The violent content in the Marxist theory has alienated Western people from accepting it. Therefore, the Western socialists modified Marxism, completely abandoning its certain principles and supporting a more humanitarian socialism.' They do not want to wipe out the entire social structure. On the other hand they want slow and gradual reforms to achieve socialism. This is called the theory of incremental change. The advocates of this theory belong to different shades of evolutionary socialism like Fabianism, democratic socialism, syndicalism and Guild socialism.

(2) (i) *Fabianism:* The Fabian society was formed in 1884 in England. The objective of the Fabian society was summed up as thus; "for the

right moment you must wait, as Fabius did, most patiently, when warring against Hannibal, though many censured his delays; but when the time comes you must strike hard, as Fabius did, or your waiting will be vain and fruitless." However, the fact remains that Fabius never struck hard. The Fabian society consisted of many important intellectual giants like George Bernard Shaw, Graham Wallace, H.G. Wells, Annie Besant, Mrs. and Mr. Sidney Webb, Ramsay MacDonald, Harold Laski, R.H. Tawney, Herbert Finer and Leonard Woolf. Fabianism was essentially a middle class movement designed to propagate socialism without its revolutionary contents. Sydney Webb said that socialism was already being realised in England as a result of development of democracy. The evolution to socialism from the former individualistic society was natural, democratic, gradual, ethical and peaceful. The development of democracy ensures not only the control by the masses over political institutions but also on the main instruments of wealth production. The Fabians want the anarchy of capitalistic competitive struggle to be gradually replaced by organised cooperation. They want socialism in the economic area which has to come as a gradual process. They are against rent which they think is the unearned increment of the owner. Initially there was no rent because land was the gift of the nature and there was enough productive land. But later on unproductive land was also brought under cultivation, and the good land started giving rent. The landowner plays no part in increasing the value of the land. Therefore, it is unearned rent. Unearned increment exists in industry also. The Fabians want the unearned increment to be placed before the community for common good. This is to be achieved by a suitable system of taxation and nationalising land and industry. The Fabians also voiced their concern over economic disparities existing in the society. This division of society into poor and rich is bad. The rich has no right to live luxuriously when the poor cannot afford a minimum necessity for survival. This has to be ended by the nationalisation of land and capital.

According to Laidler, Fabianism (1) regards the transition from capitalism to socialism as a gradual process; (2) it looks forward to the socialisation of industry by the peaceful economic and political agencies already at hand; (3) it sees in the middle class a group that can be utilised in developing the technique of administration on behalf of the new social order and (4) it feels that an important step in the attainment of socialism is the rousing of the social conscience of the community in favour of the socialist ideal.

The Fabians are against violent revolution. They advocate a peaceful revolution, through a policy of persuasion. They have no faith in giving shocks to the society. In fact they do not want to destroy the existing system, they only desire to change or reform it. These changes are to be brought about incremently.

(ii) *Evolutionary Socialism:* In Germany, Bernstein advocated evolutionary socialism. He also believed in the theory of incremental changes. He said, "I strongly believe in the socialist movement, in the march forward of the working classes, who step by step must work out of their emancipation by changing society from the domain of a commercial landholding oligarchy to a real democracy which in all its departments is guided by the interests of those who work and create." Thus Bernstein strongly believes in democracy. He ruled out the desirability of a revolutionary catastrophe as a solution to the ills of the society. On the contrary we must reform the society through democracy. The socialists must strive "to organise the working classes politically and develop them as a democracy, and to fight for all reforms in the state which are adapted to raise the working classes and transform the state in the direction of democracy."

Evolutionary socialism of Bernstein does not accept many of classical Marxist ideas. Criticising the economic interpretation of history, Bernstein said, "Modern society is much richer than earlier societies in ideologies which are not determined by economics and by nature operating as an economic force. Science, the arts, a whole series of social relations are nowadays much less dependent on economics than formerly they were. The point of economic development that has now been reached leaves the ideological, and especially, the ethical factors greater scope for independent activity than used to be the case." Bernstein also criticised the concept of class war. He noted that history .is characterised not by class struggle, but by class cooperation. Marx was also wrong in stating that the number of propertied class would steadily go down. Bernstein saw the number of possessing class larger. He said, "The enormous increase of social wealth is not accompanied by a decreasing number of larger capitalists, but by an increasing number of capitalists of all degrees." Bernstein saw the number of middle class increasing which was against the prediction of Marx. The worker's condition is also not deteriorating. On the contrary, it has considerably improved under the different welfare laws. Bernstein also rejected the theory of dictatorship of proletariat. He was a democrat and therefore believed that universal franchise gives equal opportunity to workers to participate in the affairs of state. He said, "The right to vote in a democracy makes its members virtually partners in the community, and this virtual partnership must in the end lead to real partnership." To him, democracy is the substance of socialism, where neither the capitalists nor the workers dominate each other. Following Bernstein, we find all the communist and socialist parties in Europe have doubted the Marxian concept of dictatorship of the proletariat. They believe in pluralism of political parties and like to come to power through democratic means. Even after ascendancy to power, they remain committed to democracy and better leave power if they lose elections. Thus there cannot be a monopoly of any political party over political power. The will of the people is supreme which has to be respected.

(iii) *Guild Socialism:* The theory of incremental changes was also advocated by the Guild Socialists. S.G. Hobson and G.D.H. Cole have been the major exponents of Guild socialism. The Guild Socialists want to achieve socialism through guilds. According to Appadorai, "The guild is a trade union modified in two ways; it will be inclusive of all workers as well as the clerical, technical and managerial workers, who are now largely excluded from trade union membership; and it will be organised to control industry, not merely to secure better conditions of work. The trade unions are the key to the situation in two respects; they will become the guilds of tomorrow, and they are the organisations by means of which the actual transition to socialism is to be achieved. The objective of guild socialism is to abolish the wage system and establishment of self-government in industry."

The Guild socialists accepted the Marxist programme of abolishing the wage system which according to them is bad morally, psychologically, economically and aesthetically. Such a system produces a slave mentality in which workers cannot become creative. The workers should be paid as human beings and not as labour. They should be protected from exploitation and miseries. For the purpose, they advocate state welfare measures. Further the industry, for the guild socialists should be managed by the workers.

The guild socialists advocate functional representation as against the existing territorial representation which is wrong because no man represents the other. Only functions can be represented. For example a farmer can represent farmers, lawyer, the lawyers. They envisage guilds of producers and guilds of consumers. The state should be limited to the political areas and other functions should be looked after by the guilds; different guilds will look after the different functions in the society. Regarding the structure of a guild socialist society, the advocates of Guild Socialism differ. But broadly speaking, as Appadorai points out, it is as follows:" (i) There will be guild for each industry which will be administered by the guild on behalf of society, (ii) Consumers' councils will cooperate with the bodies of producers to determine costs and prices, (iii) A common Parliament will (according to some authorities) look to the affairs common to all, such as defence and taxation. On this point, however, there is some difference of opinion, some thinkers, suggesting a body representing the essential functional associations to regulate such matters, (iv) There will be local regional bodies to look after matters of common interest in the locality."

These objectives are to be attained through evolutionary methods, by the trade unions. However, the Guild Socialists are suspicious of present day Parliaments in achieving their aims.

(iv) *Syndicalism:* Syndicalism developed in France. The term syndicalism is derived from syndicate which means labour union. Syndicalism wants to create a new social order through trade unions. They want to use the economic power of trade unions to destroy capitalism and establish a socialist society. Sorel and Pelloutier are the main advocates of syndicalism.

The syndicalists accept many ideas of classical Marxism. They accept the class theory that the society is divided into capitalists and proletariats, where the capitalists are dominating; the state is an instrument of class struggle in the hands of the capitalist and that the private property is evil and a root for all social ills. Therefore, they want to destroy the state. About the future society, syndicalism has not elaborated much, but they definitely want the replacement of state with a system of producers' societies. Syndicates of workers will control the means of production. These syndicates will be connected with the local union of workers and a general confederation of labour. National services such as railways and the postal services will be controlled by the General Confederation of Labour.

Thus syndicalism's objective is a stateless society. For the attainment of their objective, the syndicalists have no faith in democracy. Since economic power is the key to political power, therefore, they want to capture economic power first. Economic power is to be captured through the means of strike and general sabotage. Syndicalism gives utmost importance to strike. It has to be encouraged whenever and wherever possible. Strikes have moral, educative and practical value. Syndicalism views 'General Strike' as the final weapon for the overthrow of the capitalism. This General Strike need not be the strike of all workers; a sufficiently large numbers of workers from the key industries would be enough to achieve the overthrow of the capitalism. In such a strike, violence may become absolutely necessary. Before the General Strike, a perpetual offence against the capitalists through strikes, sabotages, destruction of machinery, boycott, label and go-slow methods are advocated by the syndicalists.

However, after the First World War, new syndicalism arose and its thinkers like Jouhaux, Perrot and Leroy abandoned the notions of class struggle and violence. They also expressed no faith in communism. They advocate reorganisation of state and modify its functions. The functions of state are reduced to the minimum. In industries, they advocate the establishment of a national, broadly representative economic council to prepare a general plan for production and. distribution. This council would also exercise control over the general policies of administration proposed by the bodies that operate the industries. New syndicalism no longer believes in revolution. It also stands for incremental change in the society.

(v) *Democratic Socialism:* The concept of democratic socialism first arose in England and then expanded to various parts of the world. However, it has developed only where we have a strong democratic traditions like in England, Holland, Belgium, Switzerland, Australia, New Zealand, Israel and India. In India democratic socialism was advocated by Jawaharlal Nehru and J.P. Narayan. In England, important thinkers like Robert Owen, R.H. Tawney, G.D.H. Cole and Harold Laski were the exponents of democratic socialism.

The concept of democratic socialism combined the advantages of both democracy as well as socialism. It means the following:

(i) It rejects the Marxian concepts of class war and state. It also rejects communism.

(ii) The state has an active role to play. The purpose of state is not the protection and promotion of class interests, but is to act as a guardian of civil and political liberties of all its citizens. The state's aim is to promote the common interest of the people. The larger interests of the society should precede the narrow interests of the individuals. The individual should not be allowed to hamper the general interests of the community. Naturally the doctrine of free trade or *laissez faire* has no place in democratic socialism.

(iii) Democratic Socialism promotes cooperation instead of competition. The objective is to eliminate all the evils of capitalism. The capitalists and the workers should cooperate with each other for mutual benefits and for the common interests of the society.

(iv) The weak should be protected against economic intimidation and starvation. The property cannot be used for exploitation. For the purpose, the state has a large area to operate. The state must embark upon welfare legislations to protect the weak, children and old people.

(v) Economic disparities are to be removed gradually. For this, the property is to be regulated. There should be d limit to individual's holdings. The monopolisation of land and capital is to be removed. The glaring inequalities of wealth have to be removed by a progressive taxation of the rich,

(vi) The important means of production or key industries should be owned by the community.

(vii) It also advocates democracy in industry which means workers' participation in the management of industry.

(viii) Democratic socialism stands for political, economic and social democracy. It gives due importance to civil and political liberties.

Thus democratic socialism stands for far-reaching changes in the society. But these changes are not to be achieved through revolution in one stroke. These changes are to be brought about slowly, gradually through peaceful and democratic methods. Thus the theory of incremental changes finds an important expression in democratic socialism.

In conclusion we can say that the theory of incremental change is a rejection of Marxian dogmatic concept of historical materialism. It does 'not believe in a violent revolution and class analysis of Marxism. With the exception of syndicalism, all of them have rejected Marxism as a dogma. Yet they have not rejected socialism which stands for the advancement of all the people in a society. They want to remove starvation and exploitation from the society. For the purpose they stand for the notion of incremental change. As against the theory of historical materialism, the theory of incremental change envisages class collaboration and cooperation and that the necessary reforms be brought about gradually, peacefully and through democratic methods. This view has also been accepted by liberals like Popper who advocates the theory of piecemeal social engineering.

III: Popper's Concept of Piecemeal Social Engineering

Karl Popper's view of piecemeal social engineering is based on his concept of rationality. Popper calls himself as a rationalist and gives a very comprehensive meaning of rationality. Rationality is an attitude of reasonableness which means. decisions should be arrived at through arguments and compromise. Nobody should be forced or coerced. Even persuasive propaganda is excluded. Rationalism means discussion, readiness to learn from others, an attitude. of give and take, intellectual humility, the acknowledgement of fallibility, respect for each individual as a potential source of argument and of reasonable information and the recognition of his right to be heard. Rationalism also means criticism. It is also the capacity to sedate means to ends. One should be clear about one's aims and be able to choose the best means to realise them. Popper stands for an open society where the rational individual pursues knowledge to solve specific problems, which he does through trial and error method.

(i) What is Social Engineering?

Before we understand piecemeal social engineering, let us understand social engineering first. According to Popper, social engineering means two things:

(i) *Absolute faith in individual and his capacities:* According to Popper, to a social engineer, individual is at the centrepoint. Everything revolves around him. He is the master of his destiny and in accordance with our aims, we can influence or change the history of man just as we have changed the face of earth'. Ends are not imposed on us by some external force but we ourselves choose our aims just as we create new thoughts or new work of art, of new houses or new machines. Therefore, Popper stands for individual's autonomy and freedom. Popper stands for democracy which is the right of people to judge and to dismiss their government, is the only known device by which we can try to protect ourselves against the misuse of political power; it is the control of the rulers by the ruled'. Popper stands for democracy because man is rational and capable enough to make choice. He is also capable of making mistake but this is all in the game. He learns by experiences and rectifies his mistake. Popper's view of man is directly in conflict with Marxian view of man which believes that man is directed and controlled by the modes of production. To Popper, man is at the helm of affairs who creates and controls everything including the modes of production. It is true that men, in many respects, are unequals. Nor can it be doubted that this inequality is of great importance and even in many respects highly desirable. But this does not mean that there should be inequality. Popper says, "... the adoption of an anti-equalitarian attitude in political life i.e. in the field of problems concerning with the power of man over man, is just what I should call criminal. For it offers a justification of the attitude that different categories of people have different rights; that the master has the right to enslave the slave; that some men have the rights to use others as their tools. Ultimately, it will be used ... to justify murder."

(ii) *Social engineering means solution to problems*—A social engineer is not interested in understanding the social institutions in terms of the origins, their development, and their present and, future significance. He knows that most of the social organisations have 'grown as the undesigned results of human actions' while only a few of them are consciously designed. To him, the problem is whether a social institution is well designed and organised to serve our aims. For example in case of institution of insurance, a social engineer will not go into the question as to how and why this institution came into being. He will think in terms of making it efficient and how to increase its profits and how to increase its benefit to the public. Similarly in case of police force, a social engineer is not interested in understanding police force as an instrument of protection of freedom and security or as an instrument of class exploitation. A social engineer is a practical man. Given his aim, he would either suggest measures 'to make it a suitable instrument for the protection of freedom or security' or he might also suggest measures by which it could be turned into a powerful weapon of class rule' The scientific basis of politics for a social engineer 'consists of the factual informations necessary for the construction or alterations of social institutions, in accordance with our wishes and aims. Such a science would have to tell us what steps we must take if we wish, for instance to avoid depressions, or else to produce depressions; or if we wish to make the distribution of wealth more even, or less even.

Thus a social engineer approaches institutions rationally as means that serve certain ends and that as a technologist he judges them wholly according to their appropriateness, efficiency, simplicity etc. Politics is like social technology, and the objective is not to seek or explore any idealism but to identify and isolate problems, to define them in precise terms and propose and criticise solutions to them .

(2) ***Two kinds of Social Engineering***

According to Popper, there are two kinds of social engineerings:
Piecemeal social engineering and Utopian social engineering. He is against the latter and wants to adopt the former.

(i) *Utopian social engineering:* According to Popper, Plato and Marx stood for utopian social engineering. Utopian social engineering means that we should have an ultimate end like Plato wanted to create an ideal state or Marxism stands for a communist society as its end. Only when we have the blueprint of the society that we aim, we can begin to consider the best ways and means for its realisation, and to draw up a plan for political action'

Popper calls utopian social engineering dangerous on many grounds. *Firstly,* it demands a strong centralised rule of the few which is likely to lead to dictatorship. *Secondly,* even if there is a benevolent dictator, he will not be able to know the results of his action which he undtrtakes to realise his ideals because dictatorship discourages criticism and even the 'benevolent dictator will not hear of complaints concerning the measures he has taken. *Thirdly,* the reconstruction of society is a big task which can be achieved in a considerable time. It may cause considerable inconvenience to many. Therefore the utopian engineer will have to ignore many complaints; 'in fact, it will be part of his business to suppress unreasonable objection. He will also suppress reasonable criticism. *Fourthly* the problems in utopian social engineering become, more acute when the benevolent' successors do not pursue the same ideal, then all the sufferings of the people for the sake of the ideal may have been in vain. *Fifthly,* since the ideals can be realised after a long period of time they may also change. 'What had appeared the ideal state to the people who made the original blueprint, may not appear so to their successors. Further when the ideal is very distant, it is very difficult to say whether the step taken was towards or away from it. *Sixthly,* use of violence is necessary for the utopian engineers to suppress those who do not accept their objectives. *Lastly,* the utopian engineer wants a total reconstruction of society 'whose practical consequences are hard to calculate, owing to our limited experiences.' He claims to plan rationally for the whole society but we do not have the necessary, factual knowledge to prove such a claim. We cannot possess such knowledge since we have insufficient practical experience in this kind of planning, and knowledge of facts must be based upon experience. At present, the sociological knowledge necessary for large-scale engineering is simply non-existent.

(ii) *Piecemeal social engineering:* The basic problem with the utopian social engineering is their belief that social experiments must be carried on in the whole society on a large scale. But the piecemeal method of social engineering can be carried out on a small scale and under realistic conditions. There is no need of revolution for the society. We should make small experiments. We can take up one particular social institution for necessary changes at a time, and make experiments on them to turn them according to our intentions. We may make mistakes and it is very natural. We analyse the reasons for the mistakes and accordingly we make a fresh experiment and see that the mistakes are not repeated. This is the method of trial and error. The advantage in this method is: we have a scope to learn from mistakes and there is no grave damage to the society as a whole. What is more important is that the mistakes or even failure do not endanger the will to future reforms because the entire society is not affected and there is no general repercussion in the society against the reforms.

Popper believes that in society such piecemeal social experiments are already taking place. For example, 'the introduction of a new kind of life-insurance, or a new kind of taxation, of a new panel reform through the whole of society without remodelling society as a whole. The liberalisation policy of Indian government can also be described as experiments in piecemeal social engineering.

The piecemeal social engineering does not have an ideal in mind, There is no blueprint of society for which sacrifices are to be made. The piecemeal social engineering is at ease. There is no illwill against the failure. This is good for politicians also. They need not make pretenses for the mistakes. Popper says, "In fact, it might lead to the happy situation where politicians begin to look out for their own mistakes instead of trying to explain them away and to prove that they have always been right." This is also the scientific method of politics, where we learn from mistakes.

Popper compares the piecemeal approach with the mechanical engineering. The mechanical engineer makes experiments in different parts of the machine. After making the different parts, he makes the whole machine. No manufacturer would be interested in producing an engine on the basis of a blueprint alone even if it is designed by the greatest expert. The mechanical engineer would first make a model and develop it after great number of piecemeal adjustments to its various parts and then only he can think of final stage of production.

However this does not mean that piecemeal engineering cannot be bold or it is confined to smallist problems. The piecemeal social engineering may pursue bold objectives as long as they are pursued in a cautious, experimental, gradual and self-critical manner. Popper says, 'We must reform .... little by little until we have more experience in social engineering.'

(3) *State Intervention for the Protection of Weak*

Popper's concept of piecemeal social engineering advocates active participation of state in the society. He agrees that injustice and inhumanity of the unrestrained capitalist system described by Marx cannot be questioned. This has been because of unlimited freedom. He says, "Unlimited freedom means that a strong man is free to bully one who is weak and to rob him of his freedom." Popper wants state action to protect the weak. 'Nobody should be at the mercy of others, but all should have a right to be protected by the state. Social institutions, designed for the protection of weak from the economically strong should be created.' The state must see to it that nobody need enter in to an inequitable arrangement out of fear of starvation, or economic ruin.' Thus Popper demands that unrestrained capitalism must give way to an economic interventionism,

Marx has given undue importance to economic factor and political power has been reduced to a third-rate place. Popper's concept of piecemeal social engineering gives primary importance to political' power. Political power is fundamental and can control economic power. 'This means an immense extension of political powers. a rational political programme should be developed for the protection of the economically weak.' We can make laws to limit exploitation. We can limit the working day; but we can do much more. By law, we can insure the workers (or better still, all citizens) against disability, unemployment and old age. In this way, we can make impossible such forms of exploitation as are based upon the helpless economic position of a workers who must yield to anything in order not to starve. 'Right to livelihood to everybody who is willing to work and in this way he can be protected from economic fear and economic intimidation. The economic power. must not be permitted to dominate political power; if necessary, it must be fought and brought under control by political power.'

(4) State power should be limited

At the same time, there should be limits to state power. Popper is against the dictatorship of the proletariat where there is no freedom: if freedom is lost everything is lost. He wants economic intervention of the state with a note of caution because interventionism is extremely dangerous which tends to increase state power. But then, the state power must always remain dangerous. It is a necessary evil. To avoid this, democracy should be strengthened and state intervention should be limited to what is really necessary for the protection of the weak: Popper wants the objects of the government to be not only limited but also negative. He is against the utilitarian theory of state according to which the aim of the state is "to maximise human happiness." According to Popper, "Of all political ideas that of making people happy is perhaps the most dangerous one". Happiness means different things to different people. It cannot be the highest political ideal. The state, in the name of promoting general happiness, may restrict individual liberty. The best course is that the government should aim at reducing the human sufferings instead of promoting happiness. The state should be protectionist and its aim should be protection of life, liberty and property from individuals and the government, the elimination of misery and sufferings and maintenance of a certain level of general welfare.

Popper's piecemeal method of social engineering makes a distinction between the two entirely different methods of economic intervention by the state. The first is the institutional method, This is a rational method and a method of indirect state intervention. The state should make laws setting limits to the powers of the property-owners. Popper says that the institutional method is best because it is the only method 'which makes it possible to apply the method of trial and error to our political actions.' "The legal framework may be slowly changed when necessary but the fact remains that the legal framework introduces a factor of certainty, security into social life and whenever it is changed, the interests of those who have made their plan in the expectation of its constancy should be protected." The second method of state intervention is discretionary, personal and irrational. It means giving power to state organs to act to achieve the temporary gains, which the rulers of the day think are necessary. Budget is the best example. In this, Popper also includes the short term decisions, which are transitory, changing from day to day, or at best from year to year. They are discretionary decisions of the rulers or civil servants. This method should be used only when the first method is inadequate. The use of discretionary power is a personal intervention and it introduces 'an ever-growing element of unpredictability into social life and with it will develop the feeling that social life is irrational and insecure.' Therefore, in short, Popper wants the state intervention through legal framework in which changes may take place according to the changing requirements. The second method of discretionary intervention should be used very sparingly only when the first method is inadequate to achieve the desired ends.

Popper is against any idealism. He is not interested in discovering social laws, as Marx did. Those who advocate such theories claim that they have freed themselves from prejudices in explaining objective social laws. But this is not true. They are prejudiced. We have to solve over practical problems by method of trial and error, and by inventing hypothesis which can be practically tested.

(5) *Criticism*

Popper's criticism of utopian social engineering is very impressive. His conception of rationalism is also very comprehensive. However his theory of piecemeal social engineering is inadequate. As Bhikhu Parekh says, "... he reduces political philosophy to social technology. He assumes that a human society is basically like a machine, its government like an engineer and governing a country like attending to the social machine by means of piecemeal engineering." This is a misleading view of society. On the basis of his views on society, he argues that the objective of political philosophy is to determine the aims of government and institutional ways of realising them. His views of the nature of government is equally false. Further, Popper is not interested in the historical study of state and government. To him; the solutions of the immediate problem is important. However a proper study of political problems would need digging history and it may have to be studied in terms of idealism and reality. But Popper's social engineer is not interested in studying the nature and structure of political life. In fact, he has oversimplified problems of politics. Bhikhu Parekh calls Popper's view of politics as a strange view. For Popper, rational politics consists in isolating and identifying problems and in providing solutions. According to Bhikhu Parekh, "In political life there are no problems in Popper's sense. Unlike theoretical problems, political problems have their origin to the ways in which men perceive and define their situations, and they disappear if men can be persuaded or induced to define them differently. If restless slaves can be persuaded that they deserve their lot in life, the problem of dealing with their potential disobedience disappears. And the problem of inflation which breaks one government may not even pose a problem for its successor, if it could somehow induce the workers to make 'patriotic' sacrifices or to believe that demands for higher wages lead to unemployment."

SUGGESTED READINGS

1. Afanasyev V., *Marxists Philosophy,* (Moscow: Foreign Languages Publishing House).
2. Ashirvatham K., *Political Theory,* (Lucknow : Upper India Publishing House).
3. Bottomore, TB, *Sociology as a Social Criticism,* (London: George Allen & Unwin Ltd.)
4. Burlatsky F., *The State and Communism,* (Moscow: Progress Publishers).
5. Carter AB, *Marx A Radical Critique,* (Sussex: Wheatsheaf Books 1988).
6. Chang H.M. *The Marxian Theory of the State* (Delhi: Anupama Publications).
7. Ganguli B.N. *Ideologies and the Social Science,* (New Delhi: Arnold Heinemann Publishers 1976).
8. Macpherson CB, *Democratic Theory,* (Oxford: Clarendon Press, 1973).
9. Miliband R. *Marxism and Politics,* (Oxford: Oxford University Press).
10. Mills C. Wright, *The Marxists,* (London: Penguin Books. 1977).
11. Parekh, Bhikhu *Contemporary Political Thinkers,* (Oxford: Martin Robertson).
12. Popper, Karl, *The Open Society and its Enemies,* Vol I & II. (London: Routledge & Kegan Paul).

16

Development and Environmentalism

The close relationship between development and environment has never been challenged. It has become too obvious today. If environment provides ground for development, it is development that helps in the maintenance, sustenance and promotion of environment. Among the numerous factors of development, environmentalism is one that provides it an essential setting. The development of environmentalism and its conservation are the prominent tasks of any developmental project.

I: Development, Underdevelopment and Modernisation

For understanding the relationship between development and environment, it is important to understand each, and with its implications.

We may take, for discussion, the concept of development first.

(a) *What* is *Development?* Development is a universal phenomenon, universal in the sense that it is a world-wide concept which means differently in different context. The Brandt Commission rightly observed: "Development never will be, and never can be, defined to universal satisfaction." For some, development means increase in national economy; for others, it implies social development; for still others, it is another name of modemisation.

The concept of development has numerous definition and, therefore, has somewhat different, though inter-related meanings. Esman says: "Development is the rational process of organising and carrying out prudently conceived and staffed programmes or projects as one would organise and carry our military or engineering operations." To Colm and Greiger, development means change, change coupled with growth. Weidner holds the view that when a process is directed towards nation-building and socio-economic progress, that process of growth is development. For Hahn-Been Lee, development is both a process and a purpose. He, therefore, says that development is "a process of acquiring a sustained growth of a system's capability to cope with new, continuous changes towards the achievement of progressive politics, economic and social objectives." Chaturvedi observes development as a process which stands for "transformation of society." Riggs gives, rather, a detailed definition: "Development involves the ability to choose whether or not to increase outputs, whether or not to raise levels of per capita income, or to direct energies to other goals, to the more equitable distribution of what is available, to aesthetic or spiritual values, or the qualitatively different kinds of outputs." Mittleman refers to development as the increasing capacity to make rational use of natural and human resources for social ends. Baran says that development means 'far-reaching transformation of society's economic, social and political structure of the dominant organisation of production, distribution and consumption.'

It may, however, be pointed out that development is a multi-dimensional process involving changes in structures, attitudes, and institutions as well as acceleration of economic growth, reduction of inequality and eradication of poverty. It is a transformation from a traditional society to modern society. The political dimension of development includes, among other things, rationalism, secularisation, participation; the social dimension of development includes, for example, elimination of social evils, all distinction, all types of discrimination, equality of status, increase in social mobility; its economic dimension means, for instance, provision for social security; absence of exploitation, sustained economic growth, attainment of plenty and prosperity. All these dimensions of development are so closely related to one another that it IS difficult to separate them: the development of one dimension or one of its aspect is bound to influence and get influenced by the other dimension or its any aspect.

(b) *What* is *Underdevelopment?* Underdevelopment is usually understood as the absence of development, the opposite of development. In other words, it is considered to be something that is static. It is too limited a meaning of underdevelopment when it is seen as static. Attempts have been made to view it as a process. Gunnar Myrdal understands it as a process, a process of cumulative circular causation among such factors as levels of living, income and productivity. Accordingly, he says that low levels of living, low levels of productivity and low incomes act in a vicious cycle to result in underdevelopment. Underdevelopment is not something static, but is something that is related to the political, economic and ecological environment. If we understand underdevelopment as a process that tends to result in low levels of life, we can reverse it, if by it we mean a process, after making changes in economic, social and political structures.

(c) *What is Modernisation?* If development is viewed as a process meaning, thereby, change with growth, it is a concept related very closely to modernisation. It is, therefore, not surprising that 'development' and 'modernisation' are more or less, interchangeable. Daniel Lerner defines the term 'modernisation' as a 'systematic' process involving complementary changes in the demographic, economic, political, communication and cultural sectors of a society." Rostow and Ward say that modernisation "involves a marked increased in geographic and social mobility, a spread of secular, scientific and technical education, a transition from ascribed to achieved status, an increase in material standards of living, and many related and subsidiary phenomena. Modernisation, therefore, is an onward phenomena, a forward movement or what Joseph and Nancy Jabbra hold, a movement towards an "economic diversification within an advanced industrial technology; heightened social mobility and the movement towards impersonal and rationalised social relationships; a concentration of the population in cities and in more comprehensive social units generally; and mobilisation of persons *en masse* through popular education, organisation and communications." Modernisation is a goal to be achieved by the countries of Asia, Africa and Latin America, for they are not modern. Development, in the context of these countries, means development in all fields of life: it is a development towards modernisation.

II: Features and Implications of Development

Development, in the context of under-developed or developing countries, means the transformation of society from its traditionality to modernity, from its crude ways of doing things to their sophisticated ways.

(1) *Development is not a static concept.* It is a *dynamic,* and hence, an ever-changing and ever-evolving concept. One can not imagine anything in a 'developed' form, for every 'developed form' still needs some improvement. Development is, thus, a continuing term,

(2) *Development is not unidimensional, but* is *a multi-dimensional process.* This means that development is not only economic development, it is also social development as also political or any other aspect. Its goals are not confined to economy merely: they touch every aspect of human and societal life: they may, to mention a few, include economic growth, social progress, and political development, nation-building and the like.

(3) *Development implies growth.* What it means is that all societies keep growing, expanding, advancing and, therefore, are in the process of chang—ever-changing. The present society of a country is different from such a society of another country; today's society is not what it was yesterday, in the past; likewise the future society would be substantially different from the society we find around us.

(4) *Development* is *closely related to technology.* In essence, a *technologically advanced* society is a developed society. Technology has changed and in fact, is changing our life, each aspect of our life. Technology has made the world very small.

(5) *Rationality constitutes yet another component of development.* What it means is that a developed society is not tradition-bound or religion-laden, but is one that stands up to reasoning and rationalism.

(6) *Development has yet other features* or *requisites as well.* Order, stability, security and the like prepare a ground for sustained growth. Countries have grown in years of peace rather than in times of wars. As development means change with growth, it implies substantial changes in the infrastructure as well. You can not run an import-export business without a developed banking system. How can you have a democracy with the institution of a dictator as the executive head?

III: Alternative Models of Development

Development, when seen in its economic dimension, is associated with the maximization of outputs, economic growth and, in one word, economic development. Any nation, including the developed or the developing, has to view its agenda of development in its contexts of social, cultural, political, demographic, educational, institutional milieu. So, in economic terms, development would be a process when an economy is transformed from one whose rate of growth of per capita income is small or negative to one in which a self-sustained rate of increase of per capita income is a permanent long-run future; (Adelman, *Theories of Economic Growth and Development,* 1961).

(a) Numerous Theories of Development

There are numerous, though loosely related, theories relating to development. Some such theories or approaches can be identified:

(i) *The 'classical' development theory* is associated with Smith, Ricardo, Malthus, Mill and others. Its assumptions are: *one,* that a country's population increases invariably with the increase of some 'minimum' standard of living of the people; *two,* any increase in population would have 'diminishing returns' in the sense that labour would increase with the increase in population, The theorists of this approach believe that agricultural land is a fixed factor and that labour would increase with the relative increase of population. This is so because the number of people and the natural resources are in balance with each other: any change in any of the two would lead to economic crisis, little or more.

This approach had its merits: it called for its relationship with environment; and it called for population control. With the population explosion on the one hand, and the shrinking of the resources on the other has made this theory irrelevant, obviously inadequate.

(ii) a. There is the other approach relating to development. It is *the 'stages' approach* advocated by the Marxists, Marx in particular. Rostow offers yet another such theory *(Politics and the Stages of Growth, 1971* and *The Stages of Economic Growth: A Non-Communist Manifesto, 1962).* Obviously, the two stages stand opposite to each other. Marx's main influence lies in his theoretical growth process—primitive society, slave-owning society, feudal society, capitalist society—as also his prophetic predictions that capitalism was bound to collapse, to be followed only by socialism and communism. However, the Marxian 'stages' theory has not been able to convince many. Rostow's stages, as against the Marxian ones, are: (1) the pre-Newtonian traditional society—a society whose structure develops within limited production-function, pre-Newtonian in the sense that we do not know the external world, nor its laws; a society which is hierarchically structured and agricultural-based; a society where power lay not as much with the central authority as with the 'region', 'local', 'man of land'. (2) Societies in the process of transition or those which have acquired the pre-conditions take-off—a kind of society which is in the process of transformation; change in structure, politics and value, and one that is ready to grow at an expanded scale; a society where aeroplane's propeller starts roaring but is one that still is stationary; a society, in Rostow's views, of 17th-18th centuries' West; a society where the old traditions are attacked, scientific advancements are made, trade and commerce get flourished, the nation-state is built; (3) the take-off stage—a type of society where the rate of national income rises from 5 per cent to 10 per cent or more; a society where there are numerous manufacturing sectors, each with a high rate of growth; a society with emerging political, social and institutional framework; a society which rose up in different countries of the West, relatively at different times: in Britain during 1783-1802 in Prance during 1830-60 in United States during 1843-60, in Sweden during 1868-90, in Germany during 1850-73, in India and China during 1952; (4) the drive to maturity—a society where with a massive and progressive structural transformation in economics, a society with 10 to 20 per cent of national income steadily invested so to attain maturity in about sixty years; a society where Rostow's aeroplane is fully airborne and is flying at a certain height; a society where economy is refined and technologically more complex; (5) the age of mass consumption—a society where goods are produced in so large quantities and varieties that the consumer gets what he wants in terms of goods and services, a society where the welfare state develops. Although Rostow's different stages seem 'logical', he does not indicate how nations actually experience pre-condition and take-off stages, nor does he justify the choice of these discrete stages. In one of the stages, he refers to the rise of 5 per cent to 10 per cent in national income. The question is as to why he laid so much stress .on increase in the rate of income, and why in so definite terms.

What is clear is the description of some selected historical events together with *'laissez faire'* bias, neither useful in understanding Marxian idea of development nor his own.

(iii) b. There is yet another 'stages' approach to development known as *The German Historical Approach.* Some German scholars such as Friedrich List, Bruno Hildebrand, Karl Bucher, Werner Sombart are associated with this approach. This approach emerged as a reaction against the English classical economists and their theories which emphasised the deductive methods and the formulation of natural laws. It also rejects the British concepts of free trade and economic liberalism. It advocated: (a) the development experience of each country is moulded by its historical circumstances, hence not subject to natural laws of economics; (b) the process of development based on actual data of different countries and after comparison, evolving a theory of pattern; (c) interventionist policies pursued by different states under their different circumstances. The historical approach, as advocated by the Germans, also refer to various stages of development. A brief description can be given below:

(A) *List:* the savage stage, the pastoral stage, the agricultural stage, the agriculture and manufacturing stage, the agricultural, manufacturing and commercial stage.

(B) *Hildebrand:* Natural or barter economy, money economy, credit economy.

(C) *Bucher:* the stage of independent domestic or house-hold economy, the stage of town economy, the stage of national economy.

(D) *Sombari:* individua1 economy, transitional economy, social economy.

The emphasis of the German Historical School with regard to development was on the use of historical observation in framing generalisations. That is why its description of stages of development was an attempt to understand the historical process of socio-economic growth of different systems. However, Hoselitz finds these historical stages as inadequate.

(iii) c. *The Gersechenkron theory of the stages of development* is yet another theory relating to numerous stages of development. Alexander Gerschenkron *(Economic Backwardness in Historical Perspective,* 1965*)* explains that all development is a voyage from backwardness to economic growth, relative backwardness to relative economic growth: less backward a country, less time it would take to attain economic growth; more backward, more time. He also says that depending upon relative backwardness of a country, there are built corresponding institutions leading to the relative rate of growth. So, for him, relative backwardness of a country works as an impetus for the creation of institutional framework in course of its voyage toward economic growth, of course via industrialisation. Accordingly, the degree of backwardness determines the stages that a country would pass: the number of these stages being larger, the more backward a country is. The Gerschenkron theory is important not as a theory of development, but as a theory relating to the rise and growth of industrialisation.

In conclusion, we may say that development is an important aspect of economic growth. By way of further discussion, the phenomenon, we may argue, of development is more important for developing countries. We may discuss below some models which may serve guides for development in the developing countries.

(iii)(a) Development Through Market

The rise of classical liberalism gave a revolutionary meaning to the concept of development. Before it; the medieval concept of development meant growth in a typical religious sense which conceived growth in terms of degeneration, decay and with a certain sense of doom. The liberals identified growth with progress which meant that civilization has moved, is moving, and will move in a desirable direction. Later on, the Marxists also accepted development as progress.

The early liberals advocated development through market. According to Bjorn Hottne, "The model implied reliance on market forces, gradual industrialisation, starting with light industries, a sufficient level of private investment derived from high profits and a low level of wages, and a stress on technological advancement, which necessitated capital accumulation and expanding markets." However, it must be kept in mind that this market model was implemented in England only. The other countries where industrialisation followed did not accept the market model. They were protectionists and relied on state power for industrialisation and the development of capitalism.

Historically, the process of development has depended upon economic growth which in turn has been determined and shaped by technological changes. In primitive society, non-food production was done by individual artisans working independently of each other. Exchange was feasible through the system of barter. Money was virtually absent. In such a system of organising production, the artisans had to do each and every activity related to production on their own. For instance, the cobbler was expected to remove the hide of dead animals, dry it and process it, design and make footwears of different sizes and then look for such buyers who could supply in return the things needed by Cobbler and his family. Similarly, a weaver had to process raw cotton, spin the yam, weave cloth, dye/print it and then look for possible customers who could give him things needed by his family in exchange of that cloth. There was no time for innovations. Survival was the sole concern of such artisans.

Some traders persuaded number of artisans engaged in similar activities to come and sit in the space provided by that trader and pursue their own line of production This way the first factory was born. In some societies, a precusor of factory system was putting-out system. Traders gave out raw materials to the artisans to make articles desired by the trader and brought them back to the traders shop. Here the artisans did not work in the place provided by the entrepreneurs. They could work at their own convenience. One feature common with the factory system is that the artisans had to hunt neither for the raw material nor for the customers. These artisans used their own tools but they were supplied raw materials by the factory owner. Some of the artisans who had keener eye for selecting materials were gradually persuaded to take to locating and acquiring materials for all the workers of the factory. Artisans were no longer required to organise barter exchange of their goods. That was the responsibility of the trader. This division of labour created circumstances in which artisans could concentrate on actual production of goods. This was the stage when they tried to do things in somewhat better manner. So process of production was sought to be modified here and there to facilitate larger production or may be better quality of the product as well. These small innovations gradually became more wide-spread and led to Industrial Revolution involving mass production of the goods. Simultaneously, increasing prosperity in some sections of the society enabled some individuals to pursue the activities which were dear to their hearts. Thus began the process of cultural development in the society. Education in itself became desirable. Fine arts of all kinds could be pursued as a whole time vocation because some patrons could be found for them.

During this period, certain other social developments were also taking place. A class of neo-rich was corning into being. These were non-feudal entrepreneurs. Their new found prosperity, their ability to influence large number of workers, working in the manufacturing units, their mobility from place to place, organising sales of the goods and procurement of raw materials gradually made these people immensely influential and powerful. They could influence the landed aristocracy into passing various laws which strengthend and perpetuated their control over the workers. In some countries they became even financiers for the aristocracy and used their acumen to induce the changes 'in social and legal framework which they found most suitable to enhancement of their own profitability. One can say that gradually balance of political power was shifting away from aristocracy and towards the nee-rich business classes in the society.

Most noteworthy feature of this free enterprise pattern of development is that nobody talked of development as such. Everyone was busy enhancing his own share in the total income generated. If some labour laws were passed in some countries, objective was to ensure supply of labour to the factories so that the owners do not suffer any erosion of their profits. For instance, in England, poor laws. did not aim at improving the lot of the poor and homeless workers, rather tied up the workers to their current employers and would not permit workers to seek more remunerative jobs elsewhere. It is another matter that business classes found commonality of interests with landed aristocracy with such kind of enactments.

This phase of social development generated its own intellectuals and thinkers. They had a firm belief in freedom to pursue the most profitable line of activity. This pursuit of profit came to be regarded as desirable activity. These intellectuals are known as mercantilists. They tried to justify earning of profit as generation of surplus. Generation of surplus, *ipso facto,* was desirable because society receive that something more. So in the domestic sphere, all the policies which severely regulated labour, forced worker to continue to work in sub-human conditions and not to demand more were justified in the name of generating more surplus. Maximum wages laws were passed when prices of all the commodities were rising sharply. Workers were forced to remain confined to their current jobs with the help of vagrancy and poor laws. In a way, market was free, i.e. without any restriction on those who wanted to earn profits. Freedoms were denied to those who just wanted to survive.

Mercantilist policies vis-a-vis international trade all reveal the tendency to justify everything in the name of surplus generation through trade. They would plead for free trade if the interests of profiteers in their country were threatened. On the other hand, they would justify banning of imports of the goods manufactured in other countries of the world, if those imports hurt the business interests of the local manufacturers.

Policies advocated vis-a-vis colonies by these mercantilists are all the more illuminating on their mind-set. They advocated severe restrictions of all kinds of freedoms in the colonies. Natives in the colonies were not to be provided with any types of opportunity for personal advancement unless it was really necessary to help colonial powers to extract more surplus from these territories. Extraction of the surplus from the territories took many forms. From countries like India were realised Home Charges (which were a third of the gross revenue collected). From colonies in North and Central Americas slave-rent was extracted from the plantation farmers. Slave trade was also justified by these liberal thinkers on the same ground that it is a source of surplus.

This profit-oriented functioning of the society is known as market oriented approach to economic and social development. Market is the place where the buyers and sellers interact with each other whereas in the initial stages of development, the market was confined to village or the nearest town only. Gradually geographic span of the market has expanded. Liberals believe that if buyers and sellers of all commodities were free to trade in the market then each of the sellers will try to maximise his surplus. He will try to obtain highest possible price for his product. On the other hand, each of the buyers and consumers will try to buy these goods which give him maximum possible satisfaction. He buys goods from those sellers who are offering more attractive (low) prices. This way consumers are maximising consumer's surplus since all the producers and consumers in the society are maximising their surpluses, social surplus which is defined as aggregation of individual surplus is maximised almost automatically. Liberals swore by efficacy of this type and perfectly competitive market mechanism in ensuring maximum satisfaction for the society. It was argued that producers who will be buyers in the markets for the factors of productions will try to buy their requirement at least possible factor prices. They will try to use different factors of production in such combination which keep the cost of production to least possible levels. This way resources of the society are deployed in most efficient manner. Therefore, it was emphasised that perfect competition in the market will develop these industries which can give higher profits i.e., more output at lower resource cost. On the other hand, the industries which fail to make efficient use of social resources will incur higher cost of production, will not be able to earn more profits and as a consequence will not be able to expand. In the long run, remunerations in such industries will become less than what can be earned elsewhere. In such situations, factors of production will move out of these industries.

The market approach to development views the state as a necessary evil. It is evil because it restraints and because all restraint is evil. But still the state is necessary because given the nature of man, a stateless society will only be anarchy where no development is possible and the life of man will become, in the words of Hobbes, 'solitary, poor, nasty, brutish and short.' Therefore, state and government cannot be ruled out. They will have to be in the market system. But then the state will be a limited state and the role of the government, most minimum. Bentham advocated a government which governs the least. According to Adam Smith the government has only three functions to perform. *Firstly,* to defend "the country from foreign aggression; *secondly* to establish administration of justice; and *thirdly,* to maintain such public works and institutions as would not be maintained by any individual or group of individuals for lack of adequate profit. Besides these, the government may also take up education and such public enterprises like roads, bridges, canals and harbours.

Adam Smith justified the minimum functions of the government on the basis of his theory of, natural order. Development takes place as a result of natural order which benefits every member of the society. Man is guided by six motives in his conduct—self-Iove, sympathy, the desire to be free, a. sense of propriety, a habit of labour and the tendency to truck, barter and exchange one thing for another. Given such motives man should be absolutely free in pursuing his self interest and while pursuing his self interest, he also contributes in the common welfare. This common welfare is never intended by the individual, but it follows because of his motives. This is what Smith called the invisible hand which leads individual to promote an end which formed no part of his intention. Therefore, individual should be left free. There should, not be any interference in the market.

Criticism

This pressure to expand the scale of production ultimately led to emergence of what is known as monopoly capital. As technological developments expanded the size of individual enterprise, the fundamental condition of perfect competition that producer shall be able to influence the market price though his individual action remained no longer valid: Some producers were too big. The other small time operators could not compete with these big industrialists. As a result the original stipulation of efficient allocation of serial resources through operation of market forces of demand and supply cannot be satisfied. It is interesting to note that accepted liberal wisdom was against the intervention of state in the day-to-day affairs of the economic system. In the initial stages of capitalist system of development, the state was regarded as the ally of the forces that generated maximum surplus. When perfect competition came to be replaced by monopolistic competition or may be even outright monopolies, the state was expected to keep its hands off the economy. Again, any intervention of the state which prevented emergence of larger and monopolistic enterprises would have not been in consonance with the guiding principle of maximum profit. However, they lost sight of the fact that emergence of monopolistic tendencies is antithetical to the perfect competition and all the virtues claimed on behalf of a perfectly competitive market equilibrium.

On social plane, unabashed pursuit of profit motive leads to certain undesirable consequences. What happens to the aged and the infirmed is no body's concern. If production of some substance is harmful for the society yet it can earn handsome profits then a competitive market will be most willing to allocate resources for this industry (narcotics included). In this system, workers are treated as suppliers of one of the factors of production namely, the labour and all technological innovations have been labour-saving in nature. By implication, attempt has all along been to displace the worker altogether from the process of production. In a system where everyone is rewarded on the basis of one's contribution to the process of production, this attempt to force worker out of the system will lead to disempowerment of working class altogether and make them totally dispensable. In such a scenario, how will the masses buy things of day-to-day consumption? In nutshell, it can be said that perfectedly competitive market system as well as its off-shoots like monopolistic tendencies are basically not oriented towards the human beings and their welfare. It results in exploitation and oppression of the workers and the weak. It only helps the property owners at the expense of the poor people.

(iii) (b) Development through Welfare State

The notion of welfare state is of rather recent origin. Upto early years of fourth decade of the twentieth century, liberal views held sway over most of the Western world. Though in the second half of 19 century in some of the countries, some definite changes were introduced with the intention of warding off some catastrophe or explosion due to inherently inequitious nature of market economy. Bismark was first to introduce labour welfare measure in the form of restriction on very long working hours. The Czar, Alexander of Russia abolished serfdom and gave it the name of revolution from above (so that there is none from below).

Rise of communism as on alternative ideology and emergence of a state professing allegiance to it, caused further challenges to the market mechanism. The remarkable achievement of first experiment with non-market based strategy of development namely, economic planning during 1920's in Russia faced liberal thinkers and economists in Western world to atleast examine the feasibilities of positive state intervention in economic affairs. Finally, the Great Depression of 1929-33 virtually sounded death-knell for the ideology of the market. During these years, Western world based on market mechanism faced never before a kind of situation. The factories were in existence. Workers were present and willing to work. Yet factories were closed. Reason: there was no demand in the market. All this while families were being forced to cut down their consumption of all kinds of commodities. Market mechanism had only one prescription for this malice-reduce rates of interests so that more investment is undertaken, more factories be set up and more people are given jobs. However, this view lost sight of the fact that those who are not able to sell production of existing factories will hardly be tempted to borrow and set up new manufacturing units. This called for a radical change. J.M. Keynes provided exactly that.

Keynes correctly diagnosed the problem of deficiency of demand and rightly pointed out that only institutions which could bail out the society from the depression was that of the government itself. He pointed out that the capitalist world was suffering from deficiency of effective demand. Large increase in investment was simply not possible. Since the crisis was not confined to just one or two countries reflection through large scale exports were ruled out and one just could not expect that families of the workers who had recently lost jobs on account of lock-outs in the factories would be able to increase their off-take of goods from the market. Only the state could come out with public works programmes financed through the budgetary deficits and create first big wave of new effective demand. This effective demand will create new jobs, new incomes and consequent demand for all kinds of goods and services which shall have all chain reaction all around in the economy. Successful implementation of this bold new approach led to development of certain models of economic growth in late 1930's. In the aftermath of World War II, the capitalist world gave up its hostility to and distrust of economic planning as well (Marshall Plan for reconstruction of war ravaged Western Europe).

So, since middle of the 20th century a new kind of systhesis between total state control of socialism and blind pursuit of profits of liberal market mechanism has been perfected. This new model of development is known as the welfare state model. One can also say that the concept of the welfare state is a manifestation of mature capitalism. Its departure from the market model of development consists in granting the state a responsibility for the stability and continuous growth of capitalist system. It means development through planning where the state is no longer an umpire but an active participant in economic activities. Market is no longer the controlling agency in the process of economic growth. The state takes over the position of market, though not fully.

Removal of economic disparities in the society is the most important task of a welfare state. For the purpose, the property is regulated to restrict its monopolisation in fewer hands. Limitations are placed on the extent of property that a person can possess. This is done in both the agriculture and the industry sectors. The property cannot be used for exploitation. Therefore, we have labour laws that protect the labour from inhuman working conditions. Positively, better working conditions have been ensured by the state through labour legislation. Public assistance, work relief, poverty programmes are designed to provide a minimum standard of living for all. It has been the state's objective to ensure the fulfilment of three basic needs of individual i.e. food, cloth and shelter. Increasing taxation on the rich is designed to mitigate the gross inequalities of income. Unemployment compensation, insurance against old age, destitution and ill-health are some of the characteristics of modem welfare state. The state also provides for free education to all.

However, it does not mean that the welfare state is concerned with only economic development of the people. It also aims at the removal of social discrimination based on sex, caste, creed, colour and other factors. The total emancipation of individual from social and economic disparities is the aim.

However, the basic tenets of capitalism and liberalism are not compromised in development through the welfare state. Competition is still there and there is a lot of scope for individual's initiative and endeavour. Only thing is that the competition of the market model is restricted in a welfare state to achieve the common good. Only thing is that the happiness of the few has given way to the happiness of all. Therefore, there cannot be any compromise with democracy. It has to continue and protected at all cost. The political and civil liberties are the pious achievements of mankind and in no case they can be limited. The objective is the complete development of man as a human being, where there are no political, economic and social stigma.

Summing up, we may say, as does Asirvatham, regarding the nature of the welfare state, "So far as the nature of the welfare state is concerned, the *first* important thing to remember is that welfare is riot a matter of charity, but of right. Welfare, as understood here, does not carry with it any stigma of pauperism. *Secondly,* if welfare is to be genuine welfare, the ground for it should have been prepared earlier by the various agencies at work in the state. Unless the minds and attitudes of men and women are attuned to the idea of a welfare state, they are apt to look upon welfare as manna from heaven falling into the mouths of an expectant people. In the *third* place, if the welfare state is to be a blessing and not a curse, it should not produce a pauper mentality on the part of its recipients. In whatever is done by the state, care should be taken not to dry up the wells of initiative and self-help."

The Welfare Model in Crisis

The concept of welfare state which arose as a result of expectations of providing basic needs to the people or atleast employment failed in its objective. Especially in 1970s and after we find welfare state in crisis. This is evident not only in the field of employment but in varied fields of trade, industrial development, social welfare, integration, domestic politics, environment, security and defence. This crisis is due to the stagnating economy which seems to be devoid of scope for further expansion. In Europe and America we witness a strong political movement opposing the welfare state. The neo-liberals want to go back to the market model of development. They are, in particular, against the increasing powers of the state. Milton Friedman said, "To the free man, the country is the collection of individuals which compose it. The scope of government must be limited to preserve law and order, to enforce private contracts, to foster competitive markets ..." Friedman has been supported by other neo-liberals like Friedrich Hayek. There is also a strong demand to cut the expenses in social security and other welfare measures. President Reagan in America and Prime-Minister Thatcher in England had started the policy of going back to the market model. This further increased unemployment and inflation resulting in a wave of political violence and racism. In India, we witness the rise of so-called dalit politics which wants quick economic and social results, and which is not contented to wait. The market model of development resulted in severe economic disparities and exploitation. It failed in satisfying the common good. The socialist developmental model also failed and now the welfare model is also witnessing the failure. The problem and the resultant crisis is very severe as there is a revolution of rising expectations among the masses. But going back to market model is no solution. It will only further anarchy. The solution to the crisis is to be found somehow in the same welfa: model of development.

(iii)(c) Development-the Socialist Model

There is much in common between socialism and communism so far as the concept of development is concerned. This is not to say that a socialist cannot be a Marxist or that a Marxist is not a socialist. The point of distinction is between a Marxian socialism and a non-Marxian socialism. By development, both mean material development; both believe that development can be achieved through social ownership of the means of production and distribution; any degree of development must, therefore, involve a measure of public ownership; both lay emphasis on providing production so to meet the demands of peoples' requirement and hence reject both the market and the welfare concepts of development; both admit a measure of equality and elimination of exploitation of man by man; both stress on right to work as a condition and right to social security as a measure of development.

But there is much that is a matter of difference between the two. Whereas for a Marxist socialist, socialism is a means to the end of communism; for a non-Marxian, socialism is an end itself. For a Marxist socialist, the abolition of capitalism is a necessary pre-requisite for development while for a non-Marxist, regulation of capitalism can yield developmental results; a Marxist socialist looks at the state as an instrument of exploitation and hence, a negative, oppressive and suppressive institution; but for a non-Marxist socialist, the existence and survival of the state provide a framework for an over-all development, and hence looks at the state as an instrument of socio-economic change; the Marxist socialist believes in social change through peaceful means if possible and through revolutionary methods if necessary while the socialist seeks changes in the society through peaceful methods, through the state and through democratic devices; the Marxist socialist expects socialism as a matter of totality while the non-Marxist socialist seeks incremental changes through successive legislations, trade-union methods, social reforms. But it is tempting to state that while Marxism is a scientific theory explaining historical stages of man's development, capitalism being only one such stage, non-Marxian socialism considers capitalism more or less a stage, without going into details of how things have moved, which has to be reformed to make it non-exploitative, non-oppressive and hence one that wants to slash capitalism, taking teeth out of it rather than abolishing it altogether, i.e., lock, stock and barrel. The non-Marxian socialism is, therefore, evolutionary socialism of Bernstein, Fabianism of Webbs, guild socialism of Cole, parliamentary or democratic socialism of Laski. It is with their model of development that we are concerned here.

The characteristic features of the socialist model of development can be briefly summed up as under:

(1) Development, being material development, needs to be managed through different and in an opposed manner as to that of capitalism. Property, as the source of profit and limitless profit leading to freezing of the wages for the labour and exploitation of the labour by the capitalist, has to be abolished. The type of property that has to be abolished is not the one we have in our clothes, households and in short what we consume. The property which has to be abolished is one we find in factories, workshops, industries, and in short through which we produce further property. *Private property is replaced by public property.*

(2) By abolition of the productive property, we mean its private ownership. This, in other words, means that all productive property would have to be made socialised or nationalised or govemmentalise. No private property would exist in farms and factories, mines and banks, in one word, in the means of production. This would imply a situation where production is done not for the few or that profit accruing from production would not be the profit of one who owns a particular means of production. What would this imply would be that the production would be done for purposes of use and not for profit, that the concept of wages for the labour would be replaced by the satisfaction of needs for each and all and that each and all would contribute in the common welfare and the development of the whole community.

(3) Social ownership of the means of production would not mean, under socialist model of development, *public ownership* of *all* the means of production, but *of the major means of production* and services and that too, most of them to be run and controlled by public enterprises and corporations. This is a fundamental difference between Marxian socialism and the non-Marxian socialism. Under Marxian socialism, all the means of production (including also the means of distribution) are owned by the society, community, state, or the working class, all in the name of the state or the party (say, the Communist Party) or in the name of the working class. In the case of non-Marxian socialism, only major means of production (say, the railways) would be owned by the state or by the public enterprises/corporations: the thrust would be general control and not the centralised control. The Marxist control of economy has to be centralised, i.e., planning to flow from top to bottom; the non-Marxist socialist control of economy

has to be decentralised, i.e., planning to flow from bottom to top-initiative from below and guidance from above.

(4) *Planning and not profit,* under the non-Marxist model of development, would be the *guiding motive.* Under capitalism, production is done with view to extract maximum profit without caring as to what the people really want, and as a consequence of it, production is never planned. But under non-Marxian socialism, as also under the Marxian socialism, production is done for purposes of fulfilling the needs of the people, and therefore, it has to be planned. Under the capitalist system, profit regulates production and ever-growing wealth goes to the employers and their associates. But under socialism, planning regulates production: what is needed is produced: production needs are matched with productive forces.

(5) Development under capitalism is *uneven development:* development for the few and deprivation for the many. This is so because wages, under capitalist mode of production, keep going down to the subsistence level and ultimately towards starvation, but under socialism, care is taken that wages match the inflatory tendencies, which ultimately leads to the labour getting full value of what is produced. Development, under socialism, is even and total development. This is not to say that all the workers would get equal wages. Wages are, indeed, unequal under socialism, for a skilled worker must get more than the unskilled, an artist more than the skilled worker. What the socialist abhors is exploitation and not inequality, inequality and not wide and wide gaps of income/grades.

(6) The question of change from: capitalism to socialism is a big question, to be solved through sustained efforts of the *democratic government* by *successive social legislations.* The change from capitalism to socialism is not a sudden change, nor the revolutionary one. This is what a Marxian socialist would like. The non-Marxian socialist seeks to change the capitalist society into socialist one, slowly and gradually, bit by bit. Hence, for a non-Marxist socialist, the path to socialism is a long distance, though a sure one at that The non-Marxist socialist would employ means like regulating capitalism, graduated taxation, slashing the exploitative powers of the capitalist, strengthening of trade-unions, passing labour legislations, promoting social security measures. There has to be a labour-movement, strong enough to combat capitalism on the one hand; and to work for workers' welfare on the other.

(7) The labour movement is an on-going movement, for socialism is *a wholesome change* in the character and structure of the capitalist society, change in so many ways and in so many aspects, and

for so many newer values. The agenda for the labour movement is extremely heavy including, among others, protection of wages, fixing hours of work, safeguarding workers against profiteering, extending social service measures, expanding education, and so on.

(8) A non-Marxist socialist society would be a society where the labour would be respected, workers' interests would be protected, individual initiative would be kept intact, cooperation would replace competition, social justice would become the measuring rod for governmental activities. Obviously, it would not be a society where the rich would be penalised for being rich, and the poor, rewarded because he is poor. It would be a society where the rich would not be permitted to become more rich and the poor, the poorer: the poor's conditions would be improved so to bring them close to the rich. It would be a *society for the equals* with minimum gap of wealth.

The non-Marxian socialism has the potentialities of providing a much better model of development than the one offered through market and the welfare state. And yet it is too much to expect that the capitalists would yield without any possible resistance. Lenin had a point when he had said that one cannot have omelette without breaking eggs.

(iii)(d) Gandhian Model of Development

Gandhi was a peculiar mixture of opposites. He was not a Marxist but he did care for the poor and the lowly; he was not a socialist but he liked to do his own work himself without employing anyone for his jobs; he was not a capitalist but he had always advocated a self-sufficient economy; he was not a liberal but he did not want. to deprive the capitalist of his property. He was a Marxist, a socialist; a liberal, an anarchist-all in his own right.

The Gandhian view of development was not, in any case, a model of material development. He was a great critic of Western capitalist system for its being exploitative and oppressive. By development, he did not mean accessibility to all material comforts but the one which leads to the development of individual, and his personality, his virtues, his values, his self. All material development which the world had attained through private property did not attract Gandhi. He regarded possession as a crime, saying: "I can only possess certain things when I know that others who also want to possess similar things, are able to do so." In a way, Gandhi's view that it is immoral to have more than one needs is a view which is more profound than Proudhan's who had said that all property was theft. Gandhi believed that it is

God who pervades everything and hence, nothing belongs to any particular being. For him, the capitalist is as good a servant of what he possesses as is the worker who produces value through his labour; at best, the capitalist is a trustee. This was the crux of Gandhi's theory of trusteeship. Following Marx, Gandhi thought of economic equality as one where the needs of all are satisfied: 'To each according to his needs'—the Marxian pronouncement, but Gandhi's conception of 'needs' was related to renunciation, 'to a situation where an individual takes as is necessary for sustenance.' But that does not mean that Gandhi. was either a Marxist or a non-Marxist socialist. His major difference with these two strands was the method through which the new social order would usher. He never thought class struggles, violence or revolutions as locomotives of history. He used to say: "This I do say, fearlessly and firmly, that every worthy object can be achieved by the use of Satyagraha. It is the highest and infallible means, the greatest force. Socialism will not be reached by any means."

With firm belief in non-violence, Gandhi's view of development was what may be termed as 'Sarvodaya'—the welfare of all, including that of the humble, the lowly, and the last as also the worker, the capitalist, the landlord. To that extent, Gandhi was close to Marx. But unlike Marx, Gandhi sought classless society without classes, classes without antagonism, antagonism without destroying the individuals, individuals with their conversion into human beings, finer human beings. Gandhi's theory of trusteeship is neither a complete abolition of capitalism, for he makes a claim for the capitalist stewardship. Nor it is a complete acceptance of Marxian, for he makes the capitalist stay—the capitalist as a trustee. It is a theory which "provides a means of transforming the present capitalist order of society into an egalitarian one. It gives no quarter to capitalism, but gives the present owning class a chance of reforming itself, to the working class a chance to contribute to the social good.

Gandhi was a simple man, a simple villager, a simple Indian villager. His view of development, measured materialistically if one insists on, would be a self-sufficient village. He said: "An ideal Indian village will be so constructed as to lend itself to perfect sanitation. It will have cottages with sufficient lights and ventilation built of a material obtainable within a radius of five miles of it... The village lanes and streets will be free of dust. It will have wells according to its needs and accessible to all. It will have houses of workshop for all.... also primary and secondary schools in which industrial education will be the central fact... It will produce its own grain, vegetables and fruit and its own khadi. This is roughly my idea of a model village." These are Gandhi's priorities and preferences of an ideal village, self-sufficient, self-evolving and self-developed-interdependence when it is necessary.

The Gandhian approach to development, if the above discussion is kept in view, would help create the following model, briefly atleast:

(1) *A pre-dominant net-work of village and cottage industries alongwith a few key industries* in the nearby towns, preferably under state or / and cooperative ownership.

(2) The Gandhian model of development is not Western-based and urban-based. The western type of industrialisation can prove to be useful for some countries, especially of the West, but what is true about one nation can not be true about the other. In the Indian. context, development has to be *rural-based* and has to follow the path of *industrialisation from bottom to top,* i.e., from villages to the towns.

(3) The Gandhian view of development never favours mass production of mass consumption. He advocates *mass production in the homes,* in the villages, and of those things which a common man requires. In other words, he advocated the means of production and distribution to be decentralised.

(4) The Gandhian model of development was an *integrated model,* one that includes, among other things, agriculture, sanitation, education, social service, industries—all these locally based and locally regulated. That is why that Gandhi never approved of large-scale industries, transportation systems, metropolises and so on and that is why that he found pre-Western Indian way of life including traditional handicrafts, village exchange system, simplicity, religious-cultural traditions acceptable under the given conditions of a backward economy as of India.

(5) Gandhi did find *planning* useful. He favoured planning as a means for transforming the Indian backward economy into a developed one, but his planning process would begin from bottom. The central planning institution would only lay guidelines and take upon itself the functioning of industries related to import and export items and which included, for example, maintenance of large-scale infrastructure, combining the efforts of the development of village communities and those of the centralised modem sectors, planning of the development of urban areas in a limited way, reestablishing of the nation-wide systems of cooperative trade.

The Gandhian model of development is realizable provided we choose to live in a traditional society, unconcerned with what is going on in other parts of the world, nay, in the other parts of the country. This is a case of choosing a cart when an automobile is available.

IV: Environmentalism

Environment constitutes a very important part of our life. To understand life without studying the impact of environment is simply impossible. The issues relating to environment have become so significant that we can ignore them only at our peril. Political philosophers from Aristotle to Montesquieu and to Marx made serious attempts to relate environment to political structures or the vice-versa. Environment facilitates life—Aristotle showed it in his description of 'polity' as the best practicable state. Environment makes and unmakes our political systems, so emphasised Montesquieu. Marx, more than anybody else, demonstrated very ably that our material development and freedom depend on our environment.

Environment—Its Spectrum: The concept of environment can include, and in fact, should include totality of all components surrounding man. It is, as the Environment Pollution Panel of US Precedent's.Science Advisory Committee observes, "the sum of all social, biological and physical or chemical factors which compose the surroundings pf man." Samuel Waugh rightly remarks: "No organism, however, simple or complex can survive on removal from its environment." Martin Clark, however, attempts to bring about some specific meanings attached to the concept of environmentalism.

(i) At one level, it means a little more than 'resource conservationism' which sees Nature as essentially a provider of raw-material, and therefore, has to be protected/conserved for future economic growth (Kahn, *The Next 200 Years,* 1978; Kahn and Simon, *The Resourceful Earth,* 1984; Stroup and Baden, *Natural Resources,* 1983). Such a meaning of environment is, entirely and purely, 'anthropocentric', declaring that 'nature is useful to man' as also assuming continuing economic growth and progress, without making major shifts in institutions and policies. Though such a meaning of environment may create critics, yet it is an improvement on 'non-conservation'.

(ii) There are, on the other hand, 'environmental protectionists' such as Brundtland *(Our Common Future,* 1987), who, like the resource conversionists are anthropocentric, are mainly concerned with public health and therefore, focus on atmospheric and water pollution, the need for public parks as also of public education. Most of them do not reject economic development, and some even use the language of welfare economics, stressing, in the process, that development should not be permitted if the real environmental or health costs are too great. Though it is the most common approach to the environmental issues, yet it does not presume or predict any economic or political upheaval.

(iii) There are still the others, known as the 'mainstream Greens' such as Carr *(The Appropriate Technology Reader,* 1985) and McRobie *(Small is Possible,* 1981) who lay stress on sustainability. They also include Brown *(Building a Sustainability Society,* 1981), Daly *(Towards a Steady State Economy,* 1973), Schumacher *(Small* is *Beautiful, 1973).* They think that sustainability is the essential limit to growth. Their, therefore, emphasis is on"renewable energy, on recycling of waste into raw-materials,' and on meeting 'real human needs'. All of them insist on the protection of environment.

(iv) Our analysis of the spectrums of environment would be incomplete if we do not turn towards what we may call "Deeper Green" thinkers such as Devall and Sessions *(Deep Ecology,* 1985) and Naess ("The Shallow and the Deep, long-range ecology movement, "Inquiry, XVI, 1973). These thinkers remark that the industrial system is destroying the planet, and therefore, the industrial system should be stopped, or otherwise, the earth would wretch revenge. They argue that Nature is not so much to be preserved as to be worshipped.

(v) There is yet an aesthetic and ethical spectrum of environment provided mostly by the Romanticist poets (such as Wordsworth (The tables turned, *Poems)* who regard Nature as the Great Teacher of Mankind, a view confirmed by Kropotkin, the anarchist. They all regard Nature as a cooperation and not a conflict.

(vi) The environmental scientists, including biologists, zoologists and ecologists, lay emphasis on the interdependence between the living organisms and their environment.

It may, thus, be concluded that environmentalism can hardly be dismissed, for it is a set of political or social ideas which can claim a scientific foundation. This is so because it covers a whole range of individual's and society's whole life: emotional or 'romanticist' appeal, an 'ethical' aspect, a rational 'scientific' combination.

V: Environment—Problems

Restricting environment's spectrum to nature, we may, for purposes of illustration, experience numerous problems. These problems may include, among others, explosive population growth, sophisticated weaponry, pollution of air, water and noise, destruction of natural resources. These problems pose a great danger to man's own survival. It should be realised, sooner than later, that conservation and improvement of the environment are vital for the survival and well-being of mankind. Natural resources of land, air and water have to be used wisely as a trust to ensure a healthy environment for the present and future generations.

Some of the notable problems of environment can be identified as under:

(1) *Population:* Population growth presses hard on the environment. The more the population grows, more is the environment endangered. Its growth taxes on the earth's resources, and, in the process, leads to poor quality of productivity, deforestation, and ecological imbalance. The population explosion destroys not only the natural environment, but it corrupts its other aspects as well-political, social, economic, cultural and civilizational.

The population of the world stood, in 1994, at about 5.5 billion and the UN estimate is that it would double itself around 2050 and the day is not far off when it would outstrip world's food supply. The population growth leads, ultimately, to population pollution and loss of all that environment gives us.

(2) *Air Pollution:* The American Clean Air Act of 1970, as amended in 1990, identifies fourteen air pollutants (six criteria, eight hazardous) and their major health effects. These are: *Criteria Pollutants* – (1) ozone – respiratory tract problems, (2) particular matter – lung diseases, (3) carbon monoxide-impaired ability of blood to carry oxygen, (4) sulfur dioxide – respiratory tract problems, (5) lead – mental retardation and brain damage, and (6) nitrogen dioxide – respiratory and lung damage; *Hazardous Air Pollutants:* (1) asbestos – a variety of lung diseases, (2) beryllium – lung diseases and a variety of cancers, (3) mercury – brain disorders, (4) vinyl chloride – lung and liver cancer, (5) arsenic – cancer, (6) radionuclides – cancer, (7) benzene – leukemia, (8) coke oven emission – respiratory cancer.

These pollutants are generally omitted by mobile sources like cars and trucks, and by stationary sources like industrial enterprises and commercial electrical power plants. All these affect adversely, in addition to human life, the plant and animal life.

(3) *Water Pollution:* Another danger to environment causes from water: both surface and underground. Water is the most used, the

most exploited, and the most polluted source. The recurring floods have their peculiar casualities. The vast oceans, after being turned into dumping grounds for all nuclear tests, and for the sewage and industrial effluents, have poisoned the whole natural environment.

(4) *Noise Pollution:* Noise pollution threatens human beings. It tells upon their psychologial, mental and physical (making people almost deaf) well-being. Ringing of the bell, vibrations of fireworks, disorderly crowd: dancing and singing-all these noise pollutants are so excessive, so offending, so persistent, so irritating that they pose a danger to normal quiet life.

(5) *Nuclear Pollution:* Of all the pollutants, nuclear pollution is the greatest. The nuclear powers, about a dozen, now, in the world, pose a grave danger to the whole universe. The United States alone possesses enough nuclear power to destroy the globe about twenty times over. The nuclear experiments have already been meddling with the environment. This is seen in the changing agricultural seasons, spread of diseases, and the whole recycling of the nature's phenomenon.

(6) *Urbanization:* Urbanization, as a source of pollution, is a threat to the environment. It means maddening race of the people from villages to the cities. Its net result is dirt, diseases, and disasters. With urbanization, environmental problems like sanitation, ill-health, housing, water-electricity, scarcity keep expanding. Indiscriminate collection of firewood, overgrazing and depletion of natural resources are the other environmental losses in the rural life

(7) *Industrialisation:* Industrialisation followed by the introduction of means of transport and communication has not only polluted the environment, but has also led to the shrinking of the natural resources. Both ways, the loss is really very heavy. Increasing levels of heat fluxes, carbon dioxide, radio-active, nuclear waste create environmental hazards. On the other, the indiscriminate consumption of conventional sources of energy leads to the gradual loss of natural resources.

(8) *Some other Pollutants:* The list of the other pollutants is; indeed, exhaustive. *Toxic and hazardous substances* such as radio-active waste, gasoline, pesticide residues, penetrate our air, water and earth, and pose a great threat to humans and their environment. *Consumer waste,* in the form of gardening and landscaping waste, books and magazines, corrugated cardboards, beer and soft drink cans and bottles, use-throw items, cellophone, plastic, paper, styrofoam and the like has created problems of how to dispose them of. *Global Climate Warning,* owing to the increasing level of

> carbon dioxide, is going to increase the earth's heat and accelerate polar icecap melt, and in the process alter world climate zones. *Acid rain,* more widespread and more acidic, pollutes both the environment and human beings. *The depletion of atmospheric ozone,* once a shield against the sun's ultraviolet rays, is likely to expose human beings to increased risks of cancer and eye damage, and on the other, produce serious derangements in existing ecological balances including a major depletion of ocean plankton which constitutes the foundation of ocean's food chains .

The problems of environment are numerous, most of them are the result of our own activities. What are we doing for our children? What are we giving to the posterity? We are giving them a depleted world which is neither a cage nor a nest.

VI: Environment—Need for Conservation

The environmental issues are great. Unless environmental issues are solved or taken care of, the coming generations may find the world not worth-living. Serious stresses involving population resources, and environment are clearly visible ahead. Despite greater material output, the world's people will be poorer in many ways than they are today." Soon, the attention of the world would turn towards environmental protection, resource rationing, population control, from 'economic rationality' of Garrett Hardin (seeking maximum individual gain) to Robert Heilbroner's 'crisis of survival' produced by environmental hazards. The liberals' see the solution of avoiding the ecological disaster in re-examining the basic axioms of liberalism and the socialists (including the Marxists), those of socialism. The ecopolitical theorists such as Mussay Bookchin and Theodore Roszak offer yet another approach for the conservation of environment—the emancipatory approach, emphasising on the ideal of human autonomy or self-determination. Roszak says: "My purpose is to suggest that the environmental anguish of the Earth has entered our lives as a radical transformation of human identity. The needs of the planet and the needs of the person have become one, and together they have begun to act upon the central institutions of our society with a force that is profoundly subversive, but which carries the promise of cultural revival." The right-left debate and those between the survivalists and their critics as also between the advocates of small-communities and large communities with regard to environmentalism still continue.

What is required is the sustenance, conservation and improvement of the changing, restless and fragile environment. Two types of possible steps can be taken to solve the environmental problems.

(1) Governments need to take steps to bring about solutions to the environmental problems because most of them are regional, national and international in scope, requiring the cooperation of many governmental units. The governments need to check the industrial enterprises from where most of the environmental problems emanate and ask them to find alternative ways and means for their activities. Difficult as it is the task for the governments to solve the ever-increasing environmental problems, there is nothing to dispair, though human ingenuity has dug us holes out of which it is not easy to climb up.

(2) Non-governmental environmental organisations can do better than the governments. These organisations may be of two sorts: (a) lobbying, those which, through education, research, litigation, seek the development and implementation of environmental legislation; (b) non-lobbying, those which, through educational programmes, grassroots organising, plans and projects, undertake the task of environmental conservation.

VII: The Concept of Sustainable Development

One of the spectrum of environment is related to what We have described above as 'mainstream Greens'. They include scholars like Carr, McRobie, Brown, Daly, Schumacher and others. They all lay stress on "sustainability" of environment together with development. In fact, 'Green' economists' condemn the whole traditional concept of growth. What they, rather, prefer is a 'steady-state' economy which is as sufficient as possible. So, the emphasis of the 'mainstream Greens' are not on pollution, but on: (1) energy and its sources may be renewed, and be kept renewing; (2) the waste be changed into raw-material, raw-material into waste, waste into raw-material: recycling of waste into raw-material; (3) Gross National Product and its growth targets need not be sought, but what should be sought is the satisfaction of 'real human needs'. The Greens say that growth means cancer, nothing more; a cancer that threatens to spread worldwide, and destroy all life. They deplore both market capitalism and state socialism as exploitative and oppressive. They accept industry if it is on small scale and is for purposes of self-sufficiency; so too, about agriculture. They advocate extensive decentralisation. Martin Clark says: This is the crux of sustainable development. "This (sustainability) strategy is, in part, he politics of community—a community that has been destroyed by modern progress, and needs to be re-created. But it is the environment that is at the centre of attention. All 'mainstream Green' groups recognise the need for major structural change in politics and society in order to protect it. The environment is one and indivisible; but it is also fragile."

(i) What is Sustainable Development?

Sustainable Development usually refers to the process of 'developing' in a sustainable way. To that extent, it is a belief in perpetuating the conventional model of development. There are two provisio to such a type of development: one which is rooted in perennial themes of responsibility to others, providing for the future, and two, dependence of life on. the natural environment. Sustainable development is development that 'meets the needs of the present without compromising the ability of 'future generations to meet their own needs' (World Commission on Environment and Development, 1987).

The concept of sustainable development provides a restriction and a goal. Development, if it has to be sustainable, has to work within constraints (say protecting and preserving the environment) which it has so far failed to observe. It is a goal because it has to achieve something (workable development) which it has so far failed to meet. Development, till now, has been development, disregarding all environmental norms; goal, till now, has been a goal without any assured living for the future generations. Sustainable development is development for the present in so far as it satisfies; its needs, but it is a development with a future-orientation, in Lockean words: 'keeping good and enough for others', (who follow).

The credit of inventing the term 'sustainable development goes to Eva Balfour and Wes Jackson. The term first came into prominence in the *World Conservation Strategy* (WCS) (1980), and had become a catchphrase of the 1990s.

The characteristic features involved in the meaning of sustainable development can be summed up as under:

(1) Sustainable development is development which not only provides, but one that sustains; it is a matter of both what 'it is' and what 'ought to be' rather what 'is not' and what 'ought-not' to be.

(2) It is essentially concerned with environmentalism in so far as it seeks development within the framework of 'environment'. It is not 'above' or 'against' or 'at the cost of' environment, but is in tune with it.

(3) It has an empirical content in so far as it permits forward movement within permissible limits; it has the prescriptive content in so far as it seeks a certain goal to be achieved. Sustainability may not be a virtue, but non-sustainability is certainly a vice; the goal is to sustain and remain rather elimination or destruction.

(4) It is a union of present and future: present in so far as the developmental course responds to the needs of today; future in so far as it gives room for accommodation and conciliation with the future.

(5) It is more a matter of policy than a programme. As such it has an ethical content. Peet says aptly: "Sustainability is not something to be defined, but to be declared. It is an ethical guiding principle."

The concept of sustainable development, David Reid says, 'strikes two chords: First, they touch on our sense of guilt about what we have done to the planet, and second, ... on a very deeply-rooted human desire to make sure our children's futures are provided for."

(ii) Issues of Global Crisis and Sustainable Development

Carley refers to the range of global issues in sustainable development.

Some of these are:

(a) Global pollution of atmosphere and oceans: consumption pattern of fossil fuels; fresh water pollution, soil degradation and erosion, chemical pollution from excessive use of fertilizers and pesticides;

(b) Loss of biodiversity and degradation of agro-ecosystem arising from deforestation, erosion and urbanization, loss of genetic diversity; trend towards comoditizing exploitable natural resources and genetically altered organisms.

(c) Growing inequality between the world's rich and poor, and the need to address poverty and basic needs on a global scale; the breakdown of traditional ecologically sound system; displacement due to rapidly growing cities resulting in under-employment.

(d) Concern about powerful trends which could contribute to unsustainable development: industrialization, the mass suburbanization, expecting doubling by the year 2025 of motor-vehicle numbers from the current 500 million.

(e) Issues of governance and mediation in development and the need for long-term holistic planning, the need for economic growth, reconciling market mechanisms which define sustainable processes of development.

The importance of the concept of sustainable development is that it is built on the realization of the need to alleviate the global crisis in a system way that integrates human, ecologial and economic factors.

(iii) Sustainable Development and Environmental Conservation

Development and conservation are the characteristic features of sustainable development. Development is development only if it is able to respond to environmentalism. Development, if it is to be sustainable, has to be environment-oriented, i.e., conservation of environment. Development and conservation have to be integrated in any scheme of sustainable development. The emphasis of 'development' is on the modification of biosphere and the application of human, financial, living and non-living resources to satisfy human needs and improve the quality of human life. The emphasis of 'conservation' is on the. management of human use of the biosphere so that it may yield the greatest sustainable benefit to present generation while maintaining its potential to meet the needs and aspirations of future generations..

The developmental aspect in the concept of sustainable development can not be ignored. Conservation hints at sustainability while the satisfaction of the needs of the people is directed towards development. Sustainable development can not sustain itself for the future unless it meets the requirements of the people living in the present, for sustenance of the future is built on the sustenance of the present.

By way of conclusion, we may say that sustainable development is all about acknowledging and where possible extending the limits which affect the welfare of both the present and future generations. These limits are ecological, technological, social, infrastructural. The sustainable development is not any fixed state of harmony, but is a process of change in which the exploitation of resources, orientation of technological development and institutional changes are made consistent with future and present needs.

(iv) Evaluation

The concept of sustainable development is too vague to be definite. It includes everything one wishes to incorporate in it. Accordingly, it lacks precision and definiteness. That is why it appears, at times, more about environment and less about development; more about stability and less about change; more about restricting one's wants and less about continuing material development; more about non-exploitative attitudes towards environment and less about harnessing it. It is not as much a concept of development with environment as it is a concept of environment without growth.

Indeed, ecological degradation should stop. But why should the pace of development stop? A disciplined use of environmental benefits go a long way for all-round development. Raman and Talwar (*Planet Protection: Imperative for Human Survival,* 1990) rightly observe: "It is generally believed that environmental degradation can be controlled and reversed only by ensuring that the parties causing the damage should be made accountable for their action and that they should participate in improving environmental conditions." What is needed is a set of norms which bring the demands of development and those of environment close to each other.

SUGGESTED READINGS

1. Adams, W.M., *Green Development* (London: Routledge, 1990).
2. Blackstone, W.T. (ed.) *Environmental* crisis (Georgia: University of Georgia Press, 1974).
3. Brown, L., *Building a Sustainable Society* (New York: Norton, 1981).
4. Carley, M and Christie, I., *Managing Sustainable Development* (London: Earthscan, 1992).
5. Dube, S.C., *Modernisation and Development: The Search for Alternative Paradigms* (London: Zed Books, 1988).
6. Elliot, J.A., *An Introduction* to *Sustainable Development* (London: Reutledge, 1994).
7. Hettne, Bjorn. *Developmental Theory and the Three Worlds,* (England, Longman Group, 1996).
8. Kay, C., *Development and Underdevelopment: A Marxist Analysis* (London: Macmillan, 1975).
9. Lele, S.M., Sustainable Development: A Critical Review, *World Development,* 19, 1991.
10. Meadows, D. *The Limits of Growth* (London: Pau, 1972)
11. Myrdal, Gunnar, *Economic Theory and Underdeveloped Regions,* (London: G. Duckworth, 1957).
    _______ *Asian Drama* (New York: Pantheon, 1968).
12. Norgaard, R.B., "Sustainable Development: A Co-evolutionary View", *Futures,* 20, 1988.
13. Norman, T.U. and Warren, F.I. (eds) *The Political Economy of Development: Theoretical and Empirical Contributions* (California: University of California Press, 1972).
14. Pearce, D., *Blueprint for a Green Economy* (London: Earthscan, 1989)
15. Raman, S. and Talwar G.N., *Planet Protection* (New Delhi: Indian Institute for Non-aligned Studies, 1990.
16. Reid, David; *Sustainable Development: An Introductionary Guide* (London: Earthscan, 1995).
17. Sharma, Sudesh Kumar (ed.) *Dynamics of Development: An International Perspective* (Delhi: Concept, 1978)
18. Sikora, R. and Barry, B. (eds) *Obligations to Future Generations* (Philadelphia: Temple University Press, 1978).
19. Tolba, M.K., *Sustainable Development: Constraints and Opportunities* (Guildford: Butterworth Scientific, 1987).
20. Rostow, W.W. *Politics and the Stages of Growth* (Cambridge: Cambridge University Press, 1971).
    _________ *Stages of Economic Growth: A Non-Communist Manifesto* (Cambridge: Cambridge University Press, 1962).

Index